T5-DGI-094

Cistercian Studies Series: Number One Hundred Sixty-Five

ACHARD OF SAINT VICTOR

WORKS

Cistercian Studies Series: Number One Hundred Sixty-Five

ACHARD OF SAINT VICTOR
WORKS

Translation and Introduction by Hugh Feiss, OSB

CISTERCIAN PUBLICATIONS
Kalamazoo, Michigan
2001

This translation has been made from
Achard de Saint-Victor, *Sermons inédits,* ed. Jean Châtillon (Paris: J. Vrin, 1970).
Achard de Saint-Victor, *L'unité de Dieu, et la pluralité des créatures,* ed. Emmanuel Martineau (Saint-Lambert des Bois: Authentica, 1987).
N. M. Häring, 'Gilbert of Poitiers, Author of the *De Discretione animae spiritus et mentis* Commonly Attributed to Achard of Saint-Victor', *Medieval Stuides,* 22 (1960) 174–191.

Available from

Cistercian Publications
Editorial Offices and Customer Service
Institute of Cistercian Studies
Western Michigan University
Kalamazoo, MI 49008

Warehouse and Distribution
Saint Joseph's Abbey
Spencer, MA 01562

British and European Customer Service
97 Loughborough Road
Thringstone, Coalville, Leic. LE67 8LZQ

http://www.spencerabbey.org/cistpub/

The work of Cistercian Publications
is made possible in part by support from Western Michigan University
to The Institute of Cistercian Studies

Library of Congress Cataloguing available upon request.
ISBN 0-87907-765-4 (hc)
0-87907-965-7 (pb)

Typeset by BookComp, Inc., Grand Rapids, Michigan
Printed by McNaughton & Gunn, Saline, Michigan

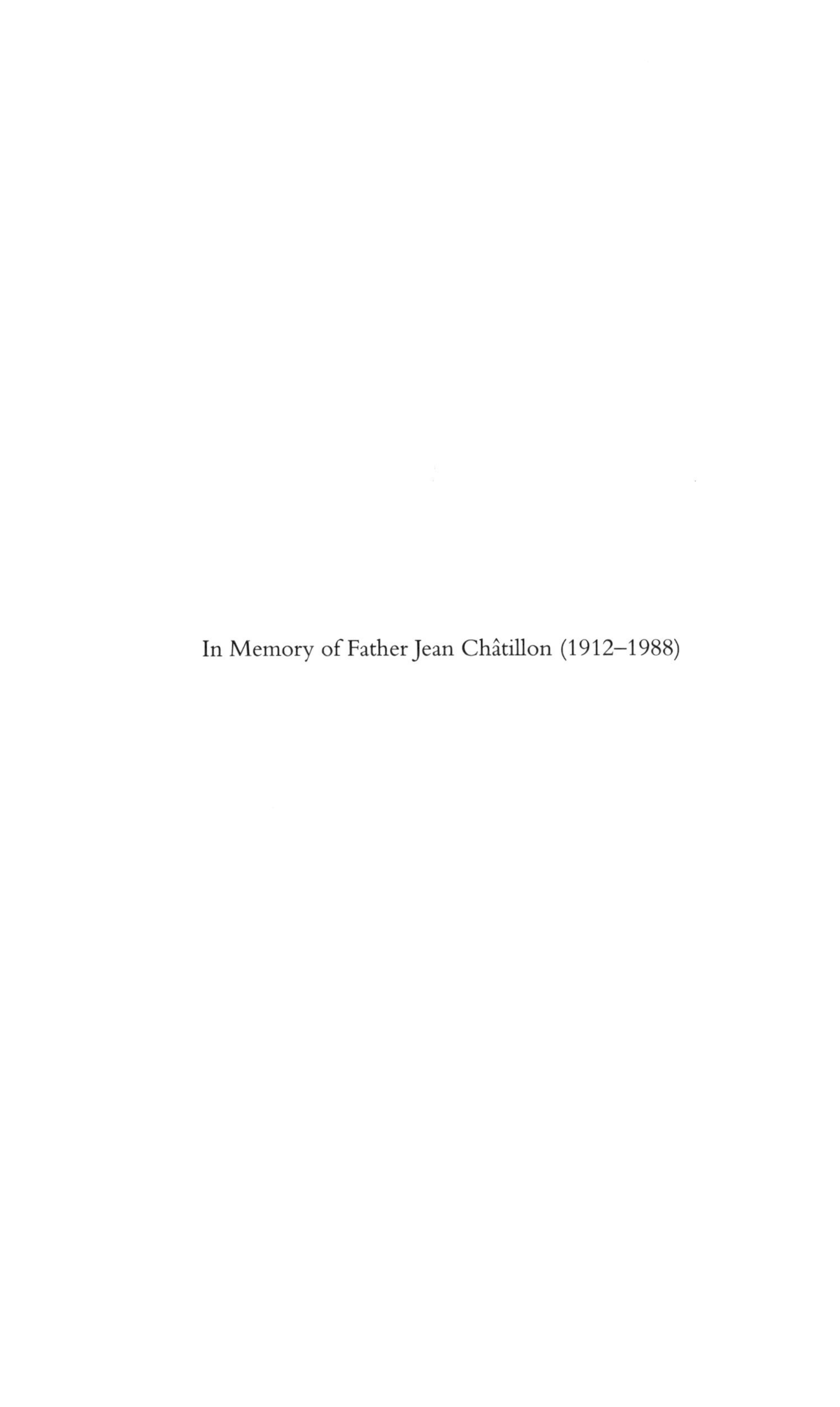

In Memory of Father Jean Châtillon (1912–1988)

TABLE OF CONTENTS

FOREWORD

THIS BOOK IS A TRIBUTE TO TWO BRILLIANT MEN, Achard of Saint Victor and Jean Châtillon. Blessed Achard of Saint Victor was *magister* and second abbot of the community of regular canons at Saint Victor in Paris, and later bishop of Avranches. The groundwork for the rediscovery of his works in the twentieth century was laid by Germain Morin, OSB. Now, one hundred years later, all of Achard's surviving works seem to have been published, and we are in a position to appreciate the breadth of his knowledge and the keenness of his mind, which was equally at home in traditional monastic theology and in the emerging scholastic theology and metaphysics of the mid-twelfth century. He was theologian and spiritual guide, brilliant preacher and astute churchman, at a time when it was still possible for someone to be all these at once.

Achard's work is known to us today primarily because of the scholarly work of Father Jean Châtillon.[1] In 1969 he published a book-length study of Achard's life, works, and thought,[2] and in 1970 he published the first printed edition of Achard's sermons.[3] These publications were the capstone of a long and brilliant career. Jean Châtillon was born in Épinal in 1912. He studied at Metz, where he was ordained priest in 1935, then at the Institut Catholique at Toulouse (S.T.D., 1939) and at the Angelicum (Ph.L., 1938). He spent the war at Nancy, then was for five years a professor of philosophy in the major seminary at Metz, before going to Paris where for the next thirty years he was on the faculty of philosophy at the Institut Catholique, and a research scholar at the Centre National de la Recherche Scientifique.

His thesis at Toulouse was on Richard of Saint Victor and the Victorines. Richard and Achard, however, were the main focus of his scholarly work. He published a number of critical editions of Richard's works, primarily of those which had never been edited before. He also edited a volume of sermons by various Victorines for the *Corpus christianorum*.[4] His productivity in this area is all the more impressive when one realizes that most of the courses he taught concerned Saints Thomas and Bonaventure, not the Victorines.

Jean Longère observed that Father Châtillon was at his best in giving guidance to students and scholars who came to him for scholarly advice. He also noted that during the last fifteen years of his life Father Châtillon became more involved in giving workshops and study sessions in monasteries of monks and canons regular. It was in these two capacities that I first came to know Father Châtillon, when he came to deliver two papers at the centennial

1. The biographical information which follows is derived from Jean Longère, 'Jean Châtillon, 1912–1988', *Revue des Etudes Augustiniennes* 34 (1989) 3–11, which also includes a bibliogprahy of Fr. Châtillon's work.

2. *Théologie, spiritualité et métaphysique dans l'oeuvre oratoire d'Achard de Saint-Victor* (Paris: J. Vrin, 1969).

3. Achard de Saint-Victor, *Sermons inédits* (Paris: J. Vrin, 1970).

4. Galteri a Sancto Victore et quorumdam aliorum, *Sermones ineditos triginta sex*. CCCM 30 (Turnhout: Brepols, 1975).

celebration of Mount Angel Abbey in 1992, during which we also had occasion to celebrate his seventieth birthday. The most vivid memory I have of that visit was his delight at seeing for the first time a pelican, which in medieval symbolism was a touching reminder of the compassion of Christ.

During that visit he advised me on two long-standing and still unfinished projects, a study of the theology of Richard of Saint Victor, and an edition of the spiritual *opuscula* of Hugh of Saint Victor. That both projects are nearing completion is the result in no small measure to Father Châtillon's advice and encouragement. Another cherished memory is a tour of Victorine sites on which he took three of us in 1984: Puiseaux, Amplonville, La Victoire, Villiers-le-Bel, Chateau-Landon, with some wonderful meals and conversation along the way.

Father Châtillon was very concerned that any translation of the Latin texts of Victorine authors be stylistically worthy of the original. Hence, it was with some trepidation that I conceived this translation project, which I wished to be a tribute and a token of gratitude to a great scholar and friend. That it is a posthumous tribute is because of other pressing duties. I am sure that now its shortcomings will matter less than the affection that prompted the undertaking.

That this book is finally seeing the light of day is thanks to the patience and kindness of Rozanne Elder, the editor of Cistercian Publications, and much of whatever merit it has it owes to her editorial oversight and that of John Leinenweber and Maureen O'Brien. Joseph Sprug very kindly compiled the index. I wish also to thank the participants in a semester-long seminar on Achard of Saint Victor at Mount Angel Seminary, which gave me the opportunity and the prodding needed to prepare the translations, and a chance to talk with intelligent people about their content. I am finally able to complete the project only because Abbot Peter Eberle, OSB, allowed me a six-week sabbatical in Unity, Oregon, and the pastor, Father James Logan, and the people of Saint Joseph's Mission housed me in their parish center and gave me the leisure to finish the project. There, surrounded by the Blue Mountains, not only could I study Achard, I could also experience something of what he meant by 'contemplating the king of glory in all his beauty'.[5]

Ascension Priory, November, 1996.

5. Châtillon, *Théologie*, 50–52.

PREFACE

THIS BOOK CONTAINS AN INTRODUCTION to the life and thought of Achard of Saint Victor (†1171) and translations of his fifteen extant sermons as well as of his treatises 'On the Distinction of Soul, Spirit, and Mind', and 'On the Unity of God and the Plurality of Creatures'. Each sermon and treatise is preceded by a special introduction, outlining its content and pointing out some interesting aspects of the work. The most important part of this book is the sermons; the rest, even the treatises, are here to make the reading of the sermons enjoyable and understandable. Only on occasion do I make reference to twentieth-century theology or spirituality in the introductions because I think this makes the sermons more interesting, and also because I think Achard's works, which make no pretense at scholarly detachment from Christian faith and life, are best understood on his own terms.

Those who are not interested in such observations can easily ignore them.

This book is a translation in a twofold sense. It is a translation of Father Châtillon's edition of Achard's Latin sermons and his two treatises. Achard's Latin is clear and elegant, more polished than that of Hugh of Saint Victor, less ornate than that of Richard of Saint Victor. Often Achard's style and thought are dense; this can make demands on the reader, and perhaps it is one reason his works are not as well known as those of Hugh and Richard. My translations aim first at accuracy, secondly at grace. I have tried to convey something of the periodic syntax of Achard's sermons, but I have not hesitated to break his sentences into smaller units in the interest of greater intelligibility.

The second way in which this book is a translation concerns the introductions and notes. There is very little in either that is original to me. Most of what is contained in them is derived either from Father Châtillon's book-length study; *Théologie, spiritualité et métaphysique dans l'oeuvre oratoire d'Achard de Saint-Victor*, or from the footnotes in his edition. The general introduction here is a condensation of the study; the footnotes to the special introductions and to the translations come mostly from the footnotes in his edition. The individual introductions to the sermons and treatises are slightly less dependent on Father Châtillon. My discussion of the treatise 'On the Unity' is based primarily on Martineau's edition, which was not available when Father Châtillon published his edition and his studies of Achard.

I have tried to read everything available on Achard. This consists, for the most part, of the edition and studies of Father Châtillon, the editions of 'On the Distinction of Soul, Spirit, and Mind' by Morin and Häring, and the edition of 'On the Unity' by Martineau. Almost everything else has been superseded by these studies and editions.

I intend this book for readers who either cannot or do not wish to read the Latin and French originals on which it depends. Hence, I have translated almost all Latin and French texts, even in the footnotes, but do not give the Latin and French originals of these translations since those who wish them can easily consult

Father Châtillon's works and the other sources. I have given the most interesting references to authors and controversies of Achard's time, especially to the works of Hugh and Richard of Saint Victor and the anonymous, but evidently Victorine, author of the *Allegoriae* and *Quaestiones* on the epistles of Saint Paul. Occasionally I make generalizations about Victorine thought, without giving documentation. After spending a great deal of the last twenty-five years—although not nearly as much as I would have liked—reading the Victorine authors, I can make these generalizations with some confidence. For corroboration one will be able to consult, God willing, the notes in my forthcoming study of Richard of Saint Victor.

Achard of Saint Victor probably intended his sermons for the community of Saint Victor first of all. Written down in polished form, they could serve also as models for preachers at Saint Victor and elsewhere, or for public reading in choir or refectory. Originally, then, Achard addressed an all-male audience. In translating his works into a new language and in a new century, I hope that he will find more readers than simply canons regular or males. To facilitate this, I have put down 'humanity' where Achard uses '*homo*' ('man', in the sense not of 'male,' but of 'human being'), and on all occasions when this could be done without obscuring the meaning, I have employed plural pronouns in place of Achard's masculine singulars.

ABBREVIATIONS

Achard, *Sermons* =	Achard de Saint-Victor, *Sermons inédits.* Ed. Jean Châtillon. Textes philosophiques du moyen age XVII. Paris: Vrin, 1970.
AHDL	*Archives d'histoire doctrinale et littéraire du moyen âge.* Paris, 1926—.
BGPTM	*Beiträge zur Geschichte der Philosophie und Theologie des Mittelalters.* Münster, 1891—.
CCCM	Corpus Christianorum, Continuatio Mediævalis. Turnhout: Brepols, 1977—.
CCSL	Corpus christianorum, Series Latina. Turnhout: Brepols, 1953—.
Châtillon, *Théologie* =	Jean Châtillon, *Théologie, spiritualité et métaphysique dans l'oeuvre oratoire d'Achard de Saint Victor.* Etudes de philosophie médiévale 58. Paris: Vrin, 1969.
CSEL	Corpus scriptorum ecclesiasticorum latinorum. Vienna, 1866—.
DSp	*Dictionnaire de spiritualité.* Paris: Letouzey et Ané, 1932—.
FS	*Franciscan Studies.* St. Bonaventure, 1941—.
MS	*Medieval Studies.* Cambridge, MA, 1939—.
PL	J. P. Migne, *Patrologia cursus completus, series latina,* 221 vols. Paris, 1844–1864.
PG	J. P. Migne, *Patrologia cursus completus, series græa,* 162 vols. Paris, 1857–1866.
RAM	*Revue d'ascétique et de mysitque.* Toulouse, 1920—.
R Ben	*Revue bénédictine.* Maredsous, Belgium, 1885—.

RTAM	*Recherches de théologie ancienne et médiévale.* Louvain, 1929—.
SCh	Sources chrétiennes series. Paris: Cerf, 1940—.
ZKTh	*Zeitschrift für katholische Theologie.* Innsbruck, 1877.

INTRODUCTION

THE LITTLE WE KNOW ABOUT THE LIFE of Achard of Saint Victor is summarized in the first part of this introduction. This is followed by a description of his works and of the modern editions in which they have appeared. The next three sections deal with Achard's theology, spirituality, and metaphysics. The section on theology, which is concerned primarily with the content of Sermons 1–12, is divided into three parts: theological anthropology, christology, and grace. The section on spirituality considers action and contemplation successively. The section on metaphysics considers the structure of uncreated being, then that of created being.

Life[1]

Achard of Saint Victor seems to have been born in England of Norman parentage around the beginning of the twelfth century. A verse epitaph from the early thirteenth century gives some hints about his origin and life span:

> An olive branch of this house, the glory of the English clergy,
> Now at last is worthy to be warmed by the heavenly light,
> Happy Achard, who flowered into a ripe old age,
> From this sheepfold was consecrated bishop of Avranches.[2]

According to the *Gallia Christiana*,[3] a much later epitaph on Achard's tomb at La Lucerne confirmed his english birth. Writing in the middle of the sixteenth century, J. Bale claimed that Achard received his first training among the canons of Saint Augustine at Bridlington. Bridlington Priory, in the East Riding of Yorkshire, was founded in 1113 or 1114 by Walter de Gant. J. E. Newman, in a recent study of its cartulary, indicates that the canons of Bridlington 'did not act as witnesses or otherwise appear in the cartulary', and no master associated directly with Bridlington appears in it until the 1170s. Newman, however, agrees that Achard was at Bridlington before going to Saint Victor in Paris, where 'he was one of the best known English masters of Paris in the twelfth century'.[4]

Apart from his birth in England early in the century, and a probable sojourn at Bridlington, we know almost nothing about Achard's life except what can be inferred from his writings or gleaned from official documents which he wrote or signed or which

1. This discussion of the life of Achard of Saint Victor is based on the exhaustive investigations of Châtillon, *Théologie*, 11–111. See also M.-T. d'Alverny, 'Achard de Saint Victor. Evêque d'Avranches—Disciple de saint Anselm', in *Analecta Anselmiana*, ed. F. S. Schmitt (Frankfurt: Minerva, 1970) 2:217–222, which emphasizes Achard's debt to the thought of Saint Anselm.

2. The biographical information which follows is derived from Jean Longère, 'Jean Châtillon, 1912–1988', *Revue des Etudes Augustiniennes* 34 (1989) 3–11, which also includes a bibliogprahy of Fr. Châtillon's work.

3. *Théologie, spiritualité et métaphysique dans l'oeuvre oratoire d'Achard de Saint-Victor* (Paris: J. Vrin, 1969).

4. Achard de Saint-Victor, *Sermons inédits* (Paris: J. Vrin, 1970).

affected him. The same is true of the other theologians of Saint Victor; Hugh's origins are a long standing issue among scholars, and for neither Hugh nor Richard, a prominent contemporary of Achard's, do we have many biographical details. The reason for this may lie in Victorine spirituality. In the *Didascalicon*, Hugh quotes Bernard of Chartres on the prerequisites for attaining wisdom: humility, hard work, a peaceful life, silent meditation, poverty, and a foreign land. Expanding on the last requirement, Hugh wrote that a courageous mind should know how to change his home voluntarily, so that one day he would be able to move on definitively.[5] In Sermon 15, Achard describes a similar passage into exile and through exile to a lasting home. Hugh, Achard, Richard, and the other canons of Saint Victor, abandoned home and family for the liberty that Christ offers. Having cut the ties that bound them to their place and family of origin, they did not look back.[6]

Achard's presence at Saint Victor is definitively established in 1155, the year in which he was elected abbot. Saint Victor was forty-seven years old in 1155; Achard may have been slightly younger. The abbey had been founded in 1108, when William of Champeaux, archdeacon of Paris and teacher at Notre-Dame, suddenly abandoned his offices. Probably with the support of Galon, bishop of Paris, William and some companions settled at Saint Victor on the outskirts of the city to live as canons regular. With the encouragement of Hildebert of Lavardin,[7] William continued his teaching at Saint Victor. This readiness to combine action and contemplation remained characteristic of Victorine theory and practice throughout the century.

In 1113 William was promoted to the bishopric of Châlons. On this occasion, he obtained for his former community from King Louis VI a rich endowment and freedom from episcopal and lay interference in its internal affairs. To Saint Victor the king transferred the endowments and privileges he had intended

5. Galteri a Sancto Victore et quorumdam aliorum, *Sermones ineditos triginta sex*. CCCM 30 (Turnhout: Brepols, 1975).

6. Châtillon, *Théologie*, 50–52.

7. Hildebert of Lavardin, *Epistolae* 1.1 (PL 171:141–143).

for a new royal foundation at Puiseaux, which now became a dependent priory of Saint Victor. In 1114 Pope Pascal II addressed a confirmation of the foundation to Prior Gilduin, who soon became the community's first abbot.[8] In his forty-two years as head of the community, Gilduin increased its endowment, saw to the construction of the church and monastery, and codified the observances of the abbey which were then transcribed in the *Liber ordinis*,[9] which was then adopted by many other canonial houses. By this diffusion of the Victorine *ordo*, by the election of members of Saint Victor to leadership roles in other canonial houses, and by the teaching and influence of members of the community, Saint Victor became a leader in the movement of ecclesiastical reform which was intertwined with the intellectual developments of the twelfth-century renaissance.

Victorine prominence in both church reform and learning was assured by the work of Hugh, who, after William of Champeaux, was the founder and inspirer of Victorine theology and the greatest teacher of the school. He died in 1141, but in the decade of his death Andrew, a pioneer of scientific exegesis, began producing his commentaries on the biblical books, and to this same decade probably belong the first works of Richard of Saint Victor. Around this time Peter the Lombard and Robert of Melun were associated with the theological teaching at Saint Victor. In his unpublished *Speculum fidei*, Robert of Crickelade mentions a debate he had with two of Peter the Lombard's disciples on their master's christology, which was witnessed by Robert of Melun and Achard. This probably occurred in 1151. We have every reason to think that at this time Master Achard was actively involved in the theological life of the Parisian schools. Echoes of that involvement are not difficult to find in his sermons.

Toward the end of April, 1155, Master Achard was elected abbot by the community of Saint Victor. It was a role he took very seriously. In Sermon 13 he discourses at length on the role of the abbot, who is judge and disciplinarian, but above all model and

8. PL 163:359–360.

9. Ludovicus Milis et Lucas Jocqué, eds., CCCM 61 (Turnhout: Brepols, 1984).

guide. In his sermons to the community we find something of the teacher who, following the pattern of Hugh of Saint Victor, makes no sharp distinction between the theology studied in the classroom and that preached in the pulpit and meditated in the cloister.

Little remains of Achard's official acts and correspondence, but we have every reason to think he was an able administrator. He maintained cordial and frequent contacts with the papal curia. Like any medieval abbot he spent much effort defending the patrimony, rights, and income of his community against encroachments by outsiders. He also had direct responsibilities for the priories dependent on Saint Victor, as well as less encompassing duties toward the independent abbeys and priories that followed the Victorine *ordo*.

Among the houses to which the observances of Saint Victor had been introduced was the cathedral chapter of Sées, where we know from contemporary sources that they were followed in 1131 under Bishop John. When he died in 1144, opponents of this reform selected as his successor (in an irregular election) one of their number, Girard. Many churchmen, including Archbishop Hugh of Rouen, Arnoul of Lisieux, and Saint Bernard, strenuously opposed the election, but their position was compromised when Girard was brutally attacked by followers of Geoffrey of Anjou. In the end, Girard was reconciled to Geoffrey and allowed to take his see, provided he made canonial profession and promised to maintain the regular life in his cathedral.[10]

When Girard died in 1157, Achard of Saint Victor was elected as his successor. Pope Adrian IV approved the election, but the English king, Henry II, would have none of it. He appointed his almoner, Frogier, to be bishop. To no avail, Thomas Becket opposed this appointment as secular interference into church affairs, while Arnoul accused Frogier of undermining the reform introduced thirty years earlier. In 1161 matters were righted, at least for Achard, when Henry II appointed him bishop of Avranches. Louis VII,

10. This Geoffrey of Anjou (Plantagenet) (1113–1151) was duke of Normandy (1135–1150) and count of Anjou (1131–1151). He turned Normandy over to his son, Henry (later Henry II of England) in 1150. Girard is mentioned by a number of chroniclers; see Châtillon, *Théologie*, 88–89.

though angry that the abbot of one of the most important french monasteries was going to an anglo-norman see, did not block the appointment. Later that year, Achard joined Robert of Torigni, abbot of Mont-Saint-Michel, at the baptism of Eleanor, the daughter of Henry II and Eleanor of Aquitaine. The rest of his six and a half years as bishop seem to have been peaceful; in fact, Achard appears several times as a conciliator between quarreling ecclesiastics.

Achard's cathedral in Avranches is no more. Substantially intact, however, are the remains of the premonstratensian abbey of La Lucerne, a few miles from Avranches, which was the object of much of Achard's care during his episcopate. Not long after he was made bishop, Achard helped strengthen the economic position of the abbey so that the canons were able to begin construction of the abbey church that still stands. Achard died on 29 March 1170, and was buried in the still uncompleted abbey church. Today he is venerated as 'blessed' in the diocese of Coutances-Avranches.

Writings

The written works of Achard of Saint Victor faired badly from the time of his death until our century. The canons of Saint Victor kept no inventory of his writings, or even copies of some of them. Apart from the few surviving letters from what must have been a voluminous correspondence, none of them appears in Migne's *Patrologia latina*; in fact, apart from fragments quoted by Barthélemy Hauréau,[11] none of them was published before the twentieth century. Even the recent scholarly recovery and publication of his works has not been without delays and difficulties.

Sermons

Of Achard's fifteen surviving sermons, the first twelve are rel-

11. *Notices et extraits de quelques manuscrits latins de la Bibliothèque nationale* (Paris, 1891) 3:27–28, 36–37, 50–51, 54–55.

atively brief. They can be read aloud in fifteen to twenty minutes. Sermons 13–15 are much longer and have a slightly different manuscript tradition. We do not know their chronology; Father Châtillon edited them in the order in which they appear in the manuscripts. Sermons 1–12 all refer to Achard as *magister* and seem to be the work of a professor. In them Achard is more theologian than popular moralist. He usually begins with a liturgical text, and this provides the starting point for an exposition of basic christian teaching on Christ or theological anthropology. It is clear from these sermons that Achard was in touch with the theology of his day.

Sermons 13–15 are much longer; reading aloud would require one to three hours. They are the work of a spiritual master and seem intended for the members of the community at Saint Victor. Achard discusses the ascetical disciplines that lead to mystical union, which he discusses in very moving terms as a mutual indwelling of God and the Christian, and as identification of the Christian with the compassionate love of Christ. Often we find allusions to Achard's metaphysics of participation and unity. Frowin of Engelberg incorporated part of Sermon 13 into his *De laude liberi arbitrii*,[12] and these sermons were also popular among Cistercians.

Barthélemy Hauréau, a nineteenth-century scholar who wrote voluminously on the manuscripts in the Bibliothèque Nationale, praised Achard's literary style and his gentle, subtle mind.[13] His praise was justified, but the content of the sermons is of greater interest. This content is a tribute both to the author and to his listeners.

The density of their content is no doubt one reason the sermons were written out and, we may presume, edited. They bear rereading. They would have been delivered at the daily community assembly in the chapter room during the part of the meeting open

12. O. Bauer, 'Frowin von Engelberg (1147–1178): *De laude liberi arbitrii libri VII*', RTAM 15 (1948) 27–75, 269–303; O. Bauer, 'Der selige Frowin im Geistesleben des zwölften Jahrhunderts', in *Der selige Frowin von Engelberg (1143–1178)*, Schriften zur Heimatkunde von Engelberg 7 (Engelberg, 1943) 18–25, or *Titlis Grüsse* 29 (1942) 48–55; Jean Châtillon, 'The *De laude liberi arbitrii* of Frowin of Engelberg and Achard of St. Victor', *American Benedictine Review* 35 (1984) 314–329.

13. *Notices et extraits* 3:24, 27, 55–56, cited in Châtillon, *Théologie*, 151–152.

to the public. In their written form they could have been used for private spiritual reading, for reading in the refectory during meals, or for reading during matins. The customary reading in all three cases was a commentary or sermon on some passage or book of the bible.

In addition to these fifteen, others of Achard's sermons may have come to us anonymously.[14] There are also some fragments of doubtful authenticity, which occur in two manuscripts in conjunction with the last three of his sermons. These were published in an appendix to the sermons in Father Châtillon's edition.[15]

At the end of the nineteenth century, Dom Germain Morin, who first published the text of Achard's *De discretione*, planned to edit Achard's sermons and had even made transcriptions. Dom Othmar Bauer, who became interested in Achard of Saint Victor through his study of Frowin of Engelberg's *De laude liberi arbitrii*, also planned to edit them, but did not complete the project. He sent his transcriptions to Father Châtillon, who finally completed the project in 1970.

De discretione animae, spiritus et mentis

The manuscripts and evidence for Achard's authorship of this treatise were first indicated in 1899 by Germain Morin, who published an edition in 1935.[16] In 1960, Nikolaus M. Häring re-edited the work, attributing it to Gilbert of Poitiers,[17] an attribution Father

14. See Jean Châtillon, 'Sermons et prédicateurs victorins de la seconde moitié du xiie siècle', AHDLMA 32 (Année 1965) 7–60, and his subsequent edition, *Sermones ineditos triginta sex*, CCCM 30 (Turnhout: Brepols, 1975).

15. This information about the sermons is derived from Châtillon, *Théologie*, 137–149.

16. G. Morin, 'Un traité faussement attribué à Adam de Saint-Victor', R Ben 16 (1899) 218–219; 'Un traité inédit d'Achard de Saint-Victor', in *Aus der Geisteswelt des Mittelalters*, BGPTM, Supplementband, 3/1 (Münster: Aschendorff, 1935) 251–262.

17. N. M. Häring, 'Gilbert of Poitiers, Author of the *"De discretione animae, spiritus et mentis"* commonly attributed to Achard of Saint Victor', MS 22 (1960) 148–191.

Châtillon subsequently refuted in favor of Achard of Saint Victor.[18] A french translation was published in 1987.[19]

De discretione animae, spiritus et mentis is a relatively brief justification of the threefold distinction among soul, spirit, and mind mentioned in the title, arguing that this distinction exists in the *substantia interior* of the human being. The author's task is to define each of these powers, describe its operations, justify the hierarchical relation of the three, and explain how this diversity of powers is compatible with the simplicity of the interior substance. Each human person is made in the image of the Trinity. The Trinity remains simple and unchanging in spite of multiple actions, acts of will, and powers. The human person, by contrast, is affected by its activities; the essence is not multiple, but what participates in the essence is. The essence, identical to its power, is involved in movement and multiplicity through its 'affections', which are qualities that 'inform' the essence. Through them the essence is diversified, not essentially, but formally, in multiple powers which are differentiated by a formal distinction. This sort of distinction occurs several times in Achard's sermons; the interest in the relationship between unity and plurality is the subject of Achard's third extant work: *De unitate Dei et pluralitate creaturarum*.[20]

De unitate Dei et pluralitate creaturarum

The existence of this work, under the titles *De Trinitate* or *De unitate divinae essentiae et pluralitate creaturarum*, has long been known. John Leland in his *Collectanea* (written in 1533) mentions that the library at Bridlington had a *De Trinitate* written by Achard. The *Eulogium ad Alexandrum III papam*, attributed to John of Cornwall and written in 1176–1177, contains two citations from this *De*

18. Jean Châtillon, 'Achard de Saint-Victor et le *De discretione animae, spiritus et mentis*', AHDLMA 31 (Année 1964) 7–35.

19. The translation is an appendix to *Achard de Saint-Victor, L'unité de Dieu et la pluralité des créatures*, ed. Emmanuel Martineau (Saint-Lambert des Bois: Authentica, 1987) 199–208.

20. This summary is derived from Châtillon, *Théologie*, 129–135.

Trinitate of Master Achard.[21] The work itself was thought to be lost, however, until a manuscript was discovered by M.-T. d'Alverny in the library of the monastery of Saint Anthony at Padua.[22] From the extracts Mlle. d'Alverny published, it became clear that some mysterious quotations in John of Ripa's *Commentary on the Sentences*, to which Monsignor A. Combes had called attention, were in fact from Achard's work.[23] Finally, in 1987, Achard's work was published in its entirety from the Padua manuscript.[24]

Other Works

As abbot and bishop Achard must have had a wide correspondence. All that survives are three letters: one to Henry II of England; one to Arnoul of Lisieux;[25] and one which he wrote with William de Passavant to Pope Alexander III.[26] Achard wrote to the english king to ask him to use his authority to ensure that his treasurer, Richard of Ely, made restitution for some money earmarked for the poor which he had diverted to his own use. To Arnoul he wrote asking for a kind reception to a certain Brother Reynier. The letter to Pope Alexander III reports that Achard and his fellow bishop had successfully settled a dispute between Arnoul of Lisieux and his treasurer, Silvester.[27] In addition to these letters from Achard, there exist four letters from Pope Adrian IV to him and the community at

21. The attribution is explicit: '*magister Acardus in libro suo De Trinitate*'. It occurs on page 267 of the edition published by N. M. Häring, 'The *Eulogium ad Alexandrum papam tertium* of John of Cornwall', MS 13 (1951) 253–300.

22. M.-T. d'Alverny, 'Note sur deux oeuvres théologiques du xiie siècle', *Bibliothèque de l'Ecole des Chartes* 102 (1954) 249–250; 'Achard de Saint-Victor, De Trinitate—De unitate et pluralitate creaturarum', RTAM 21 (1954) 299–306.

23. A. Combes, *Un inédit de saint Anselme? Le traité* De unitate divinae essentiae et pluralitate creaturarum *d'après Jean de Ripa*, Études de Philosophie Médiévale 34 (Paris: Vrin, 1944).

24. See note 19.

25. PL 196:1381–82.

26. Published, according to Father Châtillon, by R.-N. Sauvage, 'Fragments d'un cartulaire de Saint-Pierre-de-Lisieux', *Études Lexoviennes* (Paris, 1928) 3:341–342.

27. Châtillon, *Théologie*, 96.

Saint Victor written during his abbacy,[28] and a number of charters signed by him.[29]

Quite different is a collection of theological questions attributed to Achard in a thirteenth century manuscript from Cîteaux.[30] The authenticity of these *questiones* remains suspect. In addition there are early references to other works of Achard. Anonymous questions on the Pauline epistles, written between 1155 and 1165 and printed among the works of Hugh of Saint Victor, and Pseudo-Hugh's *Allegoriae* on Paul, written slightly later, both attribute to Master Achard[31] opinions the author may have heard orally. Two citations in the *Sententiae Udonis* could be references to Achard's *De unitate* or to some otherwise unknown questions of his.[32] Finally, in the *De discretione* Achard refers once[33] to arguments he has developed at greater length elsewhere, and once[34] to some of his *Quaestiones de peccato*, where, he says, he has explained something adequately.[35] This last reference seems to establish that Achard did write *questiones* which we cannot at present identify [36]

Theology

Achard was a Victorine theologian. Like Hugh and Richard he made no sharp distinction between theology and spirituality or between theology and philosophy. Reason and will, *doctrina mentis* and *disciplina cordis*, were inseparable in the quest for salvation. Faith, he taught, is the foundation of the christian life, the root from which

28. These are published in Châtillon, *Théologie*, 320–322.
29. These are discussed in Châtillon, *Théologie*, 84, 95–96; one is printed on 323.
30. Dijon B.M. ms 219, ff. 204–216.
31. *Quaestiones in epistolas Pauli* (PL 175: 431–634), references to Achard at 531; *Allegoriae in epistolas Pauli* (PL 175:879–924), references to Achard at 887A, 902B.
32. *Sententiae Udonis* 5, 6, ed. O. Lottin, in 'Le premier commentaire des Sentences de Pierre Lombard', RTAM 11 (1939) 65. The second of these *sententiae*, known from other collections as well, associates Achard and Gilbert Porreta.
33. Section 6.
34. Section 20.
35. Häring, ed., 175, 177.
36. For the information in this paragraph see Châtillon, *Théologie*, 114–119.

all else grows. It is utterly reasonable for reason to admit that there are things known to faith but beyond the grasp of reason. This desertion, even holocaust, of reason in order to live by faith is limited in both time and scope. The temporal limit is clear from Achard's theory about the relations between faith and reason; the limitation in scope is evident in his theological practice. The sacrifice of reason is limited to this life only. In the next life only faith's merit will endure; faith itself will be no more, having ceded everything to reason. The sacrifice of reason is also limited in scope. Reason does not cease to ponder and explore the most unfathomable truths which faith accepts. Drawn by a love of truth, reason examines the truths of faith from every conceivable angle in an unceasing if humble effort to understand. Achard's list of ten theological issues which earthbound human reason cannot solve[37] is clearly a checklist of theological topics on which he had spent a great deal of time and thought.

Secondly, like Hugh and Richard, Achard drew no sharp boundaries between the figurative, even playful use of theological imagination, as this had been cultivated in claustral settings since the early years of the Church, and the use of technical logic as this was being cultivated in the schools of Paris during his lifetime. The great Victorines represented a moment of precarious repose, before the balance of theological method shifted sharply from the ways of the Augustine, Gregory, and Bede to the ways of Thomas, Bonaventure, and Scotus. Achard was ready and able to write technical works of what today would be called philosophical theology, but he was also willing to allegorize on the hammer and axe used to quarry the stones for Solomon's temple. He saw no reason not to mix the two methods when this seemed appropriate. His sermons have something of the treatise about them, his treatises something of the sermon.

Achard gives us no lengthy discussion on his use of Scripture. His practice indicates that here, too, he was the follower of Hugh of Saint Victor. Scripture has both a literal sense and a spiritual sense;

37. Sermon 15.17–33.

the latter has both doctrinal and moral components. It is important to understand the literal meaning before attempting to explain the allegorical meaning. Thus, for example, it is useful to understand the architectural purposes of colonnades before allegorizing on the seven pillars Wisdom fashions for herself. Scripture never contradicts itself, and the Church and her tradition are normative guides in scriptural interpretation. Although he does not say so, he probably also agreed with Hugh that some passages in the Bible are obscure just to test the mettle of exegetes, and that the great teachers of the early Church left some standing grain when they harvested the scriptures in their commentaries just so expositors of later generations would have something to ponder.

A faithful exposition of the main lines of Achard's thought must convey both the immediate teaching and the background speculations, in so far as they are known to us. My goal is not to reconstruct a system, but to clarify the main points of his message, which emerge against the backdrop of a philosophy of platonic inspiration.

Theological Anthropology

The image and likeness of God.[38] Like many of his contemporaries, Achard makes this biblical phrase a basis of his understanding of human nature.[39] Sometimes Achard distinguishes carefully between the image (which stands for reason) and the likeness (which stands for will) but usually he is content to speak of 'image and likeness' in a global way, letting it stand for *mens*, the most profound aspect of the spiritual side of a human being.[40] Likeness implies participation. The three regions of likeness, in accord with nature, grace,

38. Genesis 1:26–27; 5:3; 9:6.

39. Two comprehensive studies of the theme are S. Otto, *Die Funktion des Bildbegriffes in der Theologie des 12. Jahrhunderts*, BGPTM 40/1 (Münster: Aschendorff, 1963), and Robert Javelet, *Image et ressemblance au douzième siècle*, 2 vols. (Paris: Letouzey & Ané, 1967). This section follows Châtillon, *Théologie*, 155–165.

40. Achard carefully discriminates between image (reason) and likeness (will) in Sermon 15.11, and *On the Distinction* 33. Thus, also Hugh of Saint Victor, *De*

and glory, correspond to Sermon 13's threefold participation of the spiritual creature in the Creator by creation, justification, and beatification.[41]

Much of Achard's interpretation of the image and likeness of God in human beings derives from Saint Augustine's trinitarian exemplarism. In Sermon 9.4 Achard says explicitly that each created thing is the image of the Trinity by its existence, beauty, and goodness.[42] The participation of the spiritual creation is special, superior, and more noble than that of the rest of creation.[43]

The spiritual creature's threefold participation in the likeness of God according to creation, justification, and beatification places it in one of three regions of likeness and unlikeness to God. The first, the natural likeness, consists in an inborn power to know, love, and rejoice in God. This image, because it is part of human nature or substance, cannot be completely destroyed, although it can be corrupted and deformed.[44] Achard views human nature as consisting of a hierarchy ranging from the exterior body through the three interior powers: soul, spirit, and mind; he locates the image and likeness of God solely in the 'interior substance' of the human being. The power of the interior substance, simple in itself and identical with the substance, is multiple in its functions.[45] Because it is identical with the substance, it is indestructible.[46] However, even apart from any corruption, the created spirit is naturally more

---

sacramentis 1.6.2 (PL 176:264) and Richard of Saint Victor, *Liber exceptionum* 1.1.1., ed. Châtillon, 104; *Sermones centum* 70 (PL 177:1119D). For the less precise use see Sermons 1.3; 2.3; 5.4; 9.4; 13.32.

41. Hugh of Saint Victor, *In Pentateuchen* 7 (PL 175:37C): 'Let us see what is meant by image, what by likeness. An image involves similar features; a likeness, participation in the same property'.

42. See Augustine, *De Trinitate* 6.10.12 (PL 42:932); Hugh of Saint Victor, *De sacramentis* 1.3.28 (PL 176:230D); Achard, Sermon 13.32.

43. Sermon 9.4; 13.32.

44. Sermon 9.4; 3.1.

45. *On the Distinction* 1–2; Sermon 2.3.

46. On the indestructibility of the image of God in the soul, see Augustine, *De Trinitate* 14.8.11 (PL 42:1044); Richard of Saint Victor, *Liber exceptionum* 2.12.5, ed. Châtillon, 464.

unlike God than it is like him.[47]

To activate this power of knowing, loving, and rejoicing in God, one needs the help of grace, which when given raises one to the level of the gratuitous image, the likeness of righteousness.[48] Achard is concerned with historical, actually existing human nature, which cannot perform any meritorious act apart from grace, and which is in fact destined to intimate union with God and so is endowed with a positive aptitude or power which grace activates. Grace is 'form' to the 'matter' of this God-directed nature. The natural image is deformed or corrupted when it is deprived of this form.[49]

The likeness according to righteousness, the gratuitous image, consists in meritorious acts of knowledge, love, and enjoyment of God.[50] Grace, a form, can only be accidental to the nature it informs.[51] It is therefore pure gift, even though without it human beings cannot reach happiness, which is their end.[52]

Loss of the Likeness: Humanity's Spiritual History. At the time of its creation, humanity received the gift of righteousness or grace; at the beginning humanity was like God in nature and grace. This twofold likeness established human beings in peace with nature, within themselves, with each other, and with God. In this original state, humanity could sin or not sin, die or not die; if human beings chose to obey God they had the possibility of avoiding suffering and death.[53] But sin they did, and through disobedience fell into

---

47. Sermon 9.4. Richard of Saint Victor, *De Trinitate* 6.1, ed. Ribaillier, 228, remarked that 'the reason for the unlikeness is incomparably greater than the reason for the likeness'.

48. One of Achard's associates seems to have drawn from this the idea that an infant who was without original sin would be able to think: *Allegoriae in epistolas Pauli* (PL 175:887B). Achard is concerned with merit, not psychology.

49. Sermon 13.15; 1.3; compare Hugh of Saint Victor, *De sacramentis* 1.1.2–3 (PL 176:187–189).

50. Sermon 1.3; 9.5.

51. *On the Distinction* 3.

52. Sermon 9.6; 13.32.

53. Sermon 7.2–3; William of Champeaux, *Sententiae* 9, ed. G. Lefèvre, *Les variations de Guilllaume de Champeaux* (Lille, 1898) 30; O. Lottin, *Psychologie et morale aux xiie et xiiie siècles* (Louvain: 1954) 4:15, 32 n. 22, and other texts cited by Châtillon, *Thólogie,* 166–167, nn. 46,47, 51.

the second region of unlikeness, that of guilt.[54] This unlikeness consisted in the loss of the form of original justice.[55] It left humanity in a pitiable state, as unlike God as possible, because only sin is totally without likeness to God. Even the third state of unlikeness, the region of punishment, adds a resemblance to divine justice. On the opposite side, given the purely theoretical choice, the blessed would choose justice, the second region of likeness, in preference to the third region of likeness, beatitude, since God's will would be preferred to ours.[56] By themselves human beings have no power to escape from this region of sin;[57] they are deprived of the likeness of grace, wounded in the natural image.[58] They cannot avoid sin and death.[59] They are weighed down by the inconveniences that result from the loss of original justice: ignorance, weakness, and need.[60] In place of the peace enjoyed by those in the state of original justice, human beings now experience inner conflicts between sense and will, will and reason. The physical world no longer serves them, but tempts them alternately with prosperity and adversity; the devils assail them. They are rushed into anger and disputes, excess in food and drink, and hypocrisy.[61]

To Restore the Likeness: Why God Became Man. Only a gracious intervention on God's part could rescue humanity from this region of unlikeness and injustice. To explain why, Achard avails himself

54. Sermon 3.2; 9,4; cp. William of Champeux, *Sententiae* 33, ed. Lefèvre, 63; Hugh of Saint Victor, *De sacramentis* 1.7.7 (PL 176:289).

55. Sermon 3.1. This theory is attributed explicitly to Achard in the *Allegoriae in epistolas Pauli* (PL 175:887A): 'According to some [1], original sin is said to be the guilt (*reatus*) [resulting from] sin; according to others [2], ignorance and concupiscence; according to others [3], original injustice; according to others [4], the kindling of sin [concupiscence]. If the first parents had not sinned, their children would have original justice, through which they would be worthy of life, the privation of which is called original sin according to Master Achard.' Here Achard sides with the opinion of Saint Anselm against [1] Abelard, [2] Hugh of Saint Victor, [4] William of Champeaux and Anselm of Laon. For references to these and other twelfth century authors, see Châtillon, *Théologie*, 168, nn. 55–58.

56. Sermon 9.5–6.

57. Sermon 9.1, 3; 15.1.

58. Sermon 1.3.

59. Sermon 7.3.

60. Sermon 1.3. On the notion of inconveniences (*incommoda*) in Hugh and Richard of Saint Victor, see Châtillon, *Théologie,* 170–71, n. 67.

61. Sermon 7.2; 9.1–3; 2.2; 13.8.

of the arguments of Saint Anselm's *Cur Deus homo*, which Hugh of Saint Victor had also drawn upon, and Richard of Saint Victor had developed.[62]

In succumbing to the devil's temptation, humanity was cheated into selling itself to the devil for nothing. By this the devil gained no rights over humanity; Achard insists on this even more strongly than did Anselm. Even if the devil had acquired some such right, he would have forfeited it by the harm he did God's creature. Humanity does indeed fall under the devil's malevolent power, but only by God's permission, as a punishment.

The Law of Moses made humanity aware of the evil it suffered, but it gave no power of escape. By sin humanity had incurred a debt to God. Since it was God who had been offended, the sinner could not hope to pay the price of redemption. Human beings could only give God what they owed him before sin—obedience to the commandment of love of God and of neighbor. They had nothing left to make the additional recompense (*pretium ad reatus expiationem*) that the sin required; hence, no prophet could redeem humanity. Achard distinguishes sin (*peccatum*), the act of disobedience to God's command, and guilt (*reatus*, a word that does not appear in Anselm), the injury toward God caused by disobedience. This Achard explains by a comparison[63] with a person who owed someone money, and then was imprisoned for offending that person. To pay back the money would not compensate for the offense. Aware that it can do nothing for itself, humanity implores God's grace.

Moved by compassionate love and by no necessity,[64] Christ comes to redeem humanity. He is conceived through the power of the Spirit, and from the first moment of his existence he is completely innocent.[65] Christ always obeyed God, and thus he paid the debt of

62. What follows is based on Sermon 3.2–3. For ample references regarding Achard's dependence on Anselm and the relation between Achard's thought and that of his contemporaries, see Châtillon, *Théologie*, 172–181, nn. 71–99.

63. See Sermon 3.2.

64. See also Sermon 1.6.

65. Achard evidently held the then common view that original sin is passed on through sexual generation. Hugh of Saint Victor expressed this view in *De vanitate mundi* 4 (PL 176:734A; *De arca Noe morali* 1.4 (PL 176:631A); but in *De sacramentis* 2.1.5 (PL 176:381–383) he explains Christ's innocence in virtue of the grace of union.

man's disobedience. However, recompense still had to be made for the injury to God. Christ did not have to suffer or to die; he did so of his own free choice, to provide this additional recompense.

Regarding the much disputed question whether humanity could have been redeemed in some other way, Achard is extremely circumspect, even contradictory. One the one hand, he cites an anonymous 'authority' to the effect that a human or an angel could not have redeemed us;[66] elsewhere, however, he cites without attribution a passage from Augustine's *De Trinitate*, by then commonly cited in the schools, which does allow for the possibility of another mode of redemption. He qualifies this somewhat by insisting, as both Augustine and Anselm had, that redemption by the God-Man is most fitting, not only because of the nature of the reparation humanity must make to God, but also because of the exemplary value of Christ's death.[67]

Christology

The Incarnation is a mystery, more to be believed than to be discussed,[68] yet it is one of Achard's constant preoccupations. Following Father Châtillon, we can summarize Achard's Christology under six subheadings:

66. He cites this authority in a slightly different form in Sermon 15.2.

67. The theologians of the school of Anselm of Laon and William of Champeaux usually remained faithful to Anselm's position that a mere human being or an angel could not have effected human redemption. Adherents of this position cited an anonymous authority: 'Man could not have been redeemed in any way except by the death of the Son of God'. Their view was criticized, e.g., by Roscelin in a letter to Abelard (PL 178:362AD, citing Augustine, *De Trinitate* 13.10.13 [PL 42:1024]) and by the school of Abelard, which said that while a human or an angel could have redeemed humanity, it was more fitting that the God-Man do it. Hugh of Saint Victor, *De sacramentis* 1.8.10 (PL 176:331D) did not mention redemption by a human being or an angel, but he agreed that 'if God had wished he could have accomplished the work of our redemption in a different way, but the Incarnation was the one which best suited our weakness'.

68. Sermon 15.16, 24–29. What follows is based on Jean Châtillon, 'Achard de Saint-Victor et les controverses christologiques du xiie siècle', in *Mélanges offerts au R. P. Cavallera* (Toulouse: Bibliothèque de l'Institut Catholique, 1948) 317–337; Châtillon, *Théologie*, 183–216.

1. *The Double Consubstantiality of the Word Incarnate.* Achard's Christology is governed by the fundamentals of christian dogma: Christ is consubstantial with Mary and with God the Father.[69] Christ's unity with the Father is greater than his unity with human nature, since he is separated from other humans by a great diversity of accidents.[70] Because the human nature of Christ is substantially identical with that of all people, the redemption of the human race is possible.

2. *The Incarnation is a Work Common to the Three Persons and Specially Attributed to the Son.* Hugh of Saint Victor discussed the reasons for the Son's incarnation, and then asked why only the Son was united to human nature when all operations of the Trinity outside itself are common to the three persons. He explains the latter point by distinguishing the action (common to the three persons) from its term (which concerned the Son alone).[71] Achard echoes this,[72] but goes on to insist on the role proper to the second person. First, it is not proper to the Father to proceed (go out) from another; the Spirit goes out, but *to* us, not *in* our nature. Moreover, the work of redemption especially befits the Son, which Achard establishes with five scriptural arguments: (i) the splendor of the Father's glory should be the light of the world; (ii) the Son of God by nature should be the source of the adoption of the children of God; (iii) it befits the Image of God to restore the image in fallen humanity; (iv) he

---

69. Sermon 1.1. Achard's *homoousion Patri et matri* is the teaching of the Council of Chalcedon (Heinrich Denzinger, *Enchiridion symbolorum*, 148) and Leo the Great, *Epistola 31 ad Pulcheriam Augustam* (PL 54:792AB). Achard's phrasing of the doctrine is found also in the *Apologia de Verbo incarnato* 11, ed. Häring, FS 16 (1956) 114. The anonymous writer of the *Apologia*, who wrote it about 1160, depended on Cassian, *De incarnatione Christi* (PL 50:171A). Walter of Saint Victor, *Contra quatuor labyrinthos Franciae*, ed. Glorieux, AHDLMA 19 (1952) 206, copied the *Apologia*.

70. Sermon 1.1. Here Achard echoes William of Champeaux's realism, according to which human nature is one; the multiplicity of individuals is explained only by the accidental determinations proper to each individual. The same theory was espoused in several Boethian commentaries attributed by N. M. Häring to Thierry of Chartres, where this teaching is inspired by Boethius, *De Trinitate* 1 (Cambridge: Harvard University Press, 1968) 6.

71. *De sacramentis* 2.1.2–3 (PL 176:371–376). This question had been in dispute between Anselm and Roscelin; see Châtillon, *Théologie*, 186–187, nn. 9–14.

72. Sermon 1.2.

who healed a deaf-mute is particularly suited to heal our ignorance and our incapacity to confess; (v) he who is the power and wisdom of God ought to be the one to heal infirmity and ignorance.[73]

3. *The Ontological Status (mode of union of the two natures in the person) of the God-Man.* Peter the Lombard mentions three opinions current in Achard's time regarding this question: (i) assumed humanity (*assumptus homo*): the human nature of Christ has all that it needs to be a person, but it is constituted a person by the person of the Word. God became a human being, and a human being became God, but neither nature lost any of its properties. Christ's humanity had by grace all the attributes of his divinity, except those incompatible with physical existence. (ii) Christ is composed of body, soul, and divinity. The person of the Word was simple before the Incarnation, but becomes composite afterward, because it subsists simultaneously in two natures. Achard does not refer to this opinion. (iii) According to some members of Abelard's school, the Word takes up a body and soul as a vesture in which to appear to humans. The body and the soul are not united in him as they are naturally in a human being; they are associated to each other because the Word has put them on simultaneously.[74] Achard represents the first opinion, although he most often approaches the subject indirectly by rejecting other formulations or by broaching related subjects.[75]

4. *The Humanity Assumed Possesses by Grace all that the Word Assuming Possesses by Nature.* Sermon 4 is a good guide to Achard's Christological thought. Achard quotes Exodus 12:8–9, which refers to

73. Sermon 1.2–3.

74. *Sententiae* 3.6, ed. Quaracchi, 2:573–582.

75. Sermons 1.5; 4.5–7; 12.2; 15.24–26. John of Cornwall, *Eulogium ad Alexandram III papam*, 4, ed. Häring, MS 13 (1951) 167, attributes the first opinion to Achard, who is the prime authority in urging the pope to condemn Christological nihilism. John was writing in 1176, and his citation of Achard is evidence of Achard's importance among the theologians of his time. Other proponents of the traditional language of *homo assumptus* were Hugh of Saint Victor, Walter of Mortagne, Gerhoh of Reichersberg and Robert of Melun. For the literature see Châtillon's *Théologie*, 190–196, notes. As Châtillon observes in 'Achard de Saint-Victor et les controverses christologiques', 318–319, n. 5, Achard rejected both the first and third opinions and came to think of the first position (his own) as leading to Nestorianism.

eating the head, feet, and entrails of the lamb during the paschal meal. Achard refers the head to Christ's divinity, the feet to his humanity, and the entrails to the personal union of divinity and humanity. He reproaches those who speak wrongly about any of the three. Regarding the divinity, Achard insists that the *homo assumptus* shares in all the positive attributes—notably knowledge and power—of the divinity.[76] Achard condemns those who denied divine knowledge and divine power to Christ's humanity.[77] He cites a dictum quoted by Walter and Hugh in their correspondence: 'The soul of Christ has through grace what God has through nature',[78] but Achard changes it slightly to encompass Christ's integral humanity. As will be noted in the introductions to Achard's Christological sermons, this is one point where his teaching is out of harmony with contemporary Christology.

5. *The Humanity of Christ and the Critique of Nihilism*. After recalling some ancient heresies, Achard attacks more recent errors, notably the opinion that Christ as man is not any thing.[79] Peter Lombard shows that the adherents of this view (condemned by Alexander III in 1177) adopted it because of difficulties they saw in the opposite

76. To defend this position Achard invokes Colossians 2:9, not only in Sermon 4.5, but also in Sermons 1.5; 15.26. See also Sermons 3.3; 5.1; *Quaestiones in epistolas Pauli* 7 (*In epistolam ad Galatas* 2:9), q. 9 (PL 175:583): 'It says "all plentitude" to indicate that in him is the fullness not only of knowledge, but also of power and goodness. This destroys the error of those who say that the humanity assumed by grace has all the knowledge which the Word has by nature, but not all power.' The last sentence may have been directed against Peter the Lombard. Châtillon, 'Achard de Saint-Victor et les controverses', 330, does not think Achard's distinction between positive and negative attributes cogent.

77. *Epistola ad Hugonem*, PL 176:1052, 1054. See the discussion in Ott, *Untersuchungen*, 340–347, and the texts cited by Châtillon, *Théologie*, 200, nn. 78–80, and 'Achard de Saint-Victor et les controverses christologiques', 327–328; for example, Hugh of Saint Victor, *De sapientia animae Christi* (PL 176:854): 'The soul of Christ, which received the fullness of the Spirit, knew these things much more, and knew them fully and perfectly'.

78. *Epistola ad Hugonem* (PL 176:1053AB); also, Roland Bandinelli, *Sententiae*, ed. Gietl, 166–167. This 'auctoritas' seems to derive from Augustine, but it is not found word for word in his works. See Jean Châtillon, '*Quidquid convenit Filio Dei per naturam convenit Filio homini per gratiam:* A propos de Jean de Ripa, *Determinationes* 1.4.4', in *Divinitas* 11 (1967) 715–728 = *Miscellanea A. Combes* (Rome: 1967) 319–331.

79. Sermon 4.6: '*Christus secundum homo non est aliquid.*'

opinion: if Christ's humanity were something, it would be a rational substance, and a rational substance is a person, according to the definition of Boethius. Since there is only one person in Christ, Christ's humanity would then be identical with his divinity. Häring thinks Gilbert of Poitiers favored the nihilist view, denying that the body and soul of Christ were united in such a way that they constituted a substance or *aliquid*.[80]

6. *The Union of the Two Natures in the Person of the Word*. Abelard had attacked traditional *assumptus homo* formulations; theologians like Achard strove to defend these statements by nuancing them properly. Achard insists that the Word assuming and the human assumed are one person, arguing that to deny this entails either saying that there are four persons in the Trinity, or that the human assumed is not a person and therefore nothing. The human assumed is a person, but the person of the Word; the Word did not assume a person, but the humanity was assumed into a person. In this Achard does not attempt to explain the traditional Christian dogma, but simply to state it plainly, and to illustrate it with a comparison in which a nude person is brought into a house and then gets dressed, so that the person brought in is clothed.[81]

The Grace of Christ

To Achard theology and spirituality are inseparable. Spirituality is a progressive and deeper participation in the being, life, and attributes of Christ. Christ is never for him simply the God-Man,

80. Peter the Lombard, *Sententiae*, 3.10.1, ed. Quaracchi, 2:593; Pope Alexlander III, letter of February 18, 1177 (Denz. 393). See R. F. Studeny, *John of Cornwall, An Opponent of Nihilism* (Moedling, Austria: St. Gabriel's Mission Press, 1939); Jean Châtillon, 'Achard de St.-Victor et les controverses christologiques', 317–337; Châtillon, *Théologie*, 203–206, notes. The term 'theological nihilism' was evidently invented by Walter of Saint Victor, who opposed it strongly in *Contra quatuor labyrinthos Franciae*, ed. Glorieux, 200.

81. Sermons 4.7; 1.2. John of Cornwall, *Eulogium* 4, ed. Häring, MS 13 (1951) 267.

the incarnate Word, savior and redeemer of the human race; he is the Sun of righteousness, the radiance of the eternal light which enlightens everyone who comes into the world, the head of the body of all the just.

Achard thinks of human nature as matter; grace is its form, restoring human nature to its original beauty and splendor. Justification is *gratificatio* and *reformatio*. The Incarnation makes possible the rejoining of the heavenly (divinely-given) form to the earthly matter of human nature. What Christ's divinity has by nature, his humanity has by the fullness of grace; all Christians participate in the gifts and attributes that Christ's humanity has in their fullness.[82]

Participation in Christ's fullness will be manifold because the attributes his divinity possesses by nature and his humanity by grace are manifold. In a sermon on the resurrection Achard speaks of the multiple meanings of the body of Christ: the sacramental body; the natural body; the virtual body—that is, the body with *virtus*, power; the intellectual body; and the spiritual body. The first two of these are familiar enough: the natural body is that which Christ received from the Virgin and which hung on the cross, and the sacramental body is that which appears under the species of bread and wine. The other three bodies of Christ are distinguished on the basis of Christ's power and wisdom. The virtual body of Christ is constituted by the totality of modes of participation in the divine power. The divine power is one, simple, and undivided in itself, but it is participated in by many. All who participate in it are members of Christ, and their totality constitutes his body. The intellectual body of Christ is closely related to his virtual body, except that it concerns not his power, but his wisdom. All who participate in his wisdom constitute his intellectual body. The spiritual body of Christ is the reunion of the virtual and intellectual bodies.[83]

We have here a distant parallel to the Greek doctrine of the divine energies. We also have an inchoate theology of the Church,

82. Sermons 13.11,14–15, 20. Latin words with the root 'form' are very frequent in Achard's sermons, evidence of the centrality of the idea of deformed human nature reformed in the image of the Son, who freely accepted the form of a slave.

83. Sermon 4.1–5.

which is constituted by Christ's power and wisdom. His power and wisdom, manifest in the totality of his members, are the basis of his presence in the world. Metaphysically, we have in Christ's multiple attributes a median between the supreme unity of his divinity and the multitude of those who constitute his spiritual body. By participation in these attributes the members of Christ become similar to God and to each other. By Christ and in Christ, their multiplicity is led back into unity.

These themes are developed at length in Achard's Sermon 13 for the feast of the dedication of a church. The metaphor is different; it is now not the body of Christ, but the interior temple that Christ builds in us and in which he makes his abode. Here the emphasis is not on the multiplicity and unity, but on the nature of Christ's spiritual activity in the depths of the Christian, and upon the mode of participation this involves.

In addition to power and wisdom, the third fundamental divine attribute is goodness or anointing. These correspond to Christ's power, his will, and his knowledge: *posse*, *velle*, *scire*. These three attributes are identical in Christ's divine simplicity and substance. They all intervene equally in the building up of the interior dwelling, but we can formally distinguish the effects proper to each in the soul in which Christ makes his dwelling. Although they are substantially one and operate causally as one, it pertains to the form and property of power to communicate power, to the form and property of anointing to procure joy, to the form and property of wisdom to give light. Achard appeals in support of this 'formal distinction' to the traditional idea of appropriating the divine attributes to each member of the Trinity. Once again, perhaps because he too is influenced by Pseudo-Dionysius, Achard parallels the later Greek theological distinction between the divine substance and its energies.

Corresponding to the three attributes of Christ are three interior dwellings, which pertain respectively to Christ's power, his anointing/goodness, and his wisdom. The first dwelling is that of power or love, the second that of anointing or spiritual joy, the third that of wisdom or contemplation. All of this shows how closely connected the spiritual development of the human being is with Christ, and indeed with the Trinity. Each of the three dwellings has seven columns, for each entails adorning the soul with a multitude of virtues.[84] The foundation of any such participation in Christ's virtues is original justice.

Original justice is what is restored to fallen humanity by the sacrament of baptism—a participation in the merits of Christ. Once a person reaches the age of reason, this original justice must be accompanied by actual justice; that is, a participation in the merits of Christ which is also the fruit of the cooperation of free will with grace.[85] Achard makes a similar distinction between prevenient or operative grace, which comes at baptism (acting in us but without us), and cooperating or subsequent grace, which acts in us, but not without the cooperation of our free will.[86] Original justice and operative grace correspond to the Incarnation, where Christ came among us, but without us; actual justice and cooperative grace he connects with Christ's second coming—his coming into us, which cannot happen without us.[87] Achard connects Christ's triumphal procession on Palm Sunday with the procession each one must make from original justice to actual justice.[88] Hence, the spiritual life is before all else an ever deeper participation in the grace of Christ; for this participation to be effective, the free will of each person must cooperate. Such cooperation is necessary because baptism does not eliminate those tendencies to sin that are part of the result of original sin.[89] The Christian's progress consists in escaping from the influence of sin in a Spirit-given flowering of the initial gift of justification, and in being penetrated with the divine energies

84. Sermon 13.2–5. Achard is evidently concerned to distinguish himself from those theologians who held that there was a real distinction between the divine substance and its attributes. On this controversy and the issues involved, see Châtillon, *Théologie*, 224–229, nn. 22, 25–29, 34.

85. Sermon 3.1; 11.3.

86. Sermons 3.1; 11.3; 15.21–22. The same distinction occurs in *Quaestiones in episolas Pauli* 1, q. 103 (PL 175:460). For further references see Châtillon, *Théologie*, 231, n. 41.

87. Sermon 3.1.

88. Sermon 11.2–3.

89. Sermon 1.3; 6.3; 7.2–3; 10.4.

flowing from Christ. Thus Christians are transformed, and become actually and effectively living members of the body of Christ.[90]

Spirituality

The Active Life

The active life is a process of interiorization, purification, and pacification. One must desert exterior things to reach interior things.[91] This desertion is an internal act, not a physical withdrawal, and leads to recovery of a power which is a participation in Christ's power. This power, or virtue, restores one's proper dominion over the material world and oneself, and this results in interior peace. Justifying grace and free will cooperate in this restoration. Sermon 13 emphasizes interiorization; Sermon 14, purification; Sermon 15 mingles these two themes with that of peace. According to this last sermon, which will provide the framework for what follows, the Christian must successively desert sin, world, flesh, self-will, and finally reason itself. As a result, proper order is restored: the universe is submitted to humanity, the flesh and senses to the will, the will to reason, and reason to God. In this way, interior peace is achieved.[92]

The First Desert: Renunciation of Sin. Sin is a distant region where one is a stranger to oneself and condemned by God. In vain does the sinner seek peace in exterior things. The devil exercises the tyranny of the seven weightier sins or principal vices. Dead in sin, sinners cannot extricate themselves by their own power; only if God's Spirit inspires them with fear of God can they begin their escape. Such

90. For this progress, see, e.g., Sermons 11; 13–15; and, in particular, Sermon 4.1.

91. Sermon 4.2; 8.4: action, distinguished from devotion and contemplation, is identified with mortification of the flesh, and this includes both ascetical denial and the practice of good works.

92. Sermon 7.2.

'initial fear' leads to 'chaste fear'—from fear of punishment to a fear rooted in the love of God.[93]

In describing this process Achard is inspired by the theological teaching regarding penitence that was just then being systematized. Achard's contemporaries distinguished three kinds of acts necessary for the remission of sins, whether venial or mortal: contrition, confession, and satisfaction.[94]

Of these, confession draws most of Achard's attention.[95] We are justified in seeing here indications of the importance of confession in the religious life of the Victorines, both in the form of private, sacramental confession, and in the form of public confession in chapter. The Victorines' insistence on confession for remission of sins was a reaction against the teaching of the school of Abelard, which de-emphasized this element of the penitential process.[96]

The Second Desert: Renunciation of the World. Sin is an evil act; the world is God's good creation. One must desert the world because it is susceptible of an evil use which leads to sin, or is sin, and so blocks the grace of Christ from penetrating the depths of the justified person. The form of the world must be replaced by the form of Christ.[97] People's relation to the world is dependent upon

93. Sermon 15.4–7. Augustine, e.g., *Enarrationes in Psalmo* 18:10 (PL 36:611), developed this distinction between two kinds of fear in order to reconcile 1 John 4:18, 'There is no fear in love, but perfect love casts out fear' with Psalm 18:10 [Psalm 19:9], 'The fear of the Lord is holy [or chaste], enduring forever'. The twelfth-century theologians wondered how fear without love could be called the beginning of (supernatural, justifying) wisdom (Psalm 111:10). See Landgraf, *Dogmengeschichte* 4/1: 176–371; Ott, *Untersuchungen*, 213–234. Hugh of Saint Victor and others were led to distinguish four kinds of fear: servile, worldly, initial, and chaste; see *De sacramentis* 2.13.5 (PL 176:528); *Miscellanea* 1.193 (PL 177:585B); Pseudo-Hugh, *Miscellanea* 6.32 (PL 177:830D-831A). Hugh thought the least of these, servile fear, was not the beginning of wisdom; Peter Lombard disagreed: *Sententiae* 3.34.4–9, ed. Quaracchi, 701–707. All agreed that initial fear was connected with grace and love. For further information, see the notes to the translation of Sermon 15.7, and Châtillon, *Théologie*, 236–237, n. 14.

94. Sermons 11.2,13; 14.5.

95. Especially in Sermon 14.5–13.

96. Châtillon, *Théologie*, 238, n. 18, cites P. Anciaux, *La théologie du sacrement de pénitence au xiie siècle* (Louvain, 1949) 186–196.

97. Sermon 13.23 is the most important text for Achard's notion of the world and 'contempt of the world', an expression that occurs in Sermons 5.4; 12.5; 15.8.

their spiritual situation, whether that be (i) sin, (ii) actual justice either in the monastery or in lay life, or (iii) glory, where the world will be seen in its divine archetype as well as in itself. In paradise, human beings were in perfect harmony with God and with nature; nature was transparent to the divine, and bore the imprint of the Trinity. That harmony was broken by sin. Sinful people do not rule the world; they are ruled by it. To sinful people, the world is opaque, devoid of transcendence. Such a world has its own sociological weight, its own seductive force, insofar as groups and societies attribute an illusory objective value to such things as self-determination, riches, the taste for earthly power, and human praise.[98] In this sense the world is sinful, ruled by the devil, something to be fled. Its prime attribute is vanity.[99] In this sense, the world has its own order and laws, which are in fact disorder and lawlessness.

The Third Desert: Renunciation of the Flesh. World and flesh are closely connected; whereas the 'world', made for people, is outside of them, the flesh is part of them. As Eve was to assist Adam, so the flesh is to assist reason; the flesh is an animal upon which reason is seated; reason needs the help of the flesh, which should provide this help. The spirit should nurture the flesh, but sensual pleasure often exerts its attractions under pretext of necessity. Among a human being's powers, reason must rule; for reason to rule, a moderate asceticism is necessary.[100]

The theme *contemptus mundi* is the object of much discussion, especially in relation to the thesis of R. Bultot that it was indicative of a theologically unjustifiable devaluation of creation. For some of the literature see Châtillon, *Théologie*, 239–240, nn. 20–21.

98. In Sermon 15.8 and 13.23, Achard sees the four elements (Colossians 2:8, 20) as a metaphor of earthly power, freedom, riches, and human praise. Cf. John 12:31; 1 John 5:19.

99. Sermon 6.1; 9.3; 13.23; 15.8, 11, most of which are inspired by biblical passages, e.g., Romans 8:20; Ecclesiastes 1:2. Achard is not as insistent on the vanity of the world as was Hugh of Saint Victor, especially in his works *Homiliae in Ecclesiasten* and *De vanitate*. For an interpretation of Hugh see Roger Baron, *Science et sagesse chez Hugues de Saint-Victor* (Paris, 1957) 178–182; H.-R. Schlette, *Die Nichtigkeit der Welt: Der philosophische Horizont des Hugo von St. Viktor* (Munich, 1961); and F. Lazzari, *Il contemptus mundi nella scuola di S. Vittore* (Naples, 1965).

100. Sermon 15.9–10; 11.4.

The Fourth Desert: Renunciation of Self-Will. The will is part of the spirit and bears resemblance to God.[101] However, the proximity of the flesh often results in the will's not following reason as it ought, but consenting to the allurements of the flesh. In the consent of the will to evil lies the essence of sin;[102] hence, one must carefully scrutinize the movements of one's will. The crucial question is whether one's will coincides with the will of God. To counter the will's self-justified vagrancies and to humble oneself, out of love for neighbor one should prefer another's will to one's own, a difficult task that can be accomplished only with the help of God.[103]

The Fifth Desert: Renunciation of Reason. To justify such a renunciation, Achard appeals to (1) the first commandment: God requires the gift of the whole person; and (2) the fact that reason is tainted by sin, fallen into darkness; it must be illumined by the judgment of God.[104] The taint results from the will's interaction with the lower powers of the soul and from its own fallacious attempts at self-justification. In the course of his argument, Achard does not carefully distinguish the roles of intellect and will, perhaps because he did not recognize a real distinction between the two.[105] So much for practical reason.

Achard gives a quite different rationale for renouncing speculative reason: the hidden things of God are not available to the gaze of human beings. Such are, for example, the beginning and end of the world, the problem of evil, the relations of grace and free will, the Eucharist, the Incarnation. In the face of such mysteries the soul is forced back by the divine light. That reason is forced back by the divine light, just as a hiker in the desert is forced back by an overpowering wind, is a theme in Augustine and Gregory the Great; they apply it to the contemplative, whereas Achard refers it

101. Sermon 15.11.

102. Sermon 1.3; 14.10, 11. Abelard had highlighted the crucial role of the consent of the will in the moral act.

103. Sermon 15.12.

104. Sermon 15.14–16.

105. See *On the Distinction* 1–2, where Achard explains his understanding of the identity of the soul and its powers, among which he does not distinguish cognitive and appetitive activities.

primarily to the theologian. This incapacity of reason is partly the result of its created nature, sublime though that nature is. Moreover, Achard insists that though nature has a radical capacity to know God, the operation of this potency requires the intervention of grace, which was lost when original justice was lost. The Christian must strive to restore actual justice to the depths of the soul's powers so that the capacity to know God may then be activated. To do this is to use reason within faith: 'unless one believes, one will not see these things', says Achard, reminding us of a phrase dear to Augustine and Anselm.[106] For Achard, this submission of reason to faith is the final step in the spiritual progress toward contemplation of the mysteries of God. To those who desert themselves totally, God will restore them with interest.

Clearly Achard's ascetical teaching is consciously based upon a theological anthropology. He also spells out the specific practical conditions under which his audience in the monastery should make these renunciations. The virtue and sacrament of penance play no negligible role. The detailed analyses of Sermon 14.5–13 regarding the conditions in which confession should be practiced in order to be effective and beneficial show that its effect was not simply to cure religious of sin, but also to aid them to avoid the snares which the world, the flesh, the will, and reason itself could lay for them.

Religious must do more than accuse themselves of faults. To make a truly voluntary, frank, and pure confession, they must not look for vain excuses for their sins, or pretexts in bad theology or pseudo-metaphysics by which to escape responsibility. They should not claim that a woman's beauty, or the complicity of a companion, or the weakness of their flesh is responsible for their evil desires to which their will consents. They should not accuse God or divine foreknowledge, the ineffectiveness of grace, the weakness of our first parents, the devil, the stars, or fate.

---

106. Sermon 15.16–33. For references see Châtillon, *Théologie*, 249–250, n. 64. Hugh of Saint Victor, *De sacramentis* 1.10.2 (PL 176:331AB) defined faith as 'a certitude regarding absent things which is above opinion but beneath knowledge (*scientia*)'. Faith for Hugh was both the grace-given enlightenment and support that make possible a subjective firmness of assent, and an objective rule, which informs the believer about truths otherwise hidden.

But Achard's asceticism employs more exterior and harsher methods, which Victorine discipline included, and which are justified by Sermon 13.17–27 in terms of the general principles of Achard's spiritual theology. In the description he gives of the first of the three interior dwellings, Achard notes that the temple was constructed with hewn stones. The quadrilateral form of the stones gives them the strength and the stability that Christ desires in the living stones of his temple. The four sides of the stones stand for wisdom, justice, sanctification, and redemption,[107] the four cardinal virtues, the four beatitudes of Luke, the four imperatives of the commandment of love. The point of these allegories is that Christ is our form, and the stones of his temple must be hewn to fit with him. Achard explains to his cloistered listeners the means by which this form of Christ is to be imprinted on them in the chapter meeting.[108] The abbot, the prior, the subprior, and the circator (whose function is to watch over observance in the monastery and publicly accuse those who are guilty of falling short of the rule) use the saw and hammer, which are faith and reason. There comes a point, however, where saw and hammer are no longer necessary. Those who have recovered peace of soul and true liberty of spirit can then participate in the building of the second dwelling, that of anointing or spiritual joy, and take their first steps on the paths of the contemplative life.[109]

The Contemplative Life and Identification with Christ

The division between active and contemplative is somewhat artificial. Achard relates the active life to the power of God and the contemplative life to his wisdom[110] but even in the highest reaches of contemplation, we must continually return to the active life. Hence, Achard says that Christians must follow the lead of Jesus

107. 1 Colossians 1:20
108. Sermon 13.24–27.
109. Sermon 13.28.
110. Sermon 4.2.

and Mary who possessed the fullness of both lives.[111] Achard does think that here below we can experience a foretaste of the vision of eternal beatitude.[112]

The Dwelling Place of Unction and Delight. At one point Achard seems to introduce devotion as an intermediate state between action and contemplation. Devotion (*devotio*) is a feeling or sentiment (*affectus*), inseparable from prayer (*oratio*), which turns a person toward God, and with charity attaches the soul, detached from exterior things, to God. Devotion is an affective seizing of the divine reality (or at least spiritual realities) which the spirit does not yet see but already feels to be very near. It engenders delight (*unctio*).[113]

This intermediate step is discussed in Sermon 13.29 in connection with the second dwelling (stopping place), the place of unction or delight. It is related not to Christ's power or his wisdom, but to his goodness. In the recipient the love of God and neighbor replaces the love of the world, the flesh, and the self. One can then rejoice in one's conscience, with a joy which is a grace, a gift of the Holy Spirit, a share in the divine sweetness.[114] This joy could be egoistic, but it should lead to a grasp of the divine perfections, first in the affectivity, then in the understanding. In the end the Christian rejoices in God's perfections, not in the joy they bring him. This leads Achard to develop a theology of pure love, whereby one rejoices not in the righteousness one has received, but in the divine righteousness in which one participates. Such a love of righteousness opens the way to contemplation.[115]

The Heaven of the Angels and Contemplation of the Eternal Reasons. This delight in unction raises the soul to contemplation, which

111. Sermon 8.3; Sermon 12.5–8.

112. Sermon 13.29, 31; 8.2. Achard speaks of experience (*experientia; experiri*) rather infrequently, by comparison to Richard of Saint Victor and other twelfth-century authors. Most of his uses of the word occur in Sermon 15, sections 9, 13, 34, 35; see also Sermon 7.2; 14.14. Achard is more generous in his use of the language of the spiritual senses, which is usually used in reference to contemplative experience.

113. Sermon 8.4; 14.18.

114. Psalm 34:9: 'Taste and see how sweet the Lord is'; older Latin translations often used *bonus* (good) instead of *suavis* (sweet).

115. Sermon 13.29–30.

in turn engenders a greater delight, and so on.[116] Contemplation is a flight of the soul 'freely suspended in God as though upon intellectual wings'.[117] For this the soul prepares by devotion, prayer, and meditation. After meditating on the works of God, the spiritual person looks upon God and remains with Christ in the heart of the Father.[118] Contemplation is both an act or power of the mind and a share in the wisdom of Christ.[119] The perfection of contemplation depends upon the degree of perfection of its object; the degrees of being and knowledge are strictly parallel. Sermon 13.32ff. distinguishes seven degrees of contemplation: (1) Creator in mirror of corporeal beings; (2–4) through spiritual creatures, according to nature, justice, and glory; (5) the eternal plan of things; (6) the predestination of the saints; (7) unity and trinity of God.[120]

Sermon 14 gives a more detailed explanation, in which various kinds of saints stand for the active life, and the nine choirs of angels mirror the stages of spiritual ascent.[121] Although artificial, this arrangement is explanatory. At the beginning the created mind must know God through the physical and spiritual things he has made,[122] and thus, for the purified soul, the created universe is not an obstacle (compare the second desert) but a mediation of the knowledge of God. This knowledge of God's attributes through the things he has made is not yet *contemplatio*, but *speculatio*.[123] It is a very limited knowledge, for created things are more dissimilar than similar to God.[124]

---

116. Sermon 13.33.
117. Sermon 15.19.
118. Sermon 12.6.
119. Sermon 13.4.
120. See also Sermon 8.4.
121. Achard does not follow exactly the arrangement of the nine choirs of angels in Pseudo-Dionysius, *Celestial Hierarchy* 6 (Colm Luibheid and Paul Rorem, ed. and tr. Pseudo-Dionysius, *The Complete Works* [New York: Paulist 1987] 160–161) nor does he assign them a purifying or illuminating role. He does call them guides who provide a ladder (Sermon 14.18).
122. Sermon 14.8 = first four modes of Sermon 13.
123. Achard seems to be aware of this distinction between direct contemplation of God and speculation of God through his manifestations and presence in creatures, but he does not adhere to it strictly: Sermon 14.18, 20.
124. Sermon 15.17; 9.4. For the idea that creatures are more dissimilar to God than similar, see Hugh of Saint Victor, *In Hierarchiam coelestem* 3 (PL 175: 961C), who was drawing on John Scotus Eriugena, *De divisione naturae* 1.66 (PL 122:510D).

Beyond this knowledge of God's attributes the soul may grasp the truth in itself. How, Achard does not explain. It is still *speculatio*, via creatures, but made possible by a divinely given and restored power, transformed into a faculty which associates the soul with the Powers and Virtues. The Christian realizes that the things it knows are still contingent (*ab alio*) and is led to their principle (Principalities). But God is not only their creator; he is also the one who governs their existence (Dominations).[125]

Then in the last three of the angelic hierarchies the contemplative arrives at a more intimate contemplation of divine reality: judicial causes (Thrones); formal causes (Cherubim), and final causes (Seraphim). Achard gives no indication how the soul knows these. The eternal reasons, which subsist in God, seem to illuminate the mind by a grace-given illumination.[126]

The Spiritual Generation of the Son of God and the Sixth Desert. Contemplation of the intellectual type that we have just analyzed is not the whole or the summit of the spiritual life. Christians are not satisfied with seeing the causes and reasons of things; they wish to be united more closely and personally to God. In Sermons 14 and 15 Achard describes a spiritual state that surpasses the preceding, and in which love and intelligence act together.

After treating of the angels, Sermon 14 discusses Mary, who possessed the perfection of both the active and contemplative lives. She is the example of a will perfectly purified through the active virtues, and a reason perfectly purified through the speculative virtues. Her purity of heart enabled her to engender and contemplate the Wisdom of God. Purity in itself was not enough, however; she needed the grace of God as well. Mary's conception of the Son of God is a symbol of what occurs in contemplatives who reach the summit of mystical union—they conceive, bear, and give birth to the Son of God.[127] In the first of these moments, love is predominant; the Holy Spirit engenders a violent love in

125. Sermon 14.19–20.
126. Sermon 14.21.
127. Sermon 14.22.

the contemplative, which expands and elevates the mind.[128] In the second, a more intellectual element dawns, and the mind passes wholly into God; in the third, it enters into the full light of day before the face of God.

In Sermon 15.34–35, Achard gives another description of the spirit's entry into mystical union, and of the mystical union itself. Earlier in the sermon Achard showed how Christians must dispossess themselves in the first five deserts. God now comes to fill the void this has left; then, paradoxically, Christians find themselves again. To go out of oneself makes possible a return to oneself: 'They leave . . . from themselves into God, so that God comes into them and they come into God'. They die to self and come to life again. The divine will and reason substitute for the created will and reason, so that the human being and God become one spirit.[129] This unity of spirit is the basis for an interior experience where love and intelligence are both involved: the spirit perceives, sees, and hears, but does not grasp the object of this experience. This experience leads to the courtyard of God, but not to the tabernacle. It corresponds to the conception theme of Sermon 14. The soul is wounded by love;[130] it longs to approach closer to its God. This desire arouses a distaste for anything—even service of neighbor—

128. See Richard of Saint Victor, *De arca Moysi* (Benjamin minor) 5.2 (PL 196:170), where Richard distinguishes three modes of contemplation: *dilatatio*, *sublevatio*, and *alienatio* or *excessus mentis*, and then proceeds to a long explanation of them. Achard, content with a rather vague use of the terms, does not draw the distinctions that Richard later did.

129. 1 Colossians 6:17; see Sermon 13.7; Gilson, *La théologie mystique de saint Bernard* (Paris, 1934) 142–147; M.-M. Davy, *Théologie et mystique de Guillaume de Saint-Thierry* I: *La connaissance de Dieu* (Paris, 1954) 156–186; Richard of Saint Victor, *De arca Moysi* (Benjamin major) 4.15 (PL 196:153D); *Adnotationes mysticae in Psalmos 30* (PL 196:273D); *De quatuor gradibus violentae caritatis* (Paris, 1955) 153, 169 (=PL1216D, 1221D). Achard differs from some other twelfth-century spiritual writers by including intellect as well as will in this *unitas spiritus*.

130. The theme of the 'the wound of love' entered Christian literature from ancient secular literature, notably because of Song of Songs 2:5. The Vulgate rendered this: 'I am languishing with love', but Augustine gives—e.g. *Enarrationes in Psalmos 37:5* (PL 36:399)—a translation closer to the Septuagint: 'I have been wounded by love'. Achard's use of the expression is close to that of Gregory the Great, *Moralia* 6.42 (PL 85:752C-753A), and Richard of Saint Victor, *De quatuor gradibus violentae caritatis*, ed. Dumeige, 131 (PL 196:1209). See A. Cabussut, 'Blessure d'amour', in DSp (1937) 1:1727–1728.

that would distract the soul from God. The renunciation of material and spiritual service (except prayer) to a neighbor, which is only provisory, is perhaps partly motivated by an awareness of the egotism that can be part of such service. In the seventh desert, contemplatives will be called to renounce contemplation and put themselves again at the service of their neighbor, with a more ardent and pure charity. But now, when such service is left behind, Christians experience a peace beyond understanding; their life is hidden within Christ; they enter into the joy of their Lord. In the first steps of contemplation, Christians saw God mirrored in physical and spiritual creatures; now they see created things in a much more sublime way in their archetypes in God. This mystical union Achard describes as *excessus mentis*, as divinization, and as reformation in the form of God. It is both affective and intellectual, but in the end, love reaches the very heart of the mystery of God, whereas the intellect stops short at the eternal reasons; there is no contemplative vision of the divine essence.[131]

The Seventh Desert: Identification with Christ. The mystical union described in Sermons 14 and 15 is not the ultimate term of the spiritual progress that Achard describes. More than contemplation of the eternal reasons, ecstasy, or spiritual inebriation, its identification with Christ is the final goal and supreme ideal. Now the love of Christ drives the contemplative to become, like Christ, a slave of all. Thus, the whole ascetical effort by which Christians turn from sin, world, flesh, and self had no other purpose than to light the fire of perfect love in them. Perfect love is love of God, but it is also a participation in that love which led the Son of God into a distant region of unlikeness in order to share the sufferings of sinners and lead them back to his Father. That the end of our salvation thus coalesces with its beginning is a warning that the steps Achard distinguishes are not to be understood in a rigid, sequential way. The same desire and hope are operative throughout the journey.

Perhaps, too, we see operative here Achard's problematic axiom, 'What belongs to the Son of God by nature, belongs to the humanity

131. See also Sermon 15.23.

of Christ by grace'. The trajectory Achard traces is not from the humanity of Christ to his divinity, but from his humanity, to his divinity, to his humanity in an endless loop. The perfect love that Christ possesses by grace in his humanity is and ever will be that in which we participate, and by which we participate in divine love. We will never cease to be his spiritual body. We will never cease to be drawn toward one another by the cords of love which drew the Son of God to become our brother.

Metaphysics

As we have seen Achard's surviving works include two philosophical works.[132] The editing and attribution of both works have been something of a scholarly saga. More will be said about both works in the introductions to the translations which follow. Here we will concentrate our attention on the background of the *De unitate Dei et pluralitate creaturarum*.

André Combes, Jean Ribaillier,[133] and Jean Châtillon all gave interpretations of Achard's metaphysics, based on the fragments of *De unitate* quoted by John of Ripa, a fourteenth-century scholastic, and what was known of the manuscript of the full work discovered by M.-T. d'Alverny in Padua. Now that the complete text of the work has been published these interpretations have all become obsolete. However, the edition has also complicated matters, because Emmanuel Martineau, the editor, has very strong opinions about the proper interpretation and importance of Achard's metaphysics.

The Victorine 'school' was a variegated group of canons regular who had in common a respect for Hugh of Saint Victor, who seems to have succeeded William of Champeaux as the chief teacher at

132. Throughout I understand 'metaphysics' in a non-technical and expansive sense, which includes philosophical psychology, that is, the *On the Distinction*.

133. In the introduction to his edition of Richard of Saint Victor's *De Trinitate* (Paris: Vrin, 1958) 27–33 . Bibliographic references to the other works mentioned in this paragraph are included in the discussion of *De unitate* in the earlier section of this introduction devoted to Achard's works.

the abbey. We know he taught extern students, and it is not fanciful to think that through him many Parisian students joined the abbey. He died in 1141, so that his impact on men like Richard of Saint Victor, and possibly even on Achard, may have been literary rather than personal. In any case, the heritage Hugh left the members of his school was a varied one, encompassing systematic and pastoral theology, both doctrinal and moral; traditional exegesis according to the literal and spiritual senses, but with a strong emphasis on the foundation provided by the literal sense, spirituality, and preaching. He was not primarily a philosopher, but he incorporated philosophy into his works. Different members of the abbey developed different aspects of Hugh's heritage. Andrew of Saint Victor pioneered the study of the literal sense of Scripture. Richard of Saint Victor was almost as versatile a thinker and author as Hugh, but he particularly devoted his talents to composing monographs on particular theological topics, e.g., *On the Trinity*; to theoretical and practical works of spirituality; and to preaching (his *Liber exceptionum* seems to be a manual for preaching). The members of Saint Victor did not feel any obligation to agree on all points with Hugh of Saint Victor or with each other; Richard criticized Andrew's interpretation of Isaiah 7:15 very stringently because it was too much influenced by Jewish interpretations.[134] At the end of the *De unitate*, Achard seems to include a tribute to Hugh of Saint Victor, whose great theological synthesis *De sacramentis* began with a distinction between God's two works: work of creation and the work of redemption.[135]

Achard's *De unitate*, Martineau thinks, contains criticism of Richard of Saint Victor's *De Trinitate*. This is a bold assertion, granted the uncertainties of the chronology of the two works, the indirectness of the evidence, and the presumably cordial relations between Abbot Achard and his subprior Richard. In any case, the two works are quite different. Richard is not primarily a philosopher; if anything, one might call his method in the *De Trinitate* a theological personalism. He tries to find in the human experience

---

134. On the Victorine school, see Patrice Sicard, *Hugues de Saint-Victor et son Ecole* (Turnhout: Brepols, 1991).

135. *De unitate* 2.21.

of love a basis for understanding and explaining something of the mystery of the Trinity. Achard, on the other hand, seldom appeals to experience. Like Richard, he is looking for necessary reasons, but he finds his 'necessary reasons' in the realm of abstract thought, beginning with the idea of unity, and in the realm of the primordial causes of things, the ideas in the divine mind.[136]

Beyond its Victorine setting, the *De unitate* betrays a fourfold debt—to Anselm, to Augustine, to Eriugena, and to Plato. The debt to Augustine is clear, both from the explicit references Achard makes in 2.3, 5, and 6, and in the many Augustinian parallels and sources to which Martineau draws attention in his notes. Treatise 2, chapter 16, is, as Martineau observes, an accurate summary of many aspects of Augustinian spirituality.[137] The debt to Anselm is primarily methodological: from him Achard (like Richard) derived the program of searching for necessary reasons for the things he accepted by faith. Achard's debt to Eriugena seems direct, and that to Plato indirect, but this combined dependence is deep, at least in what concerns the philosophy of the forms and ideas.

In the very first chapter of *De unitate* Achard draws a contrast between this world 'here' and the divine world of God and the immutable forms 'there'. 'There true plurality and unity must reside.'[138] There is where everything that is or can be has its truest being.

The largest part of the work is devoted to the formal or exemplary cause, one of the three forms or causes of all that has been or can be created. In 1.38–39 Achard explains these three kinds of causes by the analogy of the book: the final cause is the benefit the readers will gain; the formal causes is the knowledge learned by experience or revelation then given physical embodiment in the book; and the efficient cause is the *ars* or *modus scribendi*, the know-how or skill that enables the author to achieve his purpose (final cause) by putting into words the ideas (formal cause) he wishes to communicate in written form. This division of causes, all of which exist as

136. Martineau, ed., 29–36. For Richard of Saint Victor's theological method, see my forthcoming study.

137. Martineau, ed., 'Eclaircissements' 18, 251–253.

138. *De unitate* 1.1. See Châtillon, *Théologie*, 277–284.

understood in the mind of God, is derived from the four causes of Aristotle. Not only does it leave aside the material cause, it also alters in a platonic direction the meaning of the formal cause and of the efficient cause, which is no longer the agent or the instrument, but the art or skill needed by the agent. This division of forms or causes is also quite different from that in the sermons, especially Sermon 14.20. This becomes clear in 2.20, where Achard advances a division resembling that in the Sermon, which is that causes may be original (in God alone), natural, judicial (regarding merit), and final (regarding what follows from merit). This is certainly a different final cause from that in *De unitate* 1.38–39.[139]

Scattered throughout *De unitate* are references to beauty which do not seem essential to the flow of the arguments, but seem rather to indicate a pre-occupation of Achard's: the beauty of God, of God's plan, of God's creation. Achard speaks of the supreme beauty existing in God, and of the striking beauty that exists in the unity and congruence of the many things modeled on God's beauty.[140] He is fascinated by the beauty of each of the countless parts that make up the entities of the world, the beauty of each of these and of the universe in which they are united. 'The contemplation of this [conjoined] beauty would give rise to an ineffable delight', if such contemplation were possible to anyone but God.[141] Few rise to immediate contemplation of the truth in all its beauty.[142]

Finally, in the midst of his rigorous elaboration of his religious philosophy Achard several times introduces christological ideas reminiscent of the sermons. For example, in Christ 'there are two natures, each of which can be called a person per se, although there are not there two persons, but one person in two natures: in God assuming human nature—that is, in the Word—by its own nature; in the human nature assumed, by the goodness and grace of the Word assuming it'.[143]

---

139. Châtillon, *Théologie*, 284–289.
140. *De unitate* 1.5–6.
141. *De unitate* 1.48.
142. *De unitate* 2.16.
143. *De unitate* 1.14.

TEXTS IN TRANSLATION

THEOLOGY

Theological Anthropology

Sermon 9: On the Solemnity of Saint Augustine

INTRODUCTION

THIS SERMON WAS PREACHED on the feast of Saint Augustine, August twenty-eight. The canons of Saint Victor followed the Rule of Saint Augustine, although their customs were derived mainly from Benedictine, and particularly from Cluniac, practice. Augustine, the first section of this sermon indicates, was thought of as their 'father'. The text that forms the subject of the body of the sermon, 'Augustine found himself far from God, in a region of unlikeness',[1] was taken from the first response in the first nocturn of Matins for the feast as it was celebrated at Saint Victor. In its turn, the text derives from Augustine's *Confessions*:[2] 'I found myself to be far from you in a region of

1. 7.10.16

2. This text, in particular the topos 'region of unlikeness', has been the subject of a vast amount of erudition since it was first studied by Etienne Gilson in his *La théologie mystique de saint Bernard* (Paris: Vrin, 1934) 63, n. 1. For references and a summary see Châtillon, *Sermons*, 99, n. 4. The phrase echoes both a text of Plato (*Politics*, 273d) and the parable of the prodigal son (Luke 15:11–72).

unlikeness, as though I heard your voice from on high: "I am the food of the mature. Grow and you will eat me. You will not change me into yourself as you do the food of your flesh, but you will be changed into me." ' Only at the middle of his sermon, however, does Achard take up this theme, as can be seen in this brief outline: (1) Achard apologizes for the curiosity and restlessness that keep him from entering into himself and spending time on the things of God so that he can give the brethren a proper sermon. (2) The human spirit is fighting a war on several fronts. It must fight against the world and unclean spirits, yet it is torn by internal dissensions and entrenched in a sense of false security. (3) The spirit mounts the horses of anger, intemperance, and hypocrisy, and these take it to a far country, a region of wickedness. (4) There are three regions of unlikeness—nature, guilt, and punishment—and, corresponding to these, three regions of likeness—nature, righteousness (5), and beatitude (6).[3]

Achard begins with a humble declaration of inadequacy: he is troubled by restlessness and curiosity. Curiosity, the proverb says, kills cats, but today we generally think of it as a positive trait. However, for a long tradition stemming primarily from Augustine, *curiositas* is a vice. The vice still exists, unnamed, but no less malignant: it is visible in our need to be distracted and entertained at any cost, even by the inanities of most television programs, by frivolous journalism, and by mass produced fiction. *Curiositas* is whatever makes us not at home to the God who wishes to make his home in us.[4] We ride into the regions of unlikeness on 'the horses of our birth', that is to say, on the disordered powers of our soul in its fallen state, born according to the flesh, but not according to grace,[5] for, as section two explains, our inner selves are full of conflicting inclinations, desires, and wishes. The world, which God created for our benefit, now attacks us from one side, weakening us with the prosperity that puffs us up with pride, and depressing

3. These three regions are presented in an anonymous Victorine sermon, edited by Jean Châtillon in *Sermones ineditos*, CCCM 30 (Turnhout: Brepols, 1975) 276–282.

4. See the rich documentation provided by Châtillon, *Sermons*, 101–102, n. 1.

5. See the three births mentioned in Sermon 8.5.

us with misfortune. On the other side are the assaults of evil spirits. We go along oblivious of the dangers that threaten us and unaware of the internal conflicts that pull each of us apart because we are absorbed in the things around us. We ride away from our true selves into a region of unlikeness on the horses of anger, lust, and pride.[6]

In the last three sections of the sermon Achard describes three regions of unlikeness and three regions of likeness. The starting point for his discussion is the doctrine, derived from Augustine,[7] that everything God made bears at least a distant likeness to the Creator. By its nature each created thing reflects the being, beauty, and goodness of God, or, in another formulation, God's power, wisdom, and goodness. Among God's creatures, human beings are in a particular way his image and likeness because of their ability to know, love, grasp, and enjoy God.[8] On the other hand, whatever the natural likeness of creatures to God may be, we are much more unlike him than like him, and this constitutes the first, the natural, region of unlikeness.

The second region of unlikeness, that of fault, is the one most distant from God. Everything but sin has some likeness to God. To describe this second region of unlikeness Achard elaborates on the parable of the prodigal son.[9] For the prodigal, for Augustine, and for many who have recovered via the twelve steps, it was only when they reached the depths of degradation that a light arose in the darkness. The second region of likeness, which like the second region of unlikeness, is smaller than the first, consists of the region of righteousness, formed of all those whom the grace of God enables to actually use their innate capacities to know, love and embrace him. This level of likeness is as superior to the first as act is to the capacity to act.

The third region of unlikeness is that of punishment and pain, which at least resembles God in that it is just and in accord with

6. This moral application of the four horses of the Apocalypse is derived from Saint Ambrose, who may have been influenced by the myth of the winged horses in Plato's *Phaedrus*. For texts and discussion see Châtillon, *Sermons*, 104, n. 10.

7. See especially *De Trinitate* 6.10.12 (PL 42:932).

8. See Sermons 1.3; 13.32.

9. Luke 15

nature. The third region of likeness is the region of beatitude, which although smaller than the previous two, is much nearer to God. It consists in the full knowledge, love and enjoyment of God.

Finally, in an interesting development Achard asserts that the blessed, if forced to make a choice, would choose righteousness rather than happiness, because God's will is to be preferred to ours, and righteousness fulfills God's will in us, whereas beatitude fulfills our will in God. In any case, above all the regions of likeness is the Trinity; there likeness is identical to equality, and equality is unity. To contemplate that unity is the goal to which Achard prays God will bring us.

THE SERMON

On the Solemnity of Saint Augustine

SINCE I MUST FILL THE PLACE OF THE SAGE, I must become foolish. I have not prepared as I should have, and I have not foreseen in a fitting way words of exhortation appropriate for your brotherhood and suitable to the solemnity of our great father Augustine. The cause of this lack of foresight is a peculiar curiosity and restlessness of my spirit. While it should be resting within, staying at home, and spending time on the things of God, it wanders outside, restless and unstable, running here and there. In a moment, in the blink of an eye, mounted upon the horses of its birth it is led hither and yon through various regions and provinces to one battle or another. If eventually after long erroneous wanderings it returns inside to itself, it still does not pay attention to interior things and ponder them, but instead it thinks over exterior things, if not in themselves, at least in their images. While it is intent on such things and forgetful of itself, it is not attentive to the war being waged against it inside and out. Instead, the wretched spirit feels secure in the midst of war, and so its enemy finds it naked and unarmed.

2. According to the law and ordinance of nature the flesh should serve the spirit. Now, however, the flesh resists, goes against the spirit, and contradicts it; it plagues and disturbs the spirit by sensation and sensory inclination. The spirit itself is separated and divided in itself and from itself. The will departs from reason and contradicts it in many matters, and

so we do not instantly choose all that we approve by reason. Sometimes the will is even at odds with itself. Sometimes we want something in part and in part do not; since this is a family or domestic quarrel it is all the more dangerous.

On the opposite front, the world itself stands against my spirit in battle array, with the army of prosperity and adversity. With prosperity it weakens it, saps its strength, and hoists it up on the winds of pride. With adversity it breaks and crushes it. A third war also threatens, the terrible and dreadful war of the unclean spirits. 'Our struggle is not only against flesh and blood, but also against the rulers of this world, of this darkness—that is, against the
Ep 6:12 spiritual forces of evil in the heavenly places.'† The onslaught of these spirits is to be deeply feared, since they are invisible, depraved, and full of every deception and deceit. They do not enter into battle against us for an insignificant reason, but for our eternal inheritance. This they cannot acquire for themselves, but they can take it away from us, whom they wish to have as sharers in their misery.

Set among so many battle lines, and feeling secure, the spirit neglects its own salvation and wanders about unarmed and naked in the midst of its enemies. It should be totally intent on calling everything back with the help of God to the order of the first creation, on mortifying its members which are upon the earth, and on crucifying the flesh with its evil inclinations and desires, so that the subdued flesh might serve the spirit, and the world itself, which was made for humanity, might also work for humanity's good according to God's original plan. Thus might all the flaming arrows of the evil enemy be extinguished.

3. What wickedness! God's laws are despised, the spirit is trampled under the feet of its handmaid, seduced by the wiles of the enemy, drawn by the vanities of the world, tossed outside, and led far away. The horses spoken of in the Apocalypse†— Rv 6:4, 5, 8
red, black, and pale—are always ready. The red horse bears my spirit to all sorts of battles, feelings of rage, quarrels, and things like that; the black horse bears it to overeating and drunkenness; the pale horse bears it to hypocrisy and pretense. The red horse bears it through hard and harsh places, the black horse through dirty and stinking places, the pale horse through difficult and steep places. The red horse bears it through places of malice and perversity, the black horse through places of carnal desire, the pale horse through places of vainglory. Seldom or never does the spirit mount the white horse, concerning which is written: 'He went forth victorious'.† Those who do mount this horse of Rv 6:2
innocence conquer and are not conquered; those who mount the other three horses are conquered and do not conquer. Sometimes, however, it happens to mount the white horse but does not stay there long. Instead, it prefers the horses of vanity which wound it and tear it to pieces. These horses take it to a far country, a region of unlikeness, the region of Egypt, and do not bring it back from there. These horses serve Pharaoh and his army.† Ex 15:4

4. 'In a region of unlikeness', I say, in which 'Augustine found himself far from God'. Three regions of unlikeness exist: the first is of nature, the second of guilt, the third of punishment. Three regions of likeness exist: the first is of nature, the second of righteousness, the third of the blessed life. Every creature is similar to its origin insofar as it exists, is included in some species, and con-

tributes something useful to the good of the totality. Everything that exists is like that from which it comes, inasmuch as it exists, is beautiful, and is good; that is, because of its existence, beauty, and useful goodness. Every creature has the image and vestige of the supreme Trinity within itself: with regard to existence it emulates the Father, with regard to beauty the Son, with regard to usefulness the Holy Spirit.

Moreover, in the rational creature is an image much more noble and lofty than the image mentioned just now. Besides that general image found in all things, the rational creature is endowed interiorly with another image, in that it can understand him from whom it comes, love him whom it understands, embrace him whom it loves, for both implementation and enjoyment: implementation, so that it may be just; enjoyment, so that it may be blessed. Hence only the rational creature is said
Gn 1:26 to be made in the image and likeness of God,† not because no other creature has an image of God in it, but because the rational creature has such an outstanding and excellent image of its Creator, one no other nature inferior to it contains. This natural likeness is in each individual, while the region is in all. To this region of likeness is opposed a region of unlikeness of the same kind; that is, on the level of nature. Everything that exists is much more unlike him from whom it comes than similar to him; nothing, however closely it approaches him through likeness, can be his equal in all things.

5. The region of righteousness consists in usefulness brought about by an act implementing the power of understanding, loving, and embracing. This region is much worthier and more Godlike than the previous natural region, which consists in

potentiality only. This is not because it exists in many, since it is in rather few (the number of existents exceeds the number of the just), but because it involves the employment and actual use of the same power of which it has the potentiality. The likeness of righteousness is in each of the just; the region is in the totality. To this region is opposed a region of unlikeness which consists in guilt; this is much more distant from God than the regions of nature and punishment since everything that exists, with the exception of sin, has some likeness to God. Punishment has some likeness to God, either because it is just, or because at least it happens by the just judgment of God, or because such a nature is by God's doing such that it cannot be brought into contact with another nature without suffering, like a finger brought into contact with fire. This is that distant region in which the prodigal son squandered his substance with prostitutes by wanton living. This region, where pigs are fed, is slimy and full of manure. This is the region of darkness in which Augustine found himself at the moment when a light rose for him.

6. The region of beatitude, which consists in the full and thoroughly pleasant enjoyment of truth itself, fully understood and loved and embraced, is much greater, worthier, and closer to God than the previous two. It is greater than the second of them, even though it has fewer inhabitants since more are just than blessed. However, if beatitude could be possessed without righteousness, those who are already blessed would choose to be just rather than blessed, if given the choice, because through righteousness God's will is fulfilled in us and through beatitude our will is fulfilled in God. As God's will is to be preferred to the human will,

so too, even if beatitude could be possessed without righteousness, one should choose to be just rather than blessed. In accord with what was said in the other two instances, the likeness of beatitude is in each individual, the region is in the totality. To this is opposed that region of unlikeness which is called punishment.

Above all these regions of likeness is the region of the supreme and uncreated Trinity, where likeness is equality itself, and equality is unity itself. May the divine Majesty, triune and one, lead us to contemplate that unity. Amen.

Sermon 10: On Cultivating the Lord's Vineyard

INTRODUCTION

THIS SERMON ELABORATES THE LITERAL SENSE of the parable of the workers in the vineyard, and then gives a moral interpretation. (1) The opening section situates the life of the individual Christian in the wider drama of sin and grace. The Law was given to manifest sin and protect human beings from pride; grace was given so that we might keep the commandments. (2) The Church is the vineyard; we all have a responsibility to cultivate it, at least in ourselves, if not in others. (3) The first stage (hour) in the cultivation of the Christian life is to root out worldliness in works, speech, and thought. We do this through repentance and confession. During the second hour we fertilize the vineyard by cultivating compunction through the recollection of the sins we regret committing in our past life. Compunction arises from fear and gives birth to love. (4) In the third, fourth, and fifth hours we prune away superfluous habits, activities, inclinations, and feelings. (5–6) In the sixth through the eighth hours we braid a life of righteousness and love toward neighbor, God, and self. (7) Habit and expectation of reward, the tenth hour, strengthen the Christian in good. In the eleventh hour the vine is propagated through the increase of virtue. The twelfth hour is the time of our reward.

In this sermon we are presented with many spiritual terms and categories taken for granted by Christians of Achard's time and status. The outline of the spiritual journey that he presents—from repentance and confession, through fear of God, to compunction, to a life of moral reform, virtue, and righteousness informed by love—was familiar and taken for granted. So, too, were the numerical mnemonics of six works of mercy, seven gifts of the Holy Spirit, nine orders of angels. Yet, against this familiar background, several things stand out.

Right at the beginning, Achard emphasizes the primacy of grace in salvation. The stages of salvation history were designed to deprive human beings of grounds for pride. Thus at the outset Achard emphasizes the fundamental message of the parable, and then he proceeds to give the story a different twist by discussing the works through which the Spirit leads Christians to a more mature share in Christ's life.

Still in the first section, Achard puts the sober inebriation of the Spirit at the beginning of the spiritual journey; it is something initiated by baptism. In the usual outline of spiritual growth, it would appear at the end. Achard implies that because fervent and contemplative awareness of God are gifts of the Spirit, they can happen at any stage of the spiritual journey and not just to those who have advanced methodically through the active life of virtue and service.

In the second section, Achard combines the metaphor of the cultivation of the vineyard with that of Christ the vine.[1] All the vines in the vineyard are propagated from the vine which is Christ. The vineyard's vines include not just the Church on earth but the saints in heaven as well. In heaven there is no need to cultivate the

1. On the theme Christ the Vine see the apse mosaic at San Clemente (e.g., *San Clemente* [Rome: Collegio S. Clemente, 1974] fig. 3–8) and Saint Bonaventure's work, *The Mystical Vine*, in *Works of Bonaventure*, tr. José de Vinck (Paterson, NJ: Saint Anthony Guild, 1960) 1:145–205.

vine, but on earth all Christians should cultivate God's planting in themselves and in others. Throughout the sermon the Christian's responsibility toward others—in righteousness, works of mercy, and love—receives strong emphasis.[2] At the end of the section Achard speaks angrily of those who not only fail to cultivate the vineyard, but actually harm it. He mentions the detractors and murmurers who corrupt the hearts of others, especially of novices. Perhaps we are entitled to see in this admonition a hint of the spiritual malaise that seems to have struck Saint Victor under Achard's successor, Abbot Ervisius.

The opening sentences of the third section outline the agricultural elaboration Achard gives of the parable; these elaborations will be the basis for his moral interpretation. Achard begins with a description of conversion, which, consisting of inner repentance and outer confession, embraces thoughts, words, and inclinations. Compunction, the sorrowful recollection of past sins, will always have a place in the Christian's life, provided such recollection is not the occasion of renewed temptation.

Section four may be seen as an exhortation to make repentance and confession effective in a transformation of our thoughts, words and deeds. Bad habits should be eliminated first, then isolated sinful acts. Then we should try to control our feelings, in particular feelings of depression.

Achard makes some interesting observations regarding righteousness and love in section five. We should discharge all debts of righteousness by giving all their due. By giving all their due righteousness establishes a sort of proportionate equality wherein each person has what is owed to dignity and rank. However, we can never pay the debt of love; love is an abiding obligation. Fortunately, we come to possess more love the more we give it away.

In the course of this sermon Achard alludes to some arithmetical

2. Besides the obvious examples, there may be another instance near the end of section seven, where Achard speaks of the number eleven standing for 'the increase of virtues and their extension to where they had never been before'. This seems to mean that virtue increases not only intensively in those who have it, but also extensively when it is introduced into other people's lives and souls where previously it was absent. The statement could also be taken to refer to extending virtue into facets of one's own life which hitherto were not virtuous.

lore. Six is the first perfect number because it equals the sum of its parts (1+2+3). Eight is the first solid, i.e., cubic (2^3) or three-dimensional (2 x 2 x 2), number. Ten is perfection (1+2+3+4); this number will be reached when human beings join the angels to constitute the tenth heavenly choir.

THE SERMON

On Cultivating the Lord's Vineyard

THE KINGDOM OF HEAVEN IS LIKE THE HEAD OF A HOUSEHOLD who went out at dawn', at the third, sixth, ninth, and eleventh hours, 'to hire workers for his vineyard'.† In this gospel, which is read today in Mt 20:1–6
the Church, it says that the head of a household went out to cultivate his vineyard. In much the same way, next Sunday the reading will say that 'the sower went out to sow his seed'.[3] These two, namely, food and drink, make up all refection. But why is it said that he went out to cultivate his vineyard before he went out to sow his seed, as if he wished to tend to drinking before eating? In former times, to Adam in paradise and to the children of Israel in the desert, God gave food to eat, but not wine to drink. Because they ate, but did not drink, they choked. He gave them the Law, but no blessing; the letter that kills, but not the life-giving Spirit; the commandment, but not the grace to fulfill it. He did this not for himself, but for them so they would not think that they could fulfill all God's commandments by their own power without the intervention of his grace. If that happened, they would have 'glory, but not in the sight of God'.† Hence, because they would Rm 4:2
have spurned unworthily the grace that was offered them, as though they did not need it, they were given as a counterweight to their pride the Law that

3. Sermon 10, then, like Sermon 7, was given on Septuagesima Sunday. At Saint Victor in Achard's time the gospel for Sexagesima was indeed Luke 8:5–15.

showed the way, but not the grace that would have guided them along the way and led them through.

Now, in the time of grace, to us who have no occasion for pride, the wine of spiritual grace is first given us to drink in the sacrament of baptism. It consists in an overflowing abundance of charisms, an inpouring of love, and an anointing of the spirit. 'Love', the Apostle says, 'has been poured out in our hearts by the Holy Spirit who has
Rm 5:5 been given to us'.† Inebriated by this wine, as though rejoicing and exulting in the wealth of God's house, unencumbered and happy, we run with our hearts enlarged on the way of God's
Ps 119:32 commandments.† Without his grace we can do nothing, because [everything comes] 'not from the one willing, or from the one running, but from the
Rm 9:16 merciful God'.† So Augustine wrote: 'Give what you command'—that is, the power and strength that enable me to choose, and the will by which I choose, to do what you command—and once you have given me this grace, 'command what you will'.[4]

2. What is this vineyard that yields such good wine, such soberly inebriating wine? Listen to Isaiah: 'The vineyard of the Lord Sabaoth is the house
Is 5:7 of Israel'.† Everything pertaining to Israel is this vineyard, and is from this vineyard, one wholly produced and propagated from that Vine who says: 'I am the true vine and you are the branches'. Whatever good we have we have received from
Jn 15:1, 5 him. Hence, 'without me you can do nothing'.† This is the vineyard about which it is written: My
Jr 2:21 'chosen vineyard, all true seed'†—true seed indeed, because originating in Truth itself. This vineyard

4. This formula occurs several times in Saint Augustine's writings; e.g. *Confessions* 10.29.40 ('Give what you command, and command what you will.'). For other instances see Châtillon, *Sermons*, 110, n. 14.

not only extends far and wide through the whole world but is also raised up on high so that it touches the heavens; in fact, it extends its branches above the heavens. They are suspended on high; they are rooted in eternity and made eternal; they receive nourishment and fecundity from the plenty of the root. Already the multitude of the saints reigns triumphantly in God, and with God, and enjoys the most blessed sight of him.

That part of the vineyard has already been well cultivated; it needs no more cultivating. To cultivate the part that is still on earth all of us work eagerly and carefully insofar as we are able, in ourselves and in others; or at least in ourselves, since we need it, if we cannot work in another. Many do not cultivate this vineyard, but ruin it, and destroy it like foxes. Such are the detractors, murmurers, corruptors of good works, who seduce the hearts of the simple, and especially of novices. What they do not dare to do openly, they do in secret. Of them the Song says: 'Catch us the little foxes that destroy the vineyards'.† They are to be caught and Sg 2:15 bound, averted or converted. They make great strides toward the worse.

3. As I stated at the beginning, the head of the household went out at dawn, and at the third, sixth, ninth, and eleventh hours, to hire workers to cultivate this vineyard. They are to dig, then turn the soil again and a third time, fertilize the vine with manure, then prune, braid, and tie it, and finally propagate it.[5]

The workers dig the vineyard when through true repentance and pure confession they pull out the worldliness of evil deeds, base desires, and

5. For a similar descriptions of vineyard cultivation, see Richard of Saint Victor, *Liber exceptionum* 2.10.15, ed. Châtillon, 405.

worldly attractions from the roots of this vine; the vine is our heart, for from it proceeds every
Mt 15:18–19 deed,† whether good or bad. They turn the soil a second time when by repentance and confession they repel whatever worldliness has been contracted through evil and disordered speech. They turn the soil yet a third time when they wipe away every blemish from their thoughts. These blemishes must be wiped away since, when we stand before the tribunal of Christ, before God the judge, we will have to render an account of them. As the Apostle says: 'Their conscience gives
Rm 2:15 testimony to them'† of thoughts that accuse and defend them. Some will be grounds for defense, others grounds for accusation. This weeding out of worldliness and pulling up of evil inclinations are dawn and the first hour of the day. Unless the vessel is cleaned beforehand, whatever is poured into it will taste bitter.

Then the manure of sins and misdeeds is to be applied to the root of the vine to increase fertility. By frequently recalling past sins and misdeeds, and carefully meditating on them, fear is born; from fear, compunction; from compunction, the love which is the fecundity of the vine, for without it the vine produces no fruit. In this way through the grace of God even our evil deeds work together for our good;[6] God has made 'a light shine out of our
2 Co 4:6 darkness',† because out of it he has drawn good and out of the abundance of sin he brings about a
Rm 5:20 superabundance of grace.† This careful recollection is helpful only to those in whom sin is dead, not dominant. If this is not the case, remembering is harmful, infectious, and nauseating. This application of manure is the second hour. For just as the

6. See Romans 8:28 and Sermon 7.4.

dyad first receded from unity, so through sin we receded from our God.

4. Now, after the first and second hours, the time for pruning has arrived. There is to be a cutting away of superfluous growth which is too thick or extended, both in our members and in our senses. [The pruning should occur in this order:] first habits, then actions, and finally, as far as possible, even feelings—that is to say, sin dwelling in the flesh, the law of the members, carnality, the tinder of sin, the inborn concupiscence that arises partly from bad habits, partly from bad actions, and partly from the original, first corruption.

The cutting off of habits, which is easier than the others, is the third hour. It is prefigured by the third dead person whom the Lord raised to life.† The fourth hour is the cutting off of bad actions. It is indicated by the dead youth who was carried outside the city gate, whom the Lord restored alive to his mother.† The fifth hour is the cutting off of distress, at least so that it is no longer in control. It is signified by the daughter of the synagogue leader, whom the Lord raised in her father's house where few were admitted.†

Cf. Jn 11:1–44

Cf. Lk 7:11–15

Cf. Mk 5:22–23, 35–43 par.

5. Next comes the sixth hour, when the vine is braided. Once harmful things are pulled out and superfluous ones cut back, it still needs to be braided and turned so that it may bear fruit. In this braiding the higher and lower parts of the vine are made equal. To the symmetry of the braiding corresponds the position of the sun at the sixth hour: it stands in the middle to the south, equidistant from its rising and setting. The symmetrical braiding is effected through righteousness, to which it belongs to render to all what is their own and what each is owed.

What does this mean? Listen to the Apostle as
he says: 'Owe no one anything, except that you
Rm 13:8 love one another'.† Other things are rendered so
that they will not be owed; love is rendered so
that it will always be owed. Just as one cannot
render love unless one has it, so one cannot have
it unless one renders it; that is, unless one loves
God, one's neighbor, and oneself. One loves what
one is, what is next to oneself, and what is above
oneself. Scripture does not say how one should
love oneself, other than by saying: 'Those who
hate their life in this world will keep it for eternal
Jn 12.25 life';† that is, those who so govern themselves in this
present life that they may live happily for eternity
are the ones who truly love themselves. Since this
does not happen unless they treat their lives severely
and harshly, those who act this way are said to hate
their lives; their relationship to their life seems to
be such that they are persecuting it out of hatred.
In fact, this is not to hate it, but to love it truly.

6. Your neighbor is to be loved in two ways;
namely, what you do not want done to yourself you
do not do to another, and what you wish others
to do to you, that you do for your neighbor. God
is to be loved in three ways; namely, 'with all one's
Dt 6:5; Mk 12:30, etc. heart, and all one's strength, and all one's soul',†
that is, wisely, bravely and perseveringly. Notice
that there is one way to love yourself, two ways to
love your neighbor, and three ways to love God.
In this way you have the 'six' of righteousness
and love, the first perfect number, which equals
the total of its parts—unity, duality, and trinity—
without exceeding them or being exceeded by
them. In this one notes the perfect equality of
justice, whose effect is to make superiors equal
to their inferiors. It does this not by confusing

natural rank and dignity, as though a lesser were made equal to a greater (e.g., a human being made equal to God); righteousness is said to make all things equal because it renders to all what is their own, that is, whatever is owed them according to their rank and dignity. In this day of virtue of which we are speaking, the sixth hour is love of neighbor because love of neighbor consists in the six works of mercy.[7] God also completed all his works in this many days.

The seventh hour is the love of God because of the seven gifts of the Holy Spirit.[8] 'We should not be surprised that in this enumeration of the hours love of neighbor precedes love of God because the former leads to the latter. Hence John writes in his canonical epistle: 'Those who do not love a brother whom they see, how can they love God whom they do not see?'† But you say, they cannot 1 Jn 4:20
really love a neighbor unless they love God, in whom and on account of whom they love their neighbor. It is true that no one can love a neighbor without loving God also. However, no one will arrive at that perfection of love about which we speak without first loving his neighbor.

The eighth hour is the love by which we all love ourselves, since eight is the first solid number. Thus it symbolizes the fullness of love which they must have who hate their lives in this world in order to keep them for eternal life. Only those who are perfect in love of God and neighbor can do this.

7. There follows the ninth hour in which the vine is tied. This happens in us through confir-

---

7. Matthew 25:35–36 lists six works of mercy. The familiar number of seven was achieved by adding 'burying the dead' as shown in Tobit 1:17–19. Richard of Saint Victor, *Sermones centum* 35 (PL 177:986B) lists six works of mercy.

8. Isaiah 11:2 lists six gifts—wisdom, understanding, counsel, fortitude, knowledge, and godliness—to which the Vulgate adds 'the fear of the Lord' (verse 3).

mation. This confirmation happens in two ways: through habit, and through expectation of a reward. Through habit things which at first seem burdensome and unbearable, and all but impossible, first cease to be burdensome, then become easy, and are at least attractive. Thus habit, wonderfully, confirms us in the good. This confirmation through custom is the ninth hour because of the nine orders of angels who are already confirmed.

That we are confirmed through the hope and expectation of a reward is clear to all. This sort of confirmation is the tenth hour because of the denarius which is the expected reward. The denarius was said to be the coin of the census, worth ten other coins, hence its name. It bore the likeness of the king. The image of the great King consists in a tenfold rational creation embracing the nine orders of angels plus human nature. This denarius is partially incomplete as long as 'we are away from
2 Co 5:6 the Lord';† it will finally be perfect when 'all of us
Ep 4:13 reach maturity'.†

Next comes the eleventh hour in which the vine is to be propagated. To propagate a vine is to extend it, and by planting to increase and multiply it. Our vine is propagated by an increase of virtues and by extending them to where they never were before. This propagation of virtues is the eleventh hour, because eleven is the addition of unity to ten. Now all that remains is the twelfth hour, in which the owner will call his workers and render to them the reward of eternal happiness. To this may he deign to lead us. Amen.

Sermon 11: [Second] Sermon on Palm Sunday

INTRODUCTION

THE OUTLINE OF THIS SERMON CORRESPONDS to the sections: (1) Both of the principal processions of the Church year begin on the Mount of Olives, and so concern the heights of divine grace. (2) The Palm Sunday procession symbolizes the remission of original sin, and also of actual sin, both venial and mortal. Remission of actual sin requires contrition, confession, and satisfaction. (3) Original righteousness conferred in baptism is presupposed by actual righteousness, which is achieved by the simultaneous working of free choice and God's grace. (4) Jesus' Palm Sunday procession included an ass and a colt; he must rule both our bodies and our souls.

Liturgical processions were frequent at Saint Victor. Richard of Saint Victor speaks of three principal ones: Purification (February 2), Palm Sunday, and the Ascension. The Palm Sunday procession, still celebrated today, was often very elaborate in the Middle Ages.[1]

1. Richard of Saint Victor, *Sermons et opuscules spirituels inédits, 1: L'édit d'Alexandre ou les trois processions*, ed. J. Châtillon and W. J. Tulloch, tr. J. Barthlémy (Paris: Desclée de Brouwer, 1951) *passim*; *De gemino Paschate* (PL 196:1063A).

The middle two sections give a lucid summary of Achard's teaching on grace and on reconciliation, which is the return from sin to grace. Righteousness in us takes two forms: (1) original, a sharing in the merits of Christ bestowed at baptism; (2) actual, our own merits. Without original righteousness there is no actual righteousness; actual righteousness is only required of those who reach the age of discretion. Grace takes two forms: (1) prevenient or antecedent grace which restores our freedom and gives original righteousness, apart from any merit of our own; (2) subsequent or cooperating grace, which together with free will is the cause of every good work we perform, with the result that we merit actual righteousness. Grace and free will are each the cause of the one, entire, indivisible good work, which is entirely from grace and entirely from free choice. Achard's formulation of the interplay of grace and free will reflects traditional Catholic teaching; his formulation does not solve the mystery (the interaction of the infinite and the finite cannot be grasped by human reason), but states it clearly.

Twelfth-century theologians were much concerned with the theology of sacramental penance. Private sacramental confession was becoming the norm just then, and theology was interested in the interplay of conscience, consent, and act in the moral life. By the thirteenth century at least, the canons of Saint Victor had a special apostolate as confessors to the university students of Paris. Several Victorines of the early thirteenth century wrote manuals to guide confessors in this sacramental ministry. In this sermon Achard is concerned with the part of the penitent in the remission of sins, whether mortal or venial. The penitent's part is threefold: contrition in the heart, oral confession, and satisfaction. Repentance, he says, should extend to thought, word and deed. All of this is traditional Catholic teaching, as indeed is his statement that what distinguishes venial sin from mortal sin is that venial sin can coexist with the love of God and neighbor (charity). On the other hand, Achard's theory about the position of unbelievers in relation to venial and mortal sin would find no adherents today, since contemporary theology does not think that unbelievers are *ipso facto* deprived of grace (Achard's original and actual righteousness). As a generalization, one could say that Achard's theology of repentance reflects a moment in Christian history when a somewhat externalized view of sin and penance was being replaced by a more internal sense of personal responsibility, while yet a strong sense of the social and communal nature of Christian life and activity remained. Today, when the theology of repentance is once again in turmoil, we seem to be coming out of a period of extreme individualism, and rediscovering the social nature of sin, forgiveness and repentance.

The final section once again emphasizes the need for both interior virtues and external good works. The whole human being, body and soul, must be redeemed. God's grace makes our bodies his house through good works, and it makes our spirit his chamber through virtues. Beside the life of repentance, virtue, and good works, there is the life of mystical union, which begins in this life and is consummated in heaven. Of the journey (this *anagogia* or ascension) which leads from the Mount of Olives (grace) to glory in heaven, Achard declares himself unfit to speak, for he has not yet experienced it.

THE SERMON

[Second] Sermon on Palm Sunday

AMONG THE MAJOR AND PREEMINENT PROCESSIONS that the Lord celebrated, and left for those devoted to him to celebrate, are two principal ones: one done with palm branches, the other done on the day of the Lord's Ascension. They signify two spiritual realities in and through which we must advance: 'from strength to strength', and 'from glory to glory'.† The deeds of the Lord are both reality and figure: his passion and resurrection are reality, because at the historical level he really suffered and really rose; they are figure because Christ's suffering and rising not only effected but also prefigured the death by which we die to sin and the future resurrection for which we hope.

Ps 84:7; 2 Co 3:18

The first procession is from the Mount of Olives into Jerusalem; the second is from the Mount of Olives into heaven. Thus both of our processions begin from the Mount of Olives, that is, from the heights of divine grace, without which we cannot proceed anywhere. A great grace was bestowed on the angels in their creation, justification, and glorification, and upon our first parents before sin occurred. Since they did not yet exist, neither humans nor angels merited that this grace be given them. Thus, whatever good they had was the gift of grace. 'Every best gift given and every perfect gift is from above, descending from the Father of lights'.† Now, in the period of grace a much greater and more sublime grace is given to us who

Jm 1:17

are unworthy. Not only did we not merit it; we incurred demerit by sinning. The angels, on the other hand, although they did not merit to be created or justified—since they did not exist, as already said—did not incur demerit. Hence, we have been dealt with much more mercifully. From the Mount of Olives prevenient and subsequent grace have been most generously provided.[2] Note, and remember, that we have been transferred from servitude in Egypt to the freedom by which Christ
freed us,† from the power of darkness to the king- Ga 4:31
dom of the Son of God,† through whom we have Col 1:13
escaped the eternal laments and attained the company of the angels. These are the thing 'he has done for you' of which David spoke: 'Bless the Lord, O my soul, and do not forget all he has done
for you'.† No one will be blessed by God's gifts Ps 103:2
who is ungrateful to the giver.

2. Our first procession, then, is from prevenient grace, the second from subsequent grace;[3] the first from the Mount of Olives into Jerusalem, that is, into the vision of peace;[4] the second from the Mount of Olives to heaven. The first is a procession of reconciliation; the second, of salvation. Of these the Apostle wrote: 'If, when we were enemies, we were reconciled to God through the death of the Son of God, all the more will we be saved by his
life'.† Rm 5:10

Reconciliation consists both in remission of sins and in righteousness. In the remission of sins there is a certain distinction and a certain progression from the remission of original sin to the remission of actual sin. Likewise, in the remission of

2. Olives, and hence the Mount of Olives, were traditional symbols of mercy: see, e.g., Gregory the Great, *Homilia XL in Evanglia* 20.13 (PL 76:1167A).

3. See Sermon 3.1.

4. See Sermon 5.5.

original sin there is a certain progression from the remission of guilt to the remission of attraction. Guilt is remitted, especially in the sacrament of baptism, in such a way that it no longer exists at all; the attraction of original sin is not remitted completely, but is so diminished and weakened that the one reborn in Christ is no longer forced to serve under its dominion. The procession goes from the remission of original sin to the remission of actual sin.

Likewise, in the remission of actual sin there is a certain progression from the remission of venial sin to the remission of mortal sin. In the remission of venial sin there is a threefold distinction: remission of the sin takes place with respect to contrition of heart, to oral confession, and to satisfaction.[5] Similarly, in each of these there is a threefold procession and distinction in the remission involved, since contrition of the heart concerns evil works, depraved speech, and consent. Confession and satisfaction have the same three modes, for we must confess not only the evils we have done or spoken, but even those to which we gave consent, and make satisfaction for the same three things. John says:
Mt 3:8, par. Bear fruit 'worthy of repentance'.† Note that a sin is called venial if it can exist in someone together with charity and with its remedy; it is mortal if it makes someone deserve eternal death.[6] Hence, in pagans and those who do not yet have the Savior's faith no sin is venial since none has a remedy; whatever is mortal makes one deserving of death,

5. See Sermon 14.5; Richard of Saint Victor, *De potestate ligandi et solvendi* 5, in *Opsucules théologiques*, ed. J. Ribaillier (Paris: Vrin, 1967) 83–84.

6. On the distinction between mortal and venial sin in the Victorines see Hugh of Saint Victor, *De sacramentis legis naturalis et scriptae* 2.13.1 (PL 176:526BC); Richard of Saint Victor, *De differenti pena peccati mortalis et venialis*, in *Opuscules théologiques*, ed. Ribaillier, 291–293.

and will be eternally punished. However, mortal sin is remitted in the same three ways as venial sin; namely, by contrition of heart, oral confession, and satisfaction.

3. By these processions we go out of Egypt, and, with the house of Jacob [we go out] 'from a barbarous people'.† Still, we do not come im- Ps 114:1
mediately to the true land of promise, and hence we must move camp from the remission of sins to righteousness, and from original righteousness to actual righteousness. Original righteousness is what we call a certain sharing in the merits of Christ bestowed on us at our rebirth; he ceded his merits to us, so that because of them there would be done to us what would have been done to him, if he had needed it.[7] Hence, in the sacrament of regeneration even infants become not only undeserving of eternal damnation through the remission of sin, but also deserving of eternal salvation by sharing in the merits of Christ. Later, after we reach the years of discretion, this original righteousness is not sufficient for us without a certain actual righteousness, which consists in our own merits.

There is no actual righteousness, of any amount, without original righteousness, for our own merits flow from the fount of grace. The grace of God is antecedent to our will and freedom of choice, freeing and healing it, so that it may choose the good and be capable of it. Then our will, freed and healed through the grace of God, does not receive the grace of God into a void where it can rest in idleness, but cooperates with it; that is, it works together with it. The work of operant grace and the work of the cooperating will are not different

---

7. See Sermon 3.1.

things; the work of both is one. Hence, it does not follow that if the whole is from grace, nothing is from free choice, since one and the same thing is from grace and from free choice. From what has been said it follows that the work of grace alone is one thing, and the work of grace and will together is another. The work of the will by itself is only evil. Regarding the work of grace alone, the Apostle says: 'By the grace of God I am what I am'.[8] Regarding what is of grace and will together, he adds: 'And his grace in me has not been in vain'; I worked more than all the others. And, lest we take him to have done something on his own, he added: 'Not I, but the grace of God'.[9] Similarly, lest we say that everything is from God's grace and nothing from him, he adds: 'with me'. That the will can do nothing by itself without grace the same apostle declares elsewhere when he says: 'Not that we are competent to think anything of ourselves, as of
2 Co 3:5 ourselves'.†

4. In the journey of this procession it is necessary that Jesus sit upon an ass and a the colt of an ass; that is, that he rule the flesh, which is signified by the ass, and that he rule the spirit, which is signified by the colt, and guide them and lead them all the way into Jerusalem. As the Apostle says: 'Glorify
1 Co 6:20 and bear God in your body',† as if to say: 'not just inwardly in spirit, but also outwardly in the flesh'. The bride says of her spouse in the Canticle: 'I may not let him go, until I lead him into my mother's
Sg 3:4 house, and into the chamber of her who bore me'.† The grace of God is called our 'mother' insofar

8. The text of 1 Corinthians 15.10 on which Achard comments in the remainder of this section reads (in a literal translation of the Vulgate): 'By the grace of God I am what I am, and his grace in me has not been in vain. On the contrary, I have worked more abundantly than all the rest, yet not I, but the grace of God with me.'

9. See Sermon 15.22–23.

as it gives birth to us in good works outside; it is called 'her who bore' us insofar as it brings us forth inwardly in virtues. We take the house to be the body; the chamber, the spirit. Hence, we must lead the spouse into the house of our mother through imitation of the good works of Christ, and into her chamber through the practice of the virtues.

I do not know how to speak of the procession from the Mount of Olives into heaven, since I have not yet made it. It travels from misery to glory, from smallness to immensity, from temporality to eternity, from the world to the Father, from corruption to incorruption, where God himself will be seen face to face. May he deign to lead us to that vision. Amen.

Christology

Sermon 1: On the Birthday of the Lord

INTRODUCTION

THIS CHRISTMAS SERMON IS INTERESTING for both structure and content. Achard is commenting on Isaiah 7:14–15 (inserted here at the beginning). Structurally, his theme is the symbolic meaning of the butter and honey which these verses from Isaiah say constitute Emmanuel's food. A secondary theme (*protheme*) introduced right at the beginning is the meaning of Emmanuel given in Matthew 1:23: 'God with us'. As well as being a sermon, the work is also a model of medieval exegesis. Achard is most concerned with the allegorical or dogmatic meaning of his text, but in sections four and five he briefly makes a moral application, which includes as well an anagogical meaning: the moral meaning of butter is the testimony of a good conscience, the anagogic meaning of honey is internal sweetness and a foretaste of divine contemplation.

The division of the sermon into six sections corresponds to the outline of its contents: (1) Emmanuel's nourishment; his union in nature with us, and his even closer union with the Father and Holy Spirit. (2) The Incarnation was the work of the Trinity, but only the Son actually assumed human nature. (3) As the person who goes out from the Father, and as light, Son, and image, the second person of the Trinity was best qualified for the work of redemptive incarnation, whereby humanity's natural capacity for union with God is repaired, and the grace of union is restored. As the power and wisdom of God, the Son overcomes the twin afflictions of weakness and ignorance. (4) Through his incarnation, life, suffering, death, and final coming, Christ leads us to beatitude. (5) Christ's mind (*mens*) had by grace the same power, wisdom, and goodness that the Word had eternally by nature. (6) The depths of Christ's mind (*mens*) remained unmoveably united to God throughout his life and death, but by undergoing the sufferings of his soul and body, he earned for us merits which he did not need and which alone could restore us to righteousness.

Victorine exegetes often discussed this passage from Isaiah; they saw in butter a symbol of Christ's humanity, and in honey a symbol of his divinity; in the conjunction of the two lay hidden the mystery of the unity of divinity and humanity in the person of the Son. The interpretation of the text was a bone of contention between Achard's contemporaries, Andrew of Saint Victor and Richard of Saint Victor.[1]

Achard's theology of the Incarnation is firmly rooted in patristic teaching as this was known and repeated in the twelfth century.[2] To the traditional Chalcedonian Christology he brings several characteristic ideas. One is the conviction, expressed in section one, that all human beings share the same nature or substance; what differentiates one individual human being from another are accidental forms. Achard shared this Boethian realism with the founder of Saint Victor, William of Champeaux, and with Thierry of Chartres and

1. Hugh of Saint Victor, *De cibo Emmanuelis* =*Miscellanea* 12 (PL 177:477–481); Pseudo-Hugh of Saint Victor, *Miscellanea* 3.64 (PL177:675A); Richard of Saint Victor, *De Emmanuele* (PL 196:623–628); See Beryl Smalley, *The Study of the Bible in the Middle Ages* (Notre Dame, IN: University of Notre Dame Press, 1964) 163.

2. See the references given by Châtillon, *Sermons*, 24–25, n. 3.

Gilbert of Poitiers.[3] To this philosophical conviction corresponds the extremely strong sense of the unity of all human beings characteristic of Victorine theology and spirituality.

Also in section one, Achard marshals arguments regarding why it was the second person who became incarnate. That there should be reasons for the incarnation of the Son, rather than of the Father or the Spirit, was taken for granted by twelfth-century theologians;[4] Karl Rahner has endorsed and aroused renewed interest in the question.[5]

Another characteristic of Victorine Christology is the *homo assumptus* paradigm. According to Achard's use of this paradigm (Sermon 1.2, and often), the assumed humanity *(homo assumptus*) can be said to be a person *per se*, though the person is identical to that of the Word. John of Cornwall cites a passages from Achard's *De unitate* to this effect; the idea is shared by Victorine authors and others, and corresponds to the first of the three opinions cited by Peter the Lombard regarding the union of the two natures in Christ.[6]

Achard, like Hugh of Saint Victor, insists on the idea that whatever perfections (in particular, wisdom, power, and goodness) belonged to the Word by nature, belonged by grace to the human nature assumed by the Word.[7] Whatever divine attribute was not absolutely incompatible with Christ's embodied condition was

---

3. See the references given by Châtillon, *Sermons*, 25, n. 4.

4. Anselm, *De incarnatione Verbi*, ed. Schmitt 2:20–28; Hugh of Saint Victor, *De sacramentis*, II.1.2–3 (PL 176:371–376); Peter Lombard, *Sententiae* III, dist. 1, ed. Quaracchi, 551–554; Richard of Saint Victor, *Ad me clamat ex Seir*, 9, in *Opuscules théologiques*, ed. Ribaillier, 269–270.

5. K. Rahner, *The Trinity* (New York: Herder and Herder, 1970).

6. *Eulogium*, ed. Häring, MS 13 (1951) 267. See also Achard, *Sermon* 4.7; Hugh of Saint Victor, *De sacramentis*, 2.1.9, 11 (PL 176:393–399, 401–411), and *Collatio II de Verbo incarnato* (PL 177:318–320); Peter the Lombard, *Sententiae* 3, dist. 6, ed. Quarrachi, 573–582; cf. Saint Thomas Aquinas, *In Sententias* 3, dist. 6, Divisio textus.

7. This 'authority' or authoritative opinion is first quoted by Walter of Mortagne, *Epistolam ad Hugonem* (PL 1176:1053AB); see Ludwig Ott, *Untersuchungen zur theologischen Briefliteratur der Fruhscholastik: unter besonderer Berucksichtigung des Viktorinerkreises*, BGPTM 34 (Munster: Aschendorff, 1937) 340–347. Achard cites it often: Sermon 4.5, 5.1, 14.3, 15.26; *De unitate* 1.14, cited by John of Cornwall, *Eulogium*, ed. Häring, 267. See Jean Châtillon, '*Quidquid convenit Filio Dei per naturam convenit Filio hominis per gratiam*', *Divinitas* 11 (1967) 715–728 =*Miscellanea André Combes* (Rome, 1967) 2:319–331.

communicated to his humanity. This thesis, which runs counter to most twentieth-century Christology, should be seen as reflecting the convictions (1) that Christ was a perfect human being, having only the limitations (e.g., mortality) necessary to redeem us, and (2) the Trinity gave to Christ every gracious gift possible. This thesis, especially insofar as it concerns Christ's knowledge (Sermon 1.5), was shared by Saint Thomas Aquinas.[8] There seems to be a strong tension between this authoritative opinion and another which is also cited by Achard: Christ assumed all our human infirmities, except sin (Sermons 1.5; 3.3).[9]

In the final section (6), Achard declares that without Christ's merits human merit is insufficient. On the other hand, in the case of infants or adults who are baptized and die before they can do meritorious deeds, Christ's merits by themselves are sufficient. All others to whom participation in Christ's merits (*gratia preveniens vel operans* restores *justitia originalis*) is granted by baptism must embody their baptismal promises in deeds to which they are moved by grace (*gratia subsequens vel cooperans* bringing about *justitita actualis*). Achard mentions baptism seven times, but he does not explicitly discuss the fate of unbaptized infants and other vexing questions.[10]

---

8. Saint Thomas Aquinas, *Summa theologiae*, 3.9–12, 15.

9. Again it is Walter of Mortagne who cites this opinion, this time in a letter to Alberic, ed L. d'Achéry, *Spicilegium* 2:469, cited by Ott, *Untersuchungen*, 214, n. 2. The formula, *Suscepit omnes infirmitates nostras, praeter peccatum*, is found often in writings of Achard's contemporaries. Walter of Mortagne attributed it to Leo the Great; it seems to derive rather from John of Damascus, *De fide orthodoxa*, 64, Latin translations of *Burgundio* and *Cerbanus*, ed. E. M. Buytaert, Franciscan Institute Publications, Text Series 8 (Saint Bonaventure, New York: Franciscan Institute, 1955) 259, lines 4–5: *Totum enim hominem et omnia quae hominis assumpsit, praeter peccatum*.

10. See the texts cited in Châtillon, *Sermons*, 34–35, nn. 74–76; below, Sermons 10.1; 11.3; 13.17; 14.4 , 5, 16, 17; and for the correspondence between Hugh of Saint Victor and Saint Bernard regarding certain opinions of Abelard regarding baptism, see my study and translation in *Bernardus Magister* (Kalamazoo: Cistercian Publications, 1993) = *Cîteaux* 42 (1991) 349–378.

THE SERMON

On the Birthday of the Lord

[*Behold a virgin will conceive and bear a son, and will call his name Emmanuel. He will eat butter and honey that he may know how to reject evil and choose good.*†] Is 7:14–15

ON THE BIRTHDAY OF EMMANUEL it is fitting that we be refreshed by his food, which consists of butter and honey. The world has plenty of both, but of the signifiers, not of the signified; of the material, not of the spiritual. Indeed, the world abounds with what is contrary to spiritual things, notably sterility and bitterness: sterility of deeds, and bitterness of behavior. Sterility is contrary to the richness and fecundity of butter; bitterness of behavior is opposed to the sweetness of honey. Few people abound in the signified and the spiritual, because few eat the food of Emmanuel, a food that increases in the eating and decreases in fasting.

Emmanuel means 'God with us';† that is, God Mt 1:23
in our nature. He is God and man; he possesses a natural unity with God the Father, with whom he is one in nature, and he also possesses unity with his virgin mother and the rest of humanity, with whom he is one in human nature. He is *homoousios* with his Father and *homoousios* with his mother; that is, consubstantial with both. However, the natural unity he has with his Father is greater and far more excellent than that which he has with the rest of humanity, because it is divine, without any distinction of accidents. Although some diversity

is understood to exist among the persons [of the Trinity], it is very subtle and slight because only in accord with relationships that indicate not what the persons are like in themselves but how they are related to one another. Thus, for example, 'Father' does not indicate what this person is in himself, but how he is related to the Son as the Son's source and principle. Similarly, 'Son' shows how this person is related to the Father. We find there no composition of parts, no diversity of forms, no variation of accidents, and therefore the highest unity exists where there is no diversity of natures or wills. By contrast, the unity the Son has with human beings does involve variation of accidents. In this case the difference of accidents is much greater than the convergence of substances. Hence, two people, although one in nature, are said to be two diverse people, rather than one, because their difference is greater than their convergence.

2. Someone will say: Why is the Son, rather than the Father or the Holy Spirit, called 'God
Mt 1:23 with us',[†] since wherever the Son is there the Father and the Holy Spirit are also? They are inseparable. We must be aware that wherever the Son is by the inpouring of grace and the bestowal of gifts, there the Father and Holy Spirit are by the same inpouring of grace and bestowal of gifts. However, the Son exists in our nature in a unique and special way: he united it to himself personally in such a way that what was assumed and the one assuming it would be one person. What is diverse in nature is not different in power. Neither the Father nor the Holy Spirit is in us or in our nature in this way. Neither the Father nor the Holy Spirit is incarnate, although the whole Trinity brought about the Incarnation. The Father united flesh not

with himself but with the Son, and so too the Holy Spirit joined the same flesh not to himself but to the Word. Three [persons] worked as one, producing not three things but one; only the Son went out, not just to us, but into us. Just as it does not belong to the Father to go out from anyone, so it is not his to go out into anyone. The Holy Spirit went out to us when he appeared in the form of a dove and in tongues of fire, but he did not go out into us—that is, into a participation in our nature, so as to become a human being. As I said, the Son did go out into us, so that by that going out he might appear in what is ours. He went out into our exile in order to lead us into his homeland.

3. 'And who is as qualified for these things?'† 2 Co 2:16
According to what is specifically said of [the Son] in the Sacred Scriptures, it seems that neither the Father nor the Holy Spirit is as qualified to carry out and complete these things. Who is as qualified to enlighten our ignorance and destroy error as the one who is the light of the world, 'the splendor of glory', 'the brightness of eternal light'?† When Heb 1:3; Ws 7:26
truth is not recognized, there is ignorance; when falsehood is asserted, it is error. Similarly, who is as qualified to lead the children of adoption to their inheritance as the Son whose inheritance it is, without whose consent strangers could not justly be led in even by the Father himself, or the Holy Spirit? To remove all ambiguity and dispel all doubt, the Son came on behalf of his brothers [and sisters], to make us sharers in his inheritance, and thus heirs of God and joint heirs with him.† Rm 8:17
Similarly, who is as qualified to reform and restore the image of God as the one who is the image of the invisible and unchanging God?† Col 1:15

The image of God in humanity was twofold:

from nature and from grace[11] The natural image consisted in the potency or possibility of knowing, loving and enjoying God. This image was corrupted and deformed after sin and by sin, but not utterly effaced; hence 'Surely a human being passes
Ps 39:7 as an image'.† However much humanity may pass from one state to another, turning from this state to that, the created image is never totally effaced because it is natural and substantial, and what is of the substance cannot be destroyed. The image from grace consists in actual knowledge, love, and enjoyment. This has been completely effaced by transgression. Hence, we read that the man who fell in with robbers was despoiled and wounded: despoiled with respect to the image from grace, wounded with respect to the image from nature. He was completely deprived of virtues, weakened in natural gifts. In order to reform the deformed image and restore the one that was effaced, the Image of God, in every way [God's] equal, came to the image for the sake the image—that is, for the sake of humanity which is the image, he came to the image; approaching, that is, not as its equal, but from afar, by a certain likeness.

2 Co 2:16 Again, 'who is as qualified for these things'?†
Mk 7:32–37 Humanity was deaf, and therefore also mute;† deaf with respect to understanding the truth, mute with respect to its confession. Hence, it was fitting that the Word of God came to open the ears of the deaf to understanding the truth and to open the mouth of the mute to confession of the truth, for 'one believes with the heart unto righteousness,
Rm 10:10 and confesses with the mouth unto salvation'.†

In the end, all the afflictions of humanity are

11. This distinction is formulated in other terms in Sermon 9.4–5 and Sermon 13.32.

reduced to these two: infirmity and ignorance. Thus the prophet says: 'My strength has failed, and the light of my eyes is not with me'.† He does not say: 'The light of my eye has failed', and then, 'my strength', but, 'My strength has failed, and the light of my eye is not with me', for reason never sins, but the will does. In the will lies all merit, whether good or evil.[12] If reason is sometimes said to sin, it is to be understood that a person sins knowingly. But who is as qualified to heal infirmity and enlighten ignorance as the one who is the power of God and the wisdom of God?† Because he is power he can heal infirmity; because he is the wisdom he is able to enlighten ignorance.

Cf. Ps 38:11; 71:9

1 Co 1:18, 21

4. In all this 'a child is born to us, a son is given us'.† By the fact that a child is born to us, a son is given us, we come through the child to the Son, through humanity to divinity, through faith in the Incarnation to contemplation of the divinity, through the richness of butter to the sweetness of honey, through righteousness to beatitude. We come by merit to our reward, by the road to our homeland. 'A child is born to us', I say, 'a son is given us'. He accomplished his ministry of giving in all respects: by humbly serving us, by enlightening the blind, by healing lepers, by raising the dead, by curing all our infirmities. Sold for thirty coins for the sake of us who were sold under sin, he himself was sold, not under sin but for sin, not his, but ours.† Finally, for us he underwent death. What more could he have done, even if he had been purchased as a slave? Indeed, he never would have done as much. And still, passing over in the future, he will minister to us when he destroys

Is 9:6

Zc 11:12, Mt 26:15, 27:3, 9; Rm 7:14

12. The idea that sin resides in the will was inspired by Abelard, *Ethics*, ed. David Luscombe (Oxford: Clarendon, 1971) xxxxiv and passim. See below, Sermon 14.10–11.

every principality and power and virtue, and hands
1 Co 15:24 over the kingdom to his God and Father.† At present angels minister to us; in the future we will not need their ministry, when he himself will speak
Jn 16:25; 1 Co 15:28 clearly about the Father,† being all in all.†

5. Earlier I touched on the way in which Emmanuel's twofold food, butter and honey, corresponds to his twofold nature. Butter has more richness and less sweetness, whereas honey has more sweetness and less richness. Butter we interpret as the testimony of a good conscience, honey as a tasting of interior sweetness and a foretaste of divine contemplation. By these two foods we are refreshed with Christ and in Christ, as he, too, is refreshed in us and in himself. We must, however, be refreshed with the richness of butter before we are capable of being filled with the sweetness of honey.

How will those who do not delight in the testimony of their own consciences rejoice in God? Christ, from the very moment of his conception enjoyed in every way the contemplation of the divinity in his mind, which was personally united and immediately conjoined to the godhead, and in some fashion absorbed by the glory of the Lord. Clinging ineffably to this, his mind became one spirit, one person, one God, possessing all of the same power, wisdom and goodness by grace that the Word has and had from eternity by nature. The divinity bestowed itself on him to be shared completely and fully; it reserved nothing for itself which it did not give to the humanity assumed. Hence, the prophet declares: 'The mountain on which it pleased God to dwell, on it God will
Ps 68:17 dwell for ever',† that is, without end, boundary, or measure. He does not say this as though there

is an end, a boundary, or a measure in God, but to show that all the fullness of divinity dwells in him, as the Apostle clearly proclaims: 'In him dwells all the fullness of divinity'.† The meaning is this: 'all' is Col 2:9
aimed at those who say that the assumed humanity has all knowledge but not omnipotence; 'fullness' is aimed at those who say that he does not have as much power, or wisdom, or goodness as the Word himself has; and, lest someone explain all this in reference to the Word and not in reference to the assumed humanity, he adds 'bodily', that is, in the assumed humanity, which is a body. As a human being he shares fully in all that is God's, and as God he shares in all that is human, except sin.

Such was that union of human and God which made God human and a human God. As God gave everything that was his to the humanity, so he took to himself everything that is humanity's; and as the Son says to the Father: 'Everything that is yours is mine, and everything that is mine is yours',† so the assumed humanity can say to the Jn 17:10
assuming Word: 'Everything that is yours by nature is mine by grace, and everything that is mine by nature is yours by your condescension'. Because of this ineffable union of humanity and godhead, God is truly said to be human, and a human is truly said to be God. Thus Augustine says: If you concentrate on the distinction of natures, God is one thing, humanity another, and humanity and God are two; if, however, you concentrate on the personal union, there are not two but one, not in nature, but in person.[13] The Father and Son are one, not in person, but in nature; the humanity assumed and the assuming Word are

13. Châtillon cites Augustine, *Tractatus in Evangelium Ioannis* 69.3 (PL 35:1817), and *Contra Felicianum arianum,* 11 (PL 42:1166).

one, not in nature, but in person. Likewise, any of the saints who clings to God by faith and love is one with God, not in nature or in person, but in righteousness and in glory.

6. Because of this unfathomable union, the mind of Christ remained unmoved and untouched even in death; it then possessed no less glory and beatitude as far as the core of the mind was concerned. In spirit and soul and flesh[14] there was change before the passion, in the days of his flesh, that is, his mortality. We read of his spirit's muta-
Jn 11:33 bility: 'Jesus cried out in spirit';† concerning the
mutability of his soul it is written: 'My soul is sad
Mk 14:34 even unto death';† in the flesh he was hungry, he
Mt 21:18; Jn 19:28, 4:6. thirsted and was weary.†

Emmanuel was refreshed with the richness of butter, that is, the testimony of a good conscience;
Ps 21:4 because the blessings of sweetness preceded him,†
he was conscious of no evil in himself, but rather of complete good; he possessed complete innocence and the perfection of all virtues; he did nothing he should not have done and did all he should have done; he loved God and his neighbor perfectly. In all this he merited much, not for himself, but for us to whom he granted his merits, so that what would have been done to him on account of them if he had need might be done to us. These merits were great; they destroyed all evil merits and conferred good merits sufficient for salvation for infants and those with no opportunity to act, and completed what is lacking in the merits of those with opportunity to act. Whatever anyone's actual righteousness may be, it will never be of sufficient worth to merit future glory apart

14. On the distinction of mind, soul, spirit, and body, see *On the Distinction*, 31–32.

from the merits of Christ. By participating in his merits we acquire original righteousness, which is so great that without any actual righteousness it suffices in infants for salvation. Hence, no human being, however holy, nor any angel was capable of redeeming the human race. A hundred thousand humans and angels could not possess the merits to remove wrath and confer eternal life. As it is written, neither in heaven, nor on earth, nor in the nether world was found anyone who could 'open the book and break its seals' except 'the lion of the tribe of Judah'.† By the merits of his flesh Rv 5:2, 5
may he lead us to the enjoyment of his godhead. Amen.

Sermon 3: On the Coming of the Lord

INTRODUCTION

THIS SERMON CLOSELY RESEMBLES SERMON 1, but where that sermon dwelt at length on the classical theology of the Incarnation, Sermon 3 deals principally with the doctrine of the redemption. In so doing it adopts the theological reasoning of Anselm of Canterbury's *Cur Deus homo*, a doctrine less than a century old when Achard wrote, which found special favor among the Victorines before its almost universal adoption by the Western church. At the end of the sermon, Achard returns to the Christological ideas of Sermon 1 and to the image of butter and honey.

The outline of Sermon 3 is as follows: (1) If we love Christ, we long for his advent. There are three advents of Christ: into the flesh, in the spirit, and in the flesh. To the first two correspond prevenient or operant grace, which Christ earns and bestows apart from any merit of ours, and subsequent or cooperative grace, which cooperates with our free will to bring about good intentions, deeds, and virtues. (2) As a result of the sin of the first human beings, the human race was placed under the power of the demon as a punishment. The demon had no right to this domination. Humanity was left with nothing to make restitution for the offense (*reatus*) given to God. (3) God then sent his Son into humanity. He was under no obligation to suffer and die; he offered his sufferings and death on humanity's behalf. (4) Having thus come into our flesh, the incarnate Word comes into our spirit to invite us to eat the butter of good deeds and the honey of contemplation.

In section one, Achard is particularly interested in the first two comings of Christ. From the doctrinal depths of the first coming, where Christ acts without our involvement—apart from acting in our human nature—Achard draws moral conclusions regarding the second coming, by which Christ comes in spirit to cooperate with our spirit in our efforts to respond to his gift of salvation. Achard's vocabulary is his own, and does not quite correspond to the vocabulary that became standard in Catholic usage through the writings of Saint Thomas Aquinas and the Council of Trent. Achard writes that by his first coming Christ gained for us original righteousness, which is freely given to us at baptism by Christ's prevenient grace. Then, as we attempt to live out our baptismal promises, Christ gives us cooperant grace, which enables us to choose good and reject evil and so achieve actual righteousness; that is, the righteousness that results from virtuous acts sustained by Christ's cooperant grace, given subsequent to the justifying grace of baptism.[1]

Although Achard does not dwell on Christ's third coming, his description of it is noteworthy. Christ will come not *into* flesh this time, but *in* his risen flesh, in order 'to dwell among us and in us'.

---

1. See Sermon 1.6. By 'original righteousness' Achard means not that of Adam and Eve in paradise, or that which their descendants would have had if Adam and Eve had not sinned, but rather the sanctifying grace bestowed on fallen human beings at baptism. The same idea occurs in *Allegoriae in epistolas Pauli* (PL 175:887B): 'In baptism original righteousness is conferred, not that which infants would have if there had been no corruption of sin, but that which is understood to derive from participation in the merits of Christ'. Achard's understanding of prevenient and subsequent grace is found in the *Quaestiones in epistolam Pauli, ad Romanos*, q. 13 (PL 175:460).

The intimate union between Christ and humanity, which is central to Achard's theology, is the consummation and goal of creation and redemption.[2]

The second section draws explicitly on Romans, implicitly on Saint Anselm. By seducing the first human beings into sin the devil gained no claim over the human race, but God allowed him a certain power over humanity in order both to punish humanity's sin and to bring humanity to its senses. The notion of 'know thyself',[3] taken in the Pauline sense of 'know that without God's grace, you, a fallen human being, can do nothing that profits for salvation', is a constant presupposition here, as elsewhere in Achard's writings. The Old Testament law served to instruct humanity regarding its helpless state; humanity recognized that it owed to God total obedience and love, as well as the sufferings its sins deserved; nothing was left to make restitution for the offense (*reatus*)[4] given to God by humanity's sins.

The third section tells us—summarizing Anselm's argument—that the Son of God came into the world. Born of the virgin Mary through the overshadowing of the Holy Spirit, he was free of every taint of sin (in the background of the argument is the traditional Augustinian idea that sin is transmitted through human generation). However, he freely chose to bear all our infirmities, save sin and certain others (e.g., ignorance and difficulty in doing good) which were incompatible with his perfection. Christ owed nothing to suffering and death; he freely and lovingly accepted

2. The idea of a threefold coming of Christ was rather widely disseminated in Achard's time. It occurs in other texts associated with Saint Victor: *Quaestiones in Epistolas Pauli*, In 1 Thess. q. 4 (PL 275:587D); Pseudo-Hugh, *Miscellanea* 3.35; 6.80; 6.86 (PL 177:655–656; 849; 852). Achard differs slightly from these texts in connecting the third coming with reward and consummation rather than with judgment. There is, of course, liturgical warrant for connecting Advent and the judgment. See Saint Bernard, *Sermones de tempore* 3.4 (PL 183:45A).

3. Etienne Gilson, *Spirit of Medieval Philosophy* (New York: Scribners, 1936) 209–228; Colin Morris, *The Discovery of the Individual, 1050–1200* (New York: Harper and Row, 1972).

4. See Sermon 14.5. Châtillon explains (*Sermons*, 47, n. 35): 'The *reatus*, which is different from the disobedience properly so-called that constitutes sin, corresponds to the injury done to God as a result of disobedience and deserves a particular penalty'.

them and offered them to his Father as an act of restitution for his brothers and sisters. He had no need of the merits he earned by his voluntary self-giving, so he assigned them to us. At the end of the paragraph, in passing, Achard summarizes Anselm's argument that, though other ways of redemption were possible to God, none was more fitting than Christ's way, and thus it was necessary.[5] Achard argues for the suitability—and therefore the necessity—of Christ's redeeming suffering and death in two ways. His life of self-giving love not only redeemed us but also offered us both a model and an inducement to follow him. Having seen Christ's compassion for us, we will long for him to come spiritually into our souls so that we may follow his example out of compassion for the sufferings he endured for us. The second argument is that Christ's way of redemption was particularly suited to free us from both despair (at our sins) and pride (in our good deeds). Christ's way was the way of grace.

The final section takes up the theme of Sermon 1, butter and honey, Emmanuel's food. They stand for his humanity and his divinity. Having mentioned the latter, Achard enters once again into the theological controversies of his time and argues that Christ enjoyed the beatific vision of God throughout his life. His body and soul might suffer change, but his mind (*mens*) was immovably and immediately fixed on infinite truth.

---

5. For this argument, see Châtillon, *Sermons*, 50–51, n. 63–65.

THE SERMON

On the Coming of the Lord

'COME, LORD JESUS.'† John placed these three words at the end of his Apocalypse, at the end of the entire canonical Scrip- Rv 22:20
tures, in order to impress our minds more sharply and profoundly so that we might unflaggingly long for the coming of the Lord Jesus. Woe to the person who does not long for him! Whoever loves him longs for him, and the more one loves, the greater is one's longing. He should be deeply desired, because he will not come empty-handed, but will hold in his hand the kingdom and the ruling authority. We are asking for this kingdom when we say: 'Your kingdom come';† that is, that we may Mt 6:10
reign in him, or rather, he in us; he in us through righteousness, we in him through beatitude.

He will not come empty-handed, I say, because 'his right hand is full of gifts',† and in his right hand Ps 26:10
is length, that is, eternity and immortality of life, everlastingness. Also 'in his right hand is a fiery law';† whoever has this loves God and neighbor Dt 33:2
perfectly. Bountiful in mercy, he came first into flesh, having become a human being; he is going to come a second time at the end of time, not into flesh but in flesh. Between the first coming into flesh and the second in flesh, he comes invisibly in the spirit into our spirit. He came first into flesh, to dwell among us; then he comes in the spirit into our spirit, to dwell in us; finally, he will come in flesh to dwell among us and in us. He came first to act on our behalf, even apart from us; then he

comes in the spirit into our spirit, to work in us, but not apart from us; at last, he will come to reward the works he did on our behalf and apart from us as well as those he did in us, but not apart from us.

He came first to bestow on us original righteousness, which consists of participation in the merits of Christ. Christ himself granted us his merits, so that what would have been done to him on account of them, if he had need, might be done to us. We obtain this original righteousness when we are reborn in water and the spirit; through them we are made unworthy of death and worthy of everlasting life, just as through our first birth,
Ep 2:3 by which we are by nature children of wrath,† we incur a certain original unrighteousness called original sin, through which we are unworthy of life and worthy of death.[6]

My point is that he first came into flesh to confer this original righteousness on us; then he comes in spirit into our spirit to add a certain actual righteousness, which the grace of Christ effects in us, but not apart from us. First, through the grace called operant or prevenient, which works in us but apart from us, the will is healed, liberated, and given the capacity to act rightly. Then, after the will has been healed, free choice begins to act with grace. The will does not do one thing and grace another, but the will does one and the same

6. Achard teaches that original sin is the privation of a prior and primordial righteousness. According to the *Allegoriae in epistolas Pauli* (PL 175:887A): 'If the first parents had not sinned, little children would have their original righteousness through which they would be worthy of life; the privation of this is called original sin according to Master Achard'. Many opinions about the nature of original sin were current: Abelard thought it was the penalty incurred by Adam's descendants; the school of Anselm of Laon and William of Champeaux identified original sin and concupiscence; Hugh of Saint Victor thought that original sin consisted in ignorance and concupiscence. Achard follows Saint Anselm. For references and bibliography see Châtillon, *Sermons*, 44, n. 12.

thing grace does. This grace, with which the will cooperates, or which cooperates with the will, is called subsequent or cooperating grace. What is to cooperate if not to operate with another? Finally, Christ will come to glorify us on account of both kinds of righteousness. He first came into flesh in order to give for us the price of our redemption, and to liberate us from the yoke of sin and wretched slavery to the devil.[7] Then he comes in the spirit into our spirit, in order to confer on us the effect of our redemption, that is, to lead us out of prison. Finally he will come in flesh to lead us home and into all truth.

2. Once the price was paid, it was necessary that he lead the captive out of prison, where humanity had become so exhausted and weakened that it could not leave by itself, since it was carnal, 'sold
under sin'.† Hence, it is written: 'You were sold for Rm 7:14
nothing'.† The first parent sold himself for nothing Is 52:3
since he received only an apple in return for his servitude. The devil promised many things, saying: 'You will be like gods, knowing good and evil,
on the day you eat'† of the tree of the knowledge Gn 3:5
of good and evil, but in making this promise he was acting deceitfully, for no one comes to the likeness of God and the fullness of knowledge through pride and transgression of a divine decree, but through humility and observance of God's precepts. Thus, by sinning humanity was made a slave of sin, and, by the just judgment of God, handed over to the power of the devil.

For his part, the devil had no claim over humanity because he had seduced humanity; on the

7. Achard here makes his own the teaching of the Council of Sens, which in 1140 had condemned the following proposition attributed to Abelard: 'Christ did not assume flesh to free us from the yoke of the devil'. 723 (Heinrich Denzinger, *Enchiridion symbolorum*, #371).

contrary, if he had had any such right, he would have justly lost it on account of the injury he did to God by seducing his servant, and for the treachery perpetrated against humanity. It was by the permission, or rather by the judgment and sentence, of God that humanity, on account of its fault, was turned over to the power of the cruel tyrant, to the hand of the torturer, who like a ferocious tyrant began to savage and violently oppress humanity, hurling it down from one evil to another, and dragging it from one death to another.

Rm 5:14 Thus, in the world 'death reigned until Moses',†
while the devil, strong and armed, guarded his
Cf. Lk 11:21 castle.† No one opposed or resisted him, since
even the patient failed to recognize his own illness.
Hence, the apostle declared: 'I did not know sin
Rm 7:7 except that the law said, you shall not covet'.† Once
the law through which comes knowledge of sin
Rm 3:20 was given,† humanity tried to resist it, although
still ignorant of its weakness and presumptuous of
its strength. Humanity fell even more foully than
usual, like a little bird caught in a snare—the more
it struggles to fly away the more is it held ensnared.
Hence, the Apostle wrote: Before the law 'sin
was dead; but when the commandment came sin
revived', and 'seizing an opportunity through the
commandment, it produced in me every kind of
Rm 7:8–9 correctousness'.†

Humanity had nothing to give for the redemption of its soul, especially since the price was to be paid to God and not to the devil, to the judge, not to the torturer. If there was good in the prophets, it was not enough even for them, much less for others. Even if one of them had possessed perfect justice so as to covet nothing at all, and loved God with his whole heart, his whole soul, and his whole mind, and his neighbor as himself,† all this was not enough for the price of redemption. Humanity owed all this to God before sin—to covet nothing contrary to reason, and to love God and neighbor perfectly. Therefore, another price had to be sought to expiate the offense, as the following comparison makes clear. If anyone owed me money and then so offended me that I put him in prison, it would not be enough to redeem himself for him to give the money already owed; he would have to look for another means of paying. Similarly, humanity, which had become the servant of sin, had nothing to give for its liberation, to leave the prison in which it was held captive. Mt 22:37–39 par.

Hardship finally enabled humanity to understand what it heard. Instructed by the beating, humanity recognized that it could not escape from the power of darkness, from the yoke of sin and its torments, by its own power, but only by God's grace. So it fled to grace and besought its help, saying: 'Lord, I suffer violence. Answer for me.† I am not able, I am not strong enough, I am ignorant. My strength is already spent, and the light of my eyes is not with me.† Lead me out of the house of slavery; lead the captive out of prison so that you who already are its creator may be its savior as well.' Is 38:14 Ps 38:10

3. But the Lord, rich in mercy, 'whose mercies are above all his works',† did not 'in his anger shut up his mercies'.[8]† 'He bowed the heavens and came down',† coming into flesh so that the Word might become flesh, that is, a human being. He went out from the Father and came into the world, from the Father's bosom into the Virgin, in whom and from whom he was conceived, not by a man's seed but by God's divine power. He is 'the stone cut from Ps 145:9 Ps 77:9 Ps 18:9

8. See Sermon 15.1.

Dn 2:45 the mountain not by the hands'† of stone cutters, that is, he was conceived of the Virgin without the mingling of the two sexes, but solely by the action of the Holy Spirit. Hence, it is no wonder that from his conception he had every kind of innocence and perfect righteousness. Since there was no evil in him, he was perfectly innocent; all good existed in him and so perfect righteousness. Innocence is understood with reference to removing evils, just as righteousness is understood with reference to acquiring good. He coveted nothing; he loved 'God with his whole heart, his whole soul, his whole mind, his whole strength, and his neighbor

Mt 22:37–39 as himself'.† Thus he was the one capable of paying the debt of the first man and placating the wrath of God. This he did by handing himself over as a human being for humanity's sake, one who was just for the unjust.

It was still necessary that the one who paid the debt add above and beyond it the price of redemption, remove the yoke of sin, slavery, and eternal punishment from humanity's neck, and restore its lost liberty. But since he had already given his righteousness to satisfy the debt, what would he pay as the price of human redemption? After the debt was paid, there still was need to make satisfaction for the offense, so that humanity, free from the house of slavery, might leave the dark prison of the vices. Notice and understand: since Christ was perfectly innocent and just, he owed nothing to suffering and death. These are owed only because of guilt. He did not derive sin from his origin, nor did he commit sin by his will. Nevertheless, by his own choice—not from necessity but from love alone, and compassion for our misery—he bore all our infirmities except sin[9] and certain others, such as ignorance and difficulty in doing good, which are not sin, but which his perfection did not allow him to possess. Similarly, in him was the perfection of all virtues, but not penitence and faith, which have in them something of imperfection; they will all be eliminated when what is perfect comes.† Voluntarily he underwent our other weaknesses, like hunger, thirst, weariness, sadness, insults, spitting, blows, a crown of thorns, scourging with rods, and finally a most disgraceful and bitter death, at a time and place where a countless multitude of people had gathered for the paschal solemnity. Then, I say, as it is written, 'he was reckoned among the wicked' and, like a criminal, he was nailed to a cross in the midst of thieves.†

1 Co 13:10

Mk 15: 28, 27

Thus, in order to redeem us, in his humanity, in which was the fullness of divinity, he freely gave himself—his passion, his death, all the merits he earned by undergoing these things—to us as the price of our redemption. How great these were we should estimate not only from what he suffered but also from the reverence owed to his lofty dignity. Although he was God, equal to the Father in all things, 'the splendor of his glory, the imprint of his substance',† 'the brightness of eternal light',†'the image of the invisible God, the firstborn of every creature',† the worthy of worthiness, 'possessing the name that is above every name',† compassing all things by the word of his power,† he—such and so great though he was—bore so many bitter things, so many indignities, so many vile and base things, solely out of love for us who were unworthy. So great were the sins of the human

Heb 1:3; Ws 7:26

Col 1:15

Ph 2:9

Heb 1:3

9. This 'authority' was discussed above, in connection with Sermon 1.

race that they could not be redeemed otherwise than by the death of the Son of God. Neither an angel, nor a mere man, however innocent—whether a righteous descendant of Adam, or one otherwise created by God—was found suitable for the ministry of redemption. Humanity could not be otherwise redeemed. Another mode of redemption was possible to God, but none was better suited to healing our wretched state. Christ died not only as the price of redemption, but also as a model, so that we might follow in his footsteps, and as an inducement to inspire us to do so. He died as a twofold remedy: for despair, which often arises after sin and from sin, and for elation and vainglory; that is, to free us from spiritual cowardice and from the storm of elation that often arises from good deeds.

4. As was already said, he came into flesh in order to freely bestow on us original righteousness, and through it to rescue us from slavery. Then he enters into our spirit, purifying it from the stains of sin, dispelling the darkness of blindness, filling it with everything that is good, and refreshing it
Is 7:14–15 with Emmanuel's food, butter and honey[†] lest it perish on the way. Butter has more richness and less sweetness, honey more sweetness and less richness. Butter is from below and is extracted from flesh; honey is from on high and comes from the dew of heaven. Thus we can not unreasonably take the richness of butter as the perfection of all virtues, and the sweetness of honey as the contemplation
Mt 1:23 of divinity. 'Emmanuel'—'God with us'[†]—that is, [God] in our nature—namely, Christ Jesus, God and a human being, a giant of two substances—eats butter since he possesses the fullness of all virtues, deeds, and merits. He was greatly delighted and

refreshed by this best of all foods, because from his very conception and birth he was met by so many and such great blessings;† thus he 'is full of grace and truth'.† He also eats honey in the full and perfect contemplation of his divinity, for the mind of the human nature assumed, right from its beginning, fully and perfectly enjoyed the vision of God, because it saw the truth immediately in itself. The wisdom of God bestowed itself in its fullness so that the assumed humanity might participate in it, pouring itself completely into his mind.[10] Hence, no matter what was done in the body of Christ while it was still mortal, or in his soul when, according to the temporal scheme of things, it was still mutable and susceptible of joy and sorrow and other feelings, with respect to his immutable and immovable mind he remained unfailingly blessed. Once he was raised up on the cross† and, while rising from the dead, wholly deified, he drew all his garments about him, and girded himself with the strength of immortality.† May the King of glory deign to lead us to the contemplation and ineffable glory of his divinity. Amen.

Ps 21:3
Jn 1:14
Jn 12:32
Ps 18:32, 39

10. See Sermon 1.5.

Sermon 4: On the Resurrection

INTRODUCTION

SERMON 4 GIVES THE IMPRESSION of being a rewritten amalgam of several independent sermons. The following are the principal sections, which correspond only roughly to the eight into which Châtillon's edition divides text: (1) Easter brings about a new creation.[1] (2) The bodies of Christ: natural, sacramental, and spiritual (=powerful + intellectual), and their interrelations.[2] (3) Theological observations on the presence of Christ in the sacramental elements; reason's inability to grasp the mystery.[3] (4) Purge out the old yeast of wickedness and depravity and become new dough.[4] (5) Three sorts of communicants: those who receive the body and blood of Christ without sufficient love in their hearts; those who study the truth out of vanity; those who have great

1. Section one.
2. Sections one and two.
3. Section two.
4. Section three.

love for the humanity of Christ.[5] (6) A Christological discourse on the divinity of Christ,[6] his humanity,[7] and his person.[8] (7) A moral application: one's attitude toward the good things of God and of the mind should be quite different from one's attitude toward the good things of this world, which inevitably end in bitterness.[9]

Section one is governed by the Easter antiphon: 'This is the day the Lord has made';[10] section two by John 6:63: 'It is the spirit that gives life; the flesh is useless'; section four by 1 Corinthians 4:7–8: Purge out the old yeast of wickedness and depravity and become new dough. Sections five through seven give a doctrinal and, for the final phase, a moral, interpretation of Exodus 12:9, 8: Do not eat lamb raw or boiled in water, but only baked over a fire, with the head, feet, internal organs, and wild greens.

Some theological points merit attention. The Victorines, like Abelard and many others, make much of three fundamental attributes of God: power, wisdom, and goodness. In section two, Achard concentrates on two of these, power (*virtus*) and wisdom, which are attributed to Christ in 1 Corinthians 1:24. In christian Latin the word *virtus* means both power or potentiality and virtue (which in the sense of a good habit is a potentiality to do good). In accord with the metaphysics of participation developed in *De discretione* and *De unitate* Achard sees the divine substance as identical with its attributes, and hence simple and undivided. Yet in some fashion it becomes multiple when it is participated in by created beings. Achard will develop this theme more at length in Sermon 13.

In developing his teaching on the different bodies of Christ, Achard rightly emphasizes both their interrelationship and finalities: the physical and sacramental bodies of Christ are the way in which we are brought to share in his wisdom and power (his powerful and intellectual bodies), and indeed to form one spiritual body with all of those who participate in them with us. Achard states

5. Section four.
6. Section five.
7. Section six.
8. Section seven.
9. Section eight.
10. Psalm 118:24.

that the presence of Christ in the Eucharist exceeds the grasp of human reasoning, and so reason should be silent, but is not. Achard goes on to elaborate a doctrine of the real presence of the whole Christ in each eucharistic element, in contrast to the localization of Christ's risen body in some heavenly place; his opinions correspond to traditional Catholic teaching, and his exposition is lucid and well thought out. Achard is a believer for whom faith has the last word, but he is also a careful and committed thinker. The 'place' (*locus*) referred to in this connection seems to have its technical meaning as one of the Aristotelian categories. Achard's speculation that the sacraments of bread and wine differ in the graces they confer (active virtue, by the bread, contemplative wisdom, by the wine) seems a bit forced. A latter-day liturgist arguing for communion under both species might argue that since the sacraments confer grace by signifying, the richer signification of communion under both species would be likely to dispose communicants to a more devout reception of the sacrament. Perhaps what the element of wine adds is a clearer symbolic reference to the blood of Christ poured out for us on the cross.

Achard's christological views here repeat much that was found in Sermons 1 and 3. He is particularly vigorous in defense of his position that Christ's humanity possessed by grace all that belonged to the Word by nature. Once again, his argument seems to attribute to Christ's humanity powers and knowledge that seem to modern theologians to have been incompatible with the *kenosis* of Christ and his full participation in the human condition. His picture of the human Christ is much more that of the gospel of John than that of the synoptics. He recalls some of the classic heresies regarding Christ's humanity: that his body was a phantom (docetism), that he lacked soul or a mind (Apollinarianism[11]), but the main object of his attention is a twelfth-century theory called 'Christological nihilism'. The defenders of this position wished to avoid saying that the humanity of Christ was a substance, and therefore a person, distinct from Christ. They affirmed that Christ, insofar as he is

11. Achard's information on these two forms of Apollinarianism seems to derive from Augustine, *Tractatus In Joannem*, 47.10.9 (PL 35:1737).

a man, is not some-thing (*aliquid*); their critics argued that this was tantamount to saying that Christ as man was nothing (*nihil*). Peter the Lombard seems to have held this position, and he may be the object of Achard's refutation here. Christological nihilism was condemned by Pope Alexander III in 1177.[12]

12. Peter the Lombard, *Sententiae*, 3, d. 10, 1, ed. Quaracchi, 593–94. For further references see Châtillon, *Sermons*, 62 n. 55, and the doctrinal introduction.

THE SERMON

On the Resurrection

THIS DAY IS THE DAY OF CHRIST, the
day of the Lord, 'the day the Lord has
made',[13]† the Lord's day; it is a new day, Ps 118:24
illumined by a new Sun. O reality new and won-
drous! Today this new Sun has emerged for us from
the darkness, from the tomb, from the heart of the
earth, from the netherworld. This is a festive day,
a spiritual day. Just as the spirit is contained in the
body, so is this day contained in the old day, the
outer day, the ancient sun, the sun created and
illumined from the beginning of the world. Just
as everyone perceives the body, but not the spirit,
with bodily eyes, so the outer day, but not the inner
one, is perceived by everyone. The old day is com-
mon to all; only new people perceive the new day,
the festive day, the solemn day, the first fruits of our
solemnity. On this day Christ arose from the dead
and put on strength and beauty:† strength against Ps 93:1
weakness, beauty against disgrace; the strength of
immortality and incorruption, beauty by contrast
to the form in which was no beauty or comeliness.† Is 53:2
On this day Christ put aside what was old and
changed completely into a new self. Previously he
had borne the old penalty, but not the old guilt;
this he laid aside by dying, and by rising he put
on impassibility: 'In that he died to sin he died
once; in that he lives, he lives to God',† that is, Rm 6:10
in the divine manner, eternally, without end. This

13. Psalm 118:24. Achard is quoting this verse from the Easter liturgy where it is still used as an antiphon: 'This is the day the Lord has made, let us rejoice and be glad on it.'

great solemnity belongs spiritually to those who
have risen with Christ and been made new with
him who is new, those 'who have crucified their
Ga 5:24 flesh with its vices and concupiscences',† who have
put away the image of the old humanity while
putting on the image of the new humanity created
Ep 4:24 according to God.†

They should not seek refreshment from me on
this day, however, because I am not new but old,
Rm 7:14 'carnal, sold under sin'.† Let them not despair,
though, but look to the source of their newness,
who has placed before them a table replete with
many delights, and above all with the body of
Christ, not only with the sacramental body but
the natural one, and also the powerful, intellec-
tual, and spiritual body. Christ's sacramental body
is the sacrament itself, the appearances of bread
and wine, which we sometimes call the body of
Christ. The natural body is what he took from the
Virgin, which hung on the cross. The powerful
body of Christ is all the modes of participation in
the divine power. Although 'the power of God'
1 Co 1:24 is one, simple,† and indivisible in itself, it can be
shared in by many and distributed to many. Thus,
because it is shared it is, in a certain way, multiplied,
although it is simple and one, as was said. The
members of this body of Christ are each of the
modes of participation; the body itself is the totality
1 Co 1:24 of all these modes. So also 'the wisdom of God',†
although simple and indivisible, is shared by many,
and in a certain way becomes multiple. The modes
of participation in it are the members of Christ's
intellectual body; all of them are the intellectual
body itself. Just as different streams flow from a
single spring, and different rays emanate from the
one sun, so too, from the one wisdom of God many

and diverse forms of wisdom flow into us. The spiritual body of Christ consists of the powerful and the intellectual bodies.

2. The sacramental body is not received for its own sake, but for what subsists in it, the reality of Christ's body and blood. Nor should we stop there: the natural body of Christ itself is not to be received for its own sake, because 'the flesh is of no benefit'† by reason of the nature of flesh, but Jn 6:63
rather for the grace that is in it, just as we do not raise a drinking vessel for itself but rather for what is in it. The powerful and intellectual bodies—that is, the spiritual body—are received for their own sake, because 'it is the spirit who gives life'.† The Jn 6:63
sacramental body is received in order to reach the powerful, intellectual, and spiritual bodies, the life-giving spirit. Notice that the sacramental body is received with the mouth and not with the heart; the powerful, intellectual, and spiritual bodies are received with the heart and not with the mouth; the natural body is received in the mouth as a sacrament and in the heart with respect to the grace it contains.

Notice also that both the body and the blood are received under each species; the body is not separated from the blood, nor the blood from the body. Nevertheless, it may be that some grace is conferred under the sacrament of bread that is not conferred under the sacrament of the blood; or if the same grace is given by both, it may be given more amply by one than by the other. Perhaps power is given in the sacrament of the body, and wisdom in the sacrament of the blood; or if both graces are conferred by each, power may be given more abundantly in the body, wisdom more abundantly in the blood. The body, which is more

external, looks more to power, which pertains to
the active life and deals with exterior things; the
blood, which is interior, looks to wisdom which
pertains to contemplation. Moreover, we receive
the body to gain immortality for the body, the
blood in order to have beatitude for the spirit.
Similarly, the body of Christ is received so that 'the
body of our humility' may be configured to 'the
Ph 3:21 body of his glory';† we receive his blood so that our
spirit may be conformed to the spirit of Christ.

Of this sacrament of the altar let no one, by
doubting and questioning, say with the offspring
of Israel, 'Manu, manu,' that is, 'What is this? What
Ex 16:15, 31 is this?'† We are commanded to believe that the true
body and blood of Christ are present there. We are
not allowed to question what exceeds all human
reasoning, and so let reason be silent; let it not
investigate what is beyond it, what it cannot under-
stand. This is the change David underwent before
1 S 21:12–15 Achish†—Achish means 'What is this?' One thing
is seen there, another believed; the appearance of
bread and wine is seen, the truth of the body and
blood of Christ is believed. Reason ought not ask,
'Where is the head, where the foot, where this part,
where that', or whether the place is as extensive as
the body itself, or whether more of the body is
in the whole sacrament than in part of it, since
its very mode of being is beyond nature. Christ is
whole in the whole, and whole in the part; not
more in the whole than in the part, but complete
in both. Just as the accidents of bread and wine
are seen apart from what underlies them, so the
body of Christ is believed to be there apart from
such accidents. Both are wonderful, both seem
impossible to reason. The body of Christ, which
is in heaven, is in one place in such a way that it

is not simultaneously in another according to its natural mode of existing, and its place is the same size as the body. It follows that if it is in one part of heaven, it is not in another. But none of these considerations applies to its manner of being in the sacrament.

3. So that we can fittingly approach this table and not be guilty of receiving the body and blood of Christ unworthily, we should pay attention to Paul when he says: 'Purge out the old yeast . . .'† 1 Co 5:7; 11:27 Yeast corrupts the lump and makes it sour, and thus it stands for any sin that corrupts us and makes us a member of the old self. Paul divides sin into two kinds: wickedness and depravity. The body is corrupted and contaminated by two causes, that is, excessive emptying and excessive filling. Emptying consists in the removal or absence of natural humors which should be present but are not; filling consists in the condition or presence of harmful humors that corrupt nature since they are present when they should not be. As the physicians tell us, excessive emptying is cured by moderate filling, and unhealthy filling is eliminated by moderate emptying. So, too, our spirit is corrupted by two causes, namely, unhealthy emptying, called depravity,[14] which consists in the absence of the goods of the soul and the removal of virtues, and unhealthy filling, called wickedness, which consists in having vices. These two, wickedness and depravity, are cured by their contraries. Depravity is cured by truth, just as unhealthy emptiness is cured by good filling, and wickedness is cured by sincerity, just as unhealthy fullness is cured by moderate emptying. This is the meaning of 'purge

14. *Nequitia*, of which Achard says, 'hence it is called *nequam*, meaning *non quisquam* (not any), nor having any of the things that should be there'.

out the old yeast'—that is, totally abandon both wickedness and depravity, the two ways by which the inner self is corrupted—'so that you may be
1 Co 5:7 new dough'†—that is, one in charity.

Dough is flour bound together by a sprinkling of water. Those made one by the water of saving grace are new dough; as members of Christ, vivified by his spirit, they walk in newness of spirit. Those who choose evil are said to stick to each other like old dough, in accord with the statement: 'Those
1 Co 6:16 joined to a prostitute become one body'.† Note what old dough it is! But what of the saying: 'Purge out the old yeast, so that you may be new dough, as
1 Co 5:7 you are unleavened'?† If they are unleavened, how can he command that the old yeast be purged out? This can be understood as follows. The old yeast is to be purged out first; then, once it has been purged out, you will be unleavened, that is, pure and unspoiled. You should not stop there, however, but advance from good to better, until you are new dough, that is, one in love of God and neighbor, just as you are unleavened through the purging out of the old yeast. Thus you will at last be able to feast upon the paschal lamb 'who has been slaughtered
Rv 13:8 from the beginning of the world'.†

4. The law lays down how the flesh of the lamb is to be eaten: 'You are not to eat it raw or boiled in water, but only roasted over a fire, with its head, feet, and entrails, along with wild greens'.[15] The flesh of this lamb, 'who takes away
Jn 1:29 the sins of the world',† is the humanity of Christ with its sacraments and the holy Scriptures that discourse about it. Those who eat it raw are not attached to Christ by any love, and they feel no

15. This passage (Exodus 12:9, 8) is now in the sacramentary as a reading for Holy Thursday.

love when they read the Scriptures or approach the altar. Those who serve the tabernacle have no right to eat from the altar; they are cold and as good as dead when they receive it, and thus they become guilty of the body and blood of Christ because they receive unworthily. Others eat the flesh of the lamb boiled in water; they have some love, but not enough to drive out carnal attachments. It cannot be said without qualification that they have the love of God who want always to be alone and supreme. Some greedily read the Scriptures, and seek the truth with impetuous zeal, not for its own sake but for vanity, vainglory, or money. This is an alien fire; here too much comes from the water. Judas sold the body of Jesus for thirty pieces of silver;† these people, insofar as they can, Mt 26:15
sell his godhead for vanity, for evil. Those who eat the flesh roasted over a fire are those moved by a great love for the humanity of Christ, either in the Scriptures or in the reception of Christ's body and blood. Only these receive worthily, and by receiving become members of Christ; or if already members of Christ, by receiving him again they become stronger and more stable.

5. Next it says 'with its head, feet, and entrails'. The head of Christ is God; his feet, the humanity; the entrails, which are between head and feet, are the personal union of the divine and human natures. Certain persons give the Spirit to Christ within limits, whereas the Father gave it to him without limits;[16] they eat his head in a wrong way, gnawing at it and diminishing it. They do this

16. This evocation of John 3:34 ('Whoever God sends speaks the words of God; God does not measure out the Spirit') reoccurs in Sermons 5.2 and 13.2. The same text is cited in Hugh of Saint Victor, *De sapientia animae Christi* (PL 176:854C) and the *Quaestiones in epistolas Pauli* (PL 175:436B).

by denying that the assumed humanity possesses by grace all that the assuming Word possesses by nature. Whatever is said of God positively—for example, that God is 'wise', 'good', and the like—is said of the humanity [assumed] as well. I say 'positively' because certain things said of God do not attribute anything to him but rather exclude something—for example, 'eternal' and 'immense'. God is called 'eternal' because he has neither beginning nor end. Hence, although the assumed humanity is not eternal, while God is eternal, the humanity does not have less than God because, as was said, 'eternal' does not attribute anything but rather excludes something.

Why do these people not at least believe the Apostle when he says, 'In him all the fullness of
Col 2:9 divinity dwells bodily'?† When he says 'all' he includes everything in God, like power, wisdom, and goodness; when he says 'fullness' he suggests the totality of each of these—he could have them, but not in the same fullness. And lest anyone apply all this to the Word, he added 'bodily', that is, in the body of Christ. Again, the Truth says of himself: 'All authority in heaven and on earth has been
Mt 28:18 given to me'.† Clearly such a giving could only be to a lesser nature. Now if the assumed humanity did not have as much power as the Word, how would it be true that all power had been given to him. Or if he does not possess omnipotence, how is he omnipotent? And if he is not omnipotent, how is he God? O eyes that do not see! They do not dare to say that that human being is not God, and yet they say what follows from it.

These who gnaw at his godhead touch our
Jn 20:17 Christ.† If he does not possess as much divinity, how is the Word the same as God and as great

as God? Of the saints it is said: 'I said, you are gods';† they are sharers in the divine nature, as the apostle Peter says.† Of them it can be said that one is a greater or lesser god or lord than another, because they participate in different ways. There are then many gods and many lords in heaven and on earth. If they wish to agree with reason and authority they ought not presume to contradict mother Church which believes this and preaches it. Therefore, let us who are children of mother Church devoutly and with great reverence eat the head of the lamb by believing that the fullness of the godhead inheres in Christ's humanity, and by not falling short of this.

Ps 82:6
2 P 1:4

6. Certain people eat the feet of the lamb wrongly and gnaw at them irreverently. Such, for example, were those who said that Jesus' body was a phantom; those who said that the Lord assumed only a body and not a soul, while the Word itself took the place of the soul; and those who said that the Word assumed a body and soul, but not reason, while the Word took the place of the mind. There are even certain enemies of truth who say that when the Word became human nothing came to be, and in his humanity was nothing of what we are. But if this is so, how is he consubstantial with us with respect to his humanity, just as he is consubstantial with the Father with respect to his divinity? If he was nothing that the Father is, how could he be consubstantial with the Father? So also if he is nothing that we are, how can he be of the same nature, how can he have consubstantial sameness? As the former persons took away the fullness of deity from Christ's humanity, so the latter deprive his divinity of the fullness of humanity. Both are blind leaders of the blind.

Lk 3:16

7. As was stated earlier, the entrails are what lies between the head and the feet, that is, those thongs that the great John judged himself not worthy to untie.† They are the union of deity and humanity, which is well hidden, as Dionysius the Areopagite says, and unknown to every intellect, human or angelic.[17] Some dissolve this union by saying that what was assumed is not the same person as the assuming Word.[18] How was what is not the same person with the Word personally united to the Word? Again, what was assumed is either a person or not. If we say we say it is a person, and not the same person as the Word, there will be four persons in the Trinity. If it is not a person, would it be a person if the Word were not united to it? Would not something be taken away from him? We should not listen to those who say that nothing is composed of body and soul,[19] for the Church daily resounds with the words 'Perfect God and perfect man, subsisting with a rational soul and human flesh'.[20]

We should note the objection of some that if what was assumed by the Word is a person, then the Word assumed a person. This is no argument. For example, someone brought into a house a person without clothes who afterward was clothed; the one brought in is clothed; therefore a clothed person was brought in. Similarly, the Word assumed

17. Pseudo-Dionysius, *De divinis nominibus* 2.9 (PG 3:648A; in the translation of John Scotus Eriugena, PL 122:1124B). See Sermon 15.24.

18. Achard here argues for the first of the three positions outlined by Peter the Lombard, *Sententiae* 3, d. 6–7, ed. Quaracchi, 573–589. See the doctrinal introduction.

19. This is another allusion to Christological nihilism, which denied that the body and soul of Christ were united to each other as they are in every other human being Cf. *Apologia de Verbo incarnato* 13, 20, 46, ed. N. Häring, FS 16 (1956) 115, 118, 129.

20. Achard here cites the Pseudo-Athanasian creed, which was said each day at Prime by the community at Saint Victor.

humanity, not a person, but in a person in order to make it a person. We grant that the Word assumed a nature because he became of a different nature from what he had been previously. Finally, the angel Gabriel clearly accuses them of blatant error by saying to the Virgin: 'The holy one to be born
of you will be called Son of God'.[†] Is the Word of Lk 1:35
the Father called the Son of God, and is he holy, because the Holy Spirit overshadowed the Virgin? Is he not eternally holy, eternally the Son of God?

Alternatively, by the head we can understand the beginning of conception, by the feet the departure at the Lord's passion, by the entrails whatever he did between his birth and his death. All these we must reverently eat by faith and enjoy by love.

8. There follows 'with wild greens'.[†] It says Ex 12:8
'wild' because there are also garden varieties. Greens are bitter. By garden varieties we understand the bitter things that arise from ourselves and exist in ourselves; almost everything in us is matter for bitterness. Wild greens are the bitter things of the world; they are many and varied, since the whole world should be and is bitter to a healthy palate. Even if sometimes the world allures and attracts us with its sweetness, even this should
embitter us. 'The final end of joy is sorrow'[†] and Pr 14:13
'all the rivers flow into the sea';[†] that is, all delights Qo 1:7
end in grief. Therefore, we eat the good things of God, and the good things of the mind, and the good things of the world, but in different ways: by loving and enjoying the good things of God and the good things of the mind, by recollecting in bitterness the good things of the world.

Or again, we can understand the eating of wild greens as the boasting that the saints maintain in tribulations. As Paul wrote: 'Not only that, but

Rm 5:3 we also boast in our tribulations'.† Therefore, the hand that brings wild greens to our mouth[21] is the hand that rejects, whereas the hand that conveys the good things of God and of the mind is the hand that attracts. May Christ, who is the power and the wisdom of God, draw us after him, rejecting with one hand and attracting with the other, and lead us to his banquet. Amen.

21. *Manducatio*: the translation here tries to reproduce a play on words in the Latin—*manducatio*=eating and *manus*=hand.

Sermon 5: On [the Sunday of] Palm Branches

INTRODUCTION

ACHARD'S SERMON IS AN INTERPRETATION of the gospel account of Palm Sunday. (1) He begins by reiterating some themes that are familiar from other sermons of his: the three positive and substantial attributes of the divine nature: power, wisdom, and love; the authoritative opinion that the humanity assumed has by grace no less than the assuming Word has by nature.[1] (2) He then gives a brief summary of the theology of the angels.[2] (3) Charity is compared to olive oil, which in turn is seen as a figure of Christ's blood.[3] (4) Out of love, Christ became obedient even unto death, death upon a cross.[4] (5) The ass and her colt are an allegorical representation of the effects of sin and redemption on the human spirit.[5] (6) Jesus instructs some by direct inspiration

1. Section one.
2. Section one.
3. Section two.
4. Section three.
5. Section four.

and leads them to heavenly peace.[6] The outline corresponds to a physical journey from the Mount of Olives (1–3), to Bethany (4), to a walled town or castle (5), and finally to Jerusalem (6).

The christological teaching of the sermon is familiar from Sermons 1 and 4. Once again, Achard finds a way to emphasize Christ's headship over the Church, and that all graces are a participation in his fullness. The content of his brief summary of the theology of angels was traditional by his time.

Sections two and three introduce us to Achard's theology of love. Twelfth-century theologians argued about whether there could be human virtues apart from grace. Hugh of Saint Victor thought that there could be virtuous behavior apart from grace; it was not meritorious in the order of grace, but nevertheless was worthy of reward.[7] Achard, however, believes that without grace a human being is incapable of those acts of knowledge, love, and enjoyment to which human existence is ordered. He concludes that apart from love virtue is powerless.[8]

The complicated allegory of the ass and her colt provides further access to Achard's anthropology. Human beings have two principal powers: knowledge and affectivity; these are ordered, respectively, to the knowledge of truth and to the love of virtue.[9] Here Achard calls them the interior sense and the will. The will (*voluntas*, feminine) should be guided by reason (*sensus interior*, masculine). If the opposite happens, there is a reversal of gender. Dropping this aspect of his metaphor, Achard says that the sin bridles the mind with ignorance and error (they are the devil's tack, so to speak). Made for contemplation, humanity has fallen from the highest level of understanding to the depths of error. The human mind is hobbled by ignorance of self and neighbor, the world and hell. For its part, the will is reined in by idolatry and demon worship, and hobbled

6. Section five..

7. See *De sacramentis legis naturalis et scriptae* 1. 6. 17; 2. 113. 11; PL 176:273–175, 539.

8. Châtillon, *Sermons*, 69, n. 26, refers to the discussion in Arthur Landgraf, *Dogmengeschichte der Frühscholastik* (Regensburg:1952–1956) 1/1, 161–201.

9. Section five.

by the lure of the flesh, wickedness of heart, insatiable desire, and a harmful sense of security.

To untie the mind there must be teaching of the truth combined with exhortation and good example. These replace the bridle of ignorance and error with faith and devotion. The four kinds of ignorance that hobbled the mind are replaced with the corresponding kinds of knowledge, of which self-knowledge is the most important since it enables us to be compassionate toward our neighbor, and to evaluate the things of this world at their proper value in relation to the nature and destiny of ourselves who are made in the image and likeness of God. Impiety of will is replaced by true worship of God; the four disordered affects that hobble it are replaced by their opposites: continence, love of neighbor, contempt of the world, and fear of the Lord.

Two observations can be made about this anthropological schema. In his development of this metaphor, Achard is not entirely consistent. It would be more consistent with his own thinking elsewhere,[10] and that of Hugh and Richard of Saint Victor, if he had assigned devotion, exhortation, and good example to the will and affectivity, rather than to the mind. They are certainly perceived by the cognitive side of the self, but their use is to move the will. More positively, the cognitive and affective life of the self is placed in relation to four objects: the self, neighbor, world, and God. The broad vision and the relationality this implies are typically Victorine and essential to any Christian theological anthropology.

10. For example, Sermon 8.4.

THE SERMON

On [the Sunday of] Palm Branches

JESUS CAME TO THE MOUNT OF OLIVES
and said to his disciples: 'Go into the walled
town across from you, and you will find
an ass and the colt' of an ass tied. 'Untie them
and lead them to me.' The disciples the Lord sent
obeyed him, untied the ass and the colt of an ass,
and led them to Jesus. 'And they laid their gar-
Mt 21:1–2, 7 ments on them' and 'and made Jesus sit on them'.†
Thus seated, Jesus came into Jerusalem. The mount
came to the mount, the spiritual to the material,
the truth to the figure. He is the mountain about
which it is said: 'On the last days the mountain
of the house of the Lord will be prepared on the
Is 2:2 summit of the mountains'.† 'The house of the
Lord' is the city of God, which cannot be hidden
Mt 5:14 because it is set upon this mountain.† It is called
a city in relation to the difference between merits
and rewards; it is called a house with reference to
the unity of charity and love. The mountain is said
to be 'prepared', that is, predestined to be the Son
of God in power, of the same kind and amount of
power, wisdom, and goodness as the Word himself
to which it is personally united. The humanity
assumed has by grace no less than the assuming
Word has by nature.[11] Thus the Apostle wrote: 'In
Col 2:9 him all the fullness of divinity dwells bodily'.† He
says 'all' to include everything positively predicated
of God, such as power, wisdom, goodness, and the

11. See Sermons 1 and 4 for this 'authority'.

like. (Some things are said of God in a negative way, such as eternity, immensity, and immortality.) By 'fullness' he understands the totality of each. Lest anyone explain this totality with reference to the Word, he added 'bodily', that is, in the body of Christ. 'On the summit of the mountains', that is, so that the summit of the mountains would be not only holy, but the holy of holies. God the Father gave him to be head of the Church, and gave to him 'a name that is above every name',† that is named now and in the future.†

Ph 2:9
Ep 1:21

Certain names of angels pertain to their present status, such as Angels, Archangels, Virtues, Powers, Principalities, and Dominations. All these names are given to them in relation to ministries they perform in our regard. They are 'ministering spirits, sent on behalf of those who receive the inheritance'.† These ministries of theirs will all cease 'when Christ hands over the kingdom to the God and Father'.† Then Christ himself, as he passes over from humanity to divinity, will minister to them,† so that as the saints come and go they may find pasture.[12]† Other names of angels pertain to their future state, such as Thrones, Cherubim, and Seraphim. Certain angels are called Thrones, not because of their relationship to us but because of God's relationship to them—God sits and rests on them—or, indeed, because of their relationship to God, in whom they rest. Cherubim, too, whose name means 'fullness of knowledge', and Seraphim, whose name means 'burning', are so called because of the excellence of their knowledge

Heb 1:14
1 Co 15:24
Lk 12:37
Jn 10:9

12. John 10:9 It would be forcing the grammar, but improving the theology, to translate: 'Then Christ himself, as he passes over, will minister to them, leading them from his humanity to his divinity, so that as the saints come and go they may find pasture'.

and love.[13] These three will not be relieved of their responsibilities in the future; in fact, something may be added to their rest, love, and knowledge
Rm 8:19 by the revelation of the children of God;† they will
Heb 11:40 not be made perfect apart from us.† The dignity of Christ is raised above all these dignities because 'his going out is from the height of heaven, and
Ps 19:6 his circuit to its summit';† that is, Christ is exalted to equality with the Father. This is the dignity of all dignities, something that cannot be said of any angel.

Mt 21:1 2. He came, it says, 'to the Mount of Olives'.† The Son of God, although he could be called a 'mount' with reference to all the things that were in him, is not called the Mount of Olives in regard to all of them, but only in regard to the love of which he was full as he came 'to the Mount of Olives'. He himself is 'the rich mountain, the curdled mountain, the mountain on which God is pleased to dwell, 'where the Lord will dwell to
Ps 67:16–17 Vulgate the end',† that is, without boundary or measure. He does dwell on other mountains, but not 'to
Jn 3:34 the end'; to them the Spirit is given by measure.† The Mount of Olives was then, and perhaps still is, planted with olive trees from which oil is pressed. This liquid floats on all other liquids—it is love, preferred to all other virtues; it holds primacy over them all. Without love every virtue is tasteless, fruitless, and totally without merit. As he hung on the cross, Christ pressed this love out of his hands, feet, and side for us; even on the Mount, when he was in agony and given to lengthy prayer, drops of
Lk 22:43–44 blood flowed out of his most holy body.† Christ

13. The meaning of the names of the choirs of angels and of towns (Bethany and Jerusalem below) are found in Saint Jerome, *Liber de nominibus hebraicis* (PL 23:776, 787, 829–830, 839–40). See also Gregory the Great, *Homilia XL in Evanglia* 34.10 (PL 76:1252AB).

pressed out, as it were, the oil of gladness, by which
he was anointed beyond his companions.† To him Ps 45:7
the Spirit was given without measure.[14]† Of this oil Jn 3:34
it is written: 'Your name is oil poured out'.† Grace Sg 1:3
is measured out to the saints in accord with their participation in the full plenitude of Christ, and hence his name is called 'oil poured out'. By this grace he is Christ, and we are Christians.[15]

3. He came, it says, from Bethany,† which is Mk 11:1
interpreted 'the house of obedience'. In obedience to the Father, not by force but by his own volition, he went out from the Father and came into the
world.† Concentrate on how great was Christ's Jn 16:28
filial devotion, how great his love, to make him come down from equality with the Father's majesty
to receive the form of a servant.† He bowed the Ph 2:7
heavens and came down,† and put on our form Ps 18:9
in order to redeem us. In this form he was tired, he suffered hunger and thirst, he bore the other penalties of our weakness; finally, he reached the gibbet of the cross,[16] having become obedient to
God the Father even unto death.† What death? Ph 2:8
Death on a cross, a most squalid death, a disgraceful death. O devotion of Christ, O token of great love! Indeed, the love of the suffering Son seems greater than that of the commanding Father, although it cannot be greater.

4. Then it says that he told his disciples: 'Go into
the walled town[17] across from you'.† This walled Mt 21:2
town is the human race, which is fortified by us and against us. What does it mean that in this walled town of the human race an ass with a colt

14. See Sermon 4.5.

15. Achard is referring to the meaning of 'Christ,' which is 'anointed'.

16. See Sermon 1.6.

17. Saint Ambrose developed the theme of the walled town as a metaphor for the human race in *De Isaac vel anima* 8.69 (CSEL 32/1, 691; PL 14:529A) and *Epistola* 18/2 (CSEL 82, 142; PL 16:1241D).

is found—that is, among human beings something not human? Before sin, as long as humanity was still 'in honor', nothing in humanity was not human. By sinning humanity became 'like senseless beasts',
Ps 49:12 and, worse yet, 'became like them'† by crossing the line into a kind of bestiality.[18]

In the beginning, as Scripture says, 'God created humanity in his image and likeness, male and fe-
Gn 1:26–27 male he created them'.† Does not the male signify the inner sense, and the female the will, which ought to stay at the side of the inner sense and be informed and ruled by it? The sense is changed into an ass, the will into the colt of an ass, by acquiring similar habits. A kind of sex change even occurs: the male is changed into the female, and the female into the male.[19] The ass, the inner sense, has its head—that is, the highest part of itself, the mind—bound by two ropes: ignorance and error. Because of ignorance it does not know the truth; by error it believes falsehood. Before humanity sinned, it had God present through its understanding, and it enjoyed the contemplation of him. Then, however, it fell through its own fault from the pinnacle of divine understanding to reason, from reason to faith, from faith to opinion, from opinion to doubt, from doubt to ignorance, and from ignorance to error. This change is associated with the right hand, not
Ps 77:10 of the Most High, but of the devil.† [The ass] has its front feet bound by ignorance of itself and its neighbor, it back feet by ignorance of the world and hell. By these four bonds the four feet of the ass are constrained. The head of the colt is bound with

18. This theme is connected with that of the 'region of unlikeness' so often developed by twelfth-century theologians See Châtillon, *Sermons*, 70–71, n. 40.

19. In Latin 'ass' is feminine and 'colt' is masculine; Achard says that the (masculine) 'sense' is changed into an ass, and the (feminine) 'will' is changed into the colt.

impiety, that is, by idolatry and demon worship; two of its feet are bound by the lure of the flesh and wickedness of heart; the other two by insatiable desire and a harmful security. We must not fail to say how the bonds of the colt are produced from the bonds of the ass. The lure of the flesh is produced by ignorance of oneself; wickedness of heart by ignorance of one's neighbor; the insatiable desire of the world by ignorance of the same; and harmful security by ignorance of hell. To untie these Jesus sent his two disciples, whom we take to stand for instruction and exhortation. That we know what to do through instruction does not mean we immediately do it; so exhortation must follow.

Alternatively, we might take these two disciples to stand for the illumination of truth and the inspiration of goodness, that is, an upright spirit and a good spirit. These two disciples loosen the head of the ass from error and ignorance; they put on her head their own bonds, of faith and devotion. They untie her feet from the various types of ignorance: of self and neighbor, of the world and hell; they bind them with their opposites: self-knowledge and knowledge of neighbor, knowledge of the world and of hell. The head of the colt they loose from impiety, replacing it with its opposite, true worship of God. They untie its feet and bind them with their opposites, changing the lure of the flesh into continence, wickedness of heart into love of neighbor, concupiscence of the world into contempt of the world, and evil security into fear of the Lord.

5. And they lead them to Jesus and lay their garments on them. By knowledge of the truth and love of virtue we reach Jesus, as though by the

disciples' guidance. 'And they lay their garments on them', that is, examples of the virtues. And
Mt 21:7 they 'made Jesus sit on them'.† Those of such great perfection that Jesus sits on them no longer need another's teaching and support. Instead, they can say with Paul: 'Be imitators of me, as I am
1 Co 11:1 of Christ'.† Jesus presides over them and harnesses them with his ropes: knowledge of the works of the creator and the sacraments of the incarnation of the Word,[20] and contemplation of heavenly things. Thus he leads them into Jerusalem, into the true vision of peace, to which may Christ, who is our peace, deign to lead us. Amen.

20. The work of creation and the work of redemption, with the Incarnation and all the sacraments associated with it, are the two main divisions of theology according to Hugh of Saint Victor.

Grace of Christ

Sermon 2: [First Sermon] for the Dedication [of a Church]

INTRODUCTION

THE ANNIVERSARY OF THE DEDICATION of their church, June 5, was an important feast for the canons regular of Saint Victor, a feast graced with an octave and with festal sermons. This sermon for the dedication of the church interweaves a number of themes—tent, sun, bridegroom—drawn from the opening verses of Psalm 18 (Hebrew 19).

The outline is simple enough. (1) Christ is identified as the sun that illumines and enflames the hearts of those who are bathed in his rays. Holy men (perhaps Achard's mind turned to his predecessors at Saint Victor, William of Champeaux, Hugh, Gilduin, the martyred Prior Thomas) illumine and warm the hearts of others only because they participate in Christ's light. (2) In this phase of its existence the church is a tent and her members are pilgrims with no lasting home. They are on a military campaign, waging war against the world, the flesh, and the devil. Not by their own strength, but by grace, can they hope to conquer these formidable enemies. (3) This tent is a foreshadowing of the heavenly temple, wherein God will dwell in the bodies, souls, spirits, and minds of the blessed, and each human being will be God's bride, so united with him that together they form one spirit. (4) The soul's enjoyment of the vision of God corresponds to the feast of dedication; the octave prefigures the resurrection and glorification of the body.

This sermon makes a clear doctrinal point: only by the grace of God, by participation in the wisdom and love of Christ, can human beings be saved. God sometimes withdraws his grace deliberately in order that we may know our own powerlessness. The emphasis on grace and the dichotomies, knowledge and love, doctrine and discipline, are typically Victorine. Victorine, too, is the emphasis on the need for human examples, and the dangers of pride to which human models are subject.

As he gave the sermon, Achard may have been thinking about the human exemplars who had shaped the life of the canons of Saint Victor. He may also have been thinking of Saint Augustine, whose rule the canons followed. In the third section Achard orchestrates the Augustinian contrast between this life and the next, sight and faith, labor and rest, and he concludes with a reference to Augustine's notion of love without satiety.

This sermon also emphasizes the sublime destiny of the body. Although death is an exodus from the prison of this corruptible body,[1] redemption will only be complete when this body puts on incorruptibility and God dwells in each of the saints in respect to mind, soul, and body. The bridegroom's embrace encircles not just minds but enfleshed spirits.

Formally, the most remarkable feature of this sermon is its use of Scripture. In just a few paragraphs Achard quotes all four gospels, at least seven epistles, six different psalms, and three other Old Testament books. From beginning to end he weaves his rhetorical design with the threads of biblical metaphors.

---

1. For this theme among christian authors see the references cited by Châtillon, *Sermons,* 41, n. 38, and77–78, n. 41. It recurs in Sermon 6.3.

THE SERMON

[First Sermon] for the Dedication [of a Church]

HE PITCHED HIS TENT IN THE SUN,
and like a bridegroom' will he proceed
'from his bridal chamber'.† This visible Ps 19:4–5
sun has splendor and heat, so that in itself it shines
and warms; it illumines the world with the rays of
its brightness and fills it with warmth. Hence, it is
not without justification that we take the sun to
stand for spiritual people, who shine in themselves
and illumine others, who are ardent in themselves
and inflame others. In themselves they shine by the
splendor of their knowledge, and they are ardent
with the fire of love. They illumine others by
the word of preaching and inflame them by the
example of their good lives.[2]

Another sun exists which is much more sub-
lime than these, brighter and more ardent, who
is the true 'sun of righteousness',† 'the splendor Ml 4:2
of glory',† 'the brightness of eternal light',† 'the Heb 1:3; Ws 7:26
light that illumines every person coming into this
world',† who in his very nature and essence pos- Jn 1:9
sesses splendor and warmth. 'As the Father has
granted to the Son to have life in himself',† so Jn 5:26
he has given him to have splendor and warmth in
himself, although not from himself. Therefore, he
has splendor through a comprehensive knowledge
of all things, for to him, 'all things are naked and
open';† in him 'are all the treasures of the wisdom Heb 4:13
and knowledge'† of God. He also possesses warmth Col 2:3
by loving every good thing perfectly. Scripture says

2. The metaphor of the Sun of Justice who illumines the saints, who in turn illumine others, may be drawn from Pseudo-Dionysius, *De coelesti hierarchia* 2.5 (PG 3:144CD) and *De divinis nominibus* 4.1–4 (PG 3:693B-700C).

Ws 11:24/25 that ‘you hated none of the things you made’;† no
Ps 19:6 one can hide from his warmth.†

All holy people receive from the fullness of this sun so that they too may be suns, always shining and ardent in themselves, but not always sending out their rays to illumine others. Sometimes they even try to conceal themselves, since they are afraid they will suffer some loss of their light if they manifest it imprudently. However, because nothing ‘is hidden that will not be known, nothing concealed that
Mk 4:22 par will not be revealed’,† and because ‘a city built on
Mt 5:14 a hill cannot be hidden’,† sometimes, even when they are unwilling, they promote the praise of God and the advantage of their neighbor. They are hesitant not because they do not love God and neighbor, but because they are afraid they will destroy themselves through the arrogance of praise instead of building up others through the manifestation of their virtues.

2. So God pitches his tent in these people, in whom he dwells through true knowledge of himself and sincere love, as ‘in the sun’. A tent is for travelers, for those making a journey, for workers and soldiers. As long as we are in the present life
Lv 25:47; Ps 39:12; 1 P 2:11, etc. we are like ‘pilgrims and strangers’.† ‘We have no lasting city here, but we are seeking one that is
Heb 13:14 to come’.† This is why the existing church is compared to a tent and not to a temple. In this tent God fights for us, in us, and through us; his is the war we are waging and sustaining; to his army alone are we to attribute every victory. War is waged against us on many fronts. ‘The desires of the flesh are
Ga 5:17 against the spirit’;† the will contradicts reason; the will is even divided from itself.[3] In another phase of the conflict, the raucous world launches an attack.

3. On the conflict among the powers of the soul see also Sermons 7.2, 9.1–2, 13.8, and the doctrinal introduction.

With its delights it tries to soften human firmness and to weaken the strength of its adversaries. To strengthen the hands of our enemies against us a multitude of demons is present with the host of all the vices. All of these, united in a single great charge, armed with every sort of deceit and trickery, rise up against us to take us captive. They draw us into a lake without water containing a deathless worm and unquenchable fire.

So that we will not succumb to these minions, but rather resist valiantly, let us not presume on our own powers, but rather let us have recourse to divine help. The soldier of Christ will say to his king and commander: 'Bring out your spear against those who persecute me; take hold of arms and
shield, and rise up to help me'.† After the triumph Ps 35:3, 2
of victory is attained, let the soldiers say with voice and heart: ' "Not to us, Lord, not to us, but to your
name give glory".† You have accomplished all our Ps 115:1
deeds for us, O Lord'.

The Lord sometimes deserts us when we are engaged in this many-sided struggle. He allows us to be wounded by the spears of the enemy so that he may in this way let us see ourselves and recognize our weakness. Then we will know for certain that we were fighting valiantly against our enemies a little earlier not by our own strength but by divine protection. So the prophet says: 'Lord, by your favor you gave strength to my beauty; you turned your face from me, and I become
troubled'.† Therefore, all this depends not on our Ps 30:7
willing and running, but on God's mercy,† since we Rm 9:16
cannot even think anything good by ourselves,† 2 Co 3:5
much less do it or will it. Let us attribute every triumph of victory to divine grace.

3. This tent of which we speak is mobile, because as long as 'the corrupting body weighs down

Ws 9:15 the soul',† human beings never remain in the same
state but are always advancing and declining: advancing, when they raise their hearts by walking
from strength to strength until they see the God
Ps 84:5, 7 of gods in Zion;† declining, when by divine dispensation they are abandoned for the moment so that they may know themselves. But even then the grace of God works for their good. The Apostle says, 'We know that all things work together for good for those who love God, those who, in God's
Rm 8:28 intention, are called saints'.†

Every spiritual good given to people in the present pertains to this tent, whereas every one that will be given in the future pertains to the temple. Just as future goods will succeed present goods, so will the temple replace the tent, eternity will replace time, rest will replace labor, sight will replace
2 Co 5:7 faith,† beatitude will replace righteousness. Then will we leave the tabernacle and enter the temple of God—or rather, we ourselves will be the temple and house of God. He will dwell in us and we in him when we contemplate his beauty without interruption, enjoy his love without satiety, and are satisfied with his sweetness without any want.

In this house will be various portions and dwell-
Jn 14:2 ing places.† God will dwell in the bodies of the saints through immortality and the brightness of incorruption as in the outer part of the house; he will dwell in both soul and spirit as in the interior part of the house; he will dwell in the mind as though in a bridal chamber. Since his image and likeness[4] reside there, he will pour himself directly into the mind itself, and he will offer himself to be shared in the fullness of knowledge and love.

4. On the image and likeness of God in the soul see Sermon 1.3, the doctrinal introduction, and elsewhere. For the distinction of soul, spirit, and mind, see Sermon 1.6 and the note.

Then will the bride be joined to her spouse, and they will be two, I do not say in one flesh, but in one spirit.[5] In this bridal chamber a wedding will be celebrated. What happy, delightful, enjoyable embraces! There will be found an abundance of all delights, a fullness of joys! Because of its overflowing happiness, the mind—indeed the whole human being—will pass over into God, not by nature, but by participation in the very same glory and happiness. Then God will proceed from this inner dwelling 'like a bridegroom from his bridal chamber'; that is, then how beautiful and fair he is in himself, and in what form he offers himself to his bride will be externally apparent; then, I say, when he appears openly in all creatures, especially in the bodies of the saints, which then will shine like the sun.† Mt 13:43

4. Just as in the present all the saints are one tent, and each of the faithful exists as both body and soul, so in the future the totality of the faithful will be one temple of God, and each of the saints will be the temple of God, not only as soul and mind, but even as body. This will come about because God will dwell even in it through immortality and incorruptibility, just as he dwells in the mind filled by knowledge of the truth and made perfect by the enjoyment of every good. The dedication of this temple is celebrated, as far as the soul is concerned, in its exodus from Egypt, that is, when it is led out of the prison of the corruptible body, clothed with 'the first robe',[6] and led to the vision of God. This spiritual dedication of the spiritual

5. Genesis 2:24; 1 Corinthians 16:16–17. Like other spiritual authors of the twelfth century, Achard returns frequently to the idea of unity in spirit (*unitas spiritus*); e.g., Sermons 13.7 and 15.34. Here Achard is concerned with mystic union in heaven; in Sermons 13 and 15 he deals with mystical union here on earth.

6. Luke 15:22; see Sermon 74.

temple is signified by the first day of the dedication
of this visible temple. The octave day prefigures
the dedication of the heavenly temple, which will
occur bodily in the body, 'when this corruptible
[body] puts on incorruptibility and this mortal
1 Co 15:53 [body] puts on immortality'.† May the Cause and
Dedicator of this temple lead us to the dedication
of that temple. Amen.

Sermon 6: For Easter

INTRODUCTION

THIS SECOND EASTER SERMON situates the feast in the sweep of salvation history. The outline corresponds to the sections: (1) Christ is risen, and humanity and all creation with him. (2) Christ's death is sign and cause of the destruction of our threefold death: the death of the body, the death of the soul, and eternal damnation. Of this destruction Christ's resurrection is a cause, but not a sign. Christ's resurrection is the cause and sign of the resurrection of our souls and bodies; his death is the cause of this twofold resurrection, but not its sign. (3) The law of nature made humanity cognizant of its ignorance; the regime of the written law made clear humanity's weakness. Only grace could empower it to obey the law. (4) The three stages of salvation history—the time of the law of nature, the time of the written law, and the time of grace—are prefigured in the story of Elisha's raising to life of the son of the Shunammite woman. The Word came personally and bent down to raise us up. (5) Just as the boy's flesh became warm, so our hearts should warm when they meditate on Christ's humility and love. (6) The boy's seven yawns prefigure the Christian's sevenfold confession of sin, praise, and petition.

As he did in his first Easter sermon, Achard begins with a strongly felt declaration of new life. Characteristically, it is Christ, his members, and indeed the entire universe, which has risen. In a rare reference to the natural world around him, Achard sees a sign of this newness in nature, which seemed brown and dead in the winter a few months earlier, and now is full of life and color.[1] Our deaths and resurrections are multiple and interrelated. As Saint Thomas would later teach, and twentieth-century theology would rediscover,[2] Achard declares that Christ's death and resurrection are the cause both of our death to death and our rising to new life. His death is a sign of our death to death; his rising, a sign of our resurrection. Achard's interest here in the connection between sign and causality recalls a similar interest regarding the eucharistic elements in Sermon 4.2.

The last sentence of section two serves as a thesis for the treatment of the three ages of salvation history which follows: 'That humanity might be disposed and made capable of the knowledge of this mystery and the reception of so great a grace, its pride, which boasted of its knowledge and power, had to be checked' by the law of nature, which disclosed its ignorance, and the written law, which made manifest its inability to live virtuously. This threefold division of salvation history derives from Augustine, and was a basic element in Hugh of Saint Victor's theological synthesis.[3]

In section three, as Father Châtillon has pointed out, Achard provides a continuous, verse-by-verse commentary on Romans

1. Section one.

2. Saint Thomas, *Summa Theologiae* 3.56; F.-X. Durrwell, *The Resurrection; A Biblical Study* (New York: Sheed and Ward, 1960); David Michael Stanley, *Christ's Resurrection in Pauline Soteriology* (Rome: Pontificio Instituo Biblico, 1961). See *Quaestiones in epistolam Pauli ad Romanos* q. 124 (PL 175:464B).

3. See Hugh of Saint Victor, *De sacramentis legis naturalis et scriptae* 2.2.1 (PL 176:415BC); *Quaestiones in epistolam Pauli* (PL 175:559D-561A).

7:22–25, which resembles those of Abelard and Peter the Lombard.[4] Medieval exegesis of these verses did not endorse an ontological dualism whereby body and soul were seen as conflicting substances; one might say that according to the exegetical consensus of Achard's time, with which Achard agrees, the moral dualism that human beings experience runs perpendicular to the division between body and soul. The body is not the enemy; corruption is, and corruption concerns the soul as much as the body. According to Achard's perhaps unique way of explaining Romans 7:24, the sinner (not the soul) is in prison,[5] and the prison is the *lex peccati*. That Achard would not endorse a metaphysical dualism is clear from *On the Distinction* 34–39, where Achard says that (1) soul is essentially one with spirit and mind; (2) soul acts in the body in sensation and sensory appetition; (3) sensory desire and pleasure are natural and therefore good; they become evil only when they become disordered, that is, when sensory pleasure is preferred to higher goods.

Having given a straightforward account of the three ages of law and grace in section three, Achard then covers the same ground allegorically, using the story of Elisha and the son of the Shunammite woman as this was developed by Gregory the Great and other earlier writers.[6] After giving this doctrinal interpretation in section four, he adds two moral applications in sections five and six, which are calls to love and to confession respectively. The sevenfold confession involves not just the confession of sins and thanks, but also petition, which can be assimilated to confession insofar as it is an acknowledgment of neediness.

---

4. *Sermons*, 77, nn. 38, 41. This passage was studied by Timothy F. Merrill, 'Achard of Saint Victor and the Medieval Exegetical Tradition', *Westminster Theological Journal* 48 (1986) 47–62, from whom much of the following is derived.

5. Achard uses the prison image in Sermon 3.2–3 also. It might not be far wrong to say that Sermon 3 concerns the objective liberation of humanity from slavery to sin, whereas in this sermon emphasis has shifted to the subjective struggle to bring the effects of Christ's saving incarnation, death, and resurrection to fruition in the individual person. In Achard's view, both liberations are grace.

6. Gregory the Great, *Moralia* 19.63 (PL 75:894–895); *Quaestiones in epistolam Pauli* (PL 175:560B). For other references see Châtillon, *Sermons*, 79 n. 49.

THE SERMON

For Easter

THE PREEMINENCE OF THE WORD'S
RESURRECTION, the solemnity of such
a great feast, the celebration of what is
at once our redemption and our salvation, all this
arouses us, moves and touches us, and fills us in-
wardly with an inpouring of spiritual joy, so that
we may know 'the things that are above, not the
Col 3:2 things on earth'.[†] On this day that the Lord has
Ps 118:24 made,[†] in our Head our nature has put aside the
oldness not only of death and suffering but of
mortality and the capacity to suffer; it has been
totally transformed and renewed from corruption
Rm 6:10 to incorruption. 'What lives, lives for God',[†] that
is, in the likeness of God, divinely, unchangingly,
and without corruption. O wondrous new thing,
unheard of throughout the ages! Today darkness
has produced light, the earth has sent forth the
sun. Whoever heard of such things? The earth, for-
merly cursed, usually produced briars and stickers,
but now, by the Lord's generosity, it has yielded its
Ps 85:12 fruit.[†] Therefore, let us celebrate this great solem-
nity, let us rejoice with spiritual joy, and so that the
joys of this day may be multiplied, let us consider
more diligently how great will be the joy and
exultation at the future resurrection of all, and how
great will be the splendor when as many suns rise
from the heart of the earth as there are children of
the resurrection; made anew out of the dust of the
earth, they will proceed into eternal life and will
1 Th 4:17 be caught up to meet Christ in the air.[†]

Christ himself is going to come like lightning
from heaven, and thousands of the saints with him.
Then we ourselves, restored from the dust of the
earth, will hasten unto the perfect man,[†] for when Ep 4:13
we are stripped of our oldness nothing about us
will be imperfect. Then 'the mediator between
God and humanity'[†] will be full and complete in 1 Tm 2:5
his members, just as he will possess all his members
perfect and complete. Then it will be manifest that
'God is wondrous in his saints',[†] especially when Ps 68:35
the wicked have been taken away so as not to
see the glory of God, and all the citizens of the
heavenly Jerusalem have been assembled together
for the heavenly banquet, raised above the stars to
the third heaven. 'One day there in the courts of
the Lord will be better than a thousand others';[†] Ps 84:10
that is, the brightness the saints will possess in their
bodies, which will have been configured to the
body of brightness,[†] will be more brilliant than any Ph 3:21
brightness, sweeter than any delight, more pleasant
than any joy we have or can have at present. Of that
day which will come to pass in God's house or
marriage chamber (that is, in the spirits and minds
of the saints) it is not within our capacity to speak,
because that day 'eye has not seen, nor ear heard,
nor has it entered the human heart'.[†] 1 Co 2:9

To increase newness and joy, the world—which
fell when humanity fell—will rise when humanity
rises, and its very elements will be changed for
the better. The form of this world will pass away,[†] 1 Co 7:31
and so 'we are awaiting new heavens and a new
earth'.[†] 'The created world itself has been subjected 2 P 3:13
against its will to vanity, but on account of him
who subjected it in hope; it too will be freed
from the slavery of corruption into the freedom
of the children of God'.[†] Now the world itself Rm 8:20–21

celebrates and echoes the Lord's resurrection with its own partial resurrection and renewal. Think what the face of the earth was like a while ago, in the winter. Was it not shapeless, unattractive,
Gn 1:2 and in a way empty and void?† Now see what it has become, covered and graced with plants and trees, and embellished with flowers.

2. Let us return to the Lord's resurrection through which we hope for our own resurrection, not just the resurrection of our body in the future, but also that of our mind in the present. Through his single and simple death our three deaths—of soul, body, and eternal damnation—are destroyed, and so too, through his single and simple resurrection—of the body, and not of the soul—we are the recipients of two resurrections, of the soul in the present and of the body in the future. I say two and not three, because no one will rise from the death of eternal damnation. Christ, as the Apostle says, died 'for our sins and rose for our
Rm 4:25 justification'.† 'By dying he destroyed our death and by rising he restored our life.'[7]

But, someone says, the Lord's resurrection not only bestows life on us but takes away death, and his death not only takes away death but also bestows life. So then, each is the cause of both effects. Why is a distinction made when it says that he
Rm 4:25 'died for our sins and rose for our justification'?† To this we can say: although the cause of both lies in each, there is a difference in the signs and their significance. The Savior's death is not only the cause but also the sign of our death to sin; it is equally a cause, but not the sign, of our walking
Rm 6:4 in newness of life.† So too Christ's resurrection is

7. Achard here quotes an Easter Preface; this text has been adapted for use as part of the second memorial acclamation in the current Roman rite.

the cause and the sign of our rising from death of soul; our dying to sin is a cause and not a sign. Because of this difference in significance the Apostle made a distinction when he said that he 'died for our sins and rose for our justification', and so on. Without the sacrament and power of his passion and resurrection we could not avoid the threefold death or obtain the twofold resurrection. That humanity might be disposed and made capable of the knowledge of this mystery and the reception of so great a grace, its pride, which boasted of its knowledge and power, had to be checked.

3. During the period of natural law humanity was left to itself to be convinced of its ignorance of the truth. That is what happened; humanity confessed that the light of its eyes had failed.[8] To prevent humanity from saying that the one who was to fulfill the Law was not wanting, but rather the one who gave it, 'the Law was given through Moses'† to point out the way but not to Jn 1:17
provide help for walking in it. Humanity, laden with the weight of its own weakness, recognized its lack of strength and confessed not only to being sinful but also a violator of the law. Neither the natural nor the written law could free humanity from slavery to sin; the Law came in so that sin might abound all the more.† This all happened Rm 5:20
not through cruelty but as medicinal treatment. Unless sickness and discomfort increased, neither physician nor treatment would be sought. By a wondrous arrangement, God confined all things under sin so that he might have mercy on all.† Ga 3:22; Rm 11:32
What the natural law and the written Law can do together Paul clearly shows when he says: 'I delight in the law of God in my inmost self'.† What the Rm 7:22

8. See *Quaestiones in epistolam Pauli* (PL 175:559D-560A).

law could do was rouse sleeping reason to delight in the precepts of God, not to do good because of the law of the members and the inclination toward sin which fought and prevailed against the two laws. Hence the Apostle adds: 'I see in my members another law fighting against the law of my mind
Rm 7:23 and making me captive to the law of sin'.† The goad
2 Co 12:7 in our flesh† is not only a hindrance to doing the good that reason illumined by the law sees should be done; sometimes it even draws reason to consent to an act or habit of sin, and holds it captive under its sway. 'And so I am led captive into such a murky
Rm 7:24 and horrible prison,[9] unhappy being that I am.† Since neither the natural law nor the written law can free me, who will free me from the body of this death, that is, from the sin that holds sway in my flesh and brings death where it rules? The grace
Rm 7:25 of our Lord Jesus Christ!† O sweet grace, more desirable than anything else, saving medicine, our one sole remedy, our only refuge! Note to what end all things were confined under sin: that every mouth may be shut against self-glorification and the whole world may be made subject to God, since he alone gives life to the dead and calls 'things
Rm 4:17 that are not as things that are'.†

4. All this is suitably prefigured in the deed of
2 K 4:27–35 Elisha,† who sent Gehazi with his staff to raise the dead boy, the son of a Shunammite woman, commanding him to lay it on the boy's face. When it was laid there, the boy did not get up; 'there was no sound or sign of life'. Then Elisha himself came down from the mountain and went to the dead boy; he lay on top of him, drew himself together and took the boy's form so that his eyes were upon the boy's eyes, his hands on the boy's hands,

9. See Sermon 2.4 for the closely related theme of the body as prison.

his mouth on the boy's mouth. Then he walked around the house before again bending over the dead boy, and the boy's flesh became warm, he yawned seven times, and got up.

What does this boy represent if not the human race, which by sinning and taking leave of life died and remained for a long time in a foolish and puerile state? What does Elisha represent if not the Savior; the staff, if not the Law, because it is hard and stern; the boy's face, if not reason; Gehazi, if not Moses the lawgiver? Elisha sent his staff with Gehazi to raise the dead; that is, the Savior gave the Law through his servant Moses. When added to reason, the Law was like the staff laid on the face; it was unable to raise up the human race because it was not the sound of humble confession or the sign of life that is faith and love.

Then our Elisha came down from the mountain, that is, from equality to the Father—'from the highest heaven was his descent'†—and went to Ps 19:6 the dead body, bent over, 'taking the form of a slave',† and adapted and conformed himself to it, Ph 2:7 putting his eyes over its eyes by enlightening it with knowledge of the truth, his mouth over its mouth by giving it confession of the truth, and his hands upon its hands by giving it the strength to act rightly. He walked around by his loving and holy way of life because 'he was seen on earth and lived with humankind'.† Again he bent over the Bar 3:38 boy, 'having become obedient unto death, even death on a cross'.† The Father did not spare him, Ph 2:8 'but handed him over for all of us'.† Regarding the Rm 8:32 first bending, it was written: 'We do not have a high priest who is unable to sympathize with our weaknesses', and regarding the second, 'He was tempted in everything as we are, but without sin'.† Heb 4:15

5. The passage continues: 'And the boy's flesh
2 K 4:34 became warm'.† Who is so cold-hearted as not
to be moved by carefully noting and meditating
on the sublimity of the Savior, 'who, though he
was in the form of God did not think being equal
Ph 2:6 to God was robbery'†—indeed, it would not be
robbery, but nature—but became a little less than
Ps 8:5 the angels,† a mortal human being liable to suffering? He reached such a point of humility and love that he underwent the torment of the cross for the salvation of the human race, when and where people had gathered from almost the whole world for the paschal feast as the law commanded. Who, I repeat, would not be moved by such a meditation, and inflamed with the fire of divine love?

6. The passage adds: 'The boy yawned seven
2 K 4:35 times and got up'.† Truly, in order to rise, those dead in sin must seven times move their mouths in humble confession. First, they must confess the things that are around them, then themselves in them, then the things that belong to God and God in what is his own.[10] Above all, let them confess their own imperfection, which is to be noted in two areas: the things that should be there but are missing, and what belongs to them but is not fully there. Secondly, they should confess their own weakness, which also consists in two things: that they are both slothful and slow to do good, and prone to commit evil. Thirdly, let them confess their perversity, which is found in offense and in sin, that is, in not doing what is commanded, either by turning aside from the good or by doing the evil that is forbidden. In the fourth place, let them praise the grace of God by acknowledging that all

10. The four things mentioned in this sentence seem to be the circumstances, what people did in the circumstances, God's law, and what God did to and for them.

the good they have received is God's free gift. Let them not be deaf to the Scriptures: 'Every perfect gift is from above, descending from the Father of lights'.† Let them yawn a fifth time by asking for Jm 1:17
what they do not have, or for the fullness of what they possess only in part. In the sixth place let them open their mouths to draw in the good spirit and increase their desire so that they may accept the largess of the gift according to the whole extent of that desire.

But sometimes some people will begin to both live and die at once: although they recognize that 'every best gift and every perfect gift is from above, descending from the Father of lights', nevertheless, they cannot keep themselves from glorying in themselves as though they were not beneficiaries. Hence, a seventh yawn is necessary so that being humble and meek in themselves they may glory in God alone: 'Not to us, Lord, not to us, but to your name give glory';† you have performed all Ps 115:1
our works. Hence we understand how when God rewards our merits he is crowning his gifts in us, returning grace for grace.† And so the grace of Jn 1:16
God, eternal life, is given, to which may he deign to lead us, so that through him, and in him, and with him we may rejoice forever. Amen.

Sermon 7: On Septuagesima

INTRODUCTION

THE DRAMA OF THE MORAL HISTORY of the human race is considered here within a very wide framework, extending from the first human being to the resurrection of the dead. It looks at human nature before sin, after the fall, and after the resurrection.

The outline of the sections is straightforward: (1) the historical basis for Septuagesima Sunday: the seventy days between Septuagesima and the Saturday after Easter correspond to the seventy years of the captivity of the Jews in Babylon, which came to a partial end after sixty-three years (the Easter Vigil occurs on the sixty-third day after Septuagesima). (2) This captivity is a figure of the disorder that followed Adam's sin. (3) The three states of humanity relative to sin, death, and suffering. (4) The two stages in which Christ's redemption takes effect and their liturgical celebration.

When Achard says that Septuagesima recalls the seventy years of the Jewish captivity in Babylon, and extends from Septuagesima

Sunday to the Saturday after Easter, he concurs with an opinion widespread among medieval liturgists.[1] In our contemporary liturgy for the Easter Vigil, the single Alleluia and Tract that Achard describes have been replaced by a triple Alleluia.

Achard shares with Anselm and other medieval theologians a vivid sense of the physical and moral order of the universe. Human sin has disturbed that order, with disorderly repercussions throughout the universe and within the human being. Because of sin, 'everything is topsy-turvy' (*omnia versa sunt in contrarium*); confusion and disorder reign. The sense of internal conflict within the moral agent is very strong in the Victorines; it enables Richard of Saint Victor to devise elaborate allegories of the dramatic conflicts that lead a human being down the road to degradation, and the corresponding struggles of the converted sinner to reestablish order within himself.

Achard's discussion of the two trees of paradise interprets Genesis 2:9 in the light of Ecclesiasticus 1:26: 'If you desire wisdom, keep the commandments, and the Lord will lavish her upon you'. In Achard's elaboration of the Genesis story, the first human beings had to obey the divine precepts not to eat of the fruit of the tree of knowledge in order to eat the tree of life (=wisdom). It is his opinion that the name of the tree of the knowledge of good and evil was derived from no intrinsic characteristic of the fruit of the tree, but from the results which Adam and Eve experienced as a result of violating the command not to eat of it, although he notes that some (e.g., Abelard) thought the name referred to some inherent quality. Achard shared with Hugh of Saint Victor and others the idea that before eating of this fruit Adam and Eve knew good and evil differently; they came to experiential knowledge of evil only after violating God's command. In his opinion, again shared with

1. For example, Pseudo-Hugh, *De ceremoniis ecclesiasticis* 2.10 (PL 177:443B); Pseudo-Honorius, *Gemma animae* 4.2 (PL 172:689–90); Richard of Saint Victor, *Sermones centum*, 51 (PL 177:1044D-10145A); John Beleth, *Summa de ecclesiasticis officiis* 77 (CCCM 41A [Turnhout: Brepols, 1976] 139–143; PL 202:81–83). Rupert of Deutz, *De divinis officiis* 4.1–4 (CCCM 7 [Turnhout: Brepols, 1967] 103–105; PL 170:87–89) and Pseudo-Hugh of Saint Victor, *Miscellanea* 7.24 (PL 177:878BC) agree that Septuagesima contains a reference to the Babylonian Captivity, but they object to extending the period to the Saturday of Easter week, since this seems to detract from the centrality of Easter itself.

Hugh of Saint Victor, the tree of life did have one intrinsic quality, whereby its fruit inoculated one against death and suffering. This idea was suggested by Genesis 3:22, wherein God says he will expel Adam from paradise lest he reach out his hand to the tree of life, eat it, and so live forever.[2]

The state of Adam and Eve before they sinned was this: they could sin or not, die or not, depending on what they chose. If they did not eat of the fruit of the tree of life, they were liable to death and starvation; if they did eat the fruit of the tree of life before disobeying God's command, they would have been immune to both death and suffering; if, however, they had eaten the fruit of the tree of life after their sin, they would not have died, but they would have been liable to suffering. In the event, Adam and Eve did not eat of the fruit of the tree of life, but they did eat the forbidden fruit of the tree of the knowledge of good and evil. By so doing, they entered a state where they could not avoid sin, and were liable to both suffering and death. After the resurrection, risen human beings will by grace be unable to sin, to die, or to starve. If they had not sinned, human beings would have passed from the first state to the risen state, and so, in the actual first state sin and not sinning, death and not dying, suffering and not suffering were possible. In the second state, before grace, sin, death, and suffering were necessary. In the risen state, through grace, sin, death, and suffering will be impossible.

Returning to the symbolism of Septuagesima, Achard says that in the fullness of time God sent his Son to free humanity from captivity. The one Alleluia of the Easter Vigil refers to the partial salvation which humanity now enjoys, that is, the grace that enables us to choose the good and to avoid sin, even though we remain subject to death and suffering. The three Alleluias of the Saturday of Easter week refer to the state that will follow the final resurrection when sin, death, and suffering will be no more. However, even now we, the saints, can glory in our sufferings, because we know that in God's providence all things work for our good.

2. Hugh of St Victor, *De sacramentis legis naturalis et scriptae* 1.6.32 (PL 176:283A-D). For numerous other references see Châtillon, *Sermons*, 86–87, nn. 14–17, 19.

THE SERMON

On Septuagesima

SEPTUAGESIMA IS CELEBRATED BY THE DEVOUT FAITHFUL as a reminder of one thing and as the prefiguration and sign of another. This celebration is a reminder of how, because of their sins, the children of Israel were led away as captives from the land of promise into Babylon. Before that they had offended God often and deeply by transgressing his law. Although he had admonished them frequently and in many ways to return, they were unwilling, and they piled evil upon evil until they fell into idolatry. Because of this God justifiably piled on them plague upon plague, scourging upon scourging, and cast them out from his land into a foreign land, from Jerusalem into Babylon. All this occurred with God's permission, and even by his judgment and sentence. In this the Babylonians, although unwittingly, fulfilled the will of the Lord.

Israel endured this captivity for seventy years. Toward the end of this period, in the sixty-third year to be exact, when Cyrus, king of the Persians, besieged, overwhelmed, and captured Babylon, the yoke of captivity resting on the children of Israel was partially lightened and their liberty was restored. Cyrus understood that the punishment of the captive people happened entirely in accord with God's will, and to a large extent he allowed the children of Israel to go freely about his land. However, certain of them remained in captivity. In memory of this freedom one Alleluia, the song of joy, is sung during the Easter Vigil. However, because the yoke of slavery had not yet been completely removed, after the Alleluia comes a Tract, which is the sign of labor and sorrow. When the seventieth year was over, those who were still in captivity received general and communal liberty.† In memory of this, on the Saturday after Easter, the seventieth day, two Alleluias are sung. From today until the Saturday after Easter, there are ten weeks, and ten times seven, or seven times ten, make seventy days. So much for a brief indication at the historical level of the event in memory of which Septuagesima is celebrated.

2 Ch 36:22–23; Ezr 1:1–5

2. That event occurred as a figure and sign of the total and communal servitude experienced by the whole of Adam's posterity, not just in body, but also interiorly in their minds. Before sin the first human being was in Jerusalem, that is, in the vision of peace, in paradise, in the place of delights; this endured as long as the human mind was subject to its superior through loving devotion and humble obedience, the will was subject to reason, sensory activity to the will, the flesh to the senses, and the world to the flesh. While each was observing its lawful ordering, the human being experienced no contradiction within himself or without, and wherever he turned he found only peace.

Because [Adam] forgot the fear of God, however, and followed his own desires, everything turned upside down. Because the human mind no longer rendered the obedience of humble subjection due to God, it rightly lost its dominion over what was beneath it. Instantly the will ceased to obey the reason, sensory activities contradicted the will, the flesh resisted its superior, and to redress the injury to its Creator the whole world arose against

the senseless man, drew him with allurements, and afflicted him with torments. Therefore, the man was cast from the light of knowledge into the darkness of ignorance, from righteousness into iniquity, from peace into confusion, from the mountain of contemplation into the valley of tears, from liberty into slavery, from Jerusalem into Babylon. For very little, almost for nothing—for the enjoyment of one piece of fruit—he lost many great goods and found a multitude of evils. By stretching out a hand to the forbidden tree he did not achieve the likeness to God that the devil promised when he said: 'You will be like gods, knowing good and
Gn 3:5 evil'.† He ought to have eaten of the tree of life before he ate of the tree of the knowledge of good and evil, according to Solomon's statement: 'Children, you have desired wisdom; observe the
Si 1:26/33 commandments, and God will bestow it on you'.† He should first have reached out his hand to the tree of righteousness and virtue, so that afterwards he could safely approach the fullness of knowledge, not for inflation, but for edification.

We should not fail to note that the name of the tree of the knowledge of good and evil fell to it because of what followed the transgression. Before his sin, the man knew good and evil—good through prudence and experience, evil through prudence, but not through experience. After the transgression he began to know evil through experience as well. To some it seems that the tree received its name because of some innate force. This is not surprising, since it is written: 'A little wine sharpens the mind'.[3] Similarly, the tree of

3. Achard seems to be quoting a proverb It is mentioned also by Richard of Saint Victor, *Sermones centum* 43 (PL 177:1013A). For further references, see Châtillon, *Sermons*, 87–88, n. 18.

life receives its name from a certain property of its own. Its fruit has such efficacy that those using it are strengthened with everlasting firmness, and become immune to death and without experience of pain. So the Lord says, even after sin: Let us cast the human being out of paradise, 'lest perchance he reach out his hand toward the tree of life and eat of it and live forever'.† These words make it very clear that if the man had eaten from the tree of life after his sin he would not have seen death. Gn 3:22

3. Hence, we may rightly seek the difference between the status of humanity before sin and after sin. Before sin it was such that without the benefit of that tree it would not live forever, and without eating from the tree it would not have reached the state where it no longer needed the nourishment of food; and if humanity had eaten after sin, it would not have tasted death for all eternity. To this we reply that if the human being had eaten of the tree of life before sin, he would not have experienced death, that is, the dissolution of the body, or even any suffering or injury at all. If he ate it after sin, he would not indeed have died, but he would not have been without the experience of every pain.

To make the difference between the two states clear, understand that before sin the first human being could sin or not sin, and so die or not die. He was mortal, but in a certain way immortal—that is, able not to die. He had an animal body that needed the nourishment of food. After sin, however, through his own fault he became unable not to sin, even mortally; before grace he had a dead body, that is, one subject to the necessity of dying. After the resurrection, through grace he will become unable to sin or to die; he will have a spiritual body which needs no food. So, in the first state there was the possibility of sinning or not sinning, of dying or not dying; in the second, the necessity of sinning as well as of dying; in the third, the impossibility of sinning. If the man had not sinned, when the period of obedience was over he would have been transferred from the first state to the third. Because he sinned, the third state was lost; he was cast from the first to the second, from paradise into this world, from true freedom into true slavery.

4. To rescue humanity from this slavery and restore it to true freedom, in the fullness of time God sent his own Son. Through him the yoke of our captivity has already been partially taken away in the present time, and liberty restored. As a sign of this, one Alleluia is sung at the Easter Vigil. But because there are still many tribulations for the just, and because all who wish to live devoutly in Christ suffer persecutions, there follows a Tract, symbolic of labor and of patience. Again, because the saints glory in their tribulations, and say with the Apostle 'The sufferings of the present time are not worthy of comparison with the future glory that will be revealed in us', and because they know that 'to those who love God all things work together unto good, for those called to be saints according to his
Rm 8:18,28 plan',† this Tract is brief and gives praise to God:
Ps 117:1 'Praise the Lord all you peoples', and so forth.† Truly the truth of God is fortified over the saints, so that whether the devil or the world rises up against them, nothing can prevail against God's chosen, for whom all things, even evils, work together unto good.[4] On the day of the resurrection, when this mortal body puts on immortality and corruption puts on incorruption, when death, the enemy, is

4. See Sermon 10.3.

finally destroyed and swallowed up in victory,† then 1 Co 15:53–54
the yoke of every sort of misery will be lifted completely from the necks of the saints and every sort of liberty will be given them. Then 'they will shine like the sun in the kingdom of their Father',† Mt 13:43
adorned with a twofold robe.[5]† As a sign of this, on Rv 6:11
the Saturday after Easter two Alleluias are sung to designate the full and perfect joy of all the chosen, whose everlasting task will be to praise God with jubilation, as it is written: 'Blessed are they who dwell in your house, O Lord. Forever they will praise you'.† May he deign to lead us to this praise. Ps 84:4
Amen.

5. See Sermon 2.4. The twofold robe corresponds to twofold immortality, spiritual and physical.

Sermon 8: The Nativity of Blessed Mary

INTRODUCTION

ACHARD'S SERMON FOR THE FEAST OF THE NATIVITY of the Blessed Virgin (8 September) is primarily a lyrical evocation of her virtues and privileges. Its pattern is: (1) The aroma of Mary's virginity drew the Son of God to her. (2) A foretaste of affectivity and understanding is provided by prayer and meditation respectively. (3) Mary is the mediatrix of all graces. She is the sprout, her Son the flower; they bring about a righteous and blessed life. (4) She is the perfection of action, devotion, and contemplation. (5) The devotion of the faithful led to the institution of the feast. If John the Baptist was sanctified in his mother's womb, Mary must have had the same privilege.

According to the Victorines, prayer and meditation are the characteristic religious acts of the two main powers of the human spirit, affectivity and thought. Hugh of Saint Victor wrote a treatise on each: *De virtute orandi* and *De meditando*.[1] Achard insists on the

1. PL 176:977–988 and PL 176:933–998 respectively. Father Roger Baron prepared an edition of the latter in *Six opuscules spirituels*, SC 155 (Paris: Cerf, 1965). I am preparing a critical edition of the former.

interconnection between the two, implying that those who have difficulty with either meditation or prayer may not be doing the other properly.

At the beginning of section three, Achard boldly states of Mary that 'without any doubt she is the mediatrix through whom we obtain whatever grace we have'. His argument in favor of this statement seems to be that we have all grace from Christ, Christ we have from Mary, therefore we have all grace from Mary. Or, metaphorically, without the stem we would have none of the blessings that come from the flower. If Christians possess the same righteousness as Mary, they will enjoy the blessedness Christ came to bring. In itself, this is not a particularly strong version of the doctrine of Mary's mediation.[2] Another way to view this passage is to see it as an exercise in threefold exegesis, moving from the literal sense (sprout/flower), to the allegorical or doctrinal sense (Mary/Christ), to the moral or tropological sense (righteousness/blessedness).

The final section mentions three kinds of births. First, according to Achard, prior to their (super)natural births, Christ was sanctified from the moment of his conception while Jeremiah, John the Baptist, and Mary were sanctified between their conception and their delivery[3] Secondly, there is the rebirth of Paul at the time of his conversion. Finally there is the heavenly birth of each of the saints in glory at his or her death. With the exception of Jeremiah's birth, all these births have special liturgical commemorations.

2. For further references see Châtillon, *Sermons*, 95, n. 23.

3. The doctrine of Mary's immaculate conception was just developing at this time. It found support especially in England; it met with fierce opposition from some of Achard's contemporaries in France; e.g., Saint Bernard and Peter of Celle. Saint Thomas Aquinas did not accept the doctrine, either. It was finally defined in 1850 by Pope Pius IX.

THE SERMON

The Nativity of Blessed Mary

LIKE A VINE I HAVE BROUGHT FORTH THE FRUIT of a sweet aroma'.[4] The apostles were a good and sweet aroma for God, but the Virgin Mary was the sweetest aroma of all to her Spouse; even the apostles had their aroma from her. She gave herself completely to God in an aroma of sweetness; completely, I say, both in her flesh through her virginity, and in her mind through her devotion. The aroma of her sweetness not only suffused every corner of the world, but it also spread through the whole of the heavenly city, even reaching the nostrils of God, even to him who in the bosom of the Father had long awaited and desired this aroma.

Nothing like it could be found in any of the angels. To lead an angelic life in the fragile flesh, in flesh corrupted, even dead, because of sin, is more praiseworthy than to be an angel. An angel accomplishes easily and without contradiction what it does in the spirit. In the angelic nature flesh is not opposed to the spirit nor the spirit to the flesh,† since it is simple and not joined together Ga 5:17
from parts. Hence the apostate angel, who was not compelled to sin by any weakness, fell irrevocably. A human being, drawn to sin by weakness of the flesh, can offer some excuse.

4. See Ecclesiasticus 24:17. According to the liturgical usage of the abbey of Saint Victor, this verse was part of the Epistle for the feast of the Nativity of the Blessed Virgin Mary. It was also used in the *capitulum* at Vespers.

Of what praise, therefore, is the Mother of God worthy, and what praises should we bestow on her who, the first among women, without any example to guide her, offered to God the glorious gift of virginity as a most sweet aroma, and with this sweet aroma attracted the only Son of God, and totally enraptured him? He did not delay, but as soon as he was attracted and totally enraptured he came from the bosom of the Father into the womb of the Virgin. Not only did he come to her, he came into her; he came not only into the Virgin's spirit, but also into her flesh; discovering the aroma of virginity, and bearing the aroma of his deity with him, he made his handmaid his bride, his creature his mother.

2. I have used the word aroma; I have not mentioned taste yet. Whatever is perceived about God in this life is like a kind of aroma perceived at a distance, but before one possesses, holds, and enjoys the thing itself, one does not possess the taste. Although sometimes holy men[5] have a certain foretaste, yet as to its quantity and fullness it is little, almost nothing. These men are like the scouts sent by the children of Israel into the promised land to explore and examine the condition, situation, and quality of the whole land. Of all the fruits of that very fertile land they brought back only a
Nb 13:18–25 cluster of fruit.†

We can properly regard these messengers as standing for prayer and meditation. Already in this life affectivity and understanding, or will and reason, would wish, if they could, to see the condition and situation of the true land of promise, the heavenly Jerusalem, and King Solomon in his

5. Achard uses the word for 'man' (*vir*) here.

beauty.† 'No one ever has even seen God'† since, as it is written, 'No one will see me and live',† and so they send their scouts: affectivity and will send prayer; understanding and reason send meditation. These scouts bring back a kind of cluster in which is food and drink; prayer, that is, brings back the love of virtue, affectivity's and will's true food. With this food the inner self is strengthened, for love is our strength. Hence, it says in the Canticle: 'Love is strong as death', and 'many waters cannot extinguish' it.† For its part, meditation brings knowledge of the truth, the delightful drink of understanding and reason, which makes us soberly inebriated.[6] Hence the bride says in the Canticle: 'He led me into the wine cellar'† and David wrote that we will be inebriated 'by the abundance of your house, and in your light we will see light'.† The pole on which the two messengers carried the cluster of fruit fittingly represents the connection which must exist between prayer and meditation. True, it is written, 'Pray always',† but so that prayer will not grow lukewarm, the affectivity of the mind must be enkindled by a zeal for meditation in order that the fire may burn brightly in our meditation. On the other hand, so that meditation may not wander into byways of error it needs to be directed upward toward God through prayer. Thus, meditation and prayer succeed each other in turn.

Is 33:17; Jn 1:18; 1 Jn 4:12; Ex 33:20

Sg 8:6–7

Sg 2:4

Ps 36:8–9

Lk 18:1; 1 Th 5:17

3. Whatever is sent to us from above is to be attributed to the glorious mother of God. Without any doubt she is the mediatrix through whom we obtain whatever grace we have. She is the 'sprout

6. The use of 'sober inebriation' as a metaphor for mystical experience is a common one in early and medieval christian literature For further sources, see Châtillon, *Sermons,* 94–95, n. 17.

Is 11:1 from the root of Jesse',† from whose integrity 'the
Sg 2:1 flower of the field and the lily of the valleys'† rise
up. Mary is the sprout, her Son is the flower.[7] The sprout extends to us the rectitude of righteousness; the flower, the beauty of a blessed life. Behold the promise of the present and future life: an upright and blessed life! In these two is the goal of all things chastely desired: an upright life and a happy life. Let us hold on to the rectitude of the sprout so that we may reach the beauty of the flower. Let us follow the mother so that we may be worthy to reach the Son, and if we cannot imitate her through virginity, let us at least imitate her through humility. Not all the sheep 'follow the lamb wherever he goes'; this is bestowed only on virgins, on those 'who have
Rv 14:4 not defiled themselves with women'.†

In a special way the Virgin Mary followed wherever he went; the sheep followed the lamb, the mother the son. She possesses every sort of perfection of both the active and the contemplative lives. In the bible she is called not just a sprout but also a column, hence the Canticle says of her: 'Who is this who comes up from the desert, like a column of smoke of aromatical spices of myrrh, of frank-
Sg 3:6 incense, and of all the powders of the perfumers?'†
'Who'—that is, what is she like, how should she be praised, since with her aroma of sweetness she suffuses not just the world but also all of heaven? 'Who comes up', it says, step by step, advancing from strength to strength, transcending all the saints in righteousness and blessedness, 'from the desert' of the Jews' errors and infidelity, in which the synagogue was deserted by God.

---

7. This same comparison occurs in Pseudo-Hugh of Saint Victor, *Miscellanea* 3.36 (PL 177:656D–657A) and Richard of Saint Victor, *De comparatione Christi ad florem et Mariae ad virgam* (PL 196:1031–32).

4. There follows: 'like a column'; that is, thinned by heavenly disciplines, graceful, subtle in the contemplative life. A column not just of anything, but 'of smoke': light, agile, freely seeking the heights, weighed down by no load of sins. Then: 'of aromatical spices of myrrh, frankincense,[8] and of all the powder of the perfumers'. In myrrh we have the mortification of the flesh, which consists in two things: chastisement of the flesh, and the practice of good works. In both these ways carnal affectivity is mortified in us. In frankincense we have the pious devotion of prayer.[9] So David wrote: 'Let my prayer be directed as incense'.† In 'all the powders Ps 142:2
of the perfumers', we have all the other virtues, and especially contemplation. Hence, [David] does not say 'of the other spices' but 'of all powders', as though the spices are reduced to a kind of dust. He says 'of all' because of the multiplicity of the things from which contemplation is derived and rises up. Multiple are the kinds of things in which action, signified by myrrh, and devotion, signified by frankincense, occur, but far more numerous are the kinds of things about which and in which contemplation[10] occurs. Through these three, that is, myrrh, frankincense, and all the powders of the perfumers, we possess three virtues: action, devotion, and contemplation, and in these three are contained all the rest. The greatest accumulation of these which could exist in a pure human being existed in the glorious Virgin Mary, who is most

8. On the symbolism of these two spices see Gregory the Great, *Homilia XL in Evanglia* 10.6 (PL 76:1113B); Richard of Saint Victor, *Sermones centum* 96 (PL 196:1199A) and *Liber exceptionum* 2.10.17, ed. Châtillon, 408.

9. Hugh of Saint Victor, *De virtute orandi* (PL 176:979A) defines devotion as 'a pious and humble affective movement toward God'; it is the very essence of *oratio*. Achard's assigning of devotion to the cognitive side of his binary division of human nature in Sermon 5.4 seems all the more anomalous in the light of this section.

10. See Sermon 15.19.

worthy of all praise. It is her birthday we celebrate today.

5. The devotion of the faithful was not content with her Assumption and her older solemnity, so it added today's solemnity of her birth, even though we have gospel warrant to celebrate only the birthdays in the flesh of the Savior and of John the Baptist, the Lord's precursor. It is not surprising that the birth of the Mediator between God and
1 Tm 2:5 human beings† is venerated with all devotion, since when he was born the multitude of the heavenly army sang: 'Glory to God on high, and on earth peace to people of good will'.[11] Regarding the birth of the precursor, an angel declared: 'And
Lk 1:14 many will rejoice at his birth'.† Therefore, it is fitting that the birthday of the mother of God be recalled with a feast, as she is not less than John; rather, she is more sublime than all the other saints, because of her privileged virtues. We believe that she was sanctified even from her mother's womb. If Jeremiah and John were sanctified before they were born, why not Mary? Even if she had some blemish, she contracted it not from her birth but from her conception. She was not born in guilt, even though she was conceived in sorrow and punishment.

Three births exist. The first is in the flesh; it occurs in guilt and punishment, and makes us chil-
Ep 2:3 dren of wrath.† The second birth, which is properly called regeneration, is in the Spirit: it makes us chil-
Ep 5:30 dren of grace and members of Christ.† The third birth is from misery to glory, from punishment to happiness. We do not recall the birth in the spirit or the regeneration of any saint except Paul. Why is this? Because of the preeminence of his

11. See Luke 2:14, Achard is citing the Gloria of the Mass, not the Vulgate.

conversion, which occurred neither through nor by a human being, but through Jesus Christ, who was then already completely immortal and deified; also because of [Paul's] praiseworthy life following his conversion.

We religiously and devoutly venerate the birth of the saints in glory, so that with the aid of their merits and prayers we may be worthy to reach that birth of the Son of God of which it is said: 'Who will tell his generation'?† That generation has no Is 53:8
beginning and it knows no end, since it is eternal. The Son of God is born eternally of God, and lest we suppose that his birth may sometime come to an end, it is said that he is born, and ever will be born, like a ray from the sun, which as long as the sun has existed has proceeded from the sun, proceeds from it, and always will proceed from it. Thus the Son eternally proceeds and is born from the Father. To the contemplation and vision of the Father may he deign to lead us. Amen.

SPIRITUALITY

Sermons

Sermon 12: On the Transfiguration of the Lord

INTRODUCTION

THE GOSPEL FOR THE FEAST OF THE TRANSFIGURATION, Matthew 17:1–9, is the starting point for this text, which may represent the expanded form of a sermon. In the first section Achard rejects the theological opinion that the transfiguration occurred not in Christ himself but in the air around him. This opinion is mentioned in an unedited commentary on the gospel of Matthew composed by Peter Comestor. According to Peter its adherents cited paintings on walls of churches as evidence for their opinion. Aside from this, Peter says that there were two main theories about the transfiguration: first, that Christ assumed a mortal body at the incarnation, but at the transfiguration momentarily assumed an immortal body; and second, the body of Christ was naturally immortal, but this was usually hidden during Christ's life on earth. Achard agreed with Hugh of Saint Victor[1] that Christ

1. *De sacramentis legis naturalis et scriptae* 2.1.7; PL 176:390CD.

freely chose to have a mortal body.[2] Thus Achard thought that at the transfiguration on the mountain Christ showed the disciples an immortality that he had freely renounced in order to suffer for the redemption of the human race.[3]

In the second section Achard does not mention his strongly held opinions regarding the fullness of Christ's knowledge and power; instead he emphasizes Christ's full sharing in human weakness and his compassion. In section three Achard clearly asserts that Christ felt sorrow as he faced death, and pain as he underwent it.[4] This was also the opinion of Hugh of Saint Victor.[5] In this same section Achard also raises a question as to whether Christ felt sorrow during the time between his death and resurrection. Achard thinks not.[6]

Achard's discussion of Christ's nine transfigurations follows the chronology of events. Throughout these meditations on the life of Christ, a genre which was pioneered by his contemporary Aelred of Rievaulx,[7] Achard concentrates not on the historical details but on the inner motivations. His view of Christ is of a divine being who out of compassion identified himself as much as possible with humanity in its weakness and suffering. Even his discussion of the Eucharist carries with it overtones of vulnerability. The way he appeared at any given stage in his exodus from the Father and his return to the Father was adapted to human needs. Once Christ returned to his full glory, the Holy Spirit taught the disciples to think of him as he was then and will be forever, seated in glory at the right hand of the Father.

The first part of Achard's sketch of the transfiguration of the

2. Sermons 3.3; 7.3.

3. See A. Landgraf, *Dogmengeschichte* 2/1, 199–272, especially 254, summarized by Châtillon, *Sermons*, 122–124, nn. 3 and 4. Châtillon thinks that Achard adhered to the second theory, but I say he espoused the first.

4. See also Sermons 1.6; 3.3.

5. *De sacramentis legis naturalis et scriptae* 2.1.11; PL 176:404CD. On twelfth-century theological discussion of Christ's sorrow and fear at his impending death see Ott, *Untersuchungen*, 213–234

6. See Landgraf, *Dogmengeschichte* 2/1, 273–319, on the wider question whether the personal union of the divinity and humanity of Christ continued while his body and soul were separated in death.

7. *De institutione inclusarum* 29–31, in *Opera omnia*, CCCM 1 (Turnhout: Brepols, 1971) 662–673.

Christian corresponds closely to that in Sermon 10.3: active repentance followed by works of righteousness and love; however, here Achard goes on to discuss the place of contemplation at some length. The human being's transfiguration to Christ's glory begins with penance, by which one dies to the sin, the world, and one's own will. Here, as elsewhere in Achard, penance is not so much a state as a process. The next stage, righteousness on the basis of love, is Achard's personal formulation of that part of the active life that concerns good deeds. At this stage Christians should be very wary of letting their good deeds be seen by others. As the Christian's active life of penance and good works develops, meditation turns to contemplation, a resting with Christ in the bosom of the Father, wherein God is contemplated without reference to his works. Compassion will move the contemplative to reach out to others just as it moved Christ to become incarnate; at the same time, the contemplative will continue with the moral struggles of the active life, knowing that whatever progress occurs is due to grace. Such people become an example for others; their lives are spiritual food, a kind of eucharist.[8]

In sections seven and eight, while discussing the last six transfigurations that human beings undergo, Achard sketches his eschatology. This is complicated by his fascination with the interplay of soul and body in the final transformation. After death, an often miserable process, the soul leaves the body and enters a world of wondrous newness; it is freed from a multiplicity of thoughts and concerns and becomes simple and unified. At the resurrection of the dead, the wicked will rise immortal and passable to suffer forever. The bodies of the saints will put on incorruptibility, and Christ will configure them to his risen body. Once they have their glorified bodies, the saints will experience perfect joy. Finally the whole universe will be transfigured—the land, the air, the sky. The saints will see the

---

8. A composite sevenfold pattern—penitence (compunction and penance), reading, meditation, good works, prayer, contemplation and compassion—may be said to characterize Victorine spirituality, although seldom are all seven elements mentioned together. Their emphasis on good works and compassion is not as great in many other authors who used this popular outline. Here and in Sermon 10.3 Achard makes no mention of reading, although that is the basis of his sermon.

transfigured universe not just in itself but also in its archetypes, which preexisted in the mind of God.

This final reference to the archetypes introduces the topic of Achard's metaphysics, in which these archetypes play an important role. Achard will return to them in Sermon 13.32 and Sermon 14.20–21. They are discussed at length in the doctrinal introduction to Achard's metaphysics, and are a major topic in his *De unitate*.

THE SERMON

On the Transfiguration of the Lord

'JESUS TOOK PETER, JAMES AND JOHN, his brother, and he led them up a high mountain and was transfigured before them'.† In this, his transfiguration, the Lord is letting us know what we should hope, what we should desire, and to what we should direct our minds. This transfiguration of the Lord prefigured not only the glory he was to have after the resurrection but the future glory of all the saints as well. Hence, in order to indicate this twofold glory of the head and of his members ahead of time, 'his face shone like the sun and his clothes became white as snow'.†

Mt 17:1–2, par.

Mt 17:2

Some people have thought less than wisely about this transfiguration and said that the splendor appeared only in the air around his face, not that his face, laying aside its earlier form, changed into something different. If this had been so, it would be truer to say that the air was transfigured, rather than the Lord. For this reason, we say that by his divine power the Lord laid aside the form of mortality and took up at will the form of glory, and showed this to his disciples, yet without with all the greatness it was going to have. The eyes of the disciples, still weighed down by the weight of the flesh, could not yet bear it in all its glory.

2. The Lord was not transfigured just this one time: certain transfigurations preceded and followed this one. He was first transfigured when he came into the world from the bosom of the Father. 'Although he was in the form of God, he emptied

Ph 2:6–7 himself and took the form of a slave'.† The eternal became temporal; the immense became small; the Creator, a creature; God, man; the maker, what was made. This transfiguration is as great as the distance between God and man; it is immense and infinite. We should note very carefully that the Lord is not said to be transfigured in such a way that he laid aside or emptied out his previous divine form, or in some way changed it, when he accepted the form of a slave. Rather, he is called 'transfigured' because he did not appear to us in the form of God but in the human form that he assumed for our sake.

His second transfiguration occurred when 'he
Ph 2:7 was found human in appearance'.† He not only came in human likeness by truth of nature and by participation in punishment, though not in guilt, but he was also found human in appearance; that is, he appeared like other people. He lived as if he were weak and sinful, eating and drinking with
Mt 11:19 sinners so that he was called a drunkard.† This is called the transfiguration of association; by it he had compassion on the weak, and adapted himself to them, so that he could draw them to himself and impress his form upon them. This second transfiguration is much less drastic than the first. The first was from the mountain of eternity into the vale of tears; the second occurs within that vale of misery.

The third transfiguration is that which occurred on the mountain; we dealt with it earlier.

3. The fourth transfiguration is called sacramental. It first occurred when he revealed himself at the supper in the form of bread and wine and offered himself to his disciples to be eaten, saying: 'This is my body, take it and eat'. The same

transfiguration occurs each day on the altar at the hands of the priest. So he added at that time: 'Do this in memory of me'.† This transfiguration was prefigured when David changed his appearance before Achish, and pretending to be a stupid lunatic, and so transfigured himself. Scripture says that because of his fear he carried himself in his hands.[9] Similarly, the Lord carried himself in his hands, veiled under the appearance of bread and wine. 1 Co 11:24

His fifth transfiguration is that of his passion and death, by which he was transformed from having the capacity to suffer and die to actually suffering and dying; then there was 'neither beauty nor comeliness in him'.† This is more properly called a disfiguration; we read that 'his soul was sorrowful even to death'.† Doubt exists whether his sorrow was immediately laid aside at his death or stayed with him during the three days before his resurrection, not because of his passion but because of compassion for those whom he descended into the underworld to liberate. However, it does seem that his sorrow was swallowed up at death, since he said: 'My soul is sorrowful even to death', as though it would not be sorrowful after death. Therefore, only the virtue of compassion, without passion, was in Christ during those three days, just as it always is in God. Is 53:2 Mt 26:38

4. The sixth transfiguration of the Lord was that of the resurrection, when he was transfigured from passion to impassibility, from death to immortality, and put on beauty and strength. This was a vestige of what occurred on the mountain; that transfiguration was a foreshadowing of this one, as was noted above.

9. See Sermon 4.2.

The seventh transfiguration was that of the appearance in which he showed himself to his disciples after his resurrection. This appearance is called a transfiguration because he did not then show them the form of immortality, majesty, and glory which he then in fact had, but rather he appeared in the state, form, and shape he had when he was still mortal. He did this so that they would recognize him, and believe that he had truly risen. If he had appeared in that glorious form they would not have recognized him, but would have thought he was someone else.

The eighth transfiguration is that of the ascension. Although it is not set down explicitly in writing, we should believe that in the ascension when, as the apostles were watching, 'he was raised
Ac 1:9–10 into heaven and a cloud received him',† he revealed the form of his glory and majesty so that by doing so he could rouse the hearts of the disciples to follow him. Hence it is also written: 'As you have
Ac 1:11 seen him going, so will he come'.† Since he is to
Mt 25:31 come in the form of majesty;† we can conclude that he was seen to ascend in it as well.

His ninth transfiguration occurred on Pentecost day, in the spirit and hearts of his disciples, when the Holy Spirit descended upon them in tongues of fire and filled them with charity and love. When they had received these endowments they no longer thought of Christ in the usual, fleshly way, but spiritually, even when they thought of his body. They no longer thought about him as someone who worked miracles on earth in a mortal way, but as one seated in heaven at the right hand of Majesty. We should describe this as a transfiguration of the apostles rather than of the Lord.

5. In order to be able to reach this glorious transfiguration, we must start with little things so that we can proceed step by step to greater ones. The first transfiguration of a human being is that of penance, which is similar to the transfiguration of the Lord's passion. By this transfiguration we die to sin, the world, and our own will: to sin by contrition of heart and oral confession; to the world, through disdain for it and by setting aside its appearance, which happens when those who were clothed in silken clothes, precious stones, and gold, and ornamented like some kind of statue, now barely cover their limbs with sackcloth or some other poor and rough penitential garment; to our own will, when those who used to pay attention to the desire of the flesh now crucify it with its vices and desires, deny themselves, and take up
their cross.† Ga 5:24; Mt 16:24

The second transfiguration of a human being is that of righteousness, when someone does good not out of fear of punishment but out of love of righteousness. One formerly afraid of hell, who offered as a sacrifice for sin a broken spirit and a
contrite and humble heart,† is now sure of forgive- Ps 51:17
ness and offers a sacrifice of righteousness out of a desire for a heavenly home. This is similar to the transfiguration of the Lord's resurrection.

The third transfiguration happens through hidden renewal. It is not helpful, indeed it is dangerous if, as soon as someone is renewed interiorly through the grace of God, this renewal is retailed outwardly and in public, in the midst of the demons' plots. This is like carrying an open treasure chest in the sight of robbers. Especially is this the case in the first flowering of virtues,

Ep 3:17 before one is rooted and grounded in love† and protected and walled all around by an army of the other virtues. Even then one should not go outside except for the praise of God and the advantage of one's neighbor. This transfiguration imitates that of the Lord's appearing.

The fourth transfiguration of a human being occurs through meditation, when someone whose mind has been renewed begins to meditate on the works of God, not just those of the first creation, but especially those of our restoration, on the sacraments of both testaments, the precepts and promises, the glory of the saints, and the punishment of the wicked. Advancing in this way more and more and from day to day—from glory to glory, from knowledge to knowledge—and walking from strength to strength, one is renewed 'as if

2 Co 3:18; Ps 84:7 by the Spirit of the Lord'.† This transfiguration, by its sequence of stages, emulates the transfiguration of the Lord's ascension.

6. The fifth transfiguration occurs through contemplation, when someone advances so far through meditation as no longer to contemplate the works of God, or God in his works, but in so far as possible with the eye of the mind, to see God within, and in some way to abide with Christ in the bosom of the Father. This resembles the transfiguration of Pentecost which occurred in the hearts and spirits of the apostles.

The sixth occurs through a descent. Someone descending from the heights of contemplation to humble action in some way comes with Christ from the bosom of the Father into the world. One who was Israel becomes Jacob, passing from Rachel to Leah, from Mary to Martha.[10] This transfiguration is similar to the Lord's descent through all things.

The seventh occurs through association, when someone moved by the Lord's example feels compassion for the poor and associates with them, saying with Paul: 'Who is weak and I am not weak? I have become all things to all people, so that,' as far as possible for them, 'all may be saved'.† This resembles the transfiguration by which the Lord, associating himself with others, 'was found human in appearance'.†

2 Co 11:29; 1 Co 11:22

Ph 2:7

The eighth occurs through resumption of contemplation. We should not always linger in the valley through action, but should ascend with the Lord up the mountain, taking along Peter, James, and John. Peter means 'recognizing', James 'wrestler', or 'supplantor', John 'the grace of God' or 'the one in whom is God's grace'. Hence, those who want to climb the mountain of contemplation should have Peter in their company through recognition of the truth, James through the supplanting of vices, and John through removal of all presumption and trust in God's grace alone; that is, they should not presume on themselves in anything, but confidently take refuge in the grace of God. This transfiguration is like the one that occurred on the mountain.

The ninth take place through the example of a good way of life, when those of such perfection that their whole way of life is a re-creation for

10. The pairs Rachel/Leah and Mary/Martha are traditional for expressing contemplation and action. Jacob, whose name was changed to Israel, was married to both Leah and Rachel. See the elaborate allegorical interpretation of Jacob, Leah and Rachel, their children, and the children of their handmaidens, in Richard of Saint Victor, *Benjamin major.*

the weak offer themselves as bread and sweet food for the nourishment of the less perfect, 'lest they
Mt 15:32 faint on the way'† or succumb in the struggle. This transfiguration corresponds to that which is called 'sacramental'.

7. The tenth occurs in the body of each person who dies. How miserable this can be we know from experience. Notice how a dying person's facial expression is obliterated, the face grows pale, the eyes roll, all the members grow rigid, the whole outward form is changed, so that such persons can hardly be recognized even by those who have known them.

The eleventh occurs in the separation of the soul from the body. Our very spirit, as it passes from this sensible and visible world into some other spiritual region where everything it sees is new and initially unfamiliar, is struck with wonder at the novelty; in some way it is changed into another man[11] by the extreme shock of wonderment; from the kind of plurality of ideas and duties into which it had been divided while still dwelling in the flesh, it returns to a kind of simplicity of its essence, being wondrously changed.

The twelfth will occur in the common resurrection of all, both the good and the bad, when our bodies will be reformed from a show of its elements to the likeness and features of the human form. The wicked will arise in this way to be immortal and capable of suffering. They will live always, suffer always, and for them time will exist forever.

8. The thirteenth will be something spiritual and glorious occurring in the bodies of the saints, when not only will this corruptible body put

---

11. Here, uncharacteristically, Achard uses the word for male (*vir*)

on incorruptibility, but also Christ himself 'will reform the body of our humility, that it may be conformed to the body of his glory';† when even in their bodies 'the just will shine like the sun in the kingdom of their Father';† when they are going to hear that most pleasant and desirable sentence, full of every joy: 'Come, blessed of my Father, receive the kingdom prepared for you from the beginning of the world'.†

1 Co 15:53; Ph 3:21

Mt 13:43

Mt 25:34

The fourteenth will be in the spirits of the saints. Although the souls of the saints are already rejoicing with Christ in heaven, they will rejoice incomparably more when they have received back their bodies, which have been glorified and conformed to the body of Christ's glory.[12] Then, finally, they will have the fullness of joy, perfect and complete.

The fifteenth will be the transfiguration of the whole universe, for 'creation itself will be freed from its bondage to decay for the revelation of the children of God'.† Who can imagine how great will be the attractiveness of that land, how calm the air, how beautiful that sky which has no like! We are awaiting a new heaven and a new earth. Then will the saints see all things, not only in themselves, as they see them now in part, but much more surpassingly and sublimely in God, in his eternal reasons, which constitute the archetypal world that existed in the mind of God before it appeared in this sensible and visible world. Then, just as 'God will be all in all',† so in a way will all things be God in God.

Rm 8:21, 19

1 Co 15:28

See, then, twenty-three transfigurations. Eight of them are the Lord's, who could be transfigured only in the body, which is signified by the number

12. Compare Denzinger, *Enchiridion*, #414. Achard makes no mention of qualities of the risen body, such as agility.

eight[13] He himself is the primary number in solid things. Fifteen of them pertain to us, who can be transfigured in mind and body. May he who deigned to be transfigured for us deign to lead us to that most blessed transfiguration of the children of God. Amen.

13. See Sermon 10.6. At the end of the sermon Achard counts only eight transfigurations of the Lord. He may be omitting the transfiguration being celebrated in the liturgy (which occurred on the mountain), or that of Pentecost, which he says was a transformation in the disciples rather than in Christ.

Sermon 13: [Second] Sermon For the Dedication of a Church

INTRODUCTION

ACHARD GIVES A FEW CLUES ABOUT THE ORIGIN of this sermon, which in its present form has become a treatise. His text is drawn from the liturgy for the feast of the dedication of the church. As we saw in connection with Sermon 2, this feast was celebrated on June 5 at Saint Victor. Achard indicates he was speaking in the chapter room; he speaks of the enforcement of discipline in the abbey, and at some length about the duties of abbots.[1] This suggests that he might have been addressing a meeting of Victorine abbots, perhaps even a general chapter.

His topic is the participation of Christians in three of the attributes of Christ. Hence, while discoursing on spirituality, Achard takes us into the deep waters of Trinitarian theology and the metaphysics of participation.[2] One of Achard's central lessons, which is

1. Sections twenty-five and twenty-six.

2. For a somewhat lengthier commentary on the contents of this sermon see Jean Châtillon, 'The *De laude liberi arbitrii* of Frowin of Engelberg and Achard of Saint Victor', *American Benedictine Review* 35 (1984) 319–329.

particularly clear in this sermon, is that, as Eric Gill said, everything hangs together. Right from the first section he mentions the connection between time and eternity, between the point we have reached here and now, and our goal which lies ahead there and then, toward which we should meanwhile be moving. Now we are in the building stage; the dedication will come then, when the building is complete. Another recurrent theme strongly stated in the first section is the primacy of grace.

The second section quotes one of Achard's favorite New Testament verses: Christ, the one anointed with the Spirit, is 'the power and the wisdom of God'.[3] This leads him to one of the key ideas of his spirituality: Christians are Christ's dwelling place. Christ gives them a share in his fullness of grace, and thereby builds them into his house. He does this solely out of kindness. To Achard, anointing, or willing, or goodness, or utility may form the third member of a trinity of divine attributes of which wisdom and power (*virtus*) are the other two members.

Sections three through five begin with a summary of some points of Achard's Trinitarian theology. They represent his careful attempt to find philosophical concepts that will enable him to speak about the ultimately ineffable mystery of the Trinity. His purpose is to show the centrality of the Trinity in Christian existence. We can distinguish five main points. (1) The works of the Trinity are undivided. Later theology would say this applies to all the works of the Trinity *ad extra*, e.g., creation, including the creation of the humanity of Christ, but not to what concerns the divine persons rather than the divine nature. Thus, only the Son is united personally to the humanity of Christ. (2) Some works, associated with certain attributes that pertain to the divine nature, are customarily attributed to one of the persons: to the Father pertains power; to the Son pertains wisdom; to the Spirit pertains goodness. Through Christ's grace we come to participate in these attributes.

Achard chooses to speak of power (*virtue*), anointing, and wisdom, which he connects with love, delight, and contemplation respectively. The appropriation of power, wisdom, and goodness

3. 1 Corinthians 1:24

to the Father, Son, and Holy Spirit was a feature of the thinking of Abelard and Peter the Lombard. William of Saint Thierry was very critical of Abelard's use of the theory of appropriations, and instrumental in the condemnation of that use at Sens in 1140. Robert of Melun, who had close connections with Saint Victor, defended this traditional practice, and Richard of Saint Victor uses it often and defends it in his *De tribus appropriatis*.[4]

(3) All human virtues are a participation in the attributes of God, which are not diminished by being shared. (4) When a human being participates in wisdom, the efficient cause of each virtue is the divine nature in which wisdom, power, and goodness are identical, but the formal cause is divine wisdom. Achard has his own theory of formal causality to explain this. Each virtue is different formally, but the same in substance. Analogously, he maintains that the powers of the soul are not really, but only formally, distinct from the essence of the soul. (5) In the Trinity there are three persons in one substance; the house they build in us is both three and one, and corresponds to three different virtues in one soul.

Achard connects the descriptions of Christ the master-builder, who wishes to live in the house he builds in us, with the role of Christ and his disciples as peacemakers. In sections six through nine Achard gives a brief theology of peace, as Father Châtillon has written:

> The builders of God's house must be peaceful, that is, included among those whom the Gospel proclaimed blessed because they deserved to be called children of God.[5] They are not to establish just any peace, but that accorded to those of good will,[6] and 'which surpasses all understanding'.[7] This peace that they establish with the help of grace will be first of all the reconciliation between God and the world that Christ brought with him. It will also be peace with other people who are called to preserve among themselves 'the unity of the

4. Ribaillier, ed., *Opuscules théologiques*, 185–187 (=PL 196:993–994). On this controversy see Châtillon, *Sermons*, 136, n. 14.
5. Matthew 5:9
6. See Luke 2:14
7. Philippians 4:7

> Spirit'[8] in love. Finally, it will be the peace which all human beings must have with themselves, by surmounting all the contradictions sin has inscribed in them, and by restoring the order and harmony that must reign among reason, the will, and the flesh.[9]

In section six Achard anticipates his message to the abbots. Christ does not wish to work with those who are not also his imitators, people of peace. In sections eight through nine Achard returns to his idea of peace among the powers of the soul. The only people who experience perfect peace within themselves are the blessed and the totally wicked; however, the peace of the wicked is attained only at the cost of losing every shred of human dignity and decency.

In section ten Achard begins the central part of his discourse, which concerns the walls of hewn stone, cedar wood and gold which formed Solomon's temple. Achard quickly presents the literal meaning of the account in 1 Kings 5–6.

In reading of the first dwelling, the *domus virtutis*, it is important to keep in mind the multiple meanings of the word '*virtus*'. It means power, empowerment, and virtue. Thus, while discussing the participation of the Christian in the power of God, Achard draws moral lessons regarding the virtues a Christian should have. In any case, whatever *virtus* a Christian has is a participation in the *virtus* of Christ.

Achard uses the ideas of brightness or whiteness (according to Saint Jerome this is the meaning of 'Lebanon') to explain the relations and roles of the body, soul, and divinity in Christ, and the passage of the human race from its original state, in which it was informed by the brightness of grace, to the state of dark deformity into which it fell, and then to the reform or brightening effected in it by Christ. These are the topics treated in sections eleven through fifteen. Christ brought this transformation about by taking up the darkness of pain, but not the darkness of sin; this enabled him to suffer, and then to brighten his own body at the resurrection, and

8. Ephesians 4:3
9. Châtillon, 'The *De laude*', 321–322.

thereby to brighten all of his members through their participation in him, their head. Put another way, Christ's righteousness is the form of human nature, which was formed by God, deformed by sin, and is now reformed by Christ.

Near the end of section fifteen Achard speaks about the motive for the Incarnation. Humanity had no claim on divine righteousness; only kindness could move God to help fallen humanity. God's kindness would have to win out over his righteousness. Since the two are really identical in God, this could be called a victory of righteousness over righteousness.[10] The whole of section sixteen praises God's kindness and love.

Section seventeen explores the symbolic resonances of the number four, and mentions the three sacraments of initiation. Sections eighteen through twenty one further develop the meanings of the number four: the four principal virtues, the four beatitudes, the four aspects of love. Sections twenty three and twenty four talk about conversion and correction, the factors that will move a person from the lower Lebanon of worldly attachments to the higher Lebanon. Correction, Achard says, should appeal both to faith and to reason.

In section twenty five Achard mentions the chapter room, 'the house of discipline', in which the prior, subprior, and circator applied the discipline of the Victorine rule to members who violated that rule. One feature of the daily community meeting at Saint Victor and at almost all other medieval monasteries was the correction of faults. Religious could accuse themselves, or be accused by the circator, the main disciplinarian of the monastery, or by another confrere, of public violations of the common rule. The one presiding at the meeting, usually the abbot, then assigned a penance.[11] Achard is very insistent on the duty of abbots to correct and exhort by example as well as by their words. He has a

---

10. Similar discussions about the interaction of personified mercy and justice, based on Psalm 85:10, occur in Bernard of Clairvaux's *Similitudes*, and in Hugh of Saint Victor; see Maria Fumagalli, *Le quattro sorelle* (Milan: Cisalpino-La Goliardica, 1981).

11. I have discussed the role of the circator and the nature of the chapter meeting in '*Circatores:* From Benedict of Nursia to Humbert of Romans', *American Benedictine Review* 40/4 (1989) 346–379.

strong sense of hierarchy, which serves him well when he comes to allegorize the six surfaces of these living stones, hewn from Lebanon, which are now fitted to each other by the cement of the Holy Spirit and the arms of love.[12] The members of the community are united to each other by obedience and vigilance, by their joy in others' joys and their compassion for them in troubles, by imitation of good examples, and by exhortation of those who need it.

Achard's treatment of the house of cedar[13] is a theology of spiritual joy. Those who have reached the fullness of love, which is described at the end of the previous section, delight in a pure conscience. They taste the sweetness of the Lord, and rejoice in it even more than in the fact that the sweetness is directed to them. Achard considers, too, the joy of those in heaven. Joy and contemplation[14] are closely connected. God can be contemplated either in the modes of participation in him or in himself. Hence, there are seven pillars of contemplation: four concern created modes of participation (physical creation, spiritual creation, its justification, and beatification), and three have as their object God's plan or ideas for all that is outside him (formal causes), the destiny to which he has predestined them (judicial causes), and finally the Trinity itself. Delight raises the mind to contemplation, and contemplation in its turn can lead to increased delight. This reflects the relations and order between the Son and the Holy Spirit in the plan of salvation.[15]

In the conclusion Achard aptly summarizes the point of this elaborate allegory: Christ dwells in us in many ways, just as we participate in his fullness in many ways, above all in the way of virtue and discipline, in the way of sweetness and joy, and in the way of contemplation. He ends with a short but dense prayer, which asks that the image of mutual indwelling he has painted may inform his life.[16]

---

12. Section twenty-eight.
13. Sections twenty-nine through thirty-one.
14. Sections thirty-two and thirty-three.
15. This is a topic theology has recently begun to study more thoroughly; see, e.g., Jürgen Moltmann, *The Way of Jesus Christ* (San Francisco: HarperCollins, 1990) 73–78.
16. Section thirty-four.

THE SERMON

[Second] Sermon For the Dedication of a Church

I

WISDOM HAS BUILT HERSELF A HOUSE; she has hewn out seven columns.† I have announced a text Pr 9:1
that speaks of building rather than of a dedication. I am not unaware that the feast celebrated today is not of building, but of dedication, but still I know—and I think this is the direction we should take—that the house of God requires of us true and interior building and not yet a dedication. This is still the time to build this in us, rather than to dedicate it. What is not completely built cannot be dedicated yet.

The dedication of a house usually takes place, and rightly so, not at the start, or during construction, but only upon completion. Many things, and a long stretch, lie between the building of the house of God and its dedication; the distance between the two exists in place, in time, in kinds of reality, and in kinds of persons. See how much lies between the two. Note how the two are widely separated in particular aspects. In place, a great distance separates this house which is to be built on earth but dedicated in heaven. In time, a great distance separates what is to be built in this life but dedicated in the next, built in time, but dedicated in eternity. In kinds of reality there is also a great distance: building must take place now in reality, but the dedication for the time being[17] only takes place in hope; the building is in power, the dedication will be in beatitude; the building is done by grace through righteousness, the dedication will be done by righteousness through glory. Building is merit, dedication will be the reward. In the kinds of persons who do the building and dedicating, there is a great distance: humanity cooperates with God in the building, but only God will be doing the dedicating.

Since to God alone pertains the dedication of his house, let him speak of the dedication of his house himself, and let those who have the Spirit of God also speak, those who cling to God so
1 Co 6:17 that they are one spirit with him.† To them has God revealed through his Spirit the uncertain and hidden things of his wisdom that he has prepared
1 Co 2:9, 10; Ps 51:6 for those who love him.† For me it is enough to speak of the building of God's house, and would that I were equal to speaking of it as I should! Since obedience impels me to offer the brothers a word of upbuilding, I will say something to them of this building. If this does not build them up, they may at least learn how the building should take place in them, or how they themselves should build.

2. Let me return to the word I promised regarding the building of God's house. 'Wisdom has built herself a house; she has hewn out seven columns'. Christ is the power of God and the wisdom of
1 Co 1:24 God.[18]† He is the Christ, that is, the anointed one. The Spirit of God is upon him because he

17. 'Meantime' (*interim*) is almost a technical term for the fleeting moment between what has taken place and the eschatological future Achard uses the word frequently in this sermon (sections six, twenty–nine, and thirty–one), which is full of contrasts between what is and what will be. See F. Châtillon, '*Hic, ibi, interim*', RAM 25 (1949) 194–199.

18. See Sermons 4.1; 14.15; 15.20.

anointed him.† God has anointed him beyond his Lk 4:18; Is 61:1
companions† by the Holy Spirit, that is, with the Ps 45:7
abundance and fullness of graces; he gave him the Spirit without limits.[19]† From the superabundance Jn 3:34
of his anointing, by which he was drenched, he is wholly good and pleasing, wholly merciful and kind, and it pleased him to anoint us with a share in his anointing—but without any lessening of his own fullness—and through our anointing to build his house in us. Although this house is his, and he is building it to dwell in it, we also dwell there with him. He does not need it; only we do. Solely from the grace that flows into him, solely from his overflowing and superabundant anointing, that is, solely because he is the Christ whom God superabundantly anointed, does he wish to build his house in us. Since he is also wisdom, he knows how to built it as he wants; since he is power as well, he can build it as he wishes and knows how to do. Where these three—will, knowledge, and power[20]—come together concerning something to be done, there is no stopping the completion of the work and the achievement of the result.

3. Although these three cooperate with one another in building the house of God, nevertheless power builds a certain house for itself, and Christ, the anointed—or his anointing itself, builds a certain house for himself, and wisdom builds a certain house for itself, for, although the works of the Trinity are undivided, certain ones are nevertheless customarily attributed specially to the Father, certain ones specially to the Son, and certain ones specially to the Holy Spirit. As will become clear in what follows when the building of the houses

19. See Sermon 4.5.
20. See Sermon 1.4, nn. 21–22; 9.4, n. 7.

is discussed, the house that power builds for itself, for us and in us, comes first in time, though not in dignity; the house that anointing builds for itself succeeds it in second place; and the house that wisdom builds for itself follows after these two as the third. The house that power builds for itself is the house of power; the house that anointing builds for itself is the house of anointing; the house that wisdom builds for itself is the house of wisdom.

To designate the same things by other names pertinent to the same distinction: the first house is the house of love; the second house is the house of delight; the third house is the house of contemplation—power exists in love, anointing in delight, wisdom in contemplation. Moreover, the first house is the house of the way, the second is the house of life, the third is the house of truth. Christ, as he himself said, is 'the way, the truth,
Jn 14:6 and the life':† Christ is the way because he is virtue; no one comes to anointing and delight, or to wisdom and contemplation, or to eternal happiness for that matter, except through virtue and love. Christ is the truth, because he is wisdom. Christ is life, because he is the anointed one, and he is our anointing. His life is an anointing and a kind of spiritual delight: good delight is a good life; bad delight is a bad life. Spiritual delight makes a spiritual life; carnal delight makes a carnal life.

4. As wisdom hews out seven columns in her house, so power hews out seven columns in her house, and so, too, anointing hews out the same number of columns in her house. In each house the total number of columns is seven, because they are spiritual, one and all. Not only do power, anointing, and wisdom erect columns in their own

houses, they also, as it were, hew the columns out of themselves. The columns in their houses are modes of participation in themselves. Every mode is, so to speak, hewn out of the fullness of the things in which they participate. Powers are columns in the house of power. Likewise, certain spiritual anointings and certain delights are columns in the house of anointing. In the house of wisdom or contemplation, the columns are of the same kind; that is, kinds of contemplation. Indeed, the virtues, anointings and kinds of contemplation of creatures are nothing else than modes of participation and, as it were, forms of emanation from the divine power, anointing, and wisdom. In their houses, columns are hewn out of them in such a way that they are not at all diminished. The sun pours out and diffuses rays from itself in many ways, but experiences no lessening of its brightness because of this.

5. In material buildings, material columns are usually made of material for three reasons: in some they are made to keep buildings steady and solid; in others, so that they will be charming and pleasant; in others, so that they will be open and bright. For this reason, columns are sometimes used in buildings instead of walls so that the interior parts will be bathed in stronger light. Similarly, each of the three houses mentioned earlier, notwithstanding it is spiritual, has in it, as it were, spiritual columns hewn out of it spiritually for one of the same three reasons. In the house of power the columns are for the sake of solidity; in the house of anointing they are for the sake of delight; in the house of wisdom, for the sake of light. Power builds for itself a solid house; anointing builds for itself a delightful house; wisdom builds for itself a

well-lighted house. Power makes solid; anointing delights; wisdom enlightens.

Although each has its own effect, as it were formally, according to their one substance each causes all and all cause each. Power causes not only solidity, but also delight and enlightenment. Similarly, anointing is the cause not only of delight, but also of enlightenment and solidity. Wisdom, also, is the cause not only of enlightenment, but also of solidity and delight. However, insofar as by certain forms they are distinct from each in their properties, it pertains to the form and property of power to solidify, to the form and property of anointing to give delight, to the form and property of wisdom to enlighten. In this manner there occurs and is understood the distinction of houses mentioned earlier, in which the house of power is called solid, the house of anointing delightful, the house of wisdom well-lighted. Nevertheless, the house of power is not lacking in its own delight and light, nor does the house of anointing lack its light and solidity, nor the house of wisdom its solidity and delight. In its substance and nature power is not only solid, but also delightful and well-lighted; and anointing is not only delightful, but also well-lighted and solid; wisdom also is not only well-lighted, but solid and delightful as well, so that, although as was noted each one corresponds to each, as it were formally,[21] all correspond both to all and to each substantially and causally.

Since, however, all three of these houses are built in one heart, they are there joined into one house, so that in some sense they are both three and one. Three in one and one in three, one threefold

21. See *On the Distinction* 16.

house, as one might expect of the house of the one, triune God, one house which nevertheless is like Noah's ark in being divided into three. Although this house is built in us, it is not built without us. We must be God's co-workers[22] in building his house in us.

II

6. The house of God cannot be built at random and in a disorderly fashion by anyone, from just anything, or in any way whatever. Consideration must be given to the workers, the material, and the way of working. In regard to the house of God we must pay attention to by whom, of what, and in what way it is to be built. Perhaps it is to be built by people such as Solomon was, who built God's house, and of the kind of materials Solomon used, and in the way in which Solomon built it, so that what is done spiritually in our case corresponds to what was done materially in Solomon's case. For the present, in what regards the kind of person Solomon was, it is sufficient to state simply what can be gathered from the interpretation of his name. Solomon means 'peaceful'; in accord
with his name he was peaceful.† The statement of 1 Ch 22:9
God to David through the prophet Nathan gave this as the reason why in building his house he preferred Solomon to David, Solomon's father. In this respect those who wish to imitate Solomon in building the house of God should be similar to Solomon.

Such assuredly was he who came to us from the bosom of the Father to build the house of God in us, so that it might be 'the tabernacle of

22. See Sermons 3.1; 11.3; 15.22.

Rv 21:3 God among humans'.[23]† He came to dwell with them, but also in them: with them because among them, in them because within them; with them because 'he was found human in appearance, in them because he did not think it robbery but
Ph 2:6–7 natural to be equal to God'.† Who is this heavenly maker of the house of God, who is not only its maker, but its inhabitant as well? The one through whom the whole fabric of the world is established and sustained is a carpenter, and even the son of
Mt 13:55 a carpenter.† He is the craftsman, wisdom, who built and builds a house for himself. The house that wisdom builds for himself is the house of God.

In fact, this wisdom-builder is God and the Son of God. When he was in the form of God he built a house for himself in heaven; he took the form of a slave in order to build a house on earth as well. First he built a house of God among the angels; later, he came to build the house of God among humans too. This house, although at present it is being built on earth is not itself earthly, but heavenly—hence, it too is to be transferred to heaven at the appointed time, and joined and cemented to the angelic house, so that thereafter there will no longer be two houses, but one.[24] The builder of both houses is Solomon, but also
Mt 12:42 more than Solomon.† He makes all things peaceful,
Col 1:20 'whether in heaven or on earth'.† 'He himself is our
Ep 2:14 peace, who made both one',† and the discipline of our peace is upon him.

Such in their own way must be the artisans who minister, who wish to cooperate with this teacher and primary builder in constructing the house of God. This builder does not want co-

23. This verse was used in the Liturgy of the Hours for the feast of the dedication of a church.

24. See Sermon 10.7.

workers who are not his imitators. Otherwise they are not constructive but destructive; they do not gather with him, but scatter away from him and against him.† Lk 11:23

7. 'Blessed are the peacemakers, for they will be called children of God'.† It belongs to the children Mt 5:9 of God to build the house of God with the Son of God. They are not children of God unless they are peacemakers. Let them be peacemakers so they can build the house of God. Let them be peacemakers even 'with those who hate peace'.† This responsi- Ps 120:6 bility lies most of all with those who undertake to build the house of God not only in themselves but also in others. 'His place is made in peace';† the Ps 76:2 house of God is made in peace—not in the peace of the world, but in the peace of God himself, a peace that is not for the wicked but only for people of good will.† In God is 'the peace that surpasses Lk 2:14 all understanding',† and therefore, he wants peace Ph 4:7 present in his house and in those who build his house. If they cannot yet possess 'the peace that surpasses all understanding', let them at least possess peace in accord with understanding, not contrary to it; and in accord not with carnal understanding but with the understanding of reason. Their peace should be spiritual, not carnal. They should have peace toward both the one above them and the one alongside, peace with God and peace with their neighbor.

On account of these two kinds of peace, our Solomon, the source and lover of peace, says: 'I leave you peace, my own peace I give you'.† Be- Jn 14:27 cause Christ is God and man, the peace that he calls his own is to be understood as peace between God and humanity; the peace he left us is to be understood as the peace of human beings with each other. The former is superior; the latter is inferior. Only grace leads to the former; the common nature we share invites us to the latter, and to some extent draws us to it. Hence, he gives us the former as from a superior, as from what is his; he leaves us the latter as from an inferior, as in what is ours. But even for the latter what is ours is inadequate without what is his. The peace of humanity with God is that 'it is good for a human to cling to God', and by clinging to him to be one spirit.† The peace of human beings with each other is that there be for them 'one heart and one soul',† and that 'they be concerned to maintain the unity of the Spirit in the bond of peace'.† Moreover, they all must have peace not only with God and neighbor, but also with themselves.

Ps 73:28; 1 Co 6:17

Ac 4:32

Ep 4:3

8. Actually, it cannot happen that one may have peace with him who is above one, and with the one alongside, unless one also has peace within oneself. In oneself there should be peace between reason and will, and peace between will and flesh, so that the will obeys reason and the flesh obeys the will.[25] Whatever one may think about peace between reason and will, in this life there can be no perfect peace between the will and the flesh. There cannot be between them a peace that is devoid of all conflict, at least if it is a good peace.

At first a straightforward peace exists between them, but it is a bad peace, in fact the worst kind of peace; bad with respect to the flesh, worse with respect to the will, and the very worst with respect to the will and the flesh together. What is bad there is that the flesh runs away with the will; what is worse is that the will spontaneously agrees with the flesh; and the worst is the pact that comes from

25. See Sermons 2.2; 9.1–2.

the attraction of the flesh and the agreement of the will. After this straightforward peace of the worst kind there sometimes follows a straightforward and good battle, but not one that is altogether good. It is good that the will assaults the flesh, but bad that the flesh attacks the will. Next, peace and conflict come together: or rather, peace comes, but conflict does not cease right away. Conflict is lessened, but not eliminated. Both are good, but peace is better than conflict. Peace is good in both respects; conflict only in respect to the will. Finally, but only after this life, there will be a peace that is not partial but full; not good in one respect only, but best in both respects.

At first, as I said, there is a straightforward peace, peace of the worst kind, when the will acquiesces in everything to flesh and blood, when it approves nothing except what flesh and blood reveal to it,† Mt 16:17
when it relishes nothing but what the wisdom of the flesh, which is hostile to God,† dictates to it. O Rm 8:6–7
perverse peace, confused, disordered peace, confusing and perverting the order of things, subordinating the mind and exalting the flesh, trampling the image of God and putting a beast on the throne! O peace that does not make peace, but attacks nature and upsets all humanity! O concord without harmony, concord out of tune with the heart of God and deprived of all reason, O pact unseemly and foul, sordid association, love hateful to chaste love, peace in rebellion against true peace! In this peace the more the will consents to the flesh, the more it joins the flesh in dissenting from all reason and decency.

9. Sometimes, however, reason comes to meet the will and berates it about this most foul peace. It charges it that it owes more to reason than to the

flesh; indeed, that it owes nothing to flesh contrary to reason, nothing not in accord with reason. It calls to mind the ancient, divinely instituted dispensation that the will must be in the power of reason and not in the power of the flesh so as to be ruled not by the flesh but by reason. Woman is the image of man, and Eve was made to be Adam's help mate, not the serpent's. She is to help Adam against the serpent, not the serpent against Adam. Adam is reason, the serpent is the flesh; Eve is a mean between Adam and the serpent as the will is a mean between reason and flesh, inferior to reason and superior to flesh.[26] Since the will is made to help reason, not flesh, it should not be subject to flesh but to reason, so that when joined to reason it may dominate the subjected flesh. Meanwhile, the will thus instructed and admonished by reason, understands the truth and proposes to follow the truth it has understood.

But, alas! the miseries of human beings, the wretched state of sinners! Alas, those who commit sin become slaves of sin! While they are acting they do not understand this, because they are delighting in the act; they understand it when they regret the act and try to escape. Because the will has served the flesh so long, when it longs for its freedom and tries to return to reason the flesh comes against it as though it were a fugitive slave, contradicts it, and utterly opposes it. Hence a violent struggle, a serious fight arises between them. In this conflict the weakened will succumbs and is conquered unless it is rescued by the strong hand of God. Helped through grace by God's power, it prevails and conquers; it punishes the flesh and returns it

26. This analogy between Adam/Eve and reason/will occurs also in Sermon 5.4.

to the servitude it owes. The limbs that earlier brandished the weapons of iniquity for sin now display the armor of righteousness for God. Thus, not only the spirit but the body too becomes a temple of the Holy Spirit. As a result a certain peace and spiritual concord exists between the will and the flesh, but not altogether without a struggle. The flesh often complains in secret and raises its heel, at least surreptitiously, against its lord. 'I delight in the law in my inmost self, but I see another law in my members at war with the law of my mind'.† See, there is still a struggle! 'The desires of the flesh are against the spirit, and the desires of the spirit are against the flesh'.† See a very evident struggle!

Rm 7:22–23

Ga 5:17

Where, then, is peace? 'My soul thirsts for you; in how many ways my flesh thirsts for you!'.† 'My heart and my flesh exult in the living God'.† See the peace! The more this peace grows, the more the struggle decreases. Nevertheless, however much the struggle decreases, it is not completely eliminated as long as 'the corruptible body weighs down the soul'.† When what is corruptible puts on incorruptibility, when death is swallowed up in victory, when the body itself is spiritual, not by changing into the nature of the spirit but by subjecting itself totally and inseparably to the spirit's reason and will, then there will be in us 'the peace that surpasses all understanding',† peace in itself, the best peace, complete peace, eternal peace. O lovable peace, O desirable peace! Who will grant me that as I work in myself I may pass from myself and rest in you? Who will grant me that as for the moment I am fighting against myself for you, so by conquering myself I may finally be crowned in you?

Ps 63:1

Ps 84:2

Ws 9:15

1 Co 15:54, 44; Ph 4:7

III

10. These things regarding peace and peacemakers have been said for the sake of the builders of the house of God. These builders must be like Solomon in this virtue. However, because we said that not only must they be like Solomon, they must also build from similar materials in a similar way, it is our task to consider of what and how Solomon
1 K 5 and 6 built the house of God. If we consult the narrative† about these things and ask the kind of material and way of building, it answers that there were three kinds of materials: hewn stone, cedar wood, and the finest gold. There it describes this manner of building: first Solomon built the house of hewn stone; next, he overlaid the whole interior of the house with boards of cedar and in this way it is as if he built wooden walls within stone walls, a wooden house within a stone house. Thirdly, he covered everything inside with the finest gold; everywhere he used golden nails to attach gold plates to the cedar wood. We may say that he made golden walls within the cedar walls, a golden house within the cedar house. Thus he made, as it were, one house in three and three in one: he put the stone outside, the cedar inside, and the gold innermost. It seems pertinent to the manner of building that when the house of God was being built, hammer and axe were not heard in it. They were not heard there then because they had been heard enough earlier and elsewhere.

You see of how many, of what kind, and in what order and way, Solomon built the material and figurative house of God materially and figuratively. We too, as we look to Solomon for the three kinds of material, and the order and way of building, and as we draw a form and a kind of outward model from him, if we are Solomons—that is, peacemakers—by the work of our Solomon, Christ, we will build the true spiritual house of God interiorly, spiritually, and truly, 'in spirit and in truth'.† Jn 4:23

A

11. The first house, or the first part—the house we meet first—is to be built of hewn stones. Where will the hewn stones we need come from? Perhaps they will come from the same place as they did for Solomon. And where did they come from for Solomon? From Lebanon. Read the historical account, and ponder it, and you will find that then they were taken from Lebanon. Lebanon is a great mountain which has still not been worn down or stripped. Following in Solomon's footsteps, let us go to Lebanon; from it let us take the stones we seek; we have as many as are necessary. Hewn stones have two characteristics: because of one, they are called stones; because of the other, hewn. That they are called stones pertains to the material; that they are called hewn respects the form. That they are stones they have naturally; that they are hewn they have accidentally.[27]

In respect to both their material and their form they are from Lebanon, but the material is from one Lebanon, the form from another. Lebanon is interpreted 'brightening'.[28] The two Lebanons are two forms of brightening: the brightening of truth and the brightening of vanity, the Lebanon of

27. On matter and form in Achard's philosophy see *On the Distinction* 3.

28. See Saint Jerome, *Liber de nominibus hebraicis* (PL 23:821–822); Sermon 14.3, below; and Hugh of Saint Victor's *Eulogium Sponsi ad Sponsam* (PL 176.987B-994A), of which I am preparing a critical edition.

Christ and the Lebanon of the world. In regard to the Lebanon of Christ: 'The just will flourish like a palm tree, and grow like a cedar of Lebanon in
Ps 92:12–13 the house of the Lord';† in regard to the Lebanon of the world: 'The Lord will shatter the cedars
Ps 29:5 of Lebanon'.† The Lebanon of Christ has true brightness;[29] the Lebanon of the world has shaded brightness. The brightening of Christ lies mainly within and still remains hidden; the brightening of the world is wholly external and shows on the surface. The world is like a wall painted white on the outside but completely dirty and unclean inside. The brightening of Christ lies in spiritual and true goods; the brightening of the world in carnal and false goods. Hence, the brightening of Christ feasts and enlightens spiritual eyes; the brightening of the world deceives, destroys and blinds carnal eyes.

Because of these two forms of brightening, because of these two Lebanons, the groom says to the bride in the Song of Songs: 'Come from Lebanon, my bride; come from Lebanon, and you will be
Sg 4:8 crowned'.[30]† First, she is called from Lebanon to Lebanon to be a bride; then, since she is a bride she is called from the Lebanon beyond Lebanon to be crowned. The first call is from Lebanon to Lebanon; from brightening to brightening; from the illusory to the true; from outside to inside; from the carnal to the spiritual; from the Lebanon of the world to that of Christ. The second call is from a Lebanon beyond Lebanon; that is, from brightening to brightness itself, from the brigh-

29. In what follows Achard distinguishes between *candor* (brightness) and *candidatio* (brightening); and between *candidus* (bright) and *candidatus* (brightened) One could also translate 'light' and 'illumination', 'light' and 'lit', but the use of 'bright' and its cognates seems to produce less ambiguity.

30. See Sermon 14.3.

tening of Christ to the brightness of God, even from the brightening of the humanity of Christ to the brightness of Christ's own divinity. Christ is bright both according to his divinity and according to his humanity, but according to his humanity he is both bright and brightened, whereas according to his divinity he is not brightened, but simply bright or, rather, brightness itself, the brightness of eternal life.

12. The brightening in Christ's humanity is threefold. In one respect, our common nature has been brightened in Christ; in another, it is his special nature, that is, his one humanity. Since his humanity consists of both his mind and his flesh, there is one brightening with respect to his mind, and another with respect to his flesh. Our common nature has been brightened in him, in that what was dark has become bright. Before this common nature existed in him, it was dark in everyone else because of the rust and stains of sins. However, grace brought it about that this nature, which was dark in others, became bright in him as soon as it began to exist there. It was never dark in him, but always bright, since it was taken up by the Word in such a way that it was without any evil or sin. The mind of Christ is not brightened by becoming bright after being dark; it was never dark, there or elsewhere. Before it began to exist there it was nowhere else, because it was nothing before that. From the moment it began to exist it could not be dark, because it immediately inhered perfectly and personally to the Word himself. The darkness of original sin was not present there because that human being was conceived of the Holy Spirit and the Virgin. The darkness of actual sin was not there because 'he committed no sin, nor was deceit

1 P 2:22; Is 53:9 found in his mouth'.† Christ's flesh, however, was brightened from the darkness it had in him at first, and later set aside.

13. There are two darknesses: one of guilt, the other of pain. To these are opposed two brightnesses, one of righteousness, the other of glory. The darkness of guilt and the brightness of righteousness cannot exist together in a single person, if righteousness is complete and perfect as it was in Christ. Similarly, the darkness of pain and the brightness of glory cannot exist together in a single person in the same respect. Although these were together in Christ, they were not there in the same respect: the brightness of glory was there with respect to his mind, the darkness of pain was there with respect to his flesh, in such a way that the flesh did not then share in this brightness, nor did the mind ever share in the darkness; there never was any pain in the mind of Christ, and as long as there was pain in the flesh of Christ, glory was not yet there.

The darkness of guilt and the brightness of glory never exist in the same person, whether in the same respect or not. The darkness of pain and the brightness of righteousness do inhere in the same one, and hence the bride says in the Song of Songs:
Sg 1:4 'I am dark, but beautiful',† dark because of pain, beautiful because of righteousness. Because of this brightness and this darkness the bridegroom was
Ps 45:2 also simultaneously 'the most handsome of men',† and, according to the saying of another prophet,
Is 53:2 'he had neither beauty nor comeliness'.† God sent
Rm 8:3 'his own Son in the likeness of sinful flesh',† and because he was sent in the likeness of sinful flesh he shared in darkness; because he was not sent in the sinful flesh itself he shared in brightness. 'He was

tempted in everything as we are, but without sin'.† Heb 4:15
That he was tried in everything as we are pertains to the darkness; that it was without sin pertains to the brightness. On account of this brightness and darkness, the bride says of him: 'My beloved is bright and ruddy'.† In the Scriptures ruddiness and Sg 5:10
darkness usually have the same force and signify both guilt and pain. In respect to guilt it is said: 'If your sins are as red as scarlet';† in respect to Is 1:18
the pain the angels' address to Christ is 'Why is your vesture red, and your clothes like theirs who tread the wine press?'.† He answers them: 'I have Is 63:2
trod the wine press alone, and I have stained all my clothes'.† He says his clothes are stained in Is 63:3
his passion and by the pouring out of his blood. Earlier, his flesh had been dark through its capacity to suffer and die; then it become darker through his passion and death, while shortly after that it was brightened through the resurrection. Then he put on beauty and strength; then Christ's clothes which had earlier been stained became white as snow; then whiter than snow; there he left his grave 'like a bridegroom coming from his bridal-chamber'† and Ps 19:5
was glorified by the Father with the glory he had with the Father as determined beforehand before the world existed.† Jn 17:5

14. So Christ was brightened with respect to his humanity, he was brightness with respect to his divinity, and bright with respect to both. The brightness in the divinity of Christ is in accord with the fullness of his nature; the brightness in the humanity of Christ is in accord with the fullness of grace; the brightness in both is in accord with the fullness of glory. The fullness of glory in the divinity of Christ comes from his full nature; in his humanity it comes from the fullness of every

kind of grace. In Christ's members, brightness is in accord with grace, not nature, not in accord with the fullness of grace in the head, but in accord with a mode of participation in that fullness. The members do not possess their brightness as the humanity of their head possesses it directly from the divinity, but through the mediation of the humanity of the head and by participating in his fullness. 'From the fullness' of the head we who
Jn 1:16 are his members 'have all received'† not from the fullness of nature which belongs to the divinity alone, but from the fullness of grace which belongs only to the humanity of Christ. So the evangelist, to emphasize that we participate by grace and not by nature, immediately added: 'grace for grace'; that is, participation in grace for the fullness of that grace. We have not only received from his grace but also in place of his grace; not only of his fullness, but also in place of his fullness. Such grace as Christ's humanity had with God earned for us the participation we have in him. God 'has
Ep 1:6 graced us in his beloved Son';† God has graced us in Christ. What is this gracing of us in Christ if not a mode of participation in us of the grace of Christ and because of Christ? This participation of grace in us is our justification; our justification is our reformation; our reformation is the forming and hewing of living stones.

15. Now if the forming of stones is justification, and righteousness is their form—if the form really is their righteousness—what will the material be if not rational nature itself, which is capable of justification? The material is the good of human nature, the form is the gift of divine grace.[31] However good human nature may be, it is crude and unformed

31. See Sermons 3.1; 9.4–5.

material if it is not formed by supervenient grace. To be sure, this material had been formed in us by the hand of God, but it was deformed in us and by us by our hand, which reached out wickedly to what was forbidden. It could and can be reformed by no virtue or merit of ours; only by the virtue of him who formed it will it be reformed through the grace of Christ. Christ is the higher Lebanon, from whom we should look for and long for a form; the world is the lower Lebanon, where material is abundant enough. Before the higher Lebanon descended to the lower Lebanon, before Christ came into the world, material and form were separated widely from each other. Material was below on earth, form was above in heaven; material was in human beings, form existed only in God by nature and in angels by grace; material, insofar as it was earthly, heavy, and weighty, could not ascend into heaven to form, and so form had to descend to earth to material in order to impress itself on material. In this way it conformed material to itself, and this material it had conformed to itself it drew to heaven after itself and to itself. Once, form had come as grace to material, and had informed it graciously with its own imprint; ungrateful material despised the form of grace, rejected grace, and willingly deformed itself contrary to the will of the form. Therefore, there was nothing in it on the basis of which it could require the coming of form; rather, there were grounds why form rightly would not come to it after that.

However, although form was righteousness, it was not without kindness; in fact, not only was it not devoid of kindness, it was full of kindness; in fact, form was complete kindness, for in God kindness and righteousness are the same. So kindness

overcame righteousness; or rather, because righteousness was kindness, in a sense it overcame itself.
Ps 77:9 It did not 'in its anger shut up its mercies,[†] but as one forgetful of the previous injury and unmindful of the earlier rebuff at length it descended to material even lower than before, impressed itself on it more sharply, and formed, or rather, reformed it after itself. Form wished to be for a time with material in the region of material, so that afterward material might be with form eternally in the region of form.

16. O kindly righteousness, O truly divine form! It is most fitting for the most high God that while he is most just he also be most kind. Certainly it is most just that God himself be most kind. When will you be able to understand how kind he is in himself if you even fall short when you want to think how kind he is to you? Who can understand aright how great is the condescension of the divine kindness toward us, unworthy as we are! Solely out of kindness did such a beautiful form unite itself to such unformed material, which was not just unformed but even deformed, not just deformed, but misshapen, not by any necessity but solely by the willful perversity of its own will. Divine form, I say, freely came to freely deformed humanity; grace came gratis to one ungrateful for grace; moreover, medicine came unsummoned to the sick, strength to the weak, wisdom to the foolish, holiness to the impure, truth to the untruthful, mercy to the merciless, peace to the rebellious, kindness to the unkind, charity to the enemy, righteousness to the unjust—not to judge and condemn humanity in accord with its own righteousness, but to justify it after its injustice, form it after itself, and at length to glorify in itself the one it had formed after

itself. The form of God came in the flesh in order to conform to itself, first in the spirit and later also in the flesh, those whom God 'foreknew and predestined to be conformed to the image of his Son'.† Thus would we who bore the likeness of what is earthly also bear the image of the heavenly. This form is both God's and ours: God's because it is from God, ours because it is in us; it is expressed by God, and impressed by him on us. Rm 8:29

17. This form is a square, because it is stable and firm. Again, it is a square because it exists in four places: in Christ's divinity, in his humanity, in the angels, and in us. Again, it is a square because it is put before us in the four gospels; or rather, because Christ is our form—as the Apostle formed by him shows, Christ became a spiritual square for us—according to the apostle's word, Christ 'became for us wisdom from God, and righteousness, and sanctification, and redemption'.† See there a vital, heavenly square! Approach and receive it, you stones, or rather you who without it are dead and earthly. We are hewn in this form, and will thus be transformed from dead to living, from earthly to heavenly. 1 Co 1:30

In listing the four things that the one Christ has become for us, the Apostle follows the order of dignity, not of time. In the order of time he first became our redemption; secondly, our sanctification; thirdly, our righteousness; and fourthly, our wisdom. He became redemption for us when he gave himself as the price for us; he became sanctification for us in the remission of sins; righteousness, in the bestowal of gifts; wisdom, through contemplation in a kind of present reward for our merits, which merits are themselves his gifts. He became redemption for us through the sacrament of his passion

and death, sanctification through the sacrament of baptism, righteousness through the sacrament of confirmation, wisdom through the sacrament of the altar. It is this sacrament that is the object of the prophet's invitation: 'Come to him and be enlightened'; that is, 'Taste, and see how sweet the
Ps 34:5, 8 Lord is'.† Come to taste, and so be enlightened to see! In tasting is the savor of an inner sweetness; in sight is the splendor of knowledge. Wisdom consists of these two: it is savory knowledge.[32] Only knowledge of God is really savory; knowledge of God is never insipid. Only God is known with true savor, and he is never really known without savor. Those to whom God is not savory know that they do not know God.

18. In many passages of the Scriptures, many squares appear, but they all come together in one, Christ. Christ 'became for us wisdom from God'; he is God's wisdom, that universal wisdom that makes everyone wise. By participation in it every wise individual, human or angelic, is wise. A sage says of wisdom in the book of Wisdom: 'She teaches soberness and wisdom and righteousness and virtue; for human beings nothing is more
Ws 8:7 profitable in life'.† This is a good square: for human beings nothing is more profitable in life. In fact, wisdom is also the life in human beings, not life of the flesh but of the spirit; this is a profitable life, much more profitable than the life of the flesh. These are the four chief virtues: temperance, he here calls soberness; prudence, he calls wisdom; righteousness he calls by its own name; and fortitude he indicates with the word virtue. By prudence we distinguish good from evil, by

32. Achard is resorting to a much-used play on words, which saw in the word '*sapientia*' (wisdom) a connection with the words *sapor* (savor) and *sapida* (savory)

temperance we reject evil, by righteousness we choose good, and by fortitude we execute and maintain the good.

19. Elsewhere Wisdom presents to us this same square and its utility, saying in the flesh: 'Blessed are you poor, because the kingdom of heaven is yours. Blessed are you who are hungry now, because you will have your fill. Blessed are you who weep now, because you will laugh. Blessed will you be, when people hate you and ostracize you,' and so forth 'on account of the Son of man'.† Notice Lk 6:20–22
the four things: poverty, thirst, weeping, and bearing persecution. Poverty pertains to temperance, thirst to righteousness, weeping to prudence, and bearing persecution to fortitude. Poverty of spirit exists when, even if the riches and delights of the world abound, the heart is not set on them, but exercises restraint in their regard. In Matthew this is said about thirst: 'Blessed are those who hunger and thirst for righteousness'.† About pru- Mt 5:6
dence Solomon says that 'in much wisdom is much vexation', and that those set on knowledge are set on sorrow as well'.† What is more prudent in this Qo 1:18
life than to weep continuously on account both of the abundance of this life's evils and the lack of the other life's goods. These are the lower and higher pools.† Jg 1:15

20. In another place in the gospel, where Christ—who is both the one who forms us and our form—invites us to be conformed to him, he says: 'Learn from me, because I am meek and humble of heart'.† There are two things to note here: the Mt 11:29
virtue of gentleness, and humility of heart. So that this will not be two-sided, but square, two more things are added: his yoke is easy, and his burden light.† The easy yoke of Christ is the love of God, Mt 11:30

through which we are easily joined to him; the light burden of Christ is love of neighbor, through which we willingly, and therefore lightly, act on behalf of our neighbor. To this pertains what the Apostle says: 'Bear one another's burdens, and you
Ga 6:2
will fulfill the law of Christ'.† Therefore, these two are joined to the two preceding because they follow from them in some way. 'The love of God is poured forth in our hearts by the Holy Spirit', that
Rm 5:5
is, by the Spirit of God, who is given us.† Upon
Is 11:2
whom does God say 'my spirit rests'† if not upon the humble? Notice that the love of God derives from humility; love of neighbor—and especially of one's enemy, which is more perfect—proceeds from patience, that is, from gentleness. If some are not yet able to love their enemies as they ought, let them only bear with them patiently, and God will give them enough grace and love to bear with them even lightly. Indeed, by the patience shown their enemies, God will quickly expel enmity from their hearts.

21. Only in the love of God is the square proposed and imposed as something we must receive. We are commanded to love God with all our heart—that is, fervently; with all our mind—that is wisely; with all our soul, which means life—that is, perseveringly; and with all our strength—that is,
Mk 12:30; Lk 10:27; Mt 22:37; Dt 6:5
abundantly.† With all our soul—that is indefatigably; with all our strength—that is, sufficiently; the love of God is indefatigable when it is not ended or interrupted; it is sufficient when none of the things pertaining to it is neglected or omitted. By having this square in the structure, the spiritual house will be firmly attached to Christ. Where then is the square through which it is firmly attached to the neighbor as well? It must not only be attached

to the cornerstone there but also to the stones alongside it; not only to the stone of life but also to the living stone; not only to the one who hews, but also to the one who is hewn.

Examine the precept of love of neighbor which follows to see if a square is taught there also. As you know, that precept is proposed in these words: 'You shall love your neighbor as yourself'.† What should we do? There does not seem to be any square in sight here. But look more closely: perhaps a square is imposed here also, but less expressly. What do his words, 'as yourself', mean? Why and how does God teach you to love your neighbor as yourself if you have not yet been taught to love yourself? Where then does he teach you this, if not where he teaches you to love God? Mt 22:39

22. There was no preceding instruction about love, but none was needed. To love God is to love oneself in truth, that is, in God himself. Contrariwise, if one does not love God, one hates oneself. One who does not love God, loves iniquity: 'One who loves iniquity, hates his soul'.† So, if by loving God you love yourself as well, then by loving God with the four aspects of yourself mentioned above you also love yourself in your four aspects. You love yourself in loving God 'with all your heart', and in loving him 'with all your mind', and in loving him 'with all your soul', and in loving him 'with all your strength'. Therefore, since you are commanded to love your neighbor as yourself, it is enjoined on you that just as you ought to love yourself by striving to possess these four, or you love by already possessing these four, so you must love your neighbor as yourself for the sake of these four, or in them. You ought to love your neighbors so that they may love, or because they love God Ps 10:6 Vulg.

fervently; for the purpose of loving or in loving God wisely; to possess the love of God indefatigably, or because that love is possessed indefatigably; and also to possess it sufficiently, or because you possess it sufficiently.

See how the square is also contained in the twofold love. And just as the Lord says that the two precepts of love are similar, so also is the square we find in them not dissimilar. If any are looking for a more explicit square in love of neighbor, let them accept what the Apostle expounds and imposes when he says 'Correct the restless, encourage the fainthearted, support the weak, be
1 Th 5:14 patient toward all'.† This square pertains especially to prelates. Whoever accepts squares of this kind will come through them to that superior square, so as to be able 'to comprehend all the saints what
Ep 3:18 is the breadth and length and height and depth':† how great is the breadth—the breadth of God—in love, how great the length in eternity, how great the height in power, and how great the depth in wisdom.[33]

23. See how from and in the higher Lebanon, that is, from and in Christ, living stones are to be found and shaped. They are far from this hewing and shaping as long as they are detained on the lower Lebanon, as long as they are stuck in love of the world. While they bear the form of the world, to which the Apostle forbids us to be conformed, they are not formed but formless; not shapely, but misshapen. The form of the world, which 'is in the
1 Jn 5:19 power of the evil one',† is formlessness and deformity; the norm of the world, for which his stones

33. *Quaestiones in epistolam Pauli ad Ephesios* q. 17 (PL 175:572A) mentions 'the length of love, the breadth of eternity, the height of power, and the depth of wisdom'.

are shaped, is enormity; the beauty of the world is ugliness. The order of the world, 'in rioting and drunkenness, in debauchery and impurity, in strife and envy',† and other such things, is not order, Rm 13:13
but simply confusion and disorder; the equality of the world is inequality. Those, then, who adapt themselves to the equality and measure of those who are given over to the world must be 'inconstant in all their ways'† and never remain in the Jm 1:8
same state. In order to receive the beautiful form of the higher Lebanon one must first put off this deformed form of the lower Lebanon. These two forms, so different from each other, cannot exist in the same thing at the same time. 'The love of the Father is not in anyone who loves the world',† says 1 Jn 2:15
the one who was beloved of Christ. According to the teaching of Truth himself: 'No one can serve two masters'.† Mt 6:24

So that stones may be formed on the higher Lebanon, they must first be extracted from the lower Lebanon; so that they may be formed in the love of God, they must first be dug from love of the world. To entice and extract them from there is very difficult. Just as the material world is made of four elements, so these people are bound in the world of vanity as though by four bonds.[34] The very thing that was on Mount Lebanon detains them there: for them the world grows light, smiles and beguiles, because their endeavors prosper and because perhaps they are, or expect to be, raised to some height of honor there. Their own bulk also holds them back; that is, pleasures of the flesh. Their own hardness also detains them; that is, the obstinacy of their minds. Their connection with other stones holds them back; that is, the carnal

34. See Sermon 15.8.

affection they have for others and others have for
them. Then there are 'the enemies of a person's
Mt 10:36 own household':† these do not wish to enter the
spiritual building, nor do they permit those close
to them to enter. These are the overlapping scales
of which God told Job the body of Leviathan is
Jb 41:6/15 fashioned.†

24. Here, certainly, hammer and axe are needed;
1 K 6:7 here they must be seen and heard,† so that by
their blows on the rocks the form of this Lebanon, which glitters in them, can perhaps be destroyed, its bulk lightened, its hardness shattered, its relationships dissolved, so that they can be separated from the mass of perdition and wrested away from the lower Lebanon. Once wrested away, they are to be taken out, smoothed, then hewn and shaped on the higher Lebanon, and so inserted into the structure of the spiritual house. They are to be cut, sometimes by faith, sometimes more menacingly by reason; faith is to be employed for the more simple; reason, with those who are wiser and capable of reason. In them, as if in the square and weight of reason—that is, by the clear and unbreakable light of truth—error ought to be attacked, overcome, and suppressed.

The axe is employed when someone is shaped by faith; the hammer, when someone is shaped by reason. The foulness of sin and the harshness of punishment must also be put before them. Since the carnal mind abhors the harshness of punishment more than the foulness of sin, the axe is employed when the foulness of sin is expounded, the hammer when the harshness of punishment is presented. Again, with regard to sins, the axe is the exposition of the foulness in pardonable matters, while the hammer is the exposition of the foulness in deadly ones. In punishments, too, the axe is the menace of the miseries of the present life, and the hammer is the threat of the miseries of the life that follows. Also, in our present miseries alone, the axe can be spoken of when people are frightened of the loss of their things or of blow to their friends; the hammer, when they are frightened about their own personal afflictions. In what concerns future sufferings alone we can take the axe to be the terror of purgatorial fire, the hammer to be the terror of eternal fire.

By such axes and hammers, through the cooperation of the grace of the Holy Spirit, it sometimes happens that some stones are extracted from the quarries of lower Lebanon, that is, from the cupidity of the world and from a worldly and carnal way of life. Will they now be inactive, then, so that hammer and axe are no longer to be heard? Not at all. Their use is still necessary. The stones are still rough; the form of the world is more to be abandoned than already abandoned, and the oldness more to be stripped away than stripped from them. Only a beginning has been made; there is no perfect consummation yet. Many deformities, enormities, and inequalities still appear in them. The larger vices in them are to be pounded away immediately as if by a hammer; the smaller vices are to be chipped away little by little as if by an axe. Their former habits and wrong deeds are to be destroyed immediately and completely; attachments and thoughts are to be polished gradually so that what was carnal may become spiritual. What is forbidden ought to be eliminated immediately; other things, even those not forbidden, ought to be trimmed back little by little.

25. The workshop in which hammer and axe

are mainly heard among us is, I say, this house of discipline, the chapter, in which we are now assembled. Here the prior, subprior, and circator, with undaunted zeal for order and brotherly love, strike transgressors of the rule with the hammer. They proceed not against the people themselves but only transgressions, for the sake of the people; they attack wrongs done to the order and to religion, not those done to themselves. The duty of their office is to act strictly, and to apply themselves vigorously to detecting disorders and correcting them. For some, to hold the axe here, and to mention rather than to castigate what needs to be corrected, is enough.

The abbot, who remains the judge in everything, and to whose judgment all things are subject, insofar as the keys of the kingdom of heaven are entrusted to him, wields the hammer with one hand, the axe with the other. It pertains to his office to correct all things and to restore them to the rule of reason. Let him direct the hammer against greater offenses, the axe against lesser ones. With the hammer let him rebuke more sharply, with the axe let him admonish more gently. Let him impose more severe discipline with the hammer, lighter discipline with the axe. Let him use the hammer on the stubborn and rebellious, the axe on the humble and docile. The hammer is to be used on those who sin habitually, with deliberation, and in a perverse spirit; it is enough to apply the axe to those whose faults arise from surprise, ignorance, or weakness. If any are so obstinate that their stiff necks can be bowed by neither hammer nor axe they should be thrown out as unclean stones, not only useless but harmful; otherwise, they will corrupt the other stones with which they are intermingled, and disturb and disfigure the whole house.

26. Abbots should remember to bear hammer and axe not only for others but also for themselves, lest when they preach to others they themselves be rejected.[35]† Far from us be those builders who 'bind heavy and unbearable burdens and lay them on others' shoulders, while they themselves are unwilling to lift a finger to move them'.† Not only must abbots bear everything the rest bear; they must, as leaders of the way, precede others as far as possible in all rigor, austerity, and the discipline of the order. They must be an example to their flock† and mold those committed to them more by their life than by their words, more by deed than by speech. Let them carry with them in their bodies the dying of Jesus by putting to death their members that are on the earth, so that each of them can say what the Apostle said: 'Be imitators of me as I am of Jesus Christ'.†

1 Co 9:27

Mt 23:4

1 P 5:3

2 Co 4:10; Col 3:5; 1 Co 11:1

Their task is to bear in themselves the measuring rod according to which the stones are to be hewn by the Cornerstone himself, and thus to direct others regularly according to that same rule. They are under obligation for themselves and for others; they will have to give an account for both, and thus those set over others will face a very heavy judgment. Just as here they are not like others, so too there they will not be like others; as here they are not equal to others in rank, so then they will be either superior in glory to others or beneath them in reproach. They are going to receive either double honor or double punishment.

35. See the Victorine customary, *Liber ordinis* 3, 'On the manner of life of the Abbot'.

So let them now strive to have double merits so that
Sg 4:2 'all their offspring may be twins".† Let them carry the hammer and axe, not only for admonishing and correcting others, but for chastising their own bodies and humbling their hearts.

27. Let subjects for their part not be content with their superior's hammers and axes; let each carry for himself the axe of compunction of heart and the hammer of pain in the flesh. Let a subject be careful not to presume to raise the hammer of rebuke or the axe of correction against his superior; let no one dare to admonish the latter except with the fear of God and humility, and with all gentleness and reverence. Let a brother not use the hammer on his brother; even the axe he should use rarely; it is more proper for an equal to counsel his equals, whereas it is a superior's task to rebuke and admonish. The everyday axe is laid on us in the struggle 'against flesh and blood', the hammer in the struggle against 'the spiritual forces of evil in
Ep 6:12 the heavens'.† Moreover, when there are struggles without and uprisings within, the axe is outward persecution from visible enemies and the hammer
2 Co 7:5, 11:26 is inner persecution from false brethren.† Nothing plagues us more effectively than a familiar enemy.

Stones finished and hewn with hammers and axes of this kind, with trimming and pressure of this sort, fittingly and properly pass over into the spiritual edifice and are fitted into place by the artisan's hand[36] and disposed to remain in the spiritual buildings. The hand of God, the artisan, puts some of those thus formed in the upper part of the structure of his spiritual house; others he puts

36. Achard seems to be echoing a hymn used for the feast of the dedication of the church. Achard writes: '*suisque aptantur locis per manum artificis*'; the hymn has '*Aptisque juncta nexibus / locantur in fastigio*'.

below; some he puts inside, others outside; some to the right, others to the left, depending on how each is shaped and fitted to the others, and on what the overall design of the house requires. All of them, wherever they are placed, he firmly joins together in unity with spiritual mortar, the mortar of the Holy Spirit, the cement of perfect love. He teaches them 'to preserve the unity of the Spirit in the bond of peace'.† The Son of God is the mason, Ep 4:3
the cement is the Holy Spirit.

28. Here hammer and axe are now silent;† 1 K 6:7
enough that they were heard up to now. No longer do they need to be heard or seen. Those who are so perfect that they are fit to be placed in God's house arrive at all God's ordinances blamelessly.† Lk 1:6
They live without offense in their relations with those within and without; no one needs to rebuke, or reprove, or even admonish them. They are established in liberty of spirit, and as cheerful givers† they offer a voluntary sacrifice, even 2 Co 9:7; Si 35:11
a holocaust. Being fervent in spirit, they are not servants, but children who do everything out of love, not out of fear. Perfect love casts out from them the fear of incurring damnation, which is like a hammer, and the fear of losing beatitude, which is like an axe. Previously, when they were driven by others to do something against their disobedient wills it was as though a hammer had done it; when they forced themselves it was like an axe. Now, however, without any coercion from others or themselves, they are spontaneously so ready for every good, and doing good has become such a habit for them, that goodness seems to be innate. O how much such people add to the beauty of God's house! How beautifully and in order they exist there! With what regularity

in themselves, what concord with others, what fittingness for the whole house! They revere all superiors as their parents; if any are subject to them, they provide for them as children. They rejoice spiritually for those who advance from the right just as if their grace were their own; they feel compassion for those who fall from the left into some fault, temptation, or trouble of mind or body, just as if they themselves were suffering. They consider the evils and goods of others to be their own, and so they know 'how to rejoice with those who rejoice and weep with those who
Rm 12:15 weep'.† They are not moved to envy by those who go ahead of them, but to imitation; they do not spurn those who come after, but challenge and urge them to better things.

Thus, in accord with the six surfaces of a hewn stone, as though with the six measures of love poured out on the whole earth, they are fitted to the living stones from above by obedience, from below by providence, from the right by congratulation, from the left by compassion, from the front by imitation, from behind by exhortation. These are, so to speak, the six arms of brotherly love, by which it reaches out to its neighbor in the good works that correspond to the works of the six days; divine love remains more inside, simple and undivided, in the depths of the heart. These seven different virtues are the seven columns that
See Pr 9:1 power has hewn in her house.† This is the house of power, the house of the way, the house of love. Because of the difficult material, it was necessary to tarry longer to locate, extract, cut, and dress stones for this house. After this we must proceed to the second house and, as it were, enter it through this first house.

B

29. So, after the outer, stone house follows the inner, cedar house; that is, after the house of power comes the house of anointing, after the house of the way comes the house of life, after the house of love comes the house of delight. Entrance to this second house is through the first. Those for whom the yoke of Christ became easy and his burden light† in the first house from perfect love of God and neighbor delight in Christ more as they delight in the world less. Having turned from carnal joy they rejoice in the Holy Spirit. Because they do nothing for vainglory, but conduct all their affairs according to a well-founded conscience, they glory and delight in the testimony of their conscience.† They find delight because they are conscious of no evil demerit in themselves, and because they are conscious of good merit. On the basis of the present good merit they are conscious of the future good reward which is theirs. They rejoice because they have a pure conscience, because they have a righteous life, and because they expect a crown of glory.† They delight and rejoice because they have a pure heart, and because they have a full heart, and because they hope it will be filled more perfectly yet. They have a heart cleansed from the inclination to sin and from guilt: they have a heart full of the flowers of the virtues and the fruits of good works; they hope it will be filled with an abundance and fullness of heavenly joys. They have a heart full of the goods not of the world but of the spirit; they expect for it to be filled with the goods of God; they believe that they 'will see the good things of the Lord in the land of the living'.†

Mt 11:30

2 Co 1:12

1 P 5:4

Ps 27:13

Meanwhile, they perceive certain first fruits of

future beatitude; they perceive now in part what they will afterward perceive perfectly. They taste
Ps 34:8 and see 'how sweet the Lord is'.† Because they taste how sweet God is in them, they see and understand how sweet the Lord is in himself. 'How sweet he is in himself', they say, 'who is so sweet in his gift! How sweet he is in his substance, who is so sweet in his grace. How sweet he is in his fullness, who is so sweet when he is shared!' First, they rejoice that they perceive how sweet God is; then, that God is much sweeter than they can perceive. First, they rejoice that such they have in part; then they rejoice because such is what they have in this way, for, to rejoice over something because they have it is one thing, and to rejoice over the quality of the thing they have is another. A person rejoices over his enemy because he has him in prison, but not in the enemy himself, whom he has there. Thus, too, many rejoice over the knowledge they have, because they have it, but not in the knowledge they have; they do not love knowledge simply as knowledge, but because of something else they have or want to have through it.

In accord with these two kinds of joys, the saints in the other life possess a joy which is equal and one which is unequal. Two things are provided, of which one person there has more than another: the one who has more rejoices and delights more in the thing of which he has more; the one who has less rejoices less in the quality of the things of which he has less. Even so, the inferior rejoices that the superior has what the superior has and he himself does not have, just as much as he would rejoice to have it if he did have it. Thus, all the people there rejoice as much over the good of another as over their own, but not as much as in their own, or in God, the common good of all. In accord with these two ways or causes of rejoicing, those for whom I have brought up these examples rejoice, as I said, that they have a foretaste of God's sweetness in the present life, and that God, of whom they have a foretaste, is so sweet. To have this second kind of joy is much more perfect. Those who rejoice that God is sweet to them in some way restrict the joy to themselves; those who rejoice that God is so sweet in himself, indeed is sweetness itself, refer back their joy to God himself. The former rejoice over their own special good; the latter rejoice over the common and general good of all the saints.

30. Next to this latter way of rejoicing and delighting there follows another related to righteousness. Those whom the habit of righteousness first delights, afterward delight in the very form and beauty of the righteousness they possess. No longer do they rejoice that they possess righteousness, but because the righteousness they have is so beautiful in itself, and because it would be no less beautiful in itself even if neither they nor anyone else had it. They do not love righteousness solely because through it they come to their reward, but they love it for its own sake. Even if they did not hope to gain anything from it, they are still of a mind to embrace and love it. They may also happen to progress so far that they prefer to be perfectly happy in order to be perfectly just, rather than to be perfectly just in order to be perfectly happy.[37] This preference seems to be more perfect and more just. All want to be happy, but not all want to be just. Furthermore,

37. See Sermon 9.6 for another statement of Achard's theology of pure love.

those who want to be perfectly blessed seek to have their will perfectly fulfilled in God and by God, while those who want to be perfectly just desire that the will of God be perfectly fulfilled in them and by them. Who can doubt that they should prefer the fulfillment of the divine will in all matters to the fulfillment of their own will?

With respect to the same way of rejoicing, a second joy concerning purity of heart follows the first. They no longer rejoice that they possess it, but rather in the immaculate quality of that purity, which, whether they, or someone else, or no one at all should possess it, the purity would still possess in itself. They do not love purity only so that through it they may or will avoid punishment, but because of the purity itself; that is, because it is so beautiful in itself that it is to be loved for itself. Hence, even if they were not going to avoid punishment through it they would choose to pursue and to guard it as much as they could. Sometimes also they progress so much in love of it that, if they had to choose, they would prefer to become wretched rather than impure; they reckon impurity itself the highest misery.

31. These are the seven joys, the seven holy and spiritual delights, that proceed from the sevenfold Spirit, from perfect love. The first delight comes from the condition of purity, the second from the condition of righteousness, the third from a kind of certainty of possessing beatitude, the fourth from a foretaste of divine sweetness, the fifth from the quality and fullness of the sweetness which has even now been tasted, the sixth from the appearance and form of righteousness, the seventh from the immaculate quality and the beauty of spiritual purity. These seven delights, these seven anointings

of the spirit, are the seven columns hewn out in the house of anointing.

There are also other delights there, but for the present it suffices to have listed as many as there are columns, and to have selected and explained them as if we were hewing them out. These joys are in the second house, the house of cedar wood. Who does not know that in comparison to stones wood is softer? In the building and preparation of the first house there was a good deal of rigor and harshness in preparing, practicing, and perfecting virtues; here are only softness and leniency, sweetness and joy. Just as cedars are first in height and imperishable by nature, so the heart tries to extend itself upward to delight in the good and to rejoice in the Holy Spirit, and to keep itself unharmed by the rottenness of the vices. The cedar wood is attached to and supported by the hewn stones because it is impossible to have delights like this where virtues are lacking. The cedar house is also inside, the stone house outside, because virtues have a way of proceeding outward in the performance of deeds, while these delights consist entirely of interior goods.

C

32. After the first and second houses follows the third; after the exterior house and the interior house comes the inmost house; after the stone house and the cedar house comes the golden one; after the house of power and the house of anointing comes the house of wisdom; after the house of the way and the house of life comes the house of truth; after the house of love and the

house of delight comes the house of contemplation. Contemplation of the truth is gold.[38] If any falsehood is mixed in, the gold is impure; such gold is found among the heretics and among secular philosophers. Contemplation of the truth without any admixture of falsity is gold, pure gold. This kind of contemplation concerning physical creation is pure gold; concerning the spiritual creation it is purer gold; concerning the Creator himself it is the purest gold.

Many are the ways of contemplating the Creator, either by some mode of participation of him, or apart from and above every mode of participation.[39] The Creator is the highest good, and without participating in him no other good is good. Physical creation has the lowest, as it were external, and merely general mode of participation in the highest good—that by which it is said of every
Gn 1:31 creature that 'all that he had made was very good'.†
In the spiritual creation participation in the highest good is no longer general but individual; superior and more inward than general participation, but still multiple rather than simple, three, not one. In this case participation by creation, participation by justification, and participation by beatification differ.[40] The first mode of participation in the highest good belongs to the spiritual creature by reason

38. On gold as a symbol of contemplation see Gregory the Great, *Moralia* 1839 (PL 76:58); *Homilia XL in Evanglia* 10.6 (PL 76:1113); Pseudo-Hugh of Saint Victor, *Miscellanea* 3.39 (PL 177:660B).

39. On these two degrees of contemplation see Hugh of Saint Victor, *In Ecclesiastem homiliae* 1 (PL 175:117B). Richard of Saint Victor makes the same division, with subdivisions, in his *Benjamin major* 1.6–7 (PL 196.70B-75C).

40. On these three modes of participation see Sermons 1.3 and 9.4–6. The first mode consists in an aptitude for knowing and loving; compare with it the natural image of Sermon 1.3, and the first region of likeness in Sermon 9.4. The second mode consists in the actual exercise of the aptitude given in the first; compare with it the image of grace of Sermon 1.3, and the second region of likeness of Sermon 9.5. The third mode can be compared to the third region of likeness in Sermon 9.6.

of its creation, because it is made in the image and likeness of God, in that it can love and understand that very goodness. The second is by reason of justification, because, not only can it understand and love goodness, but it actually does understand and love. The third is by reason of beatification, since it enjoys the goodness it has perfectly understood and perfectly loved by perfectly contemplating it and by perfectly delighting in it. Parallel to these four modes of participation in the highest good, one in physical things, the other three in spiritual creatures, four degrees of contemplation of God are formed in those modes of participation. Beyond these a fifth degree of contemplation occurs in the eternal plan of all things;[41] a sixth, still higher and more inward, occurs in the special predestination of the saints;[42] a seventh, the highest and most inward, has no relation to any creature, but is simple and absolute, occurs in the unity and trinity of the Godhead.[43] These seven degrees of divine contemplation are perhaps the seven columns that Wisdom hews out in her house.

33. The gold plates can be taken to refer to the different degrees of contemplation one by one. The gold plates are appropriately attached to the cedar wood, because these degrees of contemplation of God should be founded on spiritual delights and supported on them. Delight raises the mind to contemplation, and supports it in contemplation once it is raised there; otherwise the mind

---

41. See the 'formal causes' of Sermons 14.20 and 12.8; whereas Sermon 12 reserves this contemplation to the blessed in heaven, Sermons 13 and 14 indicate that it can be granted to Christians while they are still on earth.

42. See the 'judicial causes' of Sermon 14.20; divine predestination or foreknowledge is often mentioned by Scotus Eriugena, e.g. *De divisione naturae* 2.2 and 2.20.

43. See Sermon 14.22.

could neither rise there nor remain there. The gold nails by which the gold plates are attached to the cedar wood are certain movements forward and back, from delight to contemplation, and from contemplation to delight. Delight leads to contemplation, and contemplation pours back greater delight; greater delight in turn leads back again to fuller contemplation.

This order is preserved and represented in the Son and the Holy Spirit. The Son is first conceived by the Holy Spirit; then the Holy Spirit is sent by the Son; at length the same Spirit is said to be going to lead into all truth as into the fullness of the Son. Just as the contemplation of the truth is referred to the Son, so spiritual delight is referred to the Holy Spirit. How happy, how luminous is this movement back and forth, how pleasant and beautiful this alternation from the Holy Spirit to the Son and from the Son to the Holy Spirit, from the sweetness of delight to the clarity of contemplation, and from the clarity of contemplation to the sweetness of delight. Because from both sides—from degrees of contemplation on the one hand, and, as we saw earlier, from virtues on the other—delights flow into the spirit, the house of cedar is justly said to be in the middle between the exterior house of stone and the interior house of gold.

34. These three houses, which were introduced above, have now finally been sufficiently explained, not in the measure befitting them but in the small measure that is mine. The first is the house of power, the house of the way, the house of love; the second is the house of anointing, the house of life, the house of delight; the third is the house of wisdom, the house of truth, the house of contemplation. O lovable house, O delightful house,

O house to be contemplated! O house one and three, built in its entirety upon a single rock! O you who dwell in a mud house, you who have built your house upon sand, where you waver and grow bitter and dark, look here and gaze upon a solid house, a joyful house, a luminous house! Look and long, admire and aspire, consider and desire, desire and hasten, hasten and enter, enter and occupy. Occupy and love, occupy and delight, occupy and contemplate. Love so that you may be firm, take delight so you may be happy, contemplate so you may be enlightened; be solid so that you may become eternal, rejoice so that you may become happy, be enlightened so that you may become glorious. Cling to God the Father by the firmness of eternity; cling to the Holy Spirit by the joy of beatitude; cling to the Son by the light of glory.

Although the Son is specially described as building the house of God, he does not build it for himself alone, but for the whole Trinity together. Hence he builds not only one house, but a triple house. As the one person of Christ subsists in three essences, that is, of the flesh, the spirit, and divinity,[44] the first house pertains in a sense to his flesh because of the power exercised through the flesh; the second pertains to his spirit because of the spiritual anointing; and the third pertains to his divinity because of divine contemplation. When these three houses are built in us, we too become wholly the house of God. Our body becomes the house of God on account of the first house; our

44. Hugh of Saint Victor writes in *De sapientia animae Christi* (PL 176:847C): 'You inquire about the soul of Christ, that is, about that rational spirit that animated the human flesh in the human Christ, which the Word united—with the flesh, and in the flesh itself—to himself in the unity of his person, so that there was one Christ in one person, two natures, three essences. . . .'

spirit, on account of the second; our mind, on account of the third. God is glorified and carried by us in our body, and there he dwells as if bodily; he dwells spiritually in our spirit, and intellectually in our mind.[45] He dwells in our flesh through his flesh, in our spirit through his spirit, in our mind through his form. He dwells in our flesh through the operation of power and love from imitation of his flesh; in our spirit through the delight of anointing or the anointing of delight, from the inpouring of his Spirit: in our mind by the contemplation of wisdom, or the wisdom of contemplation, from some manifestation of his form. He dwells in our flesh in an imitable way, in our spirit in a delightful way, in our mind in a contemplative way. In power and love he himself leads us on the way by his flesh; in anointing and delight he himself nourishes our life by the Holy Spirit; in wisdom and contemplation he sustains us on our way by his form, and perfects us in life as he himself illumines the truth. In accord with the three things David asked for himself and
Ps 119:66 set down for us to ask,[†] God dwells in our flesh through discipline, in our spirit through goodness, and in our mind through knowledge. To discipline belongs the exercise of power and love on the way; to goodness, which another translation calls sweetness, belongs the joy of anointing and delight in life and refreshment; to knowledge belongs the light of wisdom and contemplation in truth.

So, 'Teach me your goodness and discipline and knowledge', O Christ, good teacher, so that through these three you may dwell wholly in me and I may dwell wholly in you, and I may be wholly in you and you may be wholly in me, and you

45. See Sermons 4.1; 14.22.

may draw my whole self to you and fill me wholly in you and not otherwise than from you. Then wholly in me, not only wholly by me but also by your whole heavenly house, you may be praised forever for me who am wholly in you. Amen.

Sermon 14: On the Feast of All Saints

INTRODUCTION

OF ALL ACHARD'S SERMONS, this one for the feast of All Saints (November 1) is most closely connected with the liturgy. On this major feast, the liturgical service of Matins at Saint Victor had nine lessons, each followed by its own response, and Achard's sermon draws its structure and themes from these nine responses. The first of them calls down the divine blessing; the second invokes Mary; the third, the angels; the fourth, John the Baptist; the fifth, the apostles; the sixth, the martyrs; the seventh, confessors; the eighth, virgins; the ninth, all the saints. Achard adopts the reverse order, because this serves his purposes better. At the end of the sermon he refers to the gospel of the day, the beatitudes as these are given in Matthew 5:1–12, and finally the *Te deum*. The gospel passage of the day was probably read at the end of Matins, as it is today in monastic communities, and the service concluded with the singing of the *Te deum*. Although it is a liturgical commentary, the sermon as it stands is too long to have been delivered during a single liturgy. Perhaps we should think of Achard giving it in sections in a series of chapter and/or eucharistic sermons during the octave of the feast. In addition, Achard no doubt expanded his text when he prepared to circulate it in written form. The section on confession was probably expanded considerably.

In the opening section Achard declares himself unfit to speak about the saints, and he addresses his audience as fellow citizens of the saints and as the temple of God. He asks them to choose which sort of saint each of them is most suited to celebrate because of the graces within—like should celebrate like.

The first category of saints is the virgins.[1] Achard decides to speak about just one virgin who represents them all, and indeed is the mother of them all. Interestingly, this one virgin-mother could be either the Church or Mary, although Achard does not mention Mary directly.[2] Achard extends the meaning of virginity to embrace whatever sort of purity, sexual or otherwise, is necessary in the children of God, who are also the children of the Church. This leads him once again to the two Lebanons and the brightenings that the spouse of the Word has from him who is brightness itself.

Those who have lost the brightness they received in baptism are confessors.[3] Achard speaks of confession[4] as both praise and acknowledgment of sin, although the latter is of particular concern to him here. As the notes indicate, Achard very carefully threads his way through the nascent theology of private confession, which was developing during his time.

With a little imagination one can see in Achard's discussion of suffering at the end of section four, an outline of the classic stages of the spiritual life: conversion (corrects), purgation (cleanses the convert), illumination (exercises the one to be perfected), unity (tests the one perfected).

The last part of section five outlines Achard's theology of con-

1. Section two.

2. Châtillon, *Sermons*, 173, n. 13, gives a considerable list of books on the spiritual motherhood of the Virgin Mary, a notion that gained currency in the twelfth century.

3. Section four.

4. Sections five through thirteen.

fession: (1) confession of the heart = sorrow regarding the past and resolution for the future; (2) confession of the mouth (to a priest) = rejection of the sin + promise of satisfaction; (3) confession in deed = forgiveness of others + avoidance of sins confessed + performance of the penance given by the priest.

Achard's primary concern here is not to contribute to the theology of confession but to exhort his hearers to make good confessions. These must be voluntary, bare, and pure: they should not wait for someone else to proclaim their faults, but do it voluntarily;[5] they should confess their faults for pure and proper motives:[6] and Achard is concerned above all that confessions be bare,[7] that is, that penitents accept responsibility for their sins. This leads Achard into a minute investigation and refutation of the excuses people can offer to avoid taking responsibility for their sins. Later moral theology would repeat many of the same analyses when it tried to determine the extent of freedom and hence of culpability.

In discussing martyrs,[8] Achard gives another version of what might be called his theology of pure love. He detects a growth in Christians' attitude toward Truth: from fear of offending Truth, to striving to please Truth, to seeking to be so familiar with Truth's demands that they become pleasing to them, to suffering gladly for the Truth, not simply because Truth pleases them, but because they know experientially that they please Truth. The goal is to be the neighbor, friend, and lover of Truth.

In a brief section on the apostles,[9] Achard gives a compact theology of the Christian teacher. First, he offers some criteria by which one can tell whether a preacher or teacher is authorized by Truth to teach. The criteria are that the teacher or preacher says nothing that is not taught by Christ, the way Christ would teach it, and for the purposes for which Christ would teach it. Those who undertake to teach or admonish are going to meet opposition; they also run risks that others do not. To help compensate for these

5. Section six.
6. Sections twelve and thriteen.
7. Sections seven through eleven.
8. Section fourteen and fifteen.
9. Section sixteen.

risks Christ offers them both compunction to cleanse them from whatever dirt they get on them, and a spiritual anointing (unction) to soothe their bruises.

John the Baptist's baptism, Achard believed, was sign alone; Christ's was sign and reality; God's baptism (which the apostles received) is reality alone.[10] By the grace of his ministry, however, John was God's messenger (angel). Thus, he can be seen as mediating between the worlds of human beings and of angels, just as Mary, who by grace was set over all the angels, mediates between their world and the realm of the Trinity.

Like Richard of Saint Victor, Achard sees a progression in contemplation from contemplative gazing on the material and spiritual wonders God has made, to contemplation of them precisely as caused and sustained in being by God, to contemplation of things in the mind of God where their destinies, forms and purposes lie hidden. Achard maintains that the good for which all things were made is the good of the creatures themselves. Perceiving this final and infinite goodness of God, the contemplative is enkindled with the force of the divine love and tries to enkindle others with that same fire.[11]

As she does in the *Paradiso* of Dante, Mary leads the Christian into the third heaven where the Trinity dwells. Here Achard draws on the venerable image of purified Christians as the mother of the Word. When their minds are made pure by the grace of God, they not only see God, but are made fruitful by the Spirit of God and conceive the Son of God. They are rapt, expanded, and raised up by the force and attraction of divine love. They are in labor to give birth, they long to burst forth into contemplation, to pass wholly into God, who is praiseworthy, glorious, and superexalted for ever.

---

10. Section ten.
11. Section eleven.

THE SERMON

On the Feast of All Saints

IT BELONGS TO GREAT AND SPIRITUAL MEN,[12] who possess every sort of sanctification and sanctity, and who are rich in every kind of virtue, to speak of the solemnity of all the saints. I am not fit to speak of the solemnity of even one saint; to be honest, I do not find even one virtue in myself. Indeed, I cannot find in myself what is not in me. One who recognizes a single virtue in himself is then not unworthy to speak of a single saint; those who possess many virtues may speak of many saints; it is proper that one who sets out to speak of all the saints should possess all the virtues. This is as far from me as speaking about them is far above me, and hence I am not unaware of how presumptuous it could seem, and also be, for me to speak about them unless the obedience enjoined on me should excuse me. Nevertheless if it must be one or the other, I prefer to seem presumptuous rather than disobedient.

I am about to speak of the saints, but I will not follow the order in which the responses about them are arranged. That order descends from top to bottom according to certain degrees of dignity and merit. For me, since I am at the bottom, an ascent is necessary if I am not to stay there. Traveling from the lower ones, I will crawl through the higher toward the highest, and through these toward the summit of all the highest, to the Trinity, which sanctifies all the saints by its sanctity. Thus in what I

---

12. Here, Achard unusually uses the word for 'men' ('*virorum est*') as distinct from women.

say, though not in reality, 'the last will be first and
Mt 20:16, par. the first last'.† But where will I find a ladder by
which I who am on earth can reach even the last
saints among those who are in heaven? They are
exalted, and I cannot reach them. I will do what I
can; I will turn to those who are still with me in the
2 Co 5:6 body, away from the Lord.† To the extent that they
are closer I will have easier access to them; at the
same time I will put some limit to my presumption.

I must not turn away from you to whom I
am now speaking in order that those I want to
meet may meet me more quickly. 'You are citizens
Ep 2:19 with the saints and members of God's household',†
Col 1:12 sharers with the saints in the light,† sanctified by
God in the very Holy of Holies 'whom God the
Jn 10:36 Father sanctified and sent into the world'.† In the
Jn 17:19 world he sanctified himself on your behalf,† so that
1 Jn 3:3 you might be holy in him as he himself is holy,†
although not to the same measure. Among you
then, and those similar to you, who are called to
Rm 1:7 be saints,† I will attempt to go on and explain the
festival of all the saints in accordance with certain
distinctions among the virtues. 'The kingdom of
God is within you', and 'God's temple, which you
Lk 17:21; 1Co 3:17 are, is holy'.† Where God's kingdom is, and in
God's temple, the feast of God's saints is to be
celebrated and is being celebrated—that is, not
by you, but in you. Those who do not celebrate
a feast more perfectly inwardly do not celebrate
it well outwardly. Let each of you, then, recog-
nize in yourself, in accordance with the virtue in
which you excel and the grace you feel is most
effective in you, which part of the solemnity is
most suitable for you, or the part to which you
are best suited, which part you discern in yourself,
or rather in which you may discern yourself. I
consider them blessed who celebrate even one part

of such a great festival in themselves, more blessed those who celebrate several parts, and most blessed those who celebrate all of them. Lest I prolong this introduction more, let me come to the point, beginning with the virgins.

I

2. It is enough to speak about one virgin, since what will be said of one pertains to all. All are represented in and to this one. Although she is one, she is the mother of all, and through this unity she contains everyone in her womb and nourishes everyone at her breast. This is your mother too, who conceived you not of man but solely of God, 'the one who willingly begot' you in her 'by the word of his truth'.† You 'were born not of the Jm 1:18
will of the flesh, but of God',† through this your Jn 1:13
spiritual mother. You are reborn in her 'of water and the Holy Spirit':† from water on account of Jn 3:5
your mother, from the Holy Spirit on account of your Father. Water is, as it were, a kind of seed of this mother; it is clean and cleansing; the Holy Spirit is, as it were, a kind of seed of God, fertile and fertilizing. This mother of yours is the bride of the Lamb,† the bride of the Virgin's Son who Rv 21:9
is himself a virgin, so that his virgin bride—of a virgin groom, indeed—is virgin and bride.[13] His spouse comes from his side, and the virginity of his bride comes from his own virginity.[14] This is

13. This association of the two titles 'virgin' and 'bride' is founded upon Luke 1:26–27 and 2 Corinthians 11:2.

14. See Genesis 2:21 and the traditional theme of the church born from the pierced side of Christ, which may be found, for example, in Richard of Saint Victor, *Liber exceptionum* 2.1.8, ed. Châtillon, 226–227, and Jean Châtillon, 'Une ecclésiologie médiévale: L'idée de l'Eglise chez les théologiens de l'ecole de Saint-Victor', *Irénikon* 22 (1949) 134–135.

she whom the Apostle promised 'to present as a
2 Co 11:2 chaste virgin to Christ'.†

Just as this virgin has a universal significance, so too does her virginity have a kind of universality; as long as people do not share in it, they cannot be children of this virgin. Those who become children, immediately, and by that very fact, become virgins, or, if they become virgins, they become children as well. This virgin is unable to have and to bear children unless they are like herself, that is, virgins; nor can they be true virgins unless they are her children. Although she does not bear them
Gn 3:16 without pain,† she does conceive and bear them without corruption; she makes even those who are corrupt into virgins by participation in her virginity. Her universal virginity is chastity, the moral purity without which no one sees God.

To this virginity taken in a universal sense belongs not only that chastity that is customarily and particularly called virginal, but also that of widows and married people. This virgin is chaste in both flesh and spirit—chastity of the flesh is free of illicit acts; chastity of the spirit is free of illicit consent. The latter cannot exist apart from the former external kind; the former can exist without the other internal kind, but it cannot be fruitful. Although by itself it diminishes sin, it cannot by itself produce merit. Thus for a bride of Christ to be holy in body is not enough, unless, as the
1 Co 7:34 Apostle advises, she is also holy in spirit.† She must
Ep 5:27 be spotless in body and unwrinkled in spirit†—
unspotted by pollution, unwrinkled by duplicity. It would be duplicity if what appeared outside were not also inside.

3. Because of this twofold holiness or chastity of the bride, the bridegroom says to her in the

Song of Songs: 'Come from Lebanon, my bride, come from Lebanon'.† Because Lebanon means 'brightening',[15] the word Lebanon is repeated to signify the twofold brightening of the bride. Her twofold brightening is her chastity and her purity. Spiritual purity, wherever it is, is brightness, yet it is not everywhere brightening. Although brightening cannot exist where there is no brightness, brightness can exist where there is no brightening. Brightness may be said to be somewhere either naturally or accidentally; brightening can only be where brightness is accidentally. 'Wisdom reaches everywhere because of its purity'; this purity is 'the brightness of eternal light'† and is not accidental, but substantial—indeed, it is the very substance of wisdom, or wisdom itself. The bride has her brightness, not from herself, but from her spouse; the brightness of the bride is nothing else than a kind of participation in the brightness of the spouse, and so it is not simply brightness but rather a kind of brightening. What the bridegroom has by nature, the spouse only obtains through grace alone.

Sg 4:8

Ws 7:24, 26

This brightening or chastity of the bride should not be understood only in reference to physical fornication, but to spiritual fornication as well; that is, everything that could divide the bride from her spouse to keep her from clinging to him. If you ask what could do this, think of every sin in which she disdains the bridegroom, in which she prefers something else to him—that is, everything that she cannot do without detriment to her soul. The perfectly chaste bride avoids not only whatever

15. See Sermon 13.11 and the notes about the meaning of 'Lebanon'. There, as here, Achard distinguishes carefully between brightness (*candor*) and brightening (*candidatio*).

may separate her completely from her spouse, but even whatever may put her a slight distance away from him.

Hence, she must be on guard not just against
major offenses but even against lighter ones. As
long as 'the perishable body weighs down the
Ws 9:15 soul',† and 'the desires of the flesh are against the
Ga 5:17; Jm 3:2 spirit',† 'we all offend in many things'.† 'There
is no one just on the earth, who does good and
Qo 7:21 does not sin';† not even 'the stars are pure in the
Jb 15:15; 25:5 sight' of God.† One of the purer stars, that disciple
who, a chosen virgin, is beloved above the rest by
God—the one who reclined on the Lord's chest at
Jn 21:20 supper,† who as though on account of the merit
of his greater purity, comes closer and clings to
Ml 4:2 the Sun of righteousness†— this one still says of
himself and of those who are like him: 'If we say
that we have no sin, we deceive ourselves, and the
1 Jn 1:8 truth is not in us'.† To such persons confession is
necessary, so those who celebrate the loftier feast
of virgins will not disdain to join to it the feast of
confessors too.

II

4. This part of the solemnity is needed most
by those who have not preserved the brightness
they received in baptism, but have soiled their
Rv 3:4 garments.† Therefore so that they may not be al-
together foreign to the whole feast and without a
share in it, the only remedy that remains for them
is to repent and confess, and so be admitted to
the feast of confessors. If there is 'great joy for the
Lk 15:10 angels of God over one sinner who repents'†—over
someone else's salvation—how great must be the
joy of those who repent over themselves, over their
own salvation! Great is the joy, great the feast—

provided the joy is good. We all have to confess not only the things we repent but also those which we do not repent, both bad and good—the good in praise of God, the bad in self-accusation.[16]

Two good things are to be confessed to God's praise, mercy and grace: mercy which removes the bad, grace which produces the good; mercy which liberates, and grace which helps. Mercy is a species of grace: for every mercy is a grace, but not every grace is mercy. Grace has been bestowed on angels, in whom there never was misery, and so strictly speaking one cannot speak of mercy there. Since mercy and grace are joined in a single phrase, so that some difference must be noted between them, mercy is properly taken to be the remission of sins, and grace is specially understood to be present in the granting of gifts. In accord with this distinction, mercy takes away, graces puts in; mercy removes demerits, grace brings merits; mercy cleans the vessel, so to speak, and grace fills the cleansed vessel; mercy justifies us from sin and vices, grace justifies us in virtues and good works. Mercy brings it about that you are not what you were, grace that you are what you were not;† through mercy you 1 Co 15:10
change from evil to not-evil, through grace from not-good to good.

In the midst of the evils of adversity another two things are to be confessed to God's praise, fairness always, goodness sometimes. Those who suffer must always confess that they suffer as they do by God's just judgment; sometimes it is our devout duty to think that by God's provident goodness we suffer what we do for our own good.

16. Hugh of Saint Victor, *Miscellanea* 2.64 (PL 177:626A): 'Confession is twofold, one of sin, the other of praise.' This idea comes from Saint Augustine: e.g., *Enarratio in psalmum* 29.2.19 (PL 36:225); *Enar. in ps.* 94.4 (PL 37:1218).

Punishment either corrects, cleanses, exercises, or tests: it corrects one to be converted, cleanses one who has been converted, it exercises one to be perfected, and tests one who has been perfected. It corrects for repentance, cleanses for forgiveness and purity, exercises for righteousness, tests for a crown. It corrects from evil action and a bad will, it cleanses from guilt and corrupt feelings, it exercises in virtue, it tests in the fullness of virtue.

5. Therefore let people confess these four things in praise of God: two, as was said, regarding their blessings, two among the evils of their adversity. In accusing themselves, they should confess two things regarding the evils of their perversity: sin and guilt:[17] sin, because they did what they should not have done, or because they did not do what they should have done;[18] guilt, because they are undeserving of grace and glory in that they did not do good, and deserving of punishment and wrath because they did evil. They are undeserving of the former because they avoided what was to be done; they are deserving of the latter because they did what they should have avoided; undeserving of the former because when they could they did not merit good, deserving of the latter because they merited bad by acting against what they should; undeserving of the former, because they did not carry out what was worthy, deserving of the latter because they carried out what was unworthy. They are undeserving of grace lest good be granted them

17. As we have seen, Achard distinguishes between sin (*peccatum*; *delictum*) and guilt (*reatus*) Guilt is the privation of grace and glory which exposes the sinner to a penalty or punishment. See Sermon 3.1–2. Hugh of Saint Victor avoids the word *reatus*. See Landgraf, *Dogmengeschichte* 4/1, 70–134.

18. See Sermon 6.6. Achard here reduces Hugh's two definitions (*De sacramentis legis naturalis et scriptae* 1.12.10; PL 176:363A: 'Sin [*peccatum*] is when what should not be done is done; negligence [*delictum*] is when what should be done is not done'), one for *peccatum* and one for *delictum*, to one.

in the present life; they are undeserving of glory, lest they be crowned in the future. They are deserving of wrath so that good things may be taken away from them; they are deserving of punishment so that evils may be inflicted upon them, eternal evils for graver faults, temporal evils for lighter faults. In many ways the Pelagian heresy denied sin. Another heresy, while confessing sin, denied the guilt; it asserted that if baptism was received and the faith kept, however much a person might sin and however long a person might persevere in sin, no one would deserve damnation.[19]

This confession of sin and guilt is to be made not only externally, but also internally: internally before God, externally before a human being, God's vicar;[20] thus one will be a true Judah, that is a 'confessor',[21] not only openly but secretly as well. In fact, confession of heart and mouth is not enough, but there must be confession in deed as well;[22] otherwise, the one confessing will be among those who 'believe for a time, and then in time of temptation fall away',† among those Lk 8:13
who confess with words but deny by deeds.† Some Tt 1:16
people are contrite at the time and promise full amendment, but then they seem to forget what they promised, and either commit again the things

19. On the Pelagian error see Augustine, *De gestis Pelagii* 35.65 (PL 44.357–358).

20. The word 'vicar' was frequently used to designate a priest. The distinction between confession to God and to his representative was bound up with the controversy regarding the necessity of oral confession that occurred during Achard's lifetime For Abelard and his disciples, confession of the heart (=contrition) was crucial; oral confession, although obligatory in principal, was not necessary for remission of sins. The Victorines opposed this vigorously: Hugh, *De sacramentis legis naturalis et scriptae* 2.14.1 and 8 (PL 176:549–554, 564–570); Pseudo-Hugh, *Miscellanea* 6.100 (PL 177:858A); Richard, *De potestate ligandi* 12, ed. Ribaillier, in *Opuscules théologiques*, 92.

21. Jerome, *Liber de nominibus hebraicis* (PL 23:781).

22. See Sermon 11:2.

they renounced, or, if they do not do them again, they do not make fitting satisfaction for what they have done.

So, let confession be in the heart through hidden accusation, in the mouth through open accusation, and in deed through worthy satisfaction. In confession of the heart are two things: sorrow regarding the past and a resolution for the future; sorrow regarding what was committed, a resolution not to commit it; sorrow because one did it, a resolution that henceforth one is not going to do it. In confession of the mouth there are also two things: rejection of the deed and promise of satisfaction. In the satisfaction itself—that is, confession in deed—three things ought to be present, so that one dismisses a sin committed against oneself; one does not repeat one's own sin, which has been dismissed; and one performs what the priest, Christ's vicar, has imposed for what was committed.

6. Because for me, and others like me who offend in many ways and bear much guilt for many things, a confession of sin rather than of praise is needed, I wish to add something about it.[23] Would that in it and through it I may become a participant in this festival! However, one thing frightens me: I confess about my confession that I do not confess truly and perfectly enough. To be perfect, confession must have three characteristics: it must be voluntary, bare, and pure. It should be voluntary, so that those who offended voluntarily also confess voluntarily. Let them first tell their

23. Achard's insistence on oral confession reflects not just his theological preoccupations but also the practice at Saint Victor. The *Liber ordinis* devotes a whole chapter to oral confession. Some faults could be confessed to any priest, others only to the abbot or his delegate who was available in the cloister at certain hours.

iniquities themselves, so that they may be justified; they should not wait until someone else brings their fault into the open.[24] If, however, that should happen, let them not object, or resist, or give way to impatience and then erupt in anger, but rather let them turn within and in the end become contrite so that they bear with it calmly and are even thankful that another person has given them a wholesome reminder regarding what they may negligently have let slip from their mind. At least they are doing through another what they have not done by themselves. In this way it may happen that this too will be counted as a voluntary confession on their part.

7. While it is voluntary, let it also be bare. Let them not palliate their depravity and shroud it in circumstances that make it seem minor; let them tell it the way it happened and leave out nothing, regarding either the measure or the manner. Let them leave nothing of their consciences uncommunicated to the other, so that they pour out all the poison and open the whole wound. If it is hidden from humans, can it be hidden from angels, or from the one in whose sight all things are laid bare?† It cannot be hidden from humans Heb 4:13
either, though for the present one is more embarrassed before their eyes than before those of the angels or of God himself. 'Nothing is covered that will not be revealed, nothing concealed that will not become known'.† When the Lord, 'who Lk 12:2

24. Achard is telling his listeners not to wait until they are accused in chapter (see Sermon 13:25). He invokes an ancient form of Isaiah 43.26—'Tell your iniquities so that you may be justified'—a text cited by many twelth century theologians as an authority for the oral confession of sins; e.g., Abelard, *Sic et non* 151 (PL 178:1599A); Gratian, *Decretum*, II, p., XXXIII, q. 3, c. 37 and 39, in A. Friedberg, *Corpus juris canonici* (Leipzig, 1879): I:1167–1168; Peter Lombard, *Sententiae* IV, d. 17, c. 1, ed. Quaracchi, 846.

will bring to light the hidden things of darkness
1 Co 4:5 and disclose the counsels of hearts',† comes, there
everything will come into the light, as the day of the Lord announces them. If any wish that the sordid things about them be concealed there, let them disclose them here; that they may be covered there, let them open them here. Nor should they mix good things about themselves in their confession of the bad. They should disparage themselves there, not praise themselves; they should accuse, not excuse. Let them not accuse another there, or excuse themselves. If they excuse themselves, God will accuse them; if they accuse themselves, God will excuse them.

8. People to their shame look in many ways for excuses for their sins, so that these will seem to be nothing, or small. Sometimes to defend a person's wrong act they reproach and wrong God's right acting in the person. Why, they say, did God make humanity this way, able to sin rather than making
it unable to sin at all? 'Who are you, O human
Rm 9:20 being, to reply to God'?† You can destroy God's
work in you, but not set it right. Or perhaps in making you did he need you to be his counselor, so that he could make you better according to your
mind than to his? 'Who has known the mind of
Rm 11:34 the Lord? Or who has been his counselor?'† Was it
really better for humanity to be able to gain merit or not? Where there can be no sin, there can be no merit. There is no merit in being what one is,
when one cannot be anything else. The one who
Si 31:10 can transgress and does not transgress† is the one
who gains merit.

Others do not calumniate God's way of asking but do quarrel with his giving consent. Why does God, who made humanity so excellently as to

make it in his own image and likeness† allow it Gn 1:26–27
to fall into such a state of weakness—as though into the necessity of sinning—so that it is not without sin, and cannot be? As if God's just consent precipitated humanity into such a depth of evil, and not rather, humanity's own unjust will! Or as if the necessity of standing upright had to be imposed on humanity, which God had set upright with freedom of choice!

Others leave aside God's acting and giving of consent, but bitterly attack his foresight. If I sin, they say God, whose foreknowledge underlies all future things, foresees it. God's foresight cannot be shaken; while it stands, I cannot fail to sin; is what I cannot avoid, then, going to be imputed to me, or even called sin? This is a fallacious argument; if they do not take care they deceive themselves. Precedent foreknowledge adds no more force to why future things happen than does subsequent memory to why past things happened. Just as for someone to remember that something happened if it did not happen cannot be, so is it impossible for someone to foreknow that something is going to happen without its happening. But neither foreknowledge, nor divine permission—any more than memory—is the cause of why something takes place in actuality.

Others cast the fact that they offend back on God's plan and attribute it to grace and not to themselves. By God's great plan, they say, and by God's grace it happened that I fell into this disgraceful deed; otherwise I would not have fallen into it. God knew that it would do me good; he wanted me to do evil so that good might come; he wanted sin to abound in me so that where trespass first abounded grace might afterward abound all

Rm 5:20 the more.† Only on this account did I fall; this was the cause of my sinning; henceforth I will be humble and more careful, stronger and more steadfast. It is certainly true that sometimes after a sin people are brought to this state by God's superabundant and provident grace, but it is not grace but their own wicked wills that originate sin. Grace alone brings it about that good follows the evil they have done; they alone did the evil that preceded.

9. Others try to transfer to God the responsibility for their sin—not by grace dispensed but by grace withheld, not through a superabundance of grace but through a scarcity of grace; not by first making God extremely benevolent to them, but by complaining and accusing God of being less benevolent toward them, and maybe even malevolent. I know, they say, that 'this depends not on
Rm 9:16 willing or running but on God's mercy';[25]† he, and no one else, is at work in humanity, 'both to will
Ph 2:13 and to accomplish for his pleasure'.† But this too I know, that no one can 'be continent, unless God
Ws 8:21 grants it'.† What do people have whereby to will and do good, or whereby to guard against evil, which they do not receive? They would not have received it if God had not given it. But also if there were still someone who gave, there would still be someone who received. God does not choose to give me grace, and for this reason alone I do not receive it. Since I do not receive grace, the result is that I neither will nor do good, nor do I guard against evil. No one can do these things without grace. If, then, any fault exists, it seems that it must be imputed to him and not to me. I would do my part, if grace did its part.

25. See Sermon 2.2.

They say these things as though they possessed some grounds for exacting grace, or as though at least there was nothing in them making them not merely not worthy but even unworthy to possess grace; as though grace had never been offered to them only to have them reject it, or even been granted, only to have them cast it away. Even now, perhaps, grace is offered and rejected, and granted and cast away; those who do not do what they can in accord with the grace already granted them deserve by this to have no further grace conferred on them; rather, they deserve to have the grace they have diminished or completely withdrawn. Similarly, those who do not strive to be assisted as much as they can be by the goodness of nature are unworthy of the gift of grace.

Others put too much blame on Adam in order to free themselves of blame; they give too much weight to Adam's case in order to lighten their own, as if it were certain that whatever is bad in them is from Adam and nothing is from themselves. This is not the situation. After the first stirrings, whatever is of sin in them is not from Adam but from themselves. Moreover, not all first stirrings are to be imputed to Adam, but some to themselves too. When they did or do something that results in such stirrings arising in them, Adam is not the cause, but they are; nor are these stirrings from Adam originally, but from themselves actually; they should not be called original sin, but only actual sin.

Others put the blame, not on Adam, but, as Adam did on Eve,† and thereby transfer their guilt Gn 3:12
to someone else. They say: I saw it done by them, or they ordered or persuaded or even forced me to do it, and therefore I did it; for this reason, if there

is an offense, it is theirs, not mine; or if it is mine, mine is light and theirs is great. No one ought to accept bad example, nor should one assent to or obey another, except for the sake of good. Nor should fear of a mortal human being be put before fear of the living God, to fall into whose hands
Heb 10:31 'is a fearful thing'.† What excuse can or should it be that you see something done by a lying person, when you see in Truth himself that it is not to be done? That is where you see whatever you see truly. Or what defense is it if you hear a human being persuading or ordering something when you hear Truth himself dissuading and forbidding that very thing? Or what reason is there for you to fear one who can kill the body but cannot do anything to the soul, rather than one who, when the body dies, has the power to send the soul into hell fire?

Gn 3:13 10. Others, like Eve who blamed the snake,† turn the blame for their having transgressed on to the devil rather than to a human being, whether Adam or someone else. The devil, however, is the one who suggests a transgression, not the one who executes it. He can advise, but he cannot apply force. He compels no one to transgress, except perhaps those who freely submit to him first so that he can exercise such power in them.

Manichaeus introduced a second, evil nature, which he said was in him, but not so much from him as against him.[26] This, he said, is the only thing in me that sins. I do not do it; in fact, I am free from sin. Nature cannot be evil, but only the will; nor can there be two souls in one person , as he thinks, or two wills naturally contrary to each other.

The astrologer, when he accuses the stars to excuse himself, condemns not so much the stars

26. See Augustine, *Contra duas epistolas Pelagianorum* 44.5 (PL 44.612).

as the Maker of the stars. I was born under the star of Saturn, he says, and therefore I am greedy and sluggish, cool toward every good work; or, under the star of Mars, and therefore I am impetuous, quick-tempered, and wrathful; or, under the star of Venus, and therefore I am careless, lustful, and shameless; or while Mercury occupied its dwelling, and so I am wordy and garrulous. Stars do not have voluntary effects, but only natural ones. The only founder and maker of all natural things, whether causes or outcomes, is God.

Others introduce a necessity for sinning through a necessary sequence of causes that they call fate. Someone by his own choice slew himself with poison, a rope, a leap, or a sword, or in some other way laid his hand against himself and snuffed out his own life. He was fated to die thus, they say; hence he could not avoid dying thus. To avoid it, or to do something else, was impossible. Through things that were the product solely of free choice, someone had fallen into a great heap of wretchedness. Giving him up to fate, they say that from an ancient accumulation of things, when unformed matter was struggling, this load of misery was ordained by the arrangement of the fates. A common evil among people is to allege the following: Why are they inevitable? Because they were foreseen. And it is true that a sequence of causes by which the course of nature is directed is present in such things; by its impetus the things that nature alone moves are carried along. However, humans hold their heads far above by free choice; they are free from this sequence and unconstrained by any force of necessity in their minds, unless by chance they have voluntarily intertwined their wills too much with lower causes, so that subjecting themselves through love, they yielded themselves as slaves to them, and with their own hands they contrived around their necks a chain by which they can be dragged around, even against their will.

11. Others, explaining why they fell into sin, plead that not they, but their companions, caused them to do it, as though they could not or should not have been on the lookout themselves.

Others attribute their fall to circumstances: the opportunity presented itself, without a note of censure or a difficulty, and so I did it—as though what one hides from human notice were not censured by God and the angels, and by one's own conscience; and as though ability is necessity, and we do not have to avoid evil even with an effort, rather than do it without any effort.

Others refer the fact that they sin to the sin they commit, and establish as the efficient cause not the executor of the sin but its matter. The beauty of the woman overcame me, they say; because she was
Mt 5:28 so beautiful to look at, I looked at her with lust.† If you could have looked and not lusted, why did you look in order to lust instead of not looking so that you would not lust?

Others, to defend the will, hold up the weakness of the flesh as a kind of shield. Although it may be the flesh that experiences anything illicit, only the will consents. Guilt comes not from the experience but from consent.

Others excuse the fault of the will on the grounds of ignorance; when perhaps the only reason they do not know what they should do is that they do not want to understand and so act rightly.

Others use the pretense of ingrained habit, or the necessity of sinning they have contracted through habit, to excuse the will. Since these occur through the will, they do not excuse the will, but accuse it all the more.

So, let confession be bare of every cloak of excuse. Let those who confess remove their guilt by humbly accusing themselves, not stubbornly increase it by excusing themselves in the ways just mentioned, saying that is, through God's acting, through God's consent, through God's foresight or foreknowledge, through provident grace, through a lack of grace, through our first parent, through another person, through the devil, through union with another nature, through a constellation, or through a fatal sequence of causes, through chance, through circumstances, through the matter of the sin, through the weakness of the flesh, through ignorance of the mind, through habit, or through any necessity whatever.

12. That confession be voluntary and bare is not enough, if it is not pure as well. Otherwise, the barer it is the fouler it is. Some confess voluntarily and plainly, but impurely; their minds and consciences are impure. They proclaim their sin like Sodom;† they confess, not that they may be Is 3:9
ashamed of their shameful acts, but to boast of them. 'They, rejoice when they do evil, and delight in the worst things'.† Confession is pure when it Pr 2:14
is done with the proper intention and purpose so that the goods of the spirit are at issue and nothing else. The reasons for confessing are many—who can count them all? I will touch on some of them briefly.

Some mention their sins in public confession in front of many people so that others will not want to speak up. Some do so in private confession before one or several people so these will not be able to speak. Some confess not to be humbled

but rather to be esteemed—that is, so that those to whom they confess may say to themselves or to others. 'How great are these people, how little is their offense, and yet how minutely they detect and how strictly they reject such a trifle!' These are the people who strain out the gnat and swallow
Mt 23:24 the camel† in their confessions accusing themselves forcefully of the least things but hiding or excusing or even altogether denying weightier matters. Some think that they have fallen into poverty, or illness, or some other physical trouble because of what they have done, and so they confess only so that they may escape these things; others confess only so that they may not fall into them.

13. Those are five reasons for confessing that are not good. There are five good reasons: someone confesses to avoid the punishment of eternal damnation, or to take away the present torment of the person's own conscience, or out of a love for inner and spiritual purity, or from zeal for stricter personal righteousness, or for the sake of humility and self-abnegation. In these things confession is pure in relation to its purpose; if it is equally voluntary in its origin, and bare in its conditions, nothing seems to be lacking to its perfection.

Notice the form of a perfect confession in David: He says: 'I said, I will confess against myself
Ps 32:5 my unrighteousness to the Lord'.† 'I said, I will confess'; that is, I will not confess at another's prompting but at my own, by my own forethought and decision. See, there a voluntary confession. 'Against myself', not against another, so that I do not spare myself or touch another, excuse myself or accuse another. 'Unrighteousness', not righteousness in equal measure, so that by adding righteousness the unrighteousness is lightened; 'my', that is, attributing everything to myself and not to any

other person or thing. See, there a bare confession. 'To the Lord', so that the Lord is the motive. See, there a pure confession. Someone who confesses perfectly in this way is quickly changed from a confessor to a martyr, and after the festival of confessors deserves to be present at the festival of the martyrs.

III

14. Here those who previously offered a sacrifice of penitence offer a sacrifice of righteousness; those who previously suffered for a fault now suffers for righteousness; those who formerly suffered for their own sake, to avoid punishment, now suffer for Christ† so that Christ may be glorified in them Ph 1:29
and they in Christ. Now, by a rhetorical figure, we may call them martyrs. 'Martyr' means 'witness'. Even earlier they offered some testimony, but now it is more excellent: earlier they testified to their iniquity but now they testify to the truth, since those who earlier suffered for their wickedness now suffer for Truth himself. Earlier they testified to hell that it was hell; now they testify to paradise that it exists. Earlier they suffered to avoid hell; now they suffers to enter paradise.

First, they suffer for Truth in order not to offend against Truth; later they also suffer to please Truth. To want to avoid offending is one thing; to want to please is another. Someone may be so placed regarding two possibilities in relation to another person as to fear offending, but without secking or striving for favor. Others so strive for Truth that not displeasing Truth is too little for them if they do not please Truth as well. Then they seek not simply to please Truth but also that Truth may please them so that his yoke may be

Mt 11:30 easy and his burden light for them,† and they may
suffer for Truth with a kind of delight in Truth and
sweetness, not only patiently but cheerfully. They
2 Co 9:7 know that 'God loves a cheerful giver'.† When they
have reached this point, then they suffer for Truth
not, as earlier, simply that Truth may please them,
but that now Truth may so please them that it is
even congenial to them to suffer for Truth. They
Rm 5:3 boast of their tribulations† and rejoice that they are
considered worthy to suffer dishonor for the name
Ac 5:41 of Jesus.† Finally, they suffer for Truth, not only because Truth pleases them, but rather because they
please Truth; they understand, with the evidence
of experience, that they find grace in the presence
of Truth and that Truth knows them by name.
Interiorly, Truth embraces them sweetly and familiarly
Nb 12:8 because he speaks to them face to face.† He
speaks to them not as a Lord speaks to a servant, but
as neighbor to neighbor, and friend to friend. He
stations them for himself as if in a secret place, and
Ex 33:19 shows them—along with Moses†—all his goodness;
he reveals to them—along with David—the
Ps 51:6 uncertain and hidden things of his wisdom;† and
they learn—along with Paul—the sacred and secret
2 Co 12:4 things of the gospel of Jesus Christ.† They seek,
but never satisfactorily find, something that can
worthily repay Truth for his great worth.

15. There are, therefore, five reasons why these martyrs suffer for Truth. First, as was said, so as not offend to Truth, secondly, to please Truth; thirdly, so that Truth will please them; fourthly, because Truth already pleases them; fifthly, because they please Truth. At this stage, the martyrs, as though perfected and proven, boldly proclaim with the Apostle: 'Who will separate us from the love of Christ? I am certain that neither death, nor life',

nor any of the other things the Apostle lists, 'can separate us from the love of God that is in Christ Jesus Our Lord'.† Rm 8:35, 38–39

O the constancy of the martyrs! These are truly martyrs, but also wholly martyrs! You no longer detect anything in them that does not bear clear testimony to Truth. If you examine their habits, their acts, their speech, all their movements and their entire bearing, their behavior and life, everything displays a kind of form of truth, the form of Christ, the form of religion and perfect holiness. In some way God dwells in them bodily, if not personally; they always carry in their body the death and marks of Jesus, they give praise, and not only bear God in their hearts, but even in their bodies, so that you can say, not ineptly, that in some measure the power and wisdom of God are, as it were, incarnate in them.† In their very flesh you can perceive indisputable evidence of the divine power and wisdom dwelling in Christ. Col 2:9; 2 Co 4:10; Ga 6:17; 1 Co 6:20, 1:24

Those who have been so enlightened by Truth and so rooted in Truth are capable of enlightening and building up others: to enlighten them to know Truth, to build them up to love Truth; to enlighten them through teaching, to build them up through exhortation. Both pertain to preaching. But how are they to preach unless they are sent?† Rm 10:15
Accordingly, they are sent by Truth, and thus from a martyr of Truth an apostle of Truth is made, and we advance from the feast of the martyrs to the feast of apostles.

IV

16. 'Apostle' means 'sent'. We recognize whether people have been sent by Truth to preach

by the following signs: if they do not teach or advise anything not taught and advised by Truth, according to and for the purpose that Truth teaches and advises—that is, only what is required, and in accord with what is required, and for the purpose required, so that all things in their preaching are in harmony with Truth—that is, matter, form, and cause—so that they preach only the truth, in accord with the truth, and for the sake of the truth. In the ministry of preaching the apostles of Truth must be fully involved in the fight against the adversaries of Truth, sustain many things at their hands, and even contract something of the dirt and dust of common human life on the soles of their feet. Truth, however, provides for them in himself a kind of inner baptism and spiritual bath to counter the dirt and toil so that they are cleansed of the dirt and refreshed from their toil. That baptism, or bath, does two things, and so it consists of two things—that is, in devout compunction and in a kind of spiritual unction: compunction to cleanse, unction to provide refreshment.

V

17. Here, because of baptism, such a feast celebrates John the Baptist. But you are asking what is the reason for this. John, as he himself asserted,
Mt 3:11, et al. baptized in water—here is baptism in the Spirit.†
Certainly that John, a human being, baptized in water is true, but John in accord with the meaning of his name—'the grace of God'[27]—baptizes in the Spirit. The human John, because he was a human and not God, baptized only in water. John was also

27. Jerome, *Liber de nominibus hebraicis* (PL 23:886).

carrying out a figure of the Law, which had various baptisms effective only to cleanse the flesh. Those held under the Law washed the outside of the dish, but not the inside;† the Law embraced the hand, but not the mind.[28] Mt 23:25

Christ is both a human being and God; therefore he baptizes both in water and in Spirit; in water, because of his humanity; in Spirit, because of his divinity. He it is who cleanses the whole man, outside with respect to action, inside with respect to will, and embraces both hand and mind. As Christ himself said, 'God is spirit';† and because Jn 4:24 he is only spirit, therefore he baptizes only in the Spirit, to wash away interior and spiritual dirt. The disciples and apostles, whom he baptizes there, are perfect; they do not need to have their head and hands washed, that is, their intentions and actions, but only the soles of their feet,† that is, Jn 13:9–10 their thoughts and feelings. So, the baptism of John was only a figure; the baptism of God is only truth; the mean, the baptism of Christ, is both truth and figure: truth because of the Spirit, a figure because of water. What happens exteriorly in the flesh, by water, sensibly, is a figure and sign of what happens interiorly, in the mind, by the Spirit, intelligibly. Those baptized by God in the superior way are made spiritual, and hence their way of life begins to be in heaven† with the angelic spirits. They Ph 3:20 pass from the feast celebrated on earth to the feast celebrated more exaltedly in heaven; from the feast of human beings they ascend to the feast of angels.

28. This statement seems to have circulated in scholarly circles from about the middle of the twelfth century. Theologians cited it to contrast the impotence of the law with the efficacy of the gospel. The roots of the phrase seem to be in a gloss on Psalm 18:8, and in Peter Lombard's commentary on the same verse as well as in his *Sententiae* III, d. 40, 1 (ed. Quaracchi 2:734). Some, like Walter of Saint Victor, *Sermo 8 de Spiritu sancto* 3–5 (Turnhout: Brepols, 1975) substitute 'servile fear' for 'law'. For further references, see Châtillon, *Sermons*, 189–190, n. 5.

VI

18. The feast of John, who was, so to speak, both angel and human, and who is therefore a mediator between angels and humans, serves as a transition from a feast of bodily action to a feast of spiritual speculation.[29] John was a human being by nature, and he was called an angel because of the grace of his ministry. On the feast assigned to John, it is, as it were, human to be devoutly remorseful, not because of a human being, but by the grace of God; it is angelic to be spiritually anointed by God's grace. As action leads to devotion and devotion to anointing, so anointing leads to speculation. The speculators who are nearest first meet the one going there; he is taken from here by Angels, and received there by Archangels; they give him their right hands, lead him forth, and serve him. The roads of that region are not yet familiar to him, and
Ep 2:2 the powers of the air† plot from nearby against the one who is still at the edge of heaven. Because he is a creature of the world, and not yet superterrestrial, for the time being he can see the invisible things
Rm 1:20 of God only through things that have been made.† His guides are kind; they furnish a ladder for him and also certain steps to ascend. Since he is not yet capable of contemplating Truth in himself, they instruct him to gaze first on him in lower creatures. The Angels, as lower, teach him the truth and inform him about bodily creation; the Archangels do the same regarding spiritual creation.

19. Advanced by this instruction, he can now gaze upon Truth to some extent, even by himself,

29. '*Speculatio*' and '*speculator*' do not seem to be technical terms in Achard, but they became such in Richard of Saint Victor's theology of contemplation, where they stand for seeing God reflected in a created likeness—one form of contemplation.

and thus he joins the Powers by reason of this divinely received power. He exercises this power until it turns into a skill, and then he is counted among the Virtues. To the Powers it pertains to be able to speculate by oneself under all circumstances, to the Virtues, to be able to do so easily. A virtue is a power or faculty that is effective and ready, easily clarifying what is to be made clear. Having seen Truth in creatures perfectly, he sees that as they are in themselves they can never exist on their own, but must exist by means of another; not, however, out of another, but out of nothing. As he discovers their creation and principle, he is joined to the gathering of Principalities.

20. Going on from this point he ponders whether creatures that cannot exist on their own can at least continue by themselves. He comprehends that the one from whom they have their beginning must govern them if they are to continue to exist. The one he earlier found to be creator he now discovers to be the ruler as well; the one he earlier found to be God, he now finds to be Lord as well, and at this point he advances to the order of Dominations.

In the governance of things much occurs that can quickly shock the brute understanding—why, for example, God made these things and not those, and why he allows these things and not those, since the reason for making or allowing those does not seem to be less, but for the present seems to be greater. Because those who are spiritual discern all things,† he penetrates the great abyss of the 1 Co 2:15
judgments of God; he gazes upon their secrets and their hidden motives. He is then placed among the Thrones, and he himself becomes a kind of throne of God.

Stretching himself further, beyond motives and judicial causes,[30] he turns his mind to the formal reasons of things, which also comprise the ways of acting that are so many ways of God. Here he sees the creatures he had earlier seen in the world in God; those he had formerly seen in themselves he now sees in their eternal reasons and truths.[31] Here he is led into the fullness of knowledge, and so is joined to the order of Cherubim. 'Cherubim' stands for the fullness of knowledge.[32]

Finally, after the judicial and formal causes, he considers the final causes. He attends to the purpose or design that God has in doing or allowing anything, and he finds that it can only be for good and on account of good—not God's good, but ours—not because we creatures had deserved it, but because God is good to us by his own gracious choice. When he perceives how immense is the goodness of God in all things he is wholly inflamed with love of God. Here he is raised among the Seraphim, a name that means 'enkindled' or 'burning'.[33] Anyone who is enkindled within by the force and fervor of divine love tries also to enkindle others with the same fire.

21. In these three highest orders of angels, as has been shown, he gazes upon three types of reasons: judicial, formal, and final reasons or causes, and in these three he comprehends the judgments, ways,

---

30. Achard adapted the term '*causa judicialis*' from the vocabulary of judicial rhetoric, modifying it profoundly, however, to mean the unfathomable judgments of God. The 'judicial causes' concern the predestination of the saints (Sermon 13.32), and call to mind the divine forethought discussed by Eriugena, *De divisione naturae* 2.2 (PL 122:529AC). In *De musica* 6.6, 16–18; 6.8, 20, 22; 6.9, 23, Augustine wrote at length of *numeri judiciales*, the eternal numbers that measure numbers in time.

31. Sermons 12.8; 13.32.

32. Sermon 5.1.

33. Sermon 5.1.

and counsels of God. He recognizes that God is most just in his judgments, most wise in his ways, and best in his counsels. He understands that he is to be supremely feared because of his supreme righteousness, supremely revered because of his supreme wisdom, and supremely loved because of his supreme goodness. Here he is compelled to burst out totally in jubilation and to proclaim with those heavenly spirits in whose feast he is taking part: 'Holy, holy, holy, Lord God Sabaoth, who was, and who is, and who is to come'.† 'Holy, holy, holy': holy in judgments, holy in ways, holy in counsels; holy in the creation of things according to formal reasons, holy in the governance of things according to judicial reasons, holy in the consummation of things according to final reasons. 'Lord God Sabaoth': 'God' refers to creation; 'Lord' to governance or management; 'Sabaoth'—that is, 'almighty'—refers to the consummation. In creation was the beginning of things, in governance is their advancement, in might and from might will be their consummation. 'Who was, and who is, and who is to come': 'who was,' to create things that were not; 'who is', to govern what you had created; 'who is to come,' to consummate what you govern.

Rv 4:8; Is 6:3

VII

22. Those who have advanced this far through the festivals of humans and of angels, must by now have most pure hearts. On the feasts of humans they pass through the virtues of action; on the feast of angels they ascend through the virtues of speculation. Hence they also possess a most pure will on account of the active virtues, and a fully purified

reason on account of the speculative virtues. Here, then, the Virgin of virgins comes to meet them; she is the immaculacy of immaculacies, the purity of purities; that is, immaculacy and purity of heart consummated and perfected in accord with what this life allows. She is the mother of God; she bears God's Son, God's wisdom, God's contemplation.
Is 33:17 She causes us to see the King in his beauty,† to
contemplate God in himself. 'Blessed are the pure
Mt 5:8 in heart for they will see God'.† But no degree of
purity of heart is enough for this sight without the grace of God. God's Son must be conceived by the Spirit of God.

Then the pure mind is made fruitful by the Holy Spirit so that the Son of God may truly and abundantly be conceived by it when it is aroused and invited to contemplate him in himself, not by the presumption of its spirit, but by the impulse of the divine Spirit, since it is totally inflamed to see the face of God by the ineffable fire of divine love. Just as if the weight of the flesh has been put aside, it is totally rapt, expanded, and raised up[34] by the force of love and the attraction of internal sweetness. It is in labor as often as it has thus conceived a spiritual desire as if placed in the light of contemplation; it strives wholeheartedly to burst forth into contemplation and, as it were, pass wholly into God. It gives birth when it reaches what it strives for,
Mt 7:8; Lk 12:36; when [the door] is opened to the one knocking,†
Rv 3:20 when it is hidden in the hidden recesses of the
Ps 31:20 divine countenance,† when, following Paul, it is
2 Co 12:2 caught up to the third heaven.† It is in the first
heaven when it conceives, in the second when it

34. '*Tota raptatur, dilatatur atque subleratur*': Richard of Saint Victor, *Benjamin minor* 6.1–2 (PL 196:167D-175A) uses the three terms, *dilatatio, sublevatio*, and *alienatio*, to describe the three modes in which contemplation occurs.

goes into labor, in the third when it gives birth. Or again, after the first heaven of humans, and the second of angels, it reaches and enters the third heaven, that of the Trinity. Here, after the human and angelic feasts, it truly celebrates a divine feast. It carried out the first bodily; the second, spiritually; and this third, purely intellectually.[35]

VIII

23. This third feast of the Trinity is a feast in contemplation of the Father who is from no one, in contemplation of the Son who is from the Father alone, and in contemplation of the Holy Spirit who is from the Father and the Son. Just as the solemnity of Blessed John is a mean between the human solemnity and the angelic one, so is the solemnity of the Virgin Mother a mean between the angelic and divine solemnities. She belongs to the angels by reason of her virginity; she has in common with God the bringing forth of God. Hence as we pass through the solemnity of John the Baptist from the human to the angelic, so also through the solemnity of the Virgin Mother we rise from the angelic to the divine.

We distinguished four feasts in the human solemnity up to the feast of John the Baptist: the feasts of virgins, confessors, martyrs and apostles. Hence, just as in the gospel reading for today's solemnity eight virtues and beatitudes are distinguished,[36]

35. *Intellectualiter* is another technical term in the mystical theology of Richard of Saint Victor and Thomas Gallus (of Saint Victor, and then of Vercelli). It refers to mental activities that lie beyond the ordinary use of reason, a higher, mystical insight in which the distinction between knowledge and love scarcely applies. Hence, it has none of the cerebral overtones of the English 'intellectually'.

36. In the twelfth century, just as today, the gospel for the feast of All Saints was Matthew 5:1–12.

so in today's solemnity we find eight degrees or distinctions. In the first degree, that of virgins, the feast is of a kind of shared chastity and purity; in the second, of confessors, the feast is of penitence and confession; in the third, of martyrs, the feast is of righteousness and patience; in the fourth, of apostles, the feast is of learning and exhortation; in the fifth, of John the Baptist, the feast is of purification and consolation; in the sixth, of angels, the feast is of speculation and spiritual understanding; in the seventh, of the Virgin Mother, the feast is of angelic purity and divine fecundity; in the eighth, of the Trinity, the feast is of threefold contemplation and intellectual wisdom.

The ninth responsory, which is sung about all the saints together, pertains not to any distinction of solemnity but rather to the union of what has been distinguished. It can rightly be sung by those who have passed through the aforementioned feasts and joined together in themselves every kind of virtue. After this no further responsory should follow except the canticle *Te deum laudamus* ['We praise You, O God']. In all these, and for all these, it is proper to praise, glorify, and superexalt him alone, who is praiseworthy and glorious and superexalted by all and before all forever.[37] Amen.

37. Achard here echoes the *Benedicite* (Daniel 3:56–55), a canticle sung at Lauds.

Sermon 15: On Quadragesima

INTRODUCTION

THIS SERMON, WHICH SEVERAL MANUSCRIPTS refer to as a treatise, is long but easy to follow. It begins with a doctrinally dense exordium, then describes a passage through seven deserts which bring one to ever greater intimacy and likeness with God.

The exordium touches on many of the themes of Achard's theology and spirituality as these have become known to us in his other sermons. He discusses the depth of meaning and the mysteries latent in even a short text of Scripture. The Word of God is ineffable for us, but not for the Father who speaks him, or for the Spirit who scrutinizes all things—Achard is here justifying his elaborate explanation of a single scriptural verse: 'Jesus was led by the Spirit into the desert'.[1] He also anticipates the very long discussion of faith and reason that constitutes half of his sermon or treatise.

1. Matthew 4:1, the opening words of the gospel for the first Sunday of Lent.

The first section tells us that humanity deserted God before God deserted humanity; in Christ God returns to humanity before humanity returns to God, hence the principle: 'God is always first to approach, last to go away'. This does not seem to mean that there is a time when God stops loving a sinful human being, only that God cannot make his home in a person whose heart is closed to God. As always, Achard emphasizes that grace is primary in the work of salvation. The grace of God appeared most clearly in the Son's willingness to desert his divine prerogatives. Out of love alone he was prompted by the Spirit to be conceived by the Spirit, and thus he entered into the region of unlikeness whither humanity had gone. This was in order to bring sinful humanity back to God by suffering the consequences of sin himself.

Section two reminds one of the *accessus* which medieval scholars sometimes provided to a written work. Who was drawn? The Son of God. How? By bonds of love. Whither? Toward deserted humanity. In what way? The likeness of sinful flesh. Why? To condemn sin. In what manner? By assuming the penalty of sin in his flesh. He went out from the Father, he came among us, he raised us up by an *exitus-reditus*—an outgoing and return—the purpose of which was to restore the divine likeness in us by stamping his own image on us. The passage through the seven deserts will restore this likeness to every part of our nature, until finally we take on the mind of Christ, and join him in leaving the Father for the sake of fallen humanity.

Although most of what he says is applicable to any Christian at any time, Achard was writing for twelfth-century canons who were professed religious. In section three he rules out false motives for embracing the religious life: a desire for physical security, pride, and ambition, a trinity that parodies the three vows of poverty, obedience, and chastity. The only proper reasons are those connected with Jesus; the only proper prompting is the Spirit of Jesus. Those, however, who have begun through bad motives can now repent—for the wrong reason they find themselves in the desert with Jesus; for the right reason, let them proceed further. Even if someone has entered religious life for the right reason, being there is only a first step; there are more deserts to cross.

Into each of these deserts the Christian is led by one of the spirits of God, that is, by what later theology called the seven gifts of the Holy Spirit. These came into theological prominence during the twelfth century; their names are found in the Vulgate text of Isaiah 11:2–3 (Achard takes them in reverse order).[2] It was an ancient idea that there were seven evil spirits, each connected with one of seven basic inclinations toward sin. The Victorines called them seven '*vitia*'; in later times they were known as 'capital sins', that is, the 'heads' under which many subdivisions of vice and sin can be found. Achard calls the seven gifts of the Holy Spirit seven good spirits, and takes the opportunity to refer to several other scriptural 'sevens'.

In section five Achard puns on the name Lucifer, which means 'light-bearer'. He is now the shade-bearer, heralding nightfall rather than dawn. At the end of this treatise,[3] Achard will return to the symbolism of night and day, and speak of the alteration of night and day, tribulation and consolation, even in the life of those who have traversed all seven deserts. God's angels minister consolation to them, just as they did to Christ after his forty days in the desert.

Section six situates the land of promise, to be reached by crossing many deserts, in the interior of each human being. Those who have wandered off into the land of unlikeness return to the land of promise by returning to themselves. Here Achard takes up a theme that entered the tradition of Christian spirituality through Gregory the Great's life of Saint Benedict: *habitare tecum*, 'to dwell with oneself'.[4] In sinning, people become strangers to themselves, vagrants or fugitives on the earth.[5] The empty selves left behind are

---

2. The seven gifts are one of the septenaries treated by Hugh of Saint Victor in his *De quinque septenis*, ed. Baron, *Six opuscules spirtuels*, SC 155 (Paris: Cerf, 1969) 100–119 (=PL 175:405–414). See also Hugh's *De septem donis Spiritus sancti*, ed. Baron, *Six opuscules*, 120–133. Achard puts them in opposition to the seven capital sins; see Sermon 10.6.

3. Section thirty eight.

4. *Dialogues* 2.3, ed. A. de Vogüé, SC 260 (Paris: Cerf, 1979) 141–151 (=PL 66:136). Gregory connects the theme with the prodigal son (Luke 15:17) and Peter's vision in prison (Acts 12:11). See Châtillon, *Sermons*, 205–206, n. 86.

5. Genesis 3:9; 4:14. See, for example, Hugh of Saint Victor, *In Ecclesiasten homiliae* 8 (=PL 175:166CD): 'Therefore, it is said to you: Adam where are you? (Genesis 3:9), so that you may return to the truth and find the truth. . . . A

occupied by the devil. Now the devil must be cast out; they desert their false allegiance to him by abandoning mortal sin. They must return to themselves and dwell there with Christ.

The first step in the desertion of mortal sin is usually prompted by the fear of the Lord.[6] Basing himself on a tradition going back to Saint Augustine, Achard says that this initial fear is to be cast out or perfected in a chaste fear that is identical with perfect love.[7] At first the fear of hell restrains a person from serious sin, but such fear leads to the hope of glory and love of righteousness, which lead one to ever greater purity of heart. Put another way, faith, the foundation of the Christian life, has an inner tendency to expand into hope and love.[8]

As love of God increases, so love of the world and temporal things decreases.[9] For Achard, the second desert is abandonment of the world for the cloister, to which one is lead by devout affection for God. To give up a impure love of earthly power, willfulness, an abundance of riches, and a desire for human praise, however, one need not leave for the cloister; the Spirit of God can teach any Christian to abandon power and riches, willfulness, and even human esteem, or to use them in such a way as not to be possessed by them. Granted this, and Achard certainly does not deny it, all that follows can apply to any devout Christian.

Having abandoned the devil and the world in the first and second deserts, Christians are now called to abandon their very flesh.[10] Achard's moral anthropology of the body sees the body as an integral part of humanity, necessary for a human being's complete happiness

---

wanderer and fugitive, you will be unstable all the days during which you are not with and in the truth. Nor will your heart find a place where it may rest . . . . Up, down, far and near, wherever it goes, (your heart) will not find rest, until it finds (the truth).'

6. Section seven.

7. Augustine, *Enarratio in Psalmum* 127.7 CCSL 40 (Turnhout: Brepols, 1956) 1871–1872 (=PL 37:1680); Landgraf, *Dogmengeschichte* 4/1:276–371.

8. Hugh of Saint Victor, *De sacramentis legis naturalis et scriptae* (PL 176:35D): 'Faith is in some way the basis and beginning of good in the human being; from it love is born, and from love hope is conceived.' See Landgraf, *Dogmengeschichte*, 1/2:25.

9. Section eight.

10. Section ten.

in heaven.[11] To concretize the metaphor he uses next, one might say that the body is like a cowboy's prize horse—it must be taken care of because he may need to ride it a long way. One should provide what it needs, but not pamper it, keeping in mind that it is easy to mistake superfluous wants for necessary sustenance. One wants a willing partner, not a master or an enemy.

The fourth desert concerns the will, God's likeness. Achard sees the will as intermediary between flesh and reason. The promptings of the senses lead the will to want many things; the mind must discern which of these wants are legitimate. This, in the theology which was then developing, is the task of conscience. However, at times even a good will should be set aside and another's will followed. To will thus to resist one's own will requires divinely given fortitude. Religious, vowed to obedience, have good reason to submit their wills to another, although, surprisingly, Achard does not insist on this.

By far the longest section of the sermon concerns the fifth desert, wherein reason is reasonable enough to acknowledge its limitations — resulting from both nature and from sin — and to give way to faith. Here people make the ultimate sacrifice, offering not just part of themselves, but everything, a holocaust rather than just a sacrifice. The ten mysteries Achard is going to list should be believed first; then they can be discussed and studied, although they will never be fully grasped. Later, near the end of this long section,[12] Achard develops the relations between faith and reason in an original way. On these matters reason cedes to faith. Faith is meritorious, but faith, which will pass away, gains merit not for itself but for reason. Faith sows, reason will reap. When we pass from this world to the next, faith will yield to reason just as the sacraments will yield to the realities they signify. Faith and the sacraments are necessary for the beginners and proficients of this world, not for the perfect of the world to come.

The ten mysteries of faith Achard considers[13] are ten theological

11. Sermon 12.8.
12. Section twenty-nine.
13. Sections seventeen through thirty-three.

issues that deeply concerned him and other theologians of his time. That almost all of them are mysteries in a strict sense, facets of the one central mystery of the coexistence and loving union of the infinite and finite is manifest in the doctrines of creation; incarnation and eucharist; grace and freedom, predestination and judgment, and their interplay in the ontology and the drama of good and evil. Achard knows by hard effort how intractable these are to the scrutiny of reason.

In his descriptions of the last two deserts Achard reaches a rhetorical and mystical climax. These two should be taken together: it is only for those who have deserted their neighbor for God that the seventh desert, the desertion of God for neighbor, pertains. An infinite distance separates Christians who are chronically too busy with good works (which they enjoy) to pray (which is difficult for them) and Achard's contemplatives, who have experienced the joys of contemplative union with God and freely give them up because they share Christ's ecstatic compassion for their brothers and sisters. Much closer to Achard's contemplative are the parents who long to find an hour of quiet for prayer and spiritual reading in the midst of a day devoted to their small children or harried pastors hoping to spend a few days in retreat.

God finds irresistible a person who is empty of self and detached from all else. God is drawn there, like air to a vacuum. This is Achard's premise throughout this work. Now, in the sixth desert, we see what it means to be God's dwelling place. In fact, one has not so much gone outside oneself as deeper inside, into the nuptial chamber. There Christians are made one spirit with God so that they see and love with the mind and will of God. Each spiritual sense perceives the beauty and wonder of God. The splendor of God is totally absorbing; they love their brothers and sisters and commend them to God's love, but they cannot for the moment actively serve them with the spiritual and corporal works of mercy. They are at rest, utterly at peace.

To be thus absorbed is to be conformed to the likeness of Christ, to have recovered completely his image and likeness in which they were created and recreated. It brings with it mystic insight into truths of faith that hitherto had remained opaque. They begin to view earthly life from Christ's perspective. They see the misery of human beings, and wish that others could be as they are. They remember the example of Christ, who emptied himself to be among human beings, for human beings, as a human being. They would like to rest with Christ, but his very love, the love that drew him from heaven to earth, draws them, and they desert God for human beings.

THE SERMON

On Quadragesima

JESUS WAS LED BY THE SPIRIT INTO THE
Mt 4:1 DESERT'.† This much of the gospel reading
is enough; for the purposes of this sermon
we have no need to proceed further. But I am
not adequate to present adequately even this brief
passage that I have proposed. I cannot now utter
all the words that occur to me regarding this sen-
tence. I am afraid of saying too much regarding
this short sentence, because I am halting in speech
Ex 4:10; 6:12 and uncircumcised of lips.† Is this not a short and
modest sentence: 'Jesus was led by the Spirit into
the desert'? It is modest, but only on the surface: in
meaning and mystery it goes far beyond my reach.
The superficial meaning is modest, but the depth
of the understanding and the mysteries is great.

This Jesus, who is led into the desert, is the Word
of God on high—that Word, ineffable to us but not
to him whose Word he is; that great and profound
Word that was in the beginning with God, and
Jn 1:1 himself was God.† The Spirit, by whom Jesus was
led into the desert, is the one 'who searches ev-
1 Co 2:10 erything, even the depths of God',† who is himself
God no less than Jesus is. These two are not two
gods but the one God. Moreover, the desert into
which Jesus was led by the Spirit, although it is
humble and lowly, is itself deep. 'The heart of a
human being is perverse and unsearchable, and
who can understand it', if not the one who searches
Jr 17:9–10 the reins and the heart?† Jesus was led into this
desert when God came to humanity, which was
both deserted and deserting, deserted by him and

deserting him. It was not deserting because it was first deserted, but it was deserted because first it was deserting, yet later more deserting because now deserted. Humanity first deserted God, not God humanity. God is always first to approach, last to go away. From the time humanity deserted God it was rightly deserted by God, and once deserted it added desertion to desertion. Once grace was withdrawn, guilt increased and abounded all the more.† Rm 5:20

Later, however, that grace might appear as grace, and that God 'might reveal the riches of his glory'† Est 1:4; Rm 9:23 and prove his love for us,† Rm 5:8 as sin abounded all the more, grace too abounded all the more, although humanity had departed a long way from God, going away into a region of unlikeness,[14] going in spirit and not returning.[15]† Ps 78:39 God did not then 'in his anger shut up his mercies',[16]† Ps 76:10 but being rich in mercy he approached closer to humanity. What approach of God to humanity could be greater than that—God, tearing open the heavens of humanity and coming down† Is 64:1 wholly to humanity, was seen on earth by humanity and lived with humanity?† Ba 3:38 For the sake of humanity he was found in human condition,† Ph 2:7 indeed he was truly a human being.

Humanity's works were bad, exceedingly bad—not the works of some, but of all—not some works, but all of them. Indeed, there was no one to do good, there was not even one† Ps 14:3 neither a human being to do good or any good done by a human being. Humanity had no merits to draw God toward itself; rather God was repelled. But his goodness was greater than humanity's wickedness. Repulsed by our spirit, he was led back to us by his Spirit, and

14. See Sermon 9 for the region of unlikeness
15. See Sermon 9.1 and 15.25.
16. See Sermon 3.3; 13.15, where the same psalm verse is quoted.

conceived among us of the Holy Spirit. Although
merits were lacking on our part while demerits
Ho 11:4 abounded, he was drawn by cords of love,† his love,
1 Jn 4:19 not ours, because 'he first loved us'.† 'God so loved
Jn 3:16 the world, that he gave his Only-begotten';† God's
Only-begotten too so loved that he gave himself,
not only to be born in the world but even to die
in the world and for the world. No one took his
life from him, but he voluntarily and freely laid it
Jn 10:18 down.† He had come for that hour, the hour of
his suffering and dying. In the giving of the Son
the Father's love was not greater than the Son's;
in fact, the Son's love could seem greater in this
Jn 3:35 respect were it not that 'the Father loves the Son'†
no less than he loves himself. 'Out of the great love
Ep 2:4 with which he loved us',† God sent 'his own Son
in the likeness of sinful flesh', so that 'in the midst
Rm 8:3 of sin' he might 'condemn sin in the flesh'.†

2. Notice who was drawn, and in what way, where, by what, for what purpose, and how it was done. The Son of God is himself the one who was drawn. The way in which he was drawn is 'great love', the Father's and his own—the same love belongs to both and is undivided. Love is a pleasant bond that draws no one who is not willing. The desert where he was drawn is 'sinful flesh'. The way by which he was drawn is 'the likeness of sinful flesh'. The purpose for which he was drawn is to 'condemn sin in the flesh'—ours, in which good
does not dwell, not his, for 'he committed no sin,
1 P 2:22; Ps 51:5 nor did his mother conceive him in sin.† The way
of doing it—that is, of condemning sin in sinful flesh—was by means of a sin committed against his own flesh. This was like sinful flesh but only in suffering pain, not in guilt. There was 'our old self
Rm 6:6 crucified with him'† and condemned so that sin

has no dominion over and does not reign in our mortal bodies, but is arraigned and condemned by us too. God's Only-begotten was arraigned and condemned for the world's sin so that the world might know how worthy of blame and condemnation sin is since it could not be redeemed except by the death of the Only-begotten of God.[17]

'O how good and sweet is your Spirit, Lord, in' us† that you did not spare your own Son, but gave him up for all of us!† O how supereminent and overflowing is the love of Christ, which led him from the Father's bosom to us—led him out and led him in—and finally would lead him above! 'The Word became flesh'—see, the leading-in and the leading-out—'and lived among us'†—see, the leading-in! When 'he will reform the body of our lowliness, making it like the body of his glory',† that will be a kind of leading-above of him in us. All these good things were done for us by the good Jesus, not in accord with works of righteousness that we have done, but rather, as one who has received mercy says, 'he saved us according to his mercy'.† He was led by his Spirit into our desert, indeed into the desert which we are, where he left us an example so that we may follow in his steps† and be led after him and through him into the desert—not by the flesh but by the Spirit, and not by our spirit or any other one, but by his alone.

Ws 12:1; Rm 8:32; Jn 1:14; Ph 3:21; 1 Co 7:25; 1 Tm 1:13; Tt 3:5; 1 P 2:21

3. 'Anyone who does not have the Spirit of Christ does not belong to him'.† Those who desert what is to be deserted, not because it should be deserted but because of the necessities or superfluities of the flesh, or vainglory, or ambition—so that in the guise of religion they arrange for themselves a stage of some temporal advancement,

Rm 8:9

17. This same authority is cited in Sermon 3.3.

or so that they achieve some other temporal benefit or avoid some inconvenience—or any reason not connected with Jesus—they are led into the desert by the flesh and not by the Spirit, or if by a spirit, it is not by the Spirit of Jesus, but by their own spirit, or the spirit of the world, or perhaps the spirit of the devil. Those who desert what they should desert for the right reason—that is, they desert evil for a good that is not temporal but eternal—they are lead into the desert by the Spirit of Jesus, because of Jesus, and only through him. Without him we can do nothing; this depends not on the one willing or running, but on God who is merciful[18] and draws us on. 'Draw me after you',
Sg 1:3 O Lord.†

If any have been led into the desert otherwise than by the Spirit of Jesus, they should not despair. Jesus is merciful; he does not reject penitents, but willingly receives them—he himself came into the desert for this purpose. Let them repent of their motives; what they began badly let them pursue and perfect well. If they were not lead *into* the desert by the Spirit of Jesus, let them strive to be led *in* the desert by the Spirit of Jesus. Those who have been led into the desert by the Spirit of Jesus should be all the more solicitous to be led by that same Spirit in the desert. It is all too disgraceful for them to want to consummate in the flesh what they have begun with the spirit, so that they are not so much consummated as consumed. Not those who have been led by the Spirit of God, but—as one who was led by the Spirit of God even to say this said—those 'who *are* led by the Spirit of God are
Rm 8:14 children of God'.†

18. Romans 9:16; see Sermon 2.2.

Perhaps the silent thoughts of some whisper that because they have been led into the desert by the Spirit, it is already enough for them to be led in the desert by the Spirit, and they do not need to be led further into the desert by the Spirit. Are they not to be led where they are not yet? How can they still be led to where they already are? They could be led to the first destination, but not the second. Will they not have to be led out from it so that then they can be led back? But note that for such I propose and distinguish several deserts, so that they may recognize whether there is a desert they have already crossed, one they are still in, and one perhaps they have not yet reached. Let them be diligent in the one in which they are now to be led by the Spirit, and eager to be led by the Spirit into the one they do not yet grasp. As there are seven good spirits of God,† so are there seven deserts, spiritual as well as good, into one of which each of the seven spirits leads. Is 11:2–3 Vulgate; Rv 4:5

I

4. The first good desert occurs when a bad desertion, the desertion of good, is deserted, so that those who used to steal themselves away from God steal no longer,† and those who used to desert God now desert their desertion of God. They also desert the bad deserter, the transgressing angel, who did not stand in the truth but first deserted the good inhabitant and became the father of lying and the origin of the bad desert, through which one passes not into the land of promise but into a land of menace, not into the land of milk and honey† but into a land of fire and sulfur,† of darkness and Ep 4:28 Ex 3:8, 17 Rv 20:9

Ps 116:9 bitterness, into the domain not of the living† but
of the dead and dying. There death never dies, so
that those who are there are always dead. Those
who desert this bad desert, then enter the good
desert, and pass like one of the Hebrews from
slavery to freedom; they escape from Pharaoh's
power by spiritually leaving the Egypt of the spirit,
not by their own strength, but by the mighty hand
Ex 3:19–20 of God.† He and no other snatches his vessels
away from the powerful, armed man, vessels at
Rm 9:22–23 first of wrath and now of mercy.† He and no
Ps 146:7 other 'frees captives',† 'brings out the bound in
Ps 68:6 strength',† 'gives life to the dead, and calls things
Rm 4:17 that are not as those that are'.† He rescues people
'from the power of darkness' and transfers them
from the kingdom of the devil 'into the kingdom
Col 1:13 of his beloved Son',† calling them into 'his own
1 P 2:9 marvelous light'† from the palpable darkness of
Ex 10:21 Egypt.† Thus those who were darkness in the devil
Ep 5:8 may be light in the Lord,† 'in whom is no darkness
1 Jn 1:5; 1 Tm 6:16; Jn 1:9 at all,† because 'he dwells in inaccessible light',† and
'enlightens every one coming into this world'.†

5. With entry into this good desert, which occurs as soon as one leaves Egypt, seven demons—that is, more serious sins and the principal vices—leave, or rather are thrown out of a human being. These are Pharaoh's picked officers, the seven 'more evil' spirits whom the unclean spirit took with him when he returned to his former home, reentering it with them, so that 'the last state of
Mt 12:43–45 that person is worse than the first'.† Just as the
Holy Spirit has his group of seven, so too does
the unclean spirit have a debased imitation of his
own. As it is written that 'the Lamb who takes
away the sins of the world' has 'seven eyes and
Jn 1:29; Rv 5:6 seven horns',† so is the dragon who pursues the
woman, that is, the Church, described in the book

of the Apocalypse as 'having seven heads'.† Pharaoh Rv 12:3
too, in his vision, first saw seven full and beautiful ears of grain on one stalk; then he saw the same number of thin and blighted ears.† To this evil seven Gn 41:5–6
the seven nations that first inhabited and possessed the promised land belong; the Lord cast them out before the face of the children of Israel when he lead them in there.[19] We are not, however, to take this in relation to the promised land promised to us long ago, but which we are not to receive until after this life has run its course. No nation touches its borders there where sin and vice find no place; it is a glorious inheritance, which has no fellowship with darkness.† Ps 16:6; 2 Co 6:14

He too, who was made there in light, remained there as long as he was without darkness. When iniquity was found in him, he was thrown down from there, or rather he himself fell from there like a flash of lighting, pulled down by the weight of his own iniquity. This was Lucifer, who rose at dawn,† but he is no longer the 'light-bearer' but Is 14:12 Vulgate
the shade-bearer. At first he was the light-bearer in his rising, but afterward the shade-bearer in his setting; the light-bearer at dawn, the shade-bearer in the evening.

Another land of promise exists, far inferior in beauty, in situation, and in every other way. It is the first for us to enter, and those who have not been led into it will never be led into the other. Only one way leads from this to the other, so that no other passage to it lies open to us. Not just the children of Israel, but even the Canaanites—that is, virtues and vices—can inhabit and possess this one; the Canaanites are barred from the other.

19. Numbers 13:28–30 (29–31 Vulgate), the reference given by Châtillon, lists only six nations.

Gn 12:6, 13:7, etc. 6. But the Canaanites get there first.† 'What is spiritual is not first, but what is physical, and then
1 Co 15:46 what is spiritual'.† We are all by nature children
Ep 2:3 of wrath;† the old self is born before the new self is reborn. This land of promise exists in us; it is the dwelling place of our heart—that is, our inner self—which must dwell with itself in itself—or rather, it must dwell there with Christ who
Ep 3:17 dwells there through faith.† When first it sinned humanity lost this dwelling place of its own as well as that of God, which pertains to the higher land of promise. Cast away from God's face, and from the face of a certain inner land—that is, its own heart—it became a wanderer from itself and a fugitive from
Gn 4:12, 14; 5:29 God upon the land the Lord has cursed,† seeking outside the peace it had lost and never finding it.

When humanity went out from itself, the victor over humanity, its expeller, the devil, immediately entered into humanity as though into a vacant house, and as if by winner's right took possession of the whole of humanity, subjecting it in servitude
Rm 7:14 to himself as one sold under sin.† It committed
Jn 8:34 sin, and became a slave of sin† and of the author of sin as well. At length, however, through the power and grace of Christ, the prince of this world, who earlier had been cast out of heaven, was also cast out from humanity where he had set up his residence—cast out not only from the soul alone but also from the body, for our bodies, the Apostle said, have become members of Christ and a temple
1 Co 6:15, 19 of the Holy Spirit.† Finally, he will also be cast out from the upper world, to be sent to the prison of the abyss and driven down to the depths of hell. However, he never leaves willingly; he does not desert anyone, he is only deserted. Those who desert mortal sin desert him—the kind of sin in

which a living person is at the same time dead: alive in the flesh, but dead in the spirit; dead by the first death, and worthy of the second; a sharer and member of the one who is the prince and source of death, through whose envy death entered the world.† Ws 2:24

7. Desertion of mortal sin generally happens because of the fear of the Lord that is the beginning of wisdom.† This fear is the starting point, but it Ps 111:10, etc.
is perfected in the chaste fear that lasts forever, and that consists in the perfect love that casts out the initial fear; it is however necessary at the beginning. While people are entangled in the love of sin, they cannot receive the light of the love of righteousness and purity simultaneously with this dark love; through the holy love they drive out the impure love and thus destroy the reign of sin in themselves. 'What accord has Christ with Belial?'† 2 Co 6:15
People can simultaneously love a fault and fear righteousness, embrace sin and dread punishment; as long as they love impurity more than they are afraid of its penalty, the stronger love will prevail to keep in evil instead of the fear freeing them from it. If, however, fear so increases that it superabounds, it loosens the bands of iniquity and the shackles that oppress† and so leads the soul of the captive Is 58:6
out of prison and strikes off the yoke of wretched servitude.

Thus does the first spirit of God, the spirit of fear,† lead into this first desert, so that people Is 11:3
desert mortal sin at least. The fear that brings this about is not of temporal punishment but of an eternal punishment, not yet felt but only believed in. Faith does not arise from humanity; it is 'the gift of God'†—once sin has been rejected, faith Ep 2:8
introduces the fear of hell which then induces

hope of glory and love of righteousness, but the fear of hell is not yet mature enough to make a person desert the world. Often those who have disregarded what is unlawful now pursue what is lawful with more eagerness and less anxiety; they think themselves allowed now to use the world the more in that they misuse themselves less in its use as they keep themselves from graver and damning offenses, if not from lighter ones. Thus they are divided, part of them seeking the things of God, and part those of the world. God's love is greater, and so it is supreme in them, but it is not alone. Hence, they have Christ as their foundation, but
1 Co 3:11–12 they still build on it with wood, hay, and straw.†

II

8. Meanwhile, the fire of divine love, having been nurtured long and devotedly on the altar of the heart, progresses to the point that it can easily burn up these things like so much perishable stuff, doing away with the love of temporal things by its own power. Thus they move their minds on to the next level, so that those who earlier abandoned the prince of this world now despise this world itself; they now cast off vanity, just as earlier they cast off iniquity. In this way they are led into the second desert by the second spirit, the spirit of
Is 11:2 godliness,† that is, of a kind of godly and devout affection for God, arising from love and not from fear. They do not take up the habit of religion and choose a claustral or solitary life because they are afraid that if they do not do so, but stay in the world, they will perish with the world, but
2 Tm 2:4 in order 'to please the one who enlisted them'.†
Henceforth they are concerned only for the things

of God,† and seek 'the things that are above, not those on earth'.† Just as in the first desert, where in deserting the spiritual forces of evil† they deserted the seven chief demons, so here too, in disdaining the world subject to vanity, they disdain four things above all, the four elements of this world; namely, earthly power, their own freedom, an abundance of riches, and human praise—that is, vain glory.[20] These are what people gripped by the vanities of the world feed upon the most so that they may have power over others and no one may have power over them—or if they cannot rule over others at least they will not have to subject themselves to others—and that 'their storehouses may be full, overflowing from this one to that', so that from all these the words that follow may result: 'They call happy the people who have these things'.† Such people are honored with the applause of human favor and with voices calling out: 'Bravo! Bravo!'† Those who reject the world with its charms and seek to delight in the Lord shout back with a brave spirit: 'Vanity of vanities! All is vanity'† and 'Happy are the people whose God is the Lord', rather than 'Happy are the people who have these things'.†

1 Co 7:32
Col 3:1–2
Ep 6:12
Ps 144:13, 15
Ps 40:15
Qo 1:2
Ps 144:15

III

9. When people have been led this far, where can they go further? They have deserted the wicked devil; they have also deserted the vain world. What is left to desert? Do they perhaps have to desert their own flesh? But the situation of the flesh is different, for its relationship to humans is different. The devil is against humans; the world too, although made for humans, is not part of

20. See Sermon 13.23.

humans, but outside of them. By contrast, the flesh
of humans is part of them; it is in them, and in a
sense it is them, so that 'people never hate their
Ep 5:29 own flesh'.† Eve too was made as a help to Adam.[21]

The flesh is like a beast on which the spirit sits;
the spirit must provide for it lest it collapse on the
way—the Lord himself fed the crowds in the desert
Mt 15:32; Mk 8:3 so they would not collapse on the way.† It may still
have a long way to go, for the way is as long as
life; whenever life comes to an end, there the way
ends as well. Moreover, on its way it must bear the
Mt 20:12 burden of the day and the heat;† it has to worry
lest being weaker in body, it succumb under the
burden.

However, an unnecessary and harmful satisfaction of the flesh often insinuates itself under cover
of necessity and honor. People indulge it beyond
the proper measure, not just providing adequately
for necessities but for its desires as well, going after
its lusts in many things. Their minds are still carnal;
Rv 2:17 they do not yet know 'the hidden manna',† 'the
Ps 78:25 bread of angels'† that people eat in the desert; by
the strength of that food Elijah walked for forty
1 K 19:8 days'.† They do not understand that they are not
to walk on the spiritual path in the vigor of the
flesh but of the spirit, and not their own spirit but
God's. He it is who helps our weaknesses. Those
who trust 'in the Lord will renew their strength;
they will assume wings like eagles, they will run
Is 40:31 and not be weary, they will walk and not faint'.†

Meanwhile they do not know these things; they
will know them later, when distress gives them understanding of what they hear. 'The beloved grew
Dt 32:15 fat, and kicked';† the man of their peace, who ate
their bread and was luxuriously supported by them,

21. In Sermon 5.4 the feminine element represented the will. Here it corresponds to the flesh, which is identified with *sensualitas* or the outer self.

and in whom they hoped to find a faithful helper, has lifted his heel against them†—in other words the outer self is against the inner, the old self against the new, Esau against Jacob, the flesh against the spirit. It happened that Eve tripped up Adam, and Hagar, Sarah's maid, rose up against her mistress—in other words, through pride sensuality rose up against reason. In the end, however, Sarah, prudent and schooled by the teaching of her experience, knows what will help; she understands that the class of servants and maids will not be corrected except by the whip. Therefore she uses a whip; she deals with the handmaid herself; she crucifies her 'flesh with its vices and desires';† she puts to death her 'members that are on earth',† bringing her body into submission.†

Ps 41:9; Jn 13:18

Ga 5:24

Col 3:5

1 Co 9:27

10. In this way do people grasp the third desert by the guidance of the third spirit, that is, the spirit of knowledge.† Thus they no longer think according to the flesh on account of the flesh; they are not wickedly unaware of its alluring deceits and its deceitful allurements, and they know that nothing hinders spiritual knowledge as much as the enticements of the flesh. But they do not desert the flesh indiscriminently—they do not desert it over necessary nurture but over superfluous measure; not to undercut, but not to overstep; not to oppress a fellow citizen, but lest they caress an enemy; not that it may be unable to follow, but lest it lead; not that it may be unable to serve, but lest it dominate. They care for it, but do not carry out its desires; they do not eliminate the exercise of the five senses, but as far as possible their pleasures; they deny softness to touch, sweetness to taste, sweet scents to smell, pleasant and beautiful things to sight, songs and pleasant sounds to hearing. Thus, insofar as the

Is 11:2

weakness of nature permits, they desert these five things in this third desert.

IV

11. Now after three deserts—like a three days'
Jon 3:3 walk†—they arrive at the mountain of God, that is, at their own spirit. After the flesh the first thing they meet is the spirit, since the spirit is neighbor to the flesh and united to it without intermediary. The spirit is the mountain of God, because in it lies the image and likeness of God: the image in reason, the likeness in the will.[22] The will is inferior to the reason as a likeness is inferior to a image; not any sort of likeness, but a more expressive and impressive likeness, is properly called an image. The will's part is to follow reason, so that reason commands and will complies.[23] The flesh is also moved by the ministry of the will, and the will often consents to the flesh when reason dissents from their agreement. The will, as inferior, and nearer to the flesh, intercepts first what comes from the flesh to the spirit and causes steps of
Ps 84:5 ascent to arise in the hearts.† But the will does not commit itself to such directly; it is suspicious of the neighboring flesh.

Having first been seduced by the flesh, the spirit became more cautious about other things. It fears that here too other snares may be lurking, and that the will, which presents itself as good, may in fact be evil. So it debates with itself about it, and carefully turns over in its mind all its angles under

22. Cf. Hugh of Saint Victor, *De sacramentis legis naturalis et scriptae* 1.6.2 (PL 176:264D) and Richard of Saint Victor, *Liber exceptionum* 1.1.1, ed. Châtillon, 104, 2.12.5, ed.Châtillon, 464; *Sermones centum* 70 (PL 177:1119C); Achard, *On the Distinction*, 33.

23. See Sermon 5.4; 7.2.

the scrutiny of reason. It looks at what it is for, in what respect, and for what purpose. It finds everything just and honorable, wholesome, and holy. It finds the will is upright, sound, and spiritual. It is not perverse because it has deserted the head of perversity, the devil; it is not vain because it has deserted the domain of vanities, the world; it is not carnal because it has deserted the flesh, or rather fleshiness. It has deserted vice, not nature; allurements, not its own substance. There is something it ought to be for, something in respect to which it ought to be, and it should have some purpose: it is for good works, measured, and its purpose is God. This will is seen as something to be held on to and guarded, not disdained or lightly valued, not rejected or deserted. Why should something good, and only good, be deserted? The other things they deserted earlier were not deserted without cause; they had to be deserted because they were bad in themselves or bad for them. However, a will of this kind is both good in itself and fruitful for one who possess it, harmless to anyone else, and acceptable to God. Who would not say that it is to be defended with every effort of mind and body rather than dismissed?

12. But perhaps what in itself should be kept because it is upright, godly, discerning, and beneficial, should sometimes be dismissed in favor of the will of another. The will of another is either evil or good. If it is evil, then who but evil people would set aside a good will for an evil one? If it is good, it is as good as one's own good will. One rightly exchanges an evil will for a good one, but why set aside one's own good will in order to follow another's? If people subordinate an exterior substance to the spirit, and even the flesh, of a brother

or sister, or their own flesh to that one's spirit, some order of justice may be present, but to curtail their own wills in favor of another's, especially if their wills are good and holy, to put one spirit in place of another, equal for equal, their own for another's—what order of righteousness is this? What reason can require it? They remember the divine precept, that they love their neighbors as themselves—not more than themselves, but also not the same amount as themselves. It is introducing the idea of a model rather than a measure, a likeness in nature rather than an equality in amount.

Those who reason thus in defense of their own wills are being led by opinion rather than by reason. There is an appearance of reason, not its reality; fallacious reason, not trustworthy; sophistic reason, not true. The surface of the argument has been
Si 19:23/26 dressed up but 'its insides are full of deceit'.† These disputers should be careful not to fall into the pit
Ps 7:16; Pr 26:27 they have made,† or entangled in their own nets, or caught in their own traps. If they follow their own arguments they are caught and slain by the sword of pride, which is what hides traps for them. They think of themselves as spiritual, as people who have already ascended to the spirit, and therefore they conclude that others should conform to their wills instead of conforming their wills to others. Those who are spiritual judge all things, and are
1 Co 2:15 themselves judged by no one.†

Ps 36:11 Here they are met by the foot of pride,† which supplants the foot of humility on which they stood well, as well as the foot of love on which they ran well. They are not yet spiritual, or if they are they become natural, not perceiving 'what pertains
1 Co 11:14 to the Spirit of God',† or even what pertains to their own spirit. 'They are in the dark and do not

know where they are going'.† They bear a log in Jn 12:35
the eye and do not see;† their minds are still set Mt 7:3
only on the flesh.† In order to be spiritual they Rm 8:5
should immediately desert their wills in favor of their brother's or sister's will; not simply in matters that charm or harm, but also in those that are permissible and agreeable as well as in those that give aid or assistance; not only in favor of a superior person's will, but also of an equal's, or even an inferior's; not only lesser goods for greater, but also equal for equal, and sometimes even greater for lesser—doing this will not be a lesser good but a greater. There are these three steps in deserting one's own good will: in the first there is God's good will; in the second, his pleasing will; in the third,
his perfect will.† Rm 12:2

13. Who can doubt that the fourth spirit, the
spirit of fortitude,† leads into this fourth desert? Is 11:2
What else is capable of it? Only those who have not yet deserted their own wills, or tried to desert them, are ignorant of this. Those who would or could do it know from experience what opposition and what struggle it involves. Even those who have not yet learned this through their own experience are not allowed by ordinary reason to remain wholly ignorant of it. Who does not easily perceive that, since deserting other things that we want is so troublesome, how utterly hard and laborious—not only difficult but practically impossible—it is to cast off the will itself by which we will, and which we will, and to do so by that very will, and by nothing else than that will. Other things that have been cast off the will has cast off, but they were not the will itself, although they were willed; here the will casts off nothing else but the will itself. The will divides, the will is divided;

the will is that from which and by which the will divides: the will divides itself both from itself and through itself—that is, voluntarily—not by its own strength, but by the fortitude of God for whom nothing is impossible.

V

14. When the will itself has been cast off along with the flesh, what part of humanity still remains to humanity? Only reason. This portion of the self remains to it. Will it not be allowed to retain at least this. Is it of great moment if humanity keeps for itself a corner where it can stand? How can it have less than this in its possession? What will humanity have if it loses even this? If humanity is not allowed to stay here, where will it go outside of itself? Where will it regain itself? Where will it stay? Once in Adam humanity went out from itself, but to its detriment.[24] The example makes us afraid that if it goes out once again something worse will happen to it?

The beauty and dignity, and also the usability of this part, allure and detain it, preventing it from leaving this part of itself. This is the image of God in humanity, which joins it to God and to the angels through likeness,[25] and separates it from the beasts through unlikeness. This is a unique mirror for seeing God, insofar as he can be seen face to face. How, then, will it not be unreasonable to desert reason?

Finally, when people already offered absolutely everything that is theirs, and even themselves almost totally, is it not enough for them that they

24. See Sermons 9.1; 15.6.
25. See Sermon 9.4.

have not only made the offering rightly but also made the division rightly? They offered what had to be offered; they also offered more things than have been retained. They sold all that they had and gave it to the poor;† naked they follow the naked Christ.[26] They sat at the table of the rich man,† the table of Christ: they waited for what was set before them there. They knew that they must set out similar things; they prepared and set out what they had again. They did this, and although very unequally, they returned like for like as far as they could. They too took up the chalice of salvation, and they drank from the chalice from which Christ drank.† They had compassion on Christ, carrying in their bodies the marks and the death of Christ.† They presented their members as instruments of righteousness for sanctification;† they presented their bodies 'as a living sacrifice, holy and pleasing to God, their reasonable homage'.† They even offered their wills as a sacrifice 'to God for a fragrant offering'.†

Mt 19:21, par.
Lk 16:21
Ps 116:13; Mt 20:22
Ga 6:17; 2 Co 4:10
Rm 6:13, 19
Rm 12:1
Ep 5:2

15. See how many and how great were the things that they offered, that they were supposed to offer, and so rightly offered! Did they not also make the right division, those who kept for themselves only one thing out of so many and such great offerings? Is this not a great amount? Certainly it is a great amount, even excessive. If you ask how excessive, how great it is, it is total. Rightly, you who are human, can you offer God your

26. The notion of spiritual nakedness is found in Saint Jerome, *Epistola* 52.5.3 (CSEL 54, 422, lines 6–7); *Epistola* 58.2.1 (529, lines 4–5), *Epistola* 120.1.12 (CSEL 55, 478, lines 1–2); *Epistola* 125.20.5 (142, lines 8–9). Several of Jerome's texts were cited by Defensor of Ligugé, *Liber scintillarum* 11.14, 81.12, CCSL 117 (Turnhout: Brepols, 1957) 56, 231. The idea appears in twelfth-century writers (e.g., Robert of Arbrissel, Abelard, Stephen Langton) and is frequently employed by Saint Bonaventure and the spiritual Franciscans. See M. Bernards, 'Nudus nudum Christum sequi', *Wissenschaft und Weisheit*, 14 (1951) 148–15l; Châtillon, *Sermons*, 259–260; Châtillon, 'Nudus Christum nudus sequere', *S. Bonaventura* (Grottaferrata: Collegio S. Bonaventura, 1974) 4:719–792.

possessions and yourself, but with your God you cannot rightly divide yourself. From you he seeks you, alone and most of all; not a part, but all. He does not require just any sort of sacrifice from you and in you; he requires a holocaust.[27] You owe him everything, for he made and remade everything. Did the devil possess everything,[28] and will Christ not possess everything? Christ must have in you more than the devil has—if there could be more in you than the whole. If, then, Christ cannot have more, let him at least not have less.

Hence you were not told simply that you must love God but how much you must love him—that is, with your whole self—so that you do not keep back any of yourself from him, but offer him your whole self, expending your whole self in a spiritual holocaust. 'You shall love him with your whole heart', offering him you whole will; 'you shall love him with you whole soul', immolating to him all your sensual inclinations through mortification of the flesh; 'you shall love him with you whole
Mt 22:37 par mind', offering him all your reason.[29]† Your reason is human reason; it is a part of your humanity; it is not pristine, but corrupted by vice. If you live by it, you are human, and you live in a human fashion. This does not help you. A human being is blind from birth; if you follow one you fall into a ditch. Let your leader be the one who enlightens
Jn 9:1; Mt 15:14; Ps 146:8 the blind.† You are blind from birth, and you will remain blind as long as you are in yourself, for

27. The distinction between a sacrifice, in which part, and holocaust, in which a whole beast, is offered, has been made by Gregory the Great, *Homiliarum in Ezechielem* 2.8.16, CCSL 142 (Turnhout: Brepols, 1977) 348–349 (=PL 76:1037C). Hildebert of Lavardin, *Epistolam ad Willelmum de Campellis* (PL 171:142–143) alluded to this passage in the letter he wrote to William of Champeaux when the later decided to embrace the claustral life.

28. See Sermon 32.

29. See *On the Distinction*, 26–27.

'the light that is in you', your reason, 'is darkness'.† Pass over to the light that is within, that shines in the darkness, so that it not only shines in the darkness but also enlightens your darkness. This light is God's reason, the eternal truth. Its counsel is that you not rely on your own prudence, but that you desert your reason, not entrusting yourself to your own counsels, but to the counsels of others rather than your own, indeed to the counsels of God's reason, as these are presented to you by itself or by those who belong to it. Wisdom dwells in counsels—in her own, not in yours—and is present in educated thoughts†—those educated by her, not by you. It is she who teaches human beings knowledge, for they teach themselves only folly.

Mt 6:23

Pr 8:12

16. Accordingly, it is good for people not to be ruled by their own counsel but to be led into this fifth desert by the fifth spirit of God, that is, by the spirit of counsel.† Then, by humbly deserting their own sense they may abound instead with God's. This sense of God's is not high-minded, it does not judge that it knows something, it is not puffed up with knowledge,† and it admires and follows the opinion of others rather than its own. There are ten issues especially to be deserted in their own sense; or rather, their own sense is to be deserted—that is, not followed—in ten issues. They are concealed, extremely well hidden from our eyes; the sight of the human mind is blind to them, so that your gaze can do little or nothing there—the gaze that belongs to nature, not to grace, for where nature falls short, grace helps nature or lifts it up somewhat.

Is 11:2

Rm 14:5, 11:20; 1 Co 8:1, 2

In accord with the ten Hebrew names of God,[30] these ten [mysteries] seem to pertain specially to

30. Isidore of Seville, *Etymologiae* 6.19 (PL 82: 253C).

God's knowledge, so that he knows them, as do those to whom he deigns to manifest the uncertain
Ps 50:8 Vulgate and hidden things of his wisdom.† It is not safe to proceed in these things by one's own cleverness, but the simplicity and humility of faith are to be preferred to it, however subtle and sublime it may be. In faith lies the first step toward understanding. These things are to be believed before being discussed. Unless one believes, one will not see them;[31] the heart must be purified of its darkness by faith and prepared for so great a light. Let people listen to the mind of the sacred Scriptures on these things, and to what the spiritual men—who speak wisdom to the perfect, to whom God may perhaps have revealed these things through his spirit—say. If this is not enough, let them ask for wisdom from
Jm 1:5 the one who gives it generously.† Let their spirits not act rashly, but long and look out for the one who leads his people into all truth and makes the human heart ascend to those things that do not ascend into the human heart. Knowledge of them is not drawn from inferiors and creatures, but 'its
Ps 19:6 going out is from the highest heaven'.†

1–2

17. These ten mysteries, in which I think human reason, weak but still presumptuous, lame yet impetuous, is to be restrained, I will now briefly insert, by listing rather than sifting them, proposing rather than disclosing them. All that I think should be disclosed about them is what they are, and that

31. Achard here echoes Isaiah 7:9, doubtlessly recalling the older Latin version, 'Unless you believe you will not understand', often cited by Augustine (e.g. *De doctrina christiana* 2.12.17). Anselm of Canterbury helped give the statement wide currency, and it became the basis of scholastic discussions of the relationship between faith and reason.

they cannot be disclosed by a human being who is unable even to conceive them.

Four of these I find in Isaiah, not bare, but veiled under the four wings of the Seraphim, two in relation to God's face and two in relation to his feet. The Seraphim veil God's face with two wings and his feet with two wings—I am not taking away the veil so that the things veiled are exposed, but so that one thing about them may be exposed: how they are hidden. I do not know whether it would be a greater thing to lay bare or to veil, to uncover or to cover.

The two things veiled by the two anterior wings that affect God's face are perhaps two notions of prior realities: one concerns the beginning of the world, the other concerns what was before the beginning of the world; the one concerns the creation of the world, the other concerns the creator of the world—not how he now exists in the world, but how he existed before he was in the world, and how the world was in him before it existed and now exists in itself. Who can grasp how that something—indeed the whole universe—was made from nothing, and how 'the worlds were prepared by the Word of God, so that what is visible
was made from what is not visible'.[32]† 'Darkness is Heb 11:3
here over the face of the deep'[33]†—who can pene- Gn 1:2
trate it if not the one who looks into the depths and
knows what is in the darkness?† The one who does Dn 3:55, Vulgate 2:22
these things knows how he does them. He could

32. The invisible things referred to here seem to be the eternal exemplary forms. These are discussed at length in *De unitate*. On the role of the Word in the creation of the forms see *De unitate* 2.1–2.

33. Cf. John Scotus Eriugena, *De divisione nature* 2.17, (PL 122:550C-551A), for whom the darkness of the deep consisted of the primordial causes of the intelligible universe. Achard treats the question of the origin of the exemplary forms in *De unitate* 1.43–2.15.

not do them if he did not know, nor could he now fail to know what he knew then, as though the one 'with whom there is no variation or shadow
Jm 1:17 caused by change'† could forget anything. For the rest, as Ambrose says, not even the angels yet see how they were made from nothing.[34]

When, then, is humanity going to see it—
Jb 4:19 humanity that dwells in a house of clay,† 'a body, that is, that perishes, that weighs down the soul, and whose earthly dwelling burdens the mind that
Ws 9:15 ponders many things'.† Now if humanity, for whose sake the world was made, does not grasp its creation, by what art or by what power will it grasp the Creator of both itself and the world, and especially how he existed before he created humanity and the world? If humanity scarcely understands, if it understands partially how the Creator of the world is in a world already created, how will it understand how he was when he was not yet in the world, that is, how he is in himself? For as he now is in himself, so surely he was before he was in the world. He existed then only in himself, because nothing else from him existed yet. In himself he was not different then from what he is now, because
Ex 3:14 he is the same—because he is who is.† What is his mode of being in himself? Since three persons are there, who will conceive in his mind, much less profess with his mouth, how each of them is in himself, how each is in each of the others, each in the other two, and any two in the third, and also each in all and all in each? Who is wise, who will understand how each thing made in the world, before it came to be in itself, whether living or not
Jn 1:4 living in itself, was life in the Word of God?†

34. It is not certain to what text of Ambrose Achard is referring. It may be *De incarnationis dominicae sacramento* 3.16 (PL 16:822C–823A).

3–4

18. Two things at the feet are similarly concealed
and veiled from us. One concerns the end of the
world, the other what happens after the end of the
world. That the end of the world is covered up and
veiled, the Savior and cause of the world himself
uncovered. The Word that was in the beginning,
and who nevertheless was himself the beginning,
gave testimony regarding the end. The Beginning
himself† has spoken 'last of all in these days' to Jn 8:25 Vulgate
us† 'on whom the ends of the ages have come'† Heb 1:1–2; 1 Co 10:11
concerning the final end of the ages and days.
And what word did the Word of God himself
utter about this? 'About that day', he said, 'No
one knows except the Father alone'.† A huge veil Mt 24:36
indeed! Not to mention other things, to whom
has been bared what—in the Apostle's words—the
future 'removal of shaken, created things, so that
those that are unshaken may remain',† may be and Heb 12:27
how bodies, dead for so many centuries, returned
to ashes and dust, and spread thinly here and there
in the air and in all the regions of the world,
'will rise in a moment, in the twinkling of an
eye',† whole, uncorrupted, and never henceforth 1 Co 15:52
to die?

But if the end of the world, which is imminent
and almost at the door, remains hidden to us who
are in the world, what do you think about the state
that will follow after the end of the world? To recall
to mind a few of the many, or rather the countless
things that 'eye has not seen, nor ear heard, which
God has prepared' for those who love him,† is there 1 Co 2:9
anyone whose understanding grasps how God will
then be all in all?† How will they possess God, in 1 Co 15:28
whom there is no diversity, no inequality, nothing

more, nothing less, in whom and from whom some will possess more and others less?

These things pertain to the four mysteries veiled in Isaiah.

19. Solomon presents four other mysteries which he admits are veiled for him, the most insightful of men, the fourth more so than the others. Three ways seemed difficult to him, not only to walk, but even to understand: 'the way of an eagle in the sky, the way of a snake on a rock, and the way of a ship on the sea'. The fourth way, which he testifies he does not understand at all,
Pr 30:18–19 is 'the way of a man in his youth'.† In this, the wise man, because he is aware of his ignorance, is not ashamed to admit that he does not know what he does not know—perhaps this is greater wisdom than if he did know it. Would that in everything else he would have found himself equally wise! Just as I did not take off the veil in the first four mysteries, but only showed how there were veiled, so here too the difficulty of the ways is not to be removed or lessened but only shown—that is, that the human mind has little or no capacity for explaining them. Solomon chose to indicate the difficulty that the ways present to the understanding rather than to conduct. He added concerning the fourth that it was so difficult for him that he was entirely ignorant of it.

I judge that the eagle in the sky is the soul snatched from the snare of the body by contemplation and freely suspended in God as though upon intellectual wings.[35] Its 'way' is the manner of flying

35. Hugh of Saint Victor thus defined contemplation in his *In Ecclesiasten homiliae* 1 (PL 175:117A): 'Contemplation is the penetrating and free gaze of the mind directed everywhere toward things to be perceived.' Richard of Saint Victor, *De arca Moysi* (*Benjamin major*) 1.4 (PL 196.67D) altered Hugh's definition slightly: 'Contemplation is the free and penetrating gaze of the mind, rapt in wonder, on the manifestations of wisdom.'

from here, flying to there, and flying about. How the soul leaves the body, by what means and where, and where it goes once it has left the body, and by what means and how—whether it is carried off or led by another person, or borne by its own lightness of impetus, how it comports itself before the face of God, how it sees him, or an angel, or itself, or another's soul whether happy or wretched, by what insight it perceives bodily things without a bodily sense of perception, who may have flown there with the angels, who has progressed to the last day—does not everyone ask about this way, but without anyone to respond? Or if someone gives an answer to some of them, can anyone respond perfectly, or to all of them?

6

20. Concerning the way of a snake on a rock, see how it too is difficult to see and practically invisible. The snake is a devious and twisting serpent—that
is, the devil; 'the rock is Christ'.† Christ is the 1 Co 10:4
power of God, and the wisdom of God† who 1 Co 1:24
reaches everywhere because of his purity';† wis- Ws 7:24
dom is God, who fills heaven and earth and all mutable nature rests upon him as on a rock, an abiding and immovable foundation. The way of a snake on a rock is guilt and punishment. Although these are evil they can only exist in good natures, which would not be good if they were not in him who is the highest good, and in whom no evil can exist. But how can what contains evil be in him and yet no evil exist in him? How can he 'reach mightily from one end to the other' and yet not abolish every fault that resists him? How
does he 'order all things sweetly'† and nevertheless Ws 8:1
in some places not only permit but even inflict

punishment? If the highest good is everywhere, why does its presence not eliminate all evil? If it is everywhere, how can anything evil be anywhere? If it is absent somewhere, how and whence is anything good everywhere? How can evil exist with [the highest good] or be good without it? Finally, how can sin itself, which is not from it and therefore is nothing, be anywhere? If it is somewhere, how does it not exist? Or if it exists, how is it nothing? How does what is nothing exist in what is something? Or how can what is absolutely nothing harm what is something? If it cannot do harm, why is it feared, why is it hated? But, besides, who can be the creator of what is nothing? How is God the cause of every creature, and the creature the cause of a fault, but yet God, the cause of the creature, is not the cause of the fault, which is the effect of the creature effected by himself? How is he, who cannot be the cause of the effect, the Cause of the cause?

See how devious, how twisted, is the way of a snake on a rock. The way is said to be upon the rock as has been shown, because if good were not corruptible, where would evil be? Evil could not exist at all, nor could good be corruptible, if incorruptible good did not support and sustain it. There are still many other twists in this same way, but who can discover them all? And who can explain, unravel, clarify, and set in order what is discovered? Even if someone will be competent to remove some of the difficulties that turn up on this way, who will take away all of them? I do not think that even Augustine himself would be up to it, even though he was a very sharp-eyed observer of this way.[36]

---

36. Achard is probably thinking of Augustine's *De libero arbitrio.*

7

21. From here we must come now to the third way, so that its hiding places may be partially disclosed, and it may be apparent how much darkness enwraps it. Let this at least be clear about it, that it is not clear. As listed and named above, this is the way 'of a ship on the sea'.[37†] Does anyone not know that Pr 30:19
the ship on the sea is the Church among the bitter and turbulent temptations of this world? But who understands equally the way of this ship? It seems to run into storms on every side, but its unity is not dissolved but rather consolidated; it does not break up or go down, but instead it goes on. A hard storm rises against it but does not drive it from its course; instead it drives it on with greater speed; the storm does not make it regress but progress; not to sink but to rise. In the midst of evils it grows; in weaknesses it regains its strength; in straits it is expanded; under pressure it grows bold.

These things seem to happen contrary to nature, and so they do. They are caused by a hidden force, not of nature but of grace, not of human power, but of divine. Who knows how it is done? Who sees how Christ, the invisible skipper, is master of this ship,[38] how he guides it to a quiet port, and

37. The use of the stormy sea as a figure of the world was traditional; see H. Rahner, '*Antenna crucis*, II: Das Meer der Welt', ZKTh 66 (1942) 89–118. The theme is pervasive in Hugh of Saint Victor's *Homilies on Ecclesiastes* (PL 175:113B-256C). See also his *In Threnos Jeremiae* (PL 175:292B): 'What does the sea stand for, if not secular life, which seems to be stirred up by recurrent storms when, by an always unstable movement, it is drawn now from adversity to prosperity, and now from prosperity to adversity?' More briefly, Richard of Saint Victor, *Liber exceptionum* 2.10.4, ed. Châtillon, 381, says: 'Dearest brothers, the present world is the sea.' Equally familiar is the idea of the church as a ship; it is developed, for example, by Hugh of Saint Victor, *De arca Noe morali* 1.4 (PL 176:629–634), and Richard of Saint Victor, *Liber exceptionum* 2.13.27, p. 497.

38. Hugh of Saint Victor, *De arca Noe morali* 1.4 (PL 176:629D-630A): 'The Church is the ark which the supreme Noah, that is our Lord Jesus Christ, who is captain and port, steering it personally, guides us through the storms of this life to himself.'

steers it by the invisible rudder of the Holy Spirit. 'The Spirit blows where it chooses, but you do not
Jn 3:8 know where it comes from and where it goes'† or even how it comes and goes. Does anyone comprehend how invisible sailors help Jesus, the invisible skipper, to administer this boat? The angels 'are all ministering spirits, sent to serve for the sake of
Heb 1:14 those who inherit salvation'.† Similarly, who can easily understand by reason how this ship is moved partly by the winds and partly by oars—that is, from above through grace, and from below by effort? How do God and humanity, the grace of God and the freedom of human choice, join together in one in a single work and a single will? Does one do something there that the other does not? What does the one do? What does the other do? In what, and how, and to what extent does freedom of choice cooperate with grace? Likewise, on the other hand, in what, how, and to what extent does grace cooperate with freedom of choice?[39]

22. Some are exposed to danger regarding this way, either because they do not find it, or because, having found it, they desert it on account of its difficulty. They err and go astray who so add to the role of grace that they exclude freedom of choice; they err even more who so defend freedom of choice that they stand convicted of voiding the grace of God. No merit can exist without free choice, nor any merit, but only demerit, without grace. The way to salvation exists in those mature enough to be able to think neither of the latter without the former, nor of the former without the latter, neither of God without humanity, nor of humanity without God, but only of God and humanity equally. Hence these statements, truthful

39. See Sermons 3.1; 11.1–3.

witnesses to this way: 'Not I, but the grace of
God that is with me';† and 'We are God's co- 1 Co 15:10
workers'.[40]† Grace precedes choice to make it free, 1 Co 3:9; 3 Jn 8
or rather freed, so that God may be the leader on the journey, not humanity, and so that humanity may attribute completely to God, and not to itself that it can be, and is, God's co-worker. Humanity would be unable to be co-worker with God, much less work without God, in doing any good whatever, had not God anticipated it by grace alone
with blessings of sweetness† so that it might be Ps 21:3
capable of this. Hence, this statement: 'By the grace
of God I am what I am'.† 1 Co 15:10

These things are a great mystery in the God-man, and man-God, Jesus Christ. He is, as he himself testifies, 'the way' to the Father, 'the mediator
between God and humanity';† taking on human Jn 14:6; 1 Tm 2:5
nature, he is in himself God and man-God, guiding humanity, not God; from humanity, not from God; to God and not to humanity.[41] On the other hand, those who receive only grace, or only freedom of choice, rely on God alone, or on humanity alone, as their way. They establish as their way from exile to their homeland either that homeland or that exile, and therefore they neither leave here nor arrive there. Such a way—if indeed it is to be called a way and not wayward—was the way of the Jews and the Gentiles. The way of Christians is nothing else than Christ himself, who is at once God and a human being, the co-working of God's grace and our free choice—or perhaps better, the working of grace and the co-working of our freedom—restored to us through grace alone. This is the

40. See Sermon 13.5.

41. This sentence reads in Latin, *hominem suscipiens, et per se Deum et hominem Deum, hominem non Deum dirigens, ab homine non Deo, ad Deum non hominem* (Châtillon, *Sermons*, 225).

unique way between the two forms of waywardness; those who enter on this way follow the King's
Nb 21:22 Highway;† they turn neither to the right nor to the
Dt 17:11 left:† they dismiss to the right grace without the co-working of free choice, and to the left free choice without the help of grace.

23. Accept how difficult it is even for them to keep to this way. 'Narrow is the way that leads' to
Mt 7:14 heaven;† this is that way, and apart from this there is no other. Do you want to understand how narrow this may be to the understanding, and how the reason of those who walk on it by faith, intention, and deed suffers difficulties because of it. On this way freedom of choice is incapable of doing or defending good, of dismissing or avoiding evil, unless it does so by grace. So faith holds, so the Scriptures teach, and so they themselves feel. If just people lose righteousness let them answer, if they can, how in losing righteousness they become unjust, or how while losing righteousness they remain just. How will anyone be just without righteousness, and how will anyone be unjust who loses what he cannot retain unless grace causes him to retain it, and grace does not in fact cause him to retain it? If grace did this, it would have happened. If they adduce his guilt, why did grace not cause it? He objects that righteousness cannot be maintained unless grace does it, and thus, as was said, guilt cannot be avoided unless the same grace brings this about. What is his guilt, if he did not avoid a fault that he could not avoid unless grace caused this, and in fact grace did not cause it?

But if they still object and argue that another fault was the reason grace did not cause him to avoid this fault, what will they answer regarding that prior fault? If they adduce yet another preceding fault as the cause of that one, and thus always wish to posit some prior fault as the cause of the later one, they will go on to infinity and never come to a first fault. Or if they grant that there is a first fault, let them explain how it can be a fault by answering these objections. It cannot be denied that there is some explanation of this matter, but, as I think, it presents no little difficulty and obscurity. If occasionally some way by which one may perhaps escape seems to emerge and suddenly shine out among the dark hidden realms of these questions, wave after wave of objections and inquiries arises. If anything is discovered, these confound, destroy, and complicate it, so that—just as happens at sea—suddenly no trace remains of the way that fleetingly appeared.

8

24. Let the eye be directed next to a fourth
way which remains, so that there it may at least
see how it is not just as invisible as the rest, but
more so even than they. It is 'the way of a man
in his youth'.† Who should we think this man is Pr 30:19 Vulgate
if not the one of whom it was foretold, 'Behold
"the Orient" is his name',† and 'The Lord will Zc 6:12
do something new on the earth; a woman will
encompass a man'?† His youth pertains to this Jr 31:22
newness; it is his humanity. His being human is
recent, but not his being God; in humanity not
long, but in divinity from of old; from of old, not of
time, but in eternity; not from the beginning, but
in the beginning,[42]† and even before the beginning Jn 1:1

42. Christ is the beginning of the beginning; he is the principle of the archetypal divine ideas which in turn are the principle of the existing world. See Sermon 15.17.

as he is the beginning of the beginning of the
Jn 8:38 universe. His is in the Father's presence,† together
Dn 7:9, 13, 21 with God, the Ancient of Days,† God with God,
co-eternal with the eternal; he is in his mother's
presence, a new human being in the fullness of
Ep 4:24; Ga 4:4; 1 Co 10:11; Mi 4:1 time, at the end of the ages, on the last day.† Not
only was a man 'about thirty years old' seen in the
course of time, and from then on appeared as a
Lk 3:23; 24:19 man great 'in deed and word',† but also as a man
before he was a boy—a man by virtue of his mind before he was a boy in bodily age; a man not only in the world, but a man even in the Virgin's womb, changing according to the successive ages of the body, but keeping only this age unchangingly in his mind.

The way of this man in his youth is the way of Christ in his humanity, in which he became a very young man, and therefore the object of disdain. This is 'the very young Benjamin, in ecstasy of
Ps 67:28 Vulgate mind',[43]† disdained in the flesh in which there
Is 53:2 was 'no beauty or comeliness',† but exalted in
mind, reaching out to God and far transcending all created minds, not only those of humans but those of angels as well. What intellect could grasp his way, by which he became a way for us, even feebly—that is, how he comes from the bosom of the Father into the bosom of his mother?[44] How was flesh conceived of Spirit, a human being of God. How from the closed womb of the Virgin did he appear in the world 'like a bridegroom
Ps 19:5 coming out of his wedding chamber'† but with no
doorway? How did he live in the likeness of sinful

43. This reference to *excessus mentis* is developed by Richard of Saint Victor in his *De patriarchis* (*Benjamin minor*) 1.1 (PL 196:1). See below Sermon 15.35. Achard's opinion is that Christ enjoyed this state permanently, since from his conception on he contemplated the divinity and was thus constantly beyond himself in God (*excedens Deo*). See Sermon 1.5.

44. See Sermons 3.3; 8.1

flesh and without sin?† How did he lay down the flesh he had assumed when he chose and assume it again when he chose?† How did his soul leave the flesh and his divinity not put off the flesh?[45] How did his soul descend to hell and his flesh ascend above all the heavens?† And most of all, how does the same flesh come daily from heaven to us on the altar, and from the altar into us, yet without leaving the heavens whence it comes?

Rm 8:3; Heb 4:15

Jn 10:17–18

Ep 4:9–10

25. Just as Christ's divinity first came to us from heaven, so now his humanity comes to us from there; as he came from heaven by his divinity yet without leaving there, so now he comes from heaven in his humanity, which nevertheless always remains there; and, as his divinity came from there through the humanity, so also the humanity comes from there through the divinity. Then God came through his humanity in a visible way and as a human being; he now comes through his divinity in a hidden way. Then God came in a way perceptible to the senses; now a human being comes in a way not perceptible to the senses; then God came in a human way, and now a human being comes in a divine way—not as a human being only in his spirit but also in his flesh, not without his divinity, but with, in, and by it, and therefore everything is done in a divine way.

What is more divine than this: Christ's body, although it is flesh and not spirit, nevertheless is the food not of the flesh and the body but of the spirit and the mind? It is the food of the inmost

45. The *glossa ordinaria* on John 10:17 (Venice, 1588) v. 5, fol. 216, Hugh of Saint Victor, *De sacramentis legis naturalis et scriptae* 2.1.10 (PL 176:399C), and Thomas Aquinas, *Summa theologiae* 3.50.2, all agree with Achard's implied position, that Christ's body, separated from his soul at death, nevertheless remained united to his divinity. For the twelfth-century controversy on this point see Landgraf, *Dogmengeschichte*, 2/1, 273–319.

self, yet not human but divine going spiritually and divinely into the spirit, not converting itself into spirit, but feeding the spirit spiritually and divinely—entering spiritually, working spiritually, coming from heaven by a spiritual way, returning to heaven by a spiritual way.[46] Although his body is among us, it is also in heaven; among us it is in different places, on different altars, at the same time—not divided into parts, but whole and entire on each altar; not distinct as this and that, but one in number; not imaginary, but true; not only in the sacrament, but in itself. It is in only one place in the way of nature, in many places by the way of power; in one by nature, in many by grace and divine power; in one by a bodily mode, in many by a spiritual mode. It is for a spirit, not a body, to be able to be in many places at once—and perhaps it is for no one but a divine spirit, that is, one uncreated and uncircumscribed, and not also for a created and circumscribed spirit.

26. Something similar, although in reverse, happens in the divine spirit, or if it is more proper to say so, in the spirit God. As this body assumed by God, and made the body of God and so somehow deified and divine, subsists bodily and naturally in one place, but spiritually and by power in many; so by contrast, God himself, although spiritually and essentially he is in many places, indeed in all, nevertheless in one mode of existing, that is, personally,[47] he is in only one place. He is in the human nature assumed through grace by the fullness of his divinity,[48] 'dwelling bodily', as

46. Sermons 9.1, 4; 15.1.
47. Sermons 1.2; 4.7; 5.1.
48. An allusion to the *auctoritas* that the humanity of Christ has by grace what his divinity possesses by nature; see Sermon 15.

the Apostle says.† He assumes to himself what is of the body, and what is his he grants to the body, not confusing their natures but marvelously and ineffably uniting them; not changing them, but joining them. We should not understand this to mean that the supreme spirit dwells somewhere bodily, or that the supreme body dwells somewhere spiritually, as though a spirit becomes a body anywhere, or a body becomes a spirit anywhere. Rather, the uncircumscribed spirit, in a certain mode of existing—that is, through the union of the person—dwells somewhere in a circumscribed way—that is, it is there in a way in which it is nowhere else. This happens in a bodily mode, since the body's nature is to be circumscribed. However, that this body is simultaneously and completely in many places happens according to the mode of the spirit. When, then we say 'bodily' or 'spiritually' we are not referring to the natures of subsisting things but to modes of subsisting. The Apostle said that the whole fullness of the divinity dwells bodily in Christ,† not with reference to the nature of the indwelling God but with reference to the mode of indwelling.

Col 2:9

Col 2:9

27. Christ's body is not merely entire in different places, that is, on many altars, in a spiritual way, but it also has in each a mode of existing by no means unspiritual. Although it is everywhere sensible in itself because of the nature of the body, it is not sensible to us as it appears present on the altar. Hence, it may be said to be present there both sensibly and insensibly: sensibly because of the truly sensible character of the body, and because of the sacrament, which is subject to the senses; insensibly in relation to its appearance and the perception of our senses. It is not there in such a way that it can be

perceived there in its own form by our weak senses. So, as has been said, it is there bodily in one respect because of the true nature of the body and the form of the sacrament, and because of a certain mode of existing; in another respect it is there incorporeally, in relation to the act of perception and a certain mode of existing. It is on the altar in such a way that it can truly be said to be on this part of the altar and not on that part—it is on that part where its sacrament is to be found; it is not on that part on which its sacrament is not present; and in this bodily mode it is there in a circumscribed way. It is not, however, on this altar in such a way that it is not wholly elsewhere at the same time and in the same mode—that is, on some other altar; in this respect it exists in an uncircumscribed way. In this, too, it far transcends the common nature and mode of subsisting bodies, and perhaps in this it exceeds in no small measure, and overcomes, the power of subsisting not only of bodies but of spiritual creatures as well. You will not, then, in the mode of subsisting which this body has, investigate a nature which is not from nature, nor in accord with nature, but beyond nature and contrary to nature; rather, you will turn your attention to the divine power; you will not consider what a created and less powerful nature is normally able to do, but you will ponder what could be impossible for grace and for the divine power, that is, an uncreated and omnipotent nature, a nature not born, from which comes every other nature and power.

28. Human reason, accustomed to following familiar nature, may not pose and accept the accustomed queries regarding this unaccustomed and divine reality. We have no room here for investigations about things that concern natural modes of

existing in place, or modes related to power. These latter far exceed the natural modes and are far removed from them. No sense should presume to ask here the other questions it might ask: when the body of the Lord is on this altar or that, what part is in which place, what part of the body beneath what part of the sacrament, or how the parts are arranged: what is up, what is down, what is to the right, what to the left, what is before, what is behind, and whether a larger part of the body occupies a larger place and a small part a smaller place, since each part of the body is not beneath a part of sacrament, but all the parts are equally beneath each and all. In other words, one member is not beneath one part, and another beneath another, but the whole and complete body is present beneath each part. Thus when the sacrament is divided into parts, the body is not cut into parts, and as a result when the sacrament is divided and the parts received separately, the whole and undivided body is received beneath the divided parts and in each part by each of the recipients.

Reason should not suggest that if this whole body is somewhere it is not wholly somewhere else, or if the place is smaller than this body it does not hold this body that is bigger than it is. These things are true not only in other bodies, but also about this body in what concerns the mode of existing that accompanies its nature, but not according to the mode that conforms to divine power. Thus, it is true that if a woman bares a child she has certainly laid with a man—true, that is, according to the mode of bearing and conceiving that nature knows, but not according to a mode, not inherent in nature, which the Creator and founder of nature has in his power over nature. Just as the infinite and immense power of God greatly transcends every mode of nature, so does it exceed sense, especially that of human beings, which is corrupt and weak.

In no other instances of divine power does the power of human reason seem as deficient as it does regarding the sacrament of the Lord's body and blood. It may be capable of something in other instances, but what can it do here? Is it able to understand how, when the substance of bread and wine have been turned into the substance of the body and blood of the Lord, the accidents of both the bread and wine are not changed along with them, but remain unchanged without the substance of bread and wine? How can there be accidents without a subject? In what subject are these accidents?

29. Reason does not know its way in these matters, but the way is not completely unknown to faith. Here reason is totally ignorant, but faith is sure of what reason cannot grasp. Faith sets out from reason's failure; faith knows through grace that of which reason can have no experience. Here faith is as strong as reason is weak. Here where reason can do little or nothing, faith, doing more or everything, has all the more merit. Here reason willingly yields so that the merit of faith may increase. Reason is right not to envy faith, because what faith merits, it merits not for itself but for reason; faith will pass away, while reason will remain and advance by the merit of faith. Faith is only for the way; reason will exist also in the homeland. Faith sows, but reason will reap. Reason will be rewarded for the merit of faith because reason itself cooperated in some way in the merit and merited something, or rather, much. The merit of reason

is that it did not prefer itself to the simplicity of faith; it did not try to precede, but to follow. If this is beyond reason's capacity, nevertheless reason does not oppose it. Reason does not rest upon its own power, but on the grace of God. It yields to grace; it allows the victory to faith; it gives glory to God, confessing that he can do what reason itself cannot fully grasp.

Especially, in regard to this sacrament, reason experiences and recognizes its total weakness, except it sees that it is reasonable that in the secrets of God, handed on to be believed by human beings, what they cannot penetrate by reason does not escape faith. I think that Solomon had particularly in mind this way of Christ's coming in his body from heaven to us and into us daily through this sacrament, and of returning into heaven, because he asserted he was totally ignorant—as far as reason went, but not faith—of this fourth way, that is, 'the way of a man in his youth'. All the sacraments of the church pertain to the youth of Christ. When we all arrive 'at maturity, at the measure of the
full age of Christ',† of the full age of his whole Ep 4:13
self—that is, not only of the head but also of all his members—and childish things have been put
away,† then will Christ be mature. Then at the same 1 Co 13:11
time will all these sacraments too be put away. For the time being children and youths—that is, those beginning and advancing—need them, but those arriving at the goal will not need them when the truth of the sacraments has been manifested and imparted in itself.

It is enough for the present to have at least lightly touched in an external way, and by speech, on the four ways of Solomon, rather than to have walked through them fully by interior understanding.

9–10

30. In order to complete the number proposed
above as ten, after the four wings of the Seraphim
and these four ways, two mysteries in which hu-
mans are to cast aside their reason as they did in
the foregoing remain to be investigated and added.
Ask Paul what these two are. He propounds them
to you, but does not expound them. In fact, he
calls you back from rashly and vainly searching into
these unsearchable matters; you are not to think
that you can comprehend the incomprehensible
things of God, especially if you trust in human
understanding and are not yet enlightened by the
divine understanding which is above humanity.
He presents you to yourself to repress your pre-
sumption; he presents God as well, so that you
may remember human weakness and your virtual
nothingness in comparison with the domain of the
divine height and majesty. What else is he thunder-
ing out to you in these words: 'Who are you, a hu-
Rm 9:20 man being, to answer God'?† To further accuse you
of temerity, and to establish it in your sight more
compellingly so that you cannot be hidden from
yourself, with you as witness he compares you to
Rm 9:21 clay,† who then are you that you presume to answer
God regarding his works, and are able to meet his
reason on an equal footing, as though he may not
presume to do anything reasonable in your regard
the reasons and modes of which your reason cannot
grasp? These reasons of his for his works, and these
modes of his operations, are his incomprehensible
Rm 11:33 judgments and his unsearchable ways.† Although
the Apostle was caught up to the third heaven and
2 Co 12:2, 4 there heard secret words,† he was stunned by the
profundity of these things, dismissing you to admi-

ration rather than investigation of them. Admiring these things, but not revealing them, he exclaims: 'O the depths of the riches of the wisdom and knowledge of God! How incomprehensible are his judgments, and unsearchable his ways. Who has known the Lord's mind' in his judgments, 'or who has been his counselor' in his ways'?† Rm 11:33–34

31. 'The Lord's judgments are a great abyss'† Ps 36:6
because there is great obscurity and profundity in them. The Son of God, as he himself said, 'came into this world for judgment', so that those who did not see might see, and that those who saw might become blind.† Jn 9:39
Judgment occurs, then, not just in blinding but also in enlightening; not just in rejection but in election. Who comprehends why, among God's judgments, Jacob was chosen rather than Esau; although they were equals, why Esau was rejected rather than Jacob?† Gn 27; Ml 1:2–3; Rm 9:13
Even from unequals he sometimes takes the one who is worse, leaving the one who is less bad and whom therefore it seems more just to take. He called the Jews, who, once called, did not come after him but went after him; he did not call the Tyrians and Sidonians, who, had they been called would have followed.† Mt 11:21–22
He casts good seed on bad soil, where he knows it will be trampled and choked; he chose not to sow it on good soil, where it would have born fruit.† Lk 8:5–8
Sometimes he allows a person who has been faithful from childhood, obedient and devoted until the last day, to fall and be detected in the fall and damned, while another, who was always his insolent and blasphemous persecutor† 1 Tm 1:13
he finally, at death, goads, converts, regenerates, and saves. To the ungrateful he grants many things that he denies to the grateful; not only in other matters, but even in spiritual graces he often confers on the

unjust what he does not confer on the just; he gives
to an abuser what he does not give to a good user
of his goods; he grants to one who is negligent and
does not ask what he does not grant to one who
desires and asks. But who can run through all of
these one by one? Countless are his judgments of
this kind; even if they are just, their righteousness
is well hidden, so that it is safer to reverently fear
them than to discuss rashly them.

32. Moreover, his ways are exalted above our
Is 55:9 ways.† Who can come after him along these ways,
much less come up to him. Who knows how by
the skill and power of his art he not only brings
forth good out of good, but even good out of
evil, and converts disease itself into a medicine?
By the fact that some people's infirmities have
been multiplied, he makes them afterward make
Ps 15:4 Vulgate haste.† From the blindness that fell on part of Israel
he brought the light of the full number of the
Rm 11:25 Gentiles;† he sometimes more fully blinds one and
the same person in order to enlighten all the more
so that he may make the light equal the darkness;
by his eternal Word he tells the light to shine forth
from darkness itself. He strikes and thus he heals,
he kills to bring to life, 'he leads down to hell and
1 Sm 2:6 back';† those who cannot be freed in Jerusalem
he leads to Babylon in order to free them there;
he sends them into captivity that they may be
free; he allows some to fall deeper so that they
may rise higher, to go further away so that they
may approach more closely. 'Law came in so that
sin might abound', so that 'where sin abounded,
Rm 5:20 grace might all the more abound'.† 'He enclosed
Ga 3:22 everything under sin'† in order to have mercy on
Rm 11:32 all.† For those who love him, for those called holy
according to his plan, he makes all things work
Rm 8:28 together for good,† not only good things but bad
things as well, not only other people's evils but

even their own. But who is able to inquire into his manner of doing this? Human weakness humbly acknowledges his method in this even more than in the preceding nine mysteries.

33. In these ten mysteries God ascends upon the Cherubim and flies.† Let them fear a fall who would wish to imitate God's flight in these matters, and, as it were, to fly on wings like God, especially the wings of fallen reason. They will surely fall and, repelled by the light, be enfolded in denser darkness[49] if God does not spread his wings and bear them up.† In these ten mysteries, in my opinion, indeed in the opinion of truth itself and the divine reason, humanity should desert its reason. Let it not be afraid to desert itself entirely, following God completely and casting its whole self on the Lord. Let them know the one in whom they put their trust, because he is able to guard what is entrusted to him and even increase it;† he will give it back to them with interest. He accepts on earth and will give back in heaven; he accepts the humble and will give back the exalted; he accepts a diminished portion and will give back the full amount; he accepts the empty and will give back the full; he accepts the broken and will give back the whole; he accepts the ignorant and will give them back contemplating God face to face; he accepts the corrupt and will render them incorruptible; he accepts the wretched and will render them blessed, transforming the temporal into the eternal, humanity into God.

Ps 18:10

Dt 32:11

2 Tm 1:12

49. The contemplative is beaten back into the darkness by the very brightness of the divine truth contemplated. This idea was developed by Saint Augustine; e.g. *Confessions* 7.10.16; *De quantitate animae* 33.75 (PL 32:1076). The notion of *reverberatio* then became a key idea in the mystical theology of Saint Gregory the Great; e.g. *Moralia* 5.33.58, CCSL 143:259 (=PL 75:711C); 16.31.38 CSEL 143:821–822 (=PL 75:1140C). Achard applies the metaphor to the theologian who seeks to know beyond the limits of his reason.

VI

34. In the present too, from the time people leave themselves for God's sake, yielding to God
Jn 14:23 and preparing a home for him in themselves† completely and not just partially, God follows after them at once and enters secretly. O fortunate exchange! A human being leaves a human being and brings God in. How happy and how gracious a guest! The whole house he enters he fills with happiness and grace. For people to leave themselves in this way for God's sake is not so much to leave as to enter. They leave, not from the house into a courtyard, but from the house into a marriage chamber. They leave, not outward but inward, not downward but upward, not from themselves into the world but from themselves into God, so that God comes into them and they come into God. They die to themselves to live to God, and so they live more truly, not in themselves who are shadows, but in God who is truth. They no
Ga 2:20 longer live in themselves, but Christ lives in them† when they follow God's will and reason, receiving these into themselves, deserting not just their own flesh but also their wills and reason. This is the divine will and reason, that they retain nothing of themselves for themselves; hence, when they completely desert themselves God's will and reason dwell in them completely. 'They are joined to God'
1 Co 6:17 and so are 'one spirit' with him.[50]†

---

50. Achard has quoted this text several times: Sermons 2.3; 13.7. It was a favorite among twelfth-century theologians. Generally, unity of spirit (*unitas spiritus*) was referred to a union of the human will with the will of God, but Achard includes both reason and will. Returning to the metaphor of the empty house broached at the beginning of his treatise, Achard says that when the self has completely deserted itself, including its will and reason, then the will and reason of God will come to dwell there.

Now that they have become spiritual, and pos-
sess the Spirit of God, they can and do 'per-
ceive what pertains to the Spirit of God'.† This 1 Co 2:14
they could not do while they retained their own
spirit. They experience in themselves 'the beauty
of God's house'† and the great sweetness he hides Ps 26:8
there for those who fear him† and cling to him. Ps 31:19
Manna rains down on them from heaven.† They Ps 78:24
often perceive an uncommon light freely offering
itself to them and inviting them to follow. They
sometimes hear, with an ear for hearing†—an inner Mt 11:15
ear—'a tongue they did not know,'† the voice of Ps 81:5
the turtledove in their land, that is, in their hearts.
They are touched, inflamed, caught up by these
things. Their whole being longs for what is above,
it sighs for what is within. They hunger and thirst
to be inebriated by the riches of God's house† Ps 36:8
with which they are being sprinkled and watered
as with showers of rain.† They call out, inwardly Ps 72:6
transfixed with the arrows of love:[51] 'As a deer longs
for springs of water, so my soul longs for you, O
God'† and 'How lovely are your tents, O Lord of Ps 42:1
hosts! My soul longs and faints for the courts of the
Lord'.† They feel distaste for everything that draws Ps 84:1–2
them back from this; they cut off all occupations
that can interfere with their inward course. Human
interchange becomes irritating to them. They take
'wings like a dove's', flying away to find rest; they
flee far away and lodge in the wilderness.† Those Ps 55:6–7
who had earlier deserted themselves for the sake
of a neighbor now desert even a neighbor for the
sake of God.

From what has been said, it is apparent that they are led into this sixth desert by the sixth spirit, the

51. See Augustine, *Enarratio in psalmum* 37.5 (PL 36:398–399); A. Cabassut, 'Blessure d'amour', DSp (1937) 1:269–270.

Is 11:2 spirit of understanding,† so that they may be free
Ps 34:8 and at leisure to see how 'sweet the Lord is'† and to
Is 33:17 contemplate the King of glory in his beauty.† They
do not desert their neighbors in feeling or in a kind
of inner dealing, but only in outer dealing; not in
secret but in what is seen. Before God they pray for
them without ceasing, but before human beings
they cease working for them. They desert four
things about their neighbor, or rather they desert
them in what pertains to four benefits. Although
the wood is fruit-bearing, it does not bear fruit
to sustain them bodily, nor does it offer leaves of
protection; in spiritual matters too, they withdraw
two things from them: teaching and consolation.

VII

35. Those who have passed through these six
deserts have already ascended, as if by six steps, to
the throne of our Solomon, that is, to contem-
plation of the sublime divinity of Christ. There
they too have a presentiment of 'the peace that
Ph 4:7 surpasses all understanding'† and 'their place be-
Ps 76:3 comes peaceful'.† They depart from their minds to
Ph 3:20 God,[52] their way of life is in heaven,† and their 'life
Col 3:3 is hidden with Christ in God'.† There they enjoy
some of the delights and first fruits of paradise,
Heb 4:11; Mt 25:21 entering into rest and the joy of their Lord,† as far
as is possible while still in frail flesh. To a great
extent there they lay aside the form of a slave and,
Ph 2:6–7 being free, assume the form of God.† In the Spirit
they strip themselves of humanity and put on God
himself. Now there are revealed to them through
God's Spirit the things from which they humbly
restrained their own spirits. Those who had earlier

52. See above, section twenty-four and below, section thirty-five.

set their minds on spiritual things in a fleshly way now also have spiritual knowledge of bodily things, and 'if they knew Christ according to the flesh, they know him so no longer'.† What they had seen in the world earlier they now see more sublimely and truly in God; the temporal things they had first perceived below themselves by sensation they now contemplate above themselves as eternal by their intellects. They have been raised up from the earth, and they draw all earthly things to themselves, considering earthly things with a heavenly eye, not with an earthly one, and perceiving the lowest things according to their own loftiness, in a lofty, not a lowly way. When humans come to a lofty heart, God is exalted,† and everything in God. Set in such a great light, they easily apprehend in what great darkness the world, which they have under their feet, lies; in their ecstasy, they say truthfully that 'everyone is a liar'.† They see without obstruction, as though from a high mountain, how great was the affliction that depressed and oppressed their brothers and sisters in Egypt as they served Pharaoh 'with mortar and brick'.† They cannot be unmoved by compassion, because, after being brought into the cellar of wine by the spouse,† they are inebriated with love so that they want everyone to be as they are. They remember the one who, being free of all, made himself the slave of all, not seeking what was his but what belonged to the many. There comes to their minds the spiritual divine example of the Only-begotten one, who 'although he was in the form of God', equal to God the Father, 'thought it not robbery' but nature 'to be equal to God', and nevertheless 'emptied himself, taking the form of slave, and was found in human condition'† among humans

2 Co 5:16

Ps 63:7–8 Vulgate

Ps 116:11

Ex 1:14

Sg 2:4

Ph 2:6–7

and for humans. Willy-nilly, they too are drawn
from heaven to earth by a sort of strong—though
Ho 11:4 light, because they are full of love†—bonds. They
would willingly, because much more pleasingly,
rest within, among the caresses of the spouse whose
inner sweetness they have experienced, were it
not that the love of Christ, their spouse, urges
them on, and his example stirs them up to go out,
following their spouse. To this is added the bond of
brotherly love and the example of the companions
of the spouse. And so they too go out, following
the spouse wherever he goes, and with him and
with his companion Paul, they became all things
1 Co 9:22, 19 to all people in order to win them.† Those who
inside were in some way God with God, in the
form of God, take up humanity again outside with
humanity and for humanity, reassuming for them
the form of a slave. Those who first deserted their
neighbor for God, now also, in a way, desert God
for their neighbor.

36. They are led into this seventh desert by the
Is 11:2 seventh spirit, the spirit of wisdom†—that is, of
perfect love. In this they are conformed to the
wisdom of God, who did the same thing in a much
more excellent way, leaving them an example to
1 Pt 2:21 imitate or to follow.† This love is so perfect that
none more perfect can be thought of in humanity.
They only can ponder it who have themselves
learned by taste what it is that Christ deserts. Until
now they have deserted lesser things in favor of
greater, or equal for equal. Here they seem to be
deserting something incomparably greater for the
sake of something incomparably less, the Creator
in some way for the creature, God for humanity—
not, however, against God but in conformity to
God, imitating him and referring everything to

him. For the moment they choose with Paul, to be in some way anathema—that is, cut off from Christ—for the sake of their brothers and sisters,† Rm 9:3
so that their brothers and sisters may be Christ's, and Christ 'may be the firstborn of many brothers and sisters'.† And now, along with Moses, they Rm 8:29
desert the great vision they had seen in the inner desert and descend from the mountain of God into Egypt to free their brothers and sisters, the people of God, but not without a command of God. Thus, not only for their neighbors, but also as it were for God, they desert God. Just as nothing is superior to God, so nothing is ulterior to this desert.

37. In this seventh desert, in accord with the seven spirits of God, God is deserted in seven spiritual matters—or rather, human spirits desert seven spiritual goods, goods they possess from and in the Spirit of God. They do not, however, lose them completely, but they no longer possess them as frequently or profusely as before. Two of these seven are to hear God and to be heard by God, to place one's ear close to God's mouth, and one's mouth close to God's ear. The first occurred in reading, the other in prayer; in reading God spoke with them; in prayer they spoke with God. Two others are a kind of perfect tranquility and purity of soul, which they cannot make last as they did before; even the apostles' feet were spattered with dust along the way of their ministry. What rest can there be amid taxing labors and daily cares for flesh and spirit? Or if sometimes there is some, is it frequent, long-lasting or extensive? The fifth is to seek the face of God always—that is, to meditate continuously on nothing but God. The sixth and seventh are to withdraw and be withdrawn; to withdraw to God and to be withdrawn by God, to

withdraw from the creature and to be withdrawn by the Creator, to withdraw to contemplation and to be withdrawn in wonder.

38. If the things deserted in each of these seven deserts are added up, the number seven will grow to forty: seven things in the first, four in the second, five in the third, three in the fourth, ten in the fifth, four in the sixth, and seven in the seventh[53] add up to forty altogether. Those who have deserted all these and abstained from all of them have, so to speak, fasted for forty days, and for forty nights as well. They not only spent and still spend days in virtues and divine consolations, but they also suffered and perhaps still suffer some nights in their weaknesses and various tribulations. No wonder if after this great fast a great hunger follows as well. Those whose perfection is so great cannot escape hungering perfectly for perfect righteousness. It must happen that angels minister to one who so hungers; they not only minister by frequently approaching and refreshing them spiritually in their own way, but in addition they make up and complete in every way what they do not do or are incapable of. They take those going away from here in their hands, and with their hands they offer them to Jesus to be completely refreshed. Jesus makes them recline 'in the kingdom of heaven
Mt 8:11 with Abraham, Isaac, and Jacob,'† and also with his angels who first offered refreshment. Passing by there he ministers to them that they may eat and drink at his table nothing less than himself—not a

53. In section five, renunciation of the seven capital sins; in section eight renunciation of the four elements of the world; in section ten, mortification of the five senses; in section twelve, threefold obedience to superiors, equals, and inferiors; in section sixteen, renunciation of reason, in itself and in the ten mysteries; in section thirty–four, renunciation of four works of love; in section thirty seven, renunciation of seven spiritual goods.

human being, but God—that is, not according to his humanity, but according to his divinity. There they are fully satisfied by the appearance of the fullness of glory of him who is blessed and glorious forever. Amen.

METAPHYSICS

On the Distinction of Soul, Spirit, and Mind

INTRODUCTION

TREATISES ON THE SOUL WERE COMMON in the twelfth century. Hugh of Saint Victor wrote on the question 'Of the Union of the Soul and Body', and there are a number of treatises by Cistercians as well.[1] The first part of Achard's short treatise argues that the interior substance of the soul is essentially one but multiple in functions; because of these multiple functions, the created spirit is diversified formally by various qualities but remains essentially one. The rest of the treatise explores the

1. Hugh of Saint Victor, 'De unione spiritus et corporis', ed. Piazzoni, *Studi Medievali*, 3rd Ser. 1/2 (1980) 861–888 (=PL 177:285–294); *L'anima dell'uomo. Trattati sull'anima dal V al IX Secolo*, ed. Ilario Tolomio (Milan: Rusconi, 1979); *Three Treatises on Man. A Cistercian Miscellany*, ed. Bernard McGinn (Kalamazoo: Cistercian Publications, 1977); Aelred of Rievaulx, *Dialogue on the Soul* (Kalamazoo: Cistercian Publications, 1981). Some of these works are compared with Achard's treatise in Häring, 'Gilbert of Poitiers, Author of the *"De discretione animae, spiritus et mentis"* commonly attributed to Achard of Saint Victor', MS 22 (1960) 169–172.

interrelations between the three principal functions of the interior spirit, and the variations in vocabulary used to describe them.

Two things will strike the reader familiar with the subject. Unlike Hugh of Saint Victor's *De unione spiritus et corporis*, Achard's work makes no use of the ancient medical theories that had recently become available in Latin. Secondly, Achard's treatise parallels the Aristotelian treatment of the same subject found in authors like Saint Thomas.[2] For example, it is easy to compare his 'spirit' to the interior senses that form a bridge between the material knowing of the external senses and the immaterial knowing of the intellect. However, Achard's entire treatise is inspired by platonizing sources, and his philosophical positions are often at variance with those of Saint Thomas. The interior substance is one; it is united with the body, itself a substance. The interior substance is the recipient of forms. The image that is the object of the spirit or imagination is spiritual, not material.

The one underlying theme is the symmetry between God and his image in the human being. For example, in sections eleven and twelve it is shown that, granted that in both God and the human being the spiritual substance and its powers are identical even as they extend to many objects, God is different insofar as his substance remains totally unmoved (and therefore totally simple) even as relates to an innumerably greater number of objects.

Achard makes frequent reference to the interplay between things and the words used to describe them. For instance, already in sections eighteen and nineteen he speaks of the various words used to described the various powers of the simple substance. Multiple qualities have given rise to multiple words; these words, however, refer to powers, not to the essence. Because he finds in language a clue to ontological structure, Achard will spend the last part of the treatise dealing with anomalies in linguistic (biblical) usage inconsonant with his analysis.

In section twenty eight we find a peculiar statement: 'To the statement God is to be loved totally with all of these, there is added:

2. See *Summa Theologiae* 1.77.1 and 1.78.4.

"and neighbor", that is, "with all your strength". . . .'[3] Morin and Martineau suppress ' "neighbor", that is'. In any case, the point is that Achard uses 'with all your strength' (*ex tota virtute*) to interpret the early phrases—with all your heart, soul, and mind—as referring to powers. He goes on to argue that the Gospel here teacher all the powers are to be directed by love, rather than that all three are instruments by which human beings love. Only the highest power, the mind, receives the love of God directly; from the mind it is communicated to the other powers.

In section thirty five, as in Sermon 12.7–8,[4] Achard shows interest in the question of the soul separated from the body. Here he says that the separated soul has an innate capacity to be united with and act through a body, but the exercise of this capacity is impeded when the soul is apart from a body.

In sections thirty–six through thirty–eight Achard draws out the parallel existing between the powers of mind (intellect and will) and those of soul (sense and sensory appetite). The adjective 'natural' (*animalis*) is derived from soul (*anima*), so that those who desire or enjoy sensory goods immoderately, or prefer them to the goods of the 'mind', are called 'natural' or 'sensual' in a pejorative sense. In themselves, sense knowledge and sense appetite are natural and therefore good.[5]

The spirit grasps images of the things that the soul perceives through the senses. The power of spirit that does this (corresponding to sense below it and to intellect above it) is imagination. The imagination immediately perceives images, not things, but it is only things that can be imagined.[6] When I imagine the form of someone who is absent it is not his image but the person or his corporeal form that I imagine.[7] Achard declares that the imaginative image by which I know the absent corporeal being is not itself corporeal. In this

3. Here, and in the rest of this introduction, I make use of Häring's observations in 'Gilbert of Poitiers, Author of the *"De discretione animae, spiritus et mentis"* commonly attributed to Achard of Saint Victor', 157–168.

4. See also Sermons 2.4; 6.1.

5. Section thirty–nine.

6. Section forty–two.

7. Section forty–three.

Achard's view is different from the views of scholastic Aristotelians, who held that the species, as distinct from the concept, was physical. Nebuchadnezzar and Pharaoh saw images; they were dreaming, a function of spirit; Daniel and Joseph saw the meaning of images, a function of mind.

In his excursus on the Magnificat, in which both 'soul' and 'spirit' are used to mean 'mind', Achard theorizes, as he does often in his sermons, on the nature of contemplation.[8] Intellect magnifies God by rising above the objects of sense and their images, even beyond its very self, to contemplate God's immense and incomprehensible majesty. The will magnifies God by submitting entirely to God in chaste fear,[9] forgetting itself and all else, as it reaches for God's majesty. Such was true at least of Mary's contemplation. For those incapable of such heights, there are lesser ways to magnify God.[10]

---

8. Sermons 12.6; 13.32–33; 14.22 (where Mary is a model of contemplative living).

9. Sermon 15.7.

10. Sections sixty-eight and sixty-nine.

On the Distinction of Soul, Spirit, and Mind[11]

THE INTERIOR SUBSTANCE, which together with the body constitutes the human being, is usually differentiated according to its various activities or functions[12] it has or can have, into various powers, also called its virtual parts. It is, however, in and of itself a power essentially one, simple, and undivided. By itself it can do whatever it is naturally capable of. It is, then, possessed of power by itself, although not from itself. In the former respect it is like God; in the latter it is different from him. (2) God is powerful both in himself and from himself. However, insofar as it is not contradictory in God for him to be a substance although he is power, or to be power although he is a substance, so neither is it contradictory in the thing made in his image, which it bears by this very fact, that its natural potency is not a quality or a form, but its very

---

11. Achard's text is not particularly difficult to read in Latin, but it is very condensed. It could be made easier for the reader by being expanded in the translation, but I have for the most part refrained from doing that. There are also a few Latin words that give the translator trouble. One is *sensualitas*. By this Achard (like Richard of Saint Victor) means not sensuality but the sensory inclinations or appetites that arise directly from sensation (see sections thirty six through thirty nine). 'Sensuality' carries with it overtones of disorder and lust lacking in the Latin word; hence, I have always translated it 'sensory appetite' or 'sensory inclination'. *Affectio* and *afficere* also are difficult. They refer not just to affects (feelings, emotions and so forth), but to a wide variety of changes caused or undergone. I have sometimes translated these words woodenly, at other times tried to give them a more colloquial rendering.

This translation is made directly from the Latin edition of N. M. Häring. Occasionally, I have preferred different manuscript readings to his; these instances are mentioned in the notes. My work has been made easier by the existence of E. Martineau's thoughtful French translation; I have indicated some instances where my translation differs from his. The editions and translation of *De discretione* are discussed in the paragraph of the introduction devoted to Achard's works.

12. On the *officia* of the soul, see Augustine, *De Trinitate* 12, CCSL 50 (Turnhout: Brepols, 1968) 356–380.

essence, which is not something different from it. (3) If its power were not itself but its form, even if substantial, it would be necessary that something underlie it, to which it would come not substantially but accidentally. From the joining of these there would come about something not simple, but compounded of the power as a form, and of the matter or quasi-matter receiving the form. (4) Therefore, the composition here would exist with respect to substance also, which could be dissolved, if not in act at least in thought. What would then underlie power, constituting along with power the thing itself? Would it be a property? Would it be a substance? (5) But a property cannot underlie to a property. If it was a substance, it would be either corporeal or incorporeal—but what is corporeal cannot be a part of an incorporeal thing. If the substance were incorporeal, it would be either rational or irrational—but a rational substance cannot have either one as a part of it. (6) However, because by this reason and others it has been shown elsewhere that the substance which is now under consideration cannot be other than a certain power, I propose to conclude these matters here.

(7) As we said, this power is simple in its essence and multiple in its functions, so that, taking both aspects into consideration, the power is said to be one in many and many in one, or rather, one is said to be many and many are said to be one. (8) So too in God, whose image this is, although power or will is simple and one with respect to substance, yet with respect to the many, which both underlie, each is multiplied, with the result that many powers and wills are reckoned to exist there. You have a scriptural witness to this fact where you read: 'Who will tell the powers of the

Lord?'† And again: 'Great are the works of the Lord sought out in all his wills'.† (9) Although that whereby [God] wills or is powerful is only one, what he wills or is powerful for is not one. To will or be powerful for this or that is not the same, although by the same he wills or is powerful for both. For a similar reason in the Book of Wisdom the spirit of wisdom is called 'multiple',† and in the Apostle's letter to the Ephesians the wisdom of God is called 'multiform'.[13]† (10) But, you will say, if these, in what concerns unity and multiplicity, are related to each power in the same way, where in this is the simplicity of the Creator greater than that of the creature, and how, in this power, is the unity of the Truth greater than that of the image. (11) Therefore consider in each power, not to how many things it is related, but rather how it is related. If you attend to the numerical character of the things to which each is related or can be extended, multiplicity will be as much greater there than here in proportion as God is capable of more things than a human being is. (12) But this multiplicity is as it were extrinsic. It is to found in those things which exist or can exist as a result of the powers and not in those things which exist or can exist in the powers. If, however, you look at how each is or can be related when it acts, you will here an intrinsic multiplicity while you find there no plurality there.

Ps 106:2
Ps 111:2
Ws 7:22
Ep 3:10

(13) God's power remains immobile in everything he does. It is not affected in different ways by its different actions, because nothing ever affects it. Therefore, it both moves all things without itself moving, and in acting and in not acting it always

13. See *De unitate* 2.18 and 2.5; Sermon 13.1–2, 32.

remains the same.[14] (14) By contrast, not only is an inferior power affected in various ways according to various effects, but it also is, or can be, subject to multiple forms of alteration because of various passions.[15] Therefore, although there is no multiplicity in it by reason of its essence, nevertheless multiplicity exists in it by reason of the things that are in its essence. (15) Its essence, or rather the essence it is, receives into itself various affections by which it—though simple in and by itself—is moved, changed, and differentiated in multiple ways. (16) These affections that occur in it are certain qualities by which the same essence or power is variously informed so that it is multiplied into various powers formally, although not essentially. Although all of these are in essence that one power, because of the formal distinction by which their plurality is determined none of them can be said[16] to be another.

(17) Hence the will is not and cannot be called the reason, nor the sense imagination, nor understanding the memory, and in general none of them is or can be called by any other name. This is not without justification. (18) Their names were invented because of the affections, which are diverse, rather than because of the essence, which is the same in all. Hence, the significance of the names looks more to the affections than to the essence, so that they are denied to each other because of the variety of affections rather than predicated of each other because of the identity of essence. (19) For

14. *De unitate* 1.43; see Augustine, *De civitate Dei* 12.18, CCSL 48 (Turnhout: Brepols, 1955) 373–375.

15. Martineau translates: 'The inferior power, by contrast, is diversely affected, and it is submitted or can be submitted to a multiple alteration not only according to its diverse effects, but also by diverse passions.'

16. Reading *dici* with Morin and Martineau rather than *dicit*.

this reason it happens also that powers of this kind are called qualities because the whole reason for distinguishing then, whether things or words, lies in the qualities. Truth, however, shows that each of them is a substance and all are one substance. (20) Because I seem to have satisfactorily explained the assertion of this unity of two of them, that is, of the reason and the will, in certain questions regarding sin, I will not undertake to pursue it further here regarding either these or others. However, because substance or power is one in itself, while it is informed either actually or possibly in various ways by the multiplicity of affections, so it is said to be, and is, many powers, because it comprehends them all in equal measure in itself; none of them, however, can comprehend the whole of it, that is, according to all its divisions. These appear to be related to it with respect to the special nature of the parts, but by a more lively and truthful examination of the matter not only are all that one [substance or power], but each is also that whole [substance or power] with respect to the essence.

(21) Just as in what concerns God certain words pertains to a single person—such as 'Father', 'Son', and 'Holy Spirit'—but others to all—such as 'God'—and some pertain to two, as, for example, 'to proceed from the Father' pertains to the Father and the Son, and 'to be the cause or principle of the Holy Spirit' pertains to the Father and the Son, so also here some names are related to the powers individually—such as 'reason', 'will', and the like—and others to diverse ones—such as 'soul' and 'spirit' and some to several [powers]—such as 'mind'. Soul and spirit are interchangeable;[17] they

17. One may omit *accepta* with Morin, Martineau and three of the four manuscripts.

are best understood, like 'sword' and 'saber', as identical. (22) Both designate indifferently an undifferentiated substance—namely, the incorporeal part of the human being, which along with the body constitutes a human—not by defining that part specifically in accord with one or the other of the powers into which it is divided, but absolutely, in accord with itself—a power simple and one, by which alone it can do what it can do by all them. This one, as was said, itself is all, and all are one, distinguished numerically by affections.

(23) It is common usage, both in Scripture and in common speech, to understand soul and spirit in this way. To take one example of each[18] from many in the Scriptures, in the Gospel Truth uses the words in this way when he says: 'Do not fear those who kill the body but cannot kill the soul, but fear the one who can destroy both soul and body
Mt 10:28 in Gehenna'.† (24) Likewise 'spirit' is understood in the same way in Ecclesiastes when it says: 'The dust', that is the flesh, 'returns to the earth it came
Qo 12:7 from, and the spirit returns to God who gave it'.† (25) When these words are not referred generally to the whole interior part of the human being, but separately and distinctly to certain of its powers, then the various words ordinarily have various meanings in accord with the realities underlying them, distinguished both from each other and from the mind. (26) The Apostle clearly divides spirit and mind in the first letter to the Corinthians, saying: 'If I pray in a tongue, my spirit prays but my mind is unprofitable. What then? I will pray with the spirit, and I will pray the my mind also; I will sing praise with the spirit, and I will sing

18. I take 'both' to refer to *anima* and *spiritus*; Martineau takes it to refer to the two testaments of the Scriptures. His translation may well be preferable.

praise with the mind also.'† In the Gospel mind is distinguished from soul when the commandment is given to love God 'with the whole heart' and 'with the whole soul' and 'with the whole mind'.† If 'heart' is taken there to mean 'spirit', this is a basis for distinguishing it from both of the others. (27) It also seems to be suggested there that the interior substance of the human being, which is capable of love, is comprehended in these three totally, that is, with all its powers, and the totality of its powers is adequately divided into these three, so that there is none of them which is not contained in one of these.

1 Co 14:14–15

Mt 22:37

(28) To the statement that God is to be loved totally with all of these there is added: 'and your neighbor', that is, 'with all your strength'.† We should note that the distinction between these three was not made with respect to substance, which is indivisible and the same in all, but with respect to the multiplicity of powers in the one substance, and that nothing of its power remains which is not included in these three. (29) This same defining addition is more evident in the Law, where from the fact that it is commanded that God be loved totally with these three, there immediately follows, as though as an explanation: 'and with all your powers'.† God is not commanded to be loved with all these because love of him can be in all of them in accord with the special nature of each, but because all of them must be exercised, regulated, and formed in accord with it. (30) Only the mind receives the love of God of itself and directly; insofar as it is possible, it pours out, as it can, [the love] it has received in accord with certain affections and effects, to the spirit, and, by the spirit's mediation, to the soul—that is, by moving,

Mk 12:31, 30

Dt 6:5

affecting, and preparing the inferior powers with it and in accord with it. (31) The power of love exists in the mind 'like oil on the head', which
Ps 133:2 runs down from the head 'on to the beard',† that is, from the mind to the spirit, as if from the beard to the 'hem of the garment': from the spirit it runs down into the soul by a kind of outpouring of itself.[19] Mind is on top, soul at the bottom, spirit in the middle. (32) Mind is the innermost of the three; spirit is exterior to mind but interior to soul. Hence it is that soul is compared to a garment, as being outermost, and to the hem, which is at the bottom. Spirit can be compared to a beard insofar as it is nearer the mind. The distinction is not to be understood as having to do with rank in terms of place but in terms of nature and perception.

(33) The mind is that which has a natural capacity, both in understanding and in affectivity, for truth, which is superior in dignity and deeper in subtlety to other things; in understanding through knowledge, in affectivity through love; it possesses the image of God in its power of knowing, and the likeness in its power of loving.[20] (34) The soul is that which can spread itself out as far as is in it, as it were downwardly and outwardly, through the instruments of the body toward the ultimate appearances of things, that is, to corporeal forms and properties, to perceive them by sense and to desire them by sensory appetite. (35) I have put down 'as far as is in it' because, although it cannot do this when separated from the body, it nevertheless retains in itself a natural faculty by which it can be united to a body and do this through a body.

19. Martineau translates: 'according to a *débordement* which is proper to it on each occasion.'

20. Genesis 1:26; See Sermon 15.11.

(36) As I have noted, the following distinction between the sense and the sensory appetite of the soul should be made. Sense is the power of perceiving corporeal things in themselves; sensory appetite is the power of desiring them and of taking delight in them. When you perceive something by sight, or hearing, or any other sense, and desire it and take delight in it, such a perception pertains to sense, while the desire and the delight pertain to sensory appetite.

(37) Even when you are not affected by delight but by a contrary emotion from what you sense, and you do not desire it but loathe and flee it, these also occur in the same sensory appetite. Thus, the soul desires things agreeable to itself and to its flesh, and for this reason it also flees from what is repugnant to it. From what its nature takes delight in when it enjoys them comes sadness when it suffers from them. (38) All these things take place naturally in the soul from and around sensory appetite just as in the mind too only by the power of the will do people naturally love what is good for them and hate what is bad, and rejoice in the one out of love and deplore the other out of hate. (39) However natural these affections of the mind and will, arising from intellectual things, and those of the soul or sensory appetite, arising from bodies, may be, it is not in relation to nature but because of vice that we call 'natural'[21]† or 'sensual' those 1 Co 2:14; Jude 19
who desire to delight, or who do take delight, by means of the sensory appetite in these inferior things from the perception of the senses, but those who in this exceed the proper measure—that is,

21. The adjective *animalis* (1 Corinthians 2:14; Jude 19), derivel from *anima* (soul), describes the lowest of the three of the three powers of the soul. Possible translations, besides 'natural', are 'sensual', 'unspiritual', and 'wordly'.

those who prefer this inferior delight of the soul to the superior and better delight of the mind. (40) Against this, the Apostle said he did not count
Ac 20:24 'his soul more precious than' himself,† calling his mind himself in accord with the saying of the philosopher that 'each one's mind is himself'.[22]
1 Co 2:14; Jude 19 'Soul', when referring to the 'natural self',† and in these words of the Apostle, is taken in accord with that so to speak partial meaning that has been defined; it is the same in the Gospel where the
Mt 6:25 Lord commands that 'we be not solicitous'† about our soul, what we will eat, and where he says that
Jn 12:27; Mt 26:38 'his soul is troubled'† and 'grieved even to death'.† What is in the spirit is related to what is in the soul; although they are not exactly the same thing, the former express a likeness of the latter.

(41) It belongs to the spirit to perceive the images of the things[23] that the soul perceives, and hence the power it has by which it does this is called 'imagination'. What sensation is in the soul, that imagination is in the spirit. The resemblance between sensible things and their images is so great that, although the latter are not the former on account of the expressed likeness of the latter to the former, when the things are perceived the images too are said to be perceived on account of them and in them. (42) The spirit does not perceive things the way the soul does, immediately in themselves, but only in their images; these, however, it perceives in themselves immediately. Therefore, it is not only truly but accurately said to perceive them. Although the spirit perceives them solely by the power of the imagination, it can be said

22. Cicero, *De republica* 6.24.26 (Cambridge: Harvard, 1951) 278–281. This adage is cited by John of Salisbury, *Metalogicon* 3.7 (Oxford: Clarendon, 1929) 146.

23. See Augustine *De Genesi ad litteram* CSEL 28 (Vienna: Tempsky, 1894) 409–411.

to imagine not the images, but only the things of which they are the images. (43) To imagine is to perceive something through its image and not through itself. Images of this kind do not have other images through which they themselves can be perceived. Thus, when I ponder within myself an image similar to the bodily form of someone, whose bodily form I do not see, I do not imagine the image but very person or the bodily form of the person. (44) The image, although it can be called a kind of form of the physical thing, is not itself physical. A thing cannot be said to be physical unless it is matter, or from matter, or in matter. You will find none of these to be the case regarding the image we are now considering.

(45) However similar they are, there is this difference between the perceptions of the soul and the spirit: although both are said to perceive the same thing, the soul perceives it in itself, and the spirit perceives it only in its image. The soul functions only with regard to matter while the spirit functions apart from matter. The soul functions only through the body, the spirit through itself. The soul works exteriorly, the spirit within. The soul does not perceive everything that the spirit perceives, whereas the spirit perceives whatever the soul perceives. (46) Whatever comes to the perception of the soul by any of its senses also falls under the perception of the spirit through its image without an interval of time. However, the images the spirit perceives cannot go out to the perception of the soul either through themselves or through their images. (47) The spirit perceives equally the images of things absent and present, and equally the images of the things that do not exist and those that do, while the soul can perceives only the prop-

erties of things existent and present. The spirit, however, can perceive nothing except according to the properties perceived by the soul. (48) As the perception of the spirit is formed according to the perception of the soul, so too its affection imitates the affection of the soul. Just as the latter is affected by the properties of bodily things, in a similar way the former is affected by the images of those properties. (49) The spirit has, then, the power of perceiving non-bodily images of bodily things according to a likeness of the senses and of being affected by them according to a likeness of the sensory appetite. Thus, to the spirit pertains whatever we do or undergo during dreams, as if we were doing or undergoing those things bodily, and whatever occurs to us then occurs as if through an external sense of the flesh.

(50) Hence Pharaoh and Nebuchadnezzar are said to have seen whatever they saw in their dreams in the spirit, but Joseph and Daniel in their minds. The former saw those things according to the images of sensible things, while the latter understood their meaning; they had neither bodily form nor an image like a bodily form. All such things pertain to the mind just as bodily forms pertain to the perception of the soul, and all their images to the perception of the spirit. Hence, the ecstasies of the saints, their revelations and visions, and whatever others things are formed from within in the way of images, are said to happen 'in the spirit'. (51) Thus,
Rv 1:10 John says he was 'in the spirit'† when he perceived his apocalypse, that is the revelation divinely made him. That revelation was either totally, or for the most part, presented in images of bodily things, but he understood that the meaning those images bore belonged not to the spirit but to the mind.

(52) For the same reason the prophets are presented as having seen what was revealed to them 'in the spirit'. They perceived most of these things from inside, with their spiritual eyes, in figures and images. The words that we read to have been directed to them did not sound bodily, be we believe that nearly all were formed by the spiritual ministry of the angels in accord with the images of bodily sounds, and were perceived by spiritual rather than carnal hearing.

(53) Why, then, since the Word is of God the Father, and God the Son is that Word—so that speech seems to refer better to their special natures—are we accustomed to say of the Holy Spirit rather than of the Father and of the Son—although it is no more true of the Spirit—that he spoke in and through the prophets?[24] My opinion is that we are accustomed to say this because of a way of speaking directed to them 'in the spirit'. To whom rather than to the Spirit of God were we to attribute spiritual speech, divinely formed in the spirit, spiritually formed by the spiritual ministry of spirits, and perceived in the spirit by the spirit in a spiritual way? (54) This spirit, which is in us and in which such speech is formed and heard, is referred to the special nature of the Holy Spirit rather than of the Father or Son not simply through sharing the same word, but on account of a likeness of nature. As that Spirit is a kind of connection between the Father and the Son, so this spirit is not unreasonably thought to be a kind of bond between mind and soul, in the middle not by its position in space but by its position in nature, so that without it they are not thought capable of

24. Achard is referring to a statement in the Nicene-Constantinopolitan Creed: 'We believe in the Holy Spirit . . . who has spoken through the prophets'.

being joined and of existing in the same thing. (55) The soul in those brute animals that lack memory seems to exist not only apart from mind but apart from spirit as well. In those, however, that possess memory, soul and spirit are found without mind. Those things incapable of reason and understanding do not possess a mind; without a soul they would not live, and without a spirit they cannot possess memory. (56) All memory resides either in the spirit or in the mind—in the spirit if it is of bodily things, either those in the soul or those in the spirit itself. From all of these is formed an imaginative memory. Other things, which cannot come to the perception of soul or of spirit and so are perceived by the mind alone, are therefore retained in memory in the mind alone. (57) In angels, who are without a soul, a spirit perhaps exists with the mind; that the soul cannot be there it is clear. Some ambiguity about the spirit, whether it is there or not, can exist; those unsure about their minds can be unsure whether they themselves have a mind—except that without a mind no one can be unsure about anything. (58) In God there is only the mind without any admixture of soul or spirit. If we refer to a soul in God, or the Spirit of God, or a spirit who is God, the meaning is different and utterly remote from that involved when we now speak of soul and spirit.

The soul is alonc without spirit and mind in some instances, and the mind is without soul and spirit in others, but the spirit does not seem to be anywhere without both of the other two. (59) Again, soul and spirit are found in one place without mind, and mind and spirit are perhaps found without soul in another, but soul and mind cannot be found anywhere without spirit. Spirit, as it is neighbor to both of the others, can be united of itself to both of them. (60) The other two, far distant from each other, do not agree to union except through the mediation of the spirit. So spirit, connecting them and leading them into a single covenant or structure, can not inappropriately be spoken of as a sort of bond between them. (61) Only in a human being does such a connection occur. Nowhere else does it happen that all these three are found together in the same thing. Of these three, soul is nearest to flesh so as to be immediately united to and infused in it. Mind is most remote from the flesh, since spirit and soul are placed between them. Spirit is nearer the flesh than is mind but more remote than soul. Soul alone is between flesh and spirit just as spirit alone is between soul and mind. (62) Although soul is connected to flesh and to spirit without any intermediary, and spirit is similarly connected to soul and to mind, by a kind of kinship soul seem to have a greater affinity to spirit than to flesh, and spirit a greater affinity to soul than to mind. Soul, although it is in flesh, is not and cannot be of the same substance with it, though it is of the same substance with spirit. Although consubstantial with soul and mind, spirit, in what concerns its perceptions and affections, is more closely conformed to soul than to mind.

(63) At times there is a shifting in terminology among these three, mind, spirit, and soul. Sometimes by 'spirit' we understand the mind, as when we read in the Apostle: 'Walk in the spirit',† and Ga 5:16
again: 'Be reformed in the spirit of your mind',† Ep 4:23
that is, in the spirit that is your mind. And also this: 'The desires of the flesh are against the spirit, and

Ga 5:17 the desires of the spirit are against the flesh'.† And in the Gospel: 'The spirit is willing, but the flesh
Mt 26:41 is weak'.†

(64) You will find many things written in this way. By the same usage, people in whom the mind rules over the others that are subject to it are called 'spiritual'. But, conversely, the spirit is sometimes, if rarely, understood by the word 'mind'. Thus in the Acts of the Apostles Peter is said to have seen in 'an ecstasy on mind' the heavens opened and a vessel descending, and the other things we
Ac 10:10ff read there.† Augustine testifies that because this was done by means of the images of bodily things it was done in the spirit, which is inferior to the mind.[25] (65) It is no different when Paul asserts that, when he was praying in the temple, 'in a trance of the
Ac 22:17 mind' he saw and heard the Lord.†

Mind is also sometimes seems to be signified by the word 'soul'. In the canticle of blessed Mary, 'soul' is perhaps to be understood as her 'mind' when, by her own testimony, it is declared that the Virgin's soul magnifies the Lord and that her
Lk 1:46 spirit exults in her savior.† (66) To magnify the Lord does not pertain to sense and sensory appetite but to intellect and will. Sensation perceives nothing besides sensible things, nor does sensory appetite desire anything except sensible things. It does not derive its delight in any other way. (67) Intellect and will magnify the Lord, when the intellect, not only surpasses the things subject to the senses and their images, but even leaves itself behind to some extent, and reaches above itself to contemplate the immense and incomprehensible majesty of the deity, presiding over all without

---

25. *De Genesi ad litteram* 12.11.24 (Vienna: Tempsky, 1894) 416–417 (=PL 34:462f.).

pride, judging all with tranquility, and arranging all with great gentleness,† and the will too subjects itself to [the majesty of the deity] with chaste fear and reaches out to it through hope and desire, disdaining everything else because of this love, and in some way forgetting itself and all other things because of joy in him. (68) Thus, when 'a human being comes to a deep heart' God is truly exalted,† so that as [God] is 'perverse with the perverted' so too he is 'holy with the holy',† lying low with the former, lifted up with the latter. Those unable to lift up and magnify God magnificently through such a great lifting up of their minds, have from the Scriptures many other lesser modes of magnifying God, about which it is not necessary to speak now. (69) I have chosen this one in preference to the others, and noted it in a special way here, because this one, which is more excellent than the others, more excellent even than can be said, cannot have been lacking to the great excellence of the Virgin Mother.

Ws 12:18

Ps 63:7–8 Vulg.

Ps 18:26, 27

As the mind magnifies the Lord, so too the spirit exults 'in God its savior'.† (70) This occurs in the spirit when it perceives divinely certain first fruits of outer salvation and is struck by a kind of sprinkling of inner sweetness; it dances and leaps, not containing itself because of the great gentleness. This sweetness or gentleness, although not bodily, nevertheless bears some likeness to [the bodily] but with a much greater abundance of purity and gladness. (71) Delight, arising from this, and striking a human being from within, forcefully and gently, is exultation of the spirit in God. It belongs to the spirit to exult, to the mind to rejoice. However, I do not recall that I have heard or read elsewhere that 'soul' refers to 'mind' or 'mind' to 'soul'. (72)

Lk 1:46–47

'Spirit' is perhaps taken for soul when, as in Genesis 6:17 where the 'spirit of life' is said to be in flesh, and elsewhere also, the spirit of flesh is mentioned.[26] However, as we have shown, soul is inferior to spirit and infused into flesh,[27] and this is the cause of its life. (73) In cases of this sort nothing hinders us from taking 'soul' or 'spirit' to stand for the whole interior substance. Wherever soul is, and whatever it does or undergoes, spirit or mind is there; it does or undergoes the same thing because this—both all and each—is itself one.[28] (74) Sometimes, however, to comprehend it totality and distinguish them sufficiently, not these three but only two words are joined. Thus in the
1 Th 5:23 first letter to the Thessalonians† it is written: 'May the God of peace himself sanctify you in all things, so that your spirit and soul and body may be kept whole and blameless at the coming of our Lord Jesus Christ'. Here therefore, either 'spirit' includes the two higher [powers] or 'soul' includes the two lower ones.

---

26. Perhaps Genesis 3:21–22.

27. Martineau translates, erroneously I believe: 'The soul is infused into the flesh, as one has said, by the inferior *spiritus*, and such is for it the cause of life.'

28. Martineau translates: 'It itself <the interior substance> undergoes the same thing, but it itself is unitarily all these <powers> together and separately.'

On the Unity of God and the Plurality of Creatures

INTRODUCTION

In *De unitate* Achard himself gives two outlines of the work, neither of which quite fits the contents.[1] It is hard not to conclude that the work is not in a polished and completed state, and may well be conflated from several fragments. On the other hand, much of it is very tightly reasoned and cohesive.

In addition to the peculiarities caused primarily by Achard's own attempts to outline his procedures, there are some other puzzles about this work. One is the title. Through the centuries it has been sometimes referred to as *De Trinitate*, which seems not unreasonable for the first 'treatise' but has little applicability to the second. At the end of the only manuscript we read: '*On the unity and plurality of creatures*'.[2] Sometimes the work has been referred to as '*On the Unity of the Divine Essence and the Plurality of Creatures*'. Martineau rejects 'of the Divine Essence' as uncharacteristic of Achard who

1. *De unitate* 1.12; 1.37–39.
2. Martineau, ed., 196.

uses 'essence' to refer to the bare substrate of the forms. He believes, however, that the insertion of 'God' for 'the Divine Essence' gives us a proper title. His arguments and edition will presumably carry the day regarding the title.[3]

Another puzzle concerns the genre of Achard's work. The two books into which it is divided are each called '*Tractatus*' ('Treatise'). Etymologically this is a good title, insofar as *tractatus* comes from *trahere* (to draw or draw out): much of Achard's effort is to draw out the meaning of words or concepts. Twice, however, Achard refers to his work as a *disputatio*.[4]

The reader of the work needs to keep in mind that much of it is elaborated with the distinction between 'there' (*ibi*) and 'here' (*hic*) to the fore. 'There' is the realm of the divine and unchanging: God, the Trinity, and God's ideas; 'here' is the world of the mutable, humanity, and the created universe. Achard is concerned with the communion and connection in difference of these two spheres of being. He is, in fact, concerned with some of the basic questions of classical philosophy.

For philosophers who believe in a God who is creator of the entire universe, the deepest and most all-embracing question is the question of the one and the many. In its metaphysical form, the question is how do the many things of this world come to co-exist with the one perfect being of God. Drawing on a long tradition of Christian Neoplatonism, Achard tries to show that the doctrines of the Trinity and the Divine Ideas make the transition from the One to the many more comprehensible. He shows that plurality as well as unity is characteristic of God, and that the Triune God knows eternally all possible kinds and instances of created being.

At a second, epistemological level, one problem is how one mind knows the single essence shared by many individuals of the same species; another related problem is how many minds know the same truth; a third problem, developed at length by Saint Augustine, is

3. Martineau, ed., 46–62.

4. *De unitate* 1.12, 1.50, ed. Martineau, 80–81, 134–135. See also a single use of the verb *disputare* in 1.42. *De unitate* is formed from a number of closely-linked chains of argument; perhaps each of these is what Achard means by *disputatio.*

how mutable human beings know eternally unchanging truths; a fourth problem is how God knows the beings and events of creation without becoming dependent upon them. Achard argues that the divine ideas, properly understood, help us answer all four questions.

Much is original and stimulating in Achard's argument. Of particular interest is his attempt to argue by reason that uncreated divine unity has in it an element of plurality. Using a much different starting point and line of argumentation, Achard attempts a philosophical analysis of the Trinity that has something of the scope and grandeur of Richard of Saint Victor's famous *De Trinitate*.

Several times[5] Achard is drawn to a consideration of beauty. For him the beauty of created things, taken individually or in their interrelatedness, is a distant hint of the infinite beauty contained in the infinite possibilities which are present to God in the divine ideas.

Methodologically, in 1.15 Achard makes an important observation about the force of converging arguments. Anticipating John Henry Newman and others, Achard notes that regarding philosophical and religious issues human beings are usually convinced by a multitude of converging arguments, not by a single line of deductive reasoning.

In 2.16, a paragraph forming a transition between the discussion of the divine ideas and the other causes of things, Achard gives a beautiful description of intellectual contemplation of the truth 'embraced naked in its beauty by the arms of the interior man'. Here Achard's highly abstract treatise joins the most elevated moments of his spiritual discourses. This coinciding is a reminder that for Achard, as for his Benedictine, Cistercian, and Victorine contemporaries, speculation on the divine ideas and on the nature of the soul as a way to understand the one and the many is also a path to help the individual enter as deeply as possible into union with the triune God. Metaphysics and spirituality are not separate quests.

In the translation that follows I have tried to follow the Latin

5. 1.5–6; 1.48.

text closely. Martineau introduces a number of words into the Latin text which he suggests were left out by inadvertence. I have not translated most of these; when I do include them I put the added words within brackets. I have profited from the copious notes to Martineau's French translation and from the translation itself.

On the Unity of God and the Plurality of Creatures

The First Tract

Chapter 1. In creatures no true plurality exists because there is no true unity. Plurality is nothing else than multiplied unity, or as many unities as are needed to equal the plurality. However, unless somewhere true plurality is to be found there will not be any plurality at all. It is impossible that plurality either exist or be spoken of properly unless it is or imitates that very unity of plurality, that is, true plurality. It cannot imitate true plurality unless true plurality exists. Hence it exists. However, it cannot exist except where there is true unity, and no true unity exists except in God. There true plurality and unity must reside, but not in the same respect.

Chapter 2. The plurality of creatures is very far from the highest unity, so that it cannot inhere in it immediately. Not only is it far from it because the former is plurality while the latter is unity, but also because the former is temporal while the latter is eternal, the former is finite while the latter is immeasurable, the former is mutable and corruptible while the latter is immutable and incorruptible, the former is created, the latter uncreated. Reason requires that besides this plurality, which is far removed from God, there be some superior plurality which coheres immediately to that highest unity, and is so to speak intermediate between that unity and this plurality. 'Intermediate' should be understood not in terms of place and dignity but with reference to cause and image—that is, that [plurality] that is from [unity] and by which this [plurality] exists is common [to both] by likeness, that is, has something common to both: with [plurality] because it is a plurality, and with [unity] because it is uncreated, because it is immutable, etc. These things are said of the nature of unity, so that this plurality, because it has something in common with that plurality, can also inhere in the unity through the mediating plurality.

Chapter 3. There is something else. Other things seem to argue that plurality exists there. Nothing, not even a created thing which does not in some way imitate the true and highest unity is or can exist. Some sort of likeness exists between every creature and that unity; this likeness is partial and imperfect. However, nothing is called imperfect except in relation to something perfect, the perfection of which it fails to attain. Hence, there subsists somewhere and in something a full and perfect likeness of that unity. Since this [likeness] cannot be in a creature, as was said, it necessarily exists above the creature, in divinity itself. However, no likeness can exist except among several, nor can it be full and total except among equals. Nothing can be equal to the highest unity which is not where it is—that is, in the supreme deity. Therefore, not only unity is found there, but also plurality.

Chapter 4. Hence, this very likeness is further evidence for that plurality we are seeking. Likeness itself, since it is one particular thing, cannot avoid being in some way like the unity proposed. Since other things are like it by some form of participation in likeness, hence partially and not fully so, likeness cannot participate in itself but is wholly like [unity] by a perfect and full likeness, and so equal to it in all respects.

Chapter 5. The unity that is in things according to a certain equality among them attains plurality, and so great a likeness with the beauty that comes from the fitting together and congruence of many—of bodies, and of spirits, and of each with the other—that it should not in any way be removed from there where the highest beauty exists. Moreover, the beauty of this unity common to many is a cause so great that the unity of each, which inheres in each of them, cannot be more beautiful, but this beauty everywhere seems inferior, at least if the creature is not united to its Creator and, 'being united to him, becomes one spirit'.[6]† While the 1 Co 6:17
unity by which they are fused into one spirit is much more eminent and gracious than that found in a single created spirit, it cannot equal the beauty that is in the superior—that is, the uncreated—spirit. It is invariably the case that although the created unity can correspond to the uncreated unity in some respects, it cannot do so in all respects. But if anything corresponds to the first and highest

6. Achard cites this text also in Sermons 2.3; 13.1 and 7; 15.34.

unity fully and completely, it is completely impossible, in this supreme harmony perfected by their highest unity, that an unequal beauty be expressed by either of them. The beauty of each would of itself coalesce into the complete unity of the other, and somehow fuse with its beauty. Hence, also, the beauty of that unity necessarily exceeds the beauty of each, unless because it is immense in both and therefore equal and one and so cannot be greater in both together than in either of them considered by itself. It is thus in creation also: the wisdom of many is one and equal, and is not found to be less in any of them than in all.

It is clear then that nothing can be or be thought which is more beautiful or greater than the beauty of the aforesaid unity and of its supreme fittingness. It is therefore necessary that it be in God—in fact, that it be God. Otherwise there would be something—whether existing or capable of being thought—more beautiful and greater than God. The same reasoning applies to mutual love. Love, like the unity just discussed, cannot exist except in several, nor can one conceive with the mind anything better or more pleasing.[7]

Chapter 6. It is clear from the foregoing that if there is such beauty as that which has been determined to exist in the unity discussed, it is beauty without measure. If it is beauty without measure, without it nothing can be beautiful. Hence, although it is impossible that anything be beautiful without a determined beauty, beauty itself exists, or nothing is beautiful. It cannot be anywhere except in God, nor can it be anything except God, by whom each

7. See Richard of Saint Victor, *De Trinitate* 3.3–4, ed. J. Ribaillier (Paris: Vrin, 1958), 137–139.

beautiful thing is beautiful, and without whom nothing beautiful can exist.

Chapter 7. In creatures the designated unity cannot be so perfect that with respect to it they are completely one. However much two bodies come together, they do not occupy the same space. Nor can a created spirit, however much it advances toward another created spirit, exist essentially in it. To penetrate created and circumscribed spirits, and to be able to be poured into them essentially, seems to be the prerogative of the uncreated and unbounded Spirit alone. Although the spirit was created earlier in the body, the body is not similarly in it, and their natures, though personally united, are quite different. Hence Truth himself, commending the supreme unity between himself and the Father, which can be found nowhere else, says: 'I am in the Father, and the Father is in me'.† Jn 14:10–11
This cannot be found in any creatures, even if they share the same nature.

Another impediment to perfect unity in them is that, even if some of them are so much one that one is nothing that the other is not—so that one does nothing that the other does not also do; so that nothing happens to the one which does not happen to the other, and nothing is in the one which is not equally in the other; and, in general, insofar as possible, they differ in nothing—it is still possible either on the part of nature, or on the part of the Author of nature who unites them, that one may do what the other does not do, or that something may happen concerning or in one which does not happen in or concerning the other. Hence, outside of and above creatures, in the very uncreated Image of things, in God himself, this unity of congruence must exist perfectly. Whatever other unity exists imitates this perfect unity and flows out of it, in accord with a certain emulation among creatures, and between them and God.

Chapter 8. It is also absurd to say that somewhere [something] exists partially which God could not make in its total being either there or elsewhere. Because of the otherness that exists in all creatures naturally—if not as common features, then at least in particulars—this unity can be imposed in none of them, much less between creature and Creator. But God cannot make something exist in the deity that is not there. This perfect unity is there, then.

Chapter 9. With the highest unity, or in the highest unity, is found the plurality that was sought earlier; at the same time the equality of this plurality was also shown. This unity, which reason has proven to be in God, is common, or, so to speak, in some way plural; and the perfect beauty of this unity, of which I spoke earlier, or even that full likeness of unity that I demonstrated, cannot avoid being several, nor can it be of them unless they are equal, nor can it itself, as will be clear from what follows, be less equal than those same equals.

Chapter 10. These matters may be investigated more fully in a different way and clarified by other reasons through the very nature of equality. If any two things are posited, and, if something is equal to one of them, it follows that it is equal to the other; and it is impossible that those two things not be equal. If, however, something is equal to the highest unity, it cannot be unequal to equality itself, otherwise their equality is not as great as that of the equal things themselves, and thus the equality is imperfect or non-existent. Equality is therefore equal to unity. Likewise, if equality is equal to the first and highest unity, it is said to be the very same.

It is not the case, however, that if it is equal to it, it is not equality itself, just as it is not the case that if the color is white, this white is not whiteness itself, because the white thing is the very substance of whiteness by participation.

It is not the case then that if equality is God, it is not equality itself; that is implied neither by the antecedent nor by the consequent. According to the same rule it is also not the case that if something is God it is not equality. God is equality, or God can be equality, for otherwise it would follow that equality is not something related to God himself. God cannot be anything, nor can anything be God, which is not God. For this reason God is equality.

As I have shown, it is not the case that if equality is equal to the highest unity it loses its very substance of equality. That would be necessary if the substance of equality were inferior to the substance of the highest unity. On the contrary, if it does not only not follow that equality, if it is equal to that unity, loses the substance of equality, then instead it retains it. Thus neither would unity be one nor wisdom wise, if either did not keep its substance. It is not by participating, but by being, that these are themselves—that is unity and wisdom—such that unity is one and wisdom is wise.

According to this pattern, if equality is itself equal to something by itself and not by equality, then another is equal to it. However, this is impossible, if it remains equality itself. So, if equality is equal to the aforesaid unity, it also retains the substance of equality which can be equal to [unity]. It is not by participation in equality that equality can be equal to anything, as are other things that are called equal, but by existing as equality itself. Again, if equality itself is equal to the aforesaid unity, it is of the same substance with it. The substance of unity and that equality is therefore the same.

Chapter 11. It has therefore been shown: if equality is equal to that unity, it is equal to it while remaining the substance of equality. If it is equal to it, then while remaining what it is, that very thing which remains what it is is itself God. Whence it is necessary that it itself be God. Otherwise, if it were equal to that unity [but were not God], it would follow that it would be God only after a fashion [=mode], and it would not remain what it is, but from the fact that it was God, it would necessarily be something else according to that mode, unless it were God in the same way as a human being is.[8] If he were a rock, he would not be not what he is, for which reason a human being is in no way a rock. If however man is an animal, it does not follow from that he is something other [than himself] because he is it after a fashion. Hence one can infer that he is in some fashion an animal. Everywhere quality exists, there is also equality. It is only after a fashion that equality can be or be said of several.

Chapter 12. Now it remains to inquire whether, with the help of grace, one can grasp by reason what we hold by faith, and what is to be held without doubting even if no reason can comprehend it

8. Martineau (81; cf. 209–211) amends and translates: 'at least it would not also be modally God as man [is himself modally animal:] that is if he were a rock . . .'

to be thus: namely, that a personal plurality exists in God. From the beginning of our disputation we proposed this order: first reason would seek and, according to its capacity, find God to be, and to be one, and what this one is and how great it is, and so forth, the very things one customarily seeks to find out in a natural progression regarding anything. Hence we have produced for consideration, in proper succession, the series of all the predicaments, paying attention in regard to each whether it can be said of God according to itself, although not truly according to itself, or from itself. Once this was finished, reason proceeded to investigate whether deity consisted solely in unity, or equally in some kind of plurality, though not in a substantial one.

This plurality being established by various and necessary arguments, there follows what has now been proposed: of what kind is [God's] nature itself, and whether it can be shown to be personal. When we have established these things, then we will have to press on to show the extent of this plurality—how many persons there are; then, how they are to be distinguished, and how the ground of their names is to be determined according to the properties of each. Finally, regarding the persons, it will be necessary to inquire regarding their names, either together or separately, either according to what they have in common or according to what is proper to each.

Chapter 13. The present inquiry into plurality—whether it is personal in God—is rendered more difficult by the plurality of pluralities itself. Plurality is substantial or natural; it is also accidental. These are eliminated where God is concerned, so of necessity there remains in God only the personal, if besides them only this kind can be found. It seems, however, that others are not others, but—which raises an even bigger question—in God himself. (The properties of being from no one, and of having a Son and Spirit, differ. Now if this plurality is different from the preceding ones, and resides in the person, then, as will be clear later, it can be found in the same person). If the reasons of things are all there, as blessed Augustine thinks, and the common and manifest opinion of philosophers has it, then perhaps one should seek the reasons, and then they will be shown in one which is not simply one but also a person, so that not only all, but each of them, and each of them singly, can be said to be, and are, persons. Whether this can be accepted regarding the aforementioned properties, or regarding none of them, is a question. It is not established between us whether a property in God is a person, but only that it is personal. Hence this plurality of reasons is different from the plurality of properties. Neither can be personal, as was shown, because each of them, or one of them, can be found in persons, or a person, but not a personal plurality, except in many and different [terms].

Chapter 14. Something else interferes with our present inquiry regarding the persons. Since, as we have shown, many exist in the one deity, all are of a rational nature. Hence personality, without which a rational nature never occurs, cannot be denied in them. From this one could infer that several persons exist there.

However, the things in the soul seem to constitute an obstacle to this conclusion, because, although they are plural, there is only one personality in them, so that all are parts of the one soul, and none of them is the whole soul. Hence none of them receives the name of person for itself, even if from these many one extracts one deity. No person results. No plurality exists there. Human personality blocks the way, because while it subsists in two, that is in the body and the soul, one of these, that is the soul, receives the name person of itself. The two do not exist there of themselves. Though the body is one person with the soul, of itself it cannot be said to be a person like the soul.

It is not thus in the divine personality. In the many of which we have been speaking, it cannot be thus, that all simultaneously receive the name of person, but none of itself (they are not parts of one person); and thus the one thing is [not] one in each that is in all. Nor is it the case that some one of them, but not the rest, is said to be a person of itself, and is such. Each one, in comparison with the rest, is complete and perfect. Among them all things are equal, so that nothing can be said of one of them according to substance which cannot equally be attributed to each of the rest. There is one undivided substance of all. The personality for any rational nature is substantial. Therefore each one of them must be capable of being called a person of itself singly, while their substance can be said to be of a rational nature. Can one therefore conclude that many persons exist there because many things exist there, each one of which receives the predicate of person? But against this, preventing this conclusion, is the consideration of that person which is in Christ. In him there are two natures, each of which can be called a person of itself, although there are not there two persons, but one person in two natures:

in God assuming human nature—that is, in the Word—by its own nature; in the human nature assumed, by the goodness and grace of the Word assuming it.

However, reason admits nothing of this sort in that first plurality, where nature cannot be diverse, nor can there be in the same nature something which is in one from grace but is in the other from nature. Hence, personality is not the same in the many as it is in the two natures of Christ. What else suggests itself to keep us from declaring that a personal plurality exists there? Will it be that plurality that was earlier identified in the eternal reasons of things? As regards the plurality in those reasons, because it is of the same nature and is not something due to grace, there are not several persons. Because none of them can be said to be of itself, and to be a person, this plurality differs from that which was uncovered above in the unity, and in the equal to the unity, and in the equality itself. Here one of the reasons is not from another; there, however, as will be shown later, what is equal to unity is from unity or must proceed from unity, and equality must proceed from both the others. Thus, it seems, in these three we are finally forced to admit a plurality of persons, or we must say that here these three are one person, and that one person is from itself, which is impossible.

Now if this reasoning turns out to be irrefutable, then, in Christ also—in whom are two natures, one from the other, the human from the divine—it would imply a number of persons; contrariwise, from the aforementioned three it would exclude the unity of nature or of substance, lest if there were one nature or one substance, the impossible would follow, that it would seem to proceed from itself.

Chapter 15. What else is left? There remains what can be said about what this [plurality] is. Is a personal plurality to be found in these many which we have found or not? Now what is there, reason cannot show; or can it be shown by another reason? Or could this reason, which of itself does not suffice, suffice when added to the reasons given above. Perhaps. For we prove things that way in many matters: arguments, insufficient by themselves, are sufficient when they are all collected together. Let what now is to be adduced regarding the procession be joined to the things established earlier regarding this plurality—namely, that there is personality in them, that each of them receives the predicate of person, that all of them are of the same nature or substance, and that from one of them exists or proceeds another and from both of these a third.

If these various statements are brought together, what is to prevent one from inferring that there are many persons there, or that unless there are many persons, it would follow that a person exists or proceeds from itself, which is impossible. Although in the Word assuming and the man assumed, one is from the other—that is, the man from the Word—there are not two persons there, nor does one follow from itself, for the man is of a different nature from the Word, and so can be from him. Hence, because of the plurality of natures there is no necessity there for a plurality of persons. For although the one is not from the other by being a different person, it can nevertheless be from it in accord with the different nature found there. However, if there were no difference of nature there, it would necessarily happen, when personality is there, and both persons are said to be of themselves (*per se*), either that another person would be there, or that neither would be from another, or that one person would be from itself.

In eternal reasons the same thing can be both substance or nature, as well as person, because in them one is not from another. This cannot be the case if each of them is a person: there either a plurality of natures must exist, or a plurality of persons. Since in the three mentioned above one of them proceeds from another, and from both of them a third, and all these are of the same nature or substance, in no way can they be of the same person. Rather, it is necessary that there be several persons, or a person proceed from itself. Since, however, there is a plurality in them, or rather they are several, of whom one proceeds from another and from those two a third, therefore, although there is one substance in them, or rather, they are one substance—it does not follow that one substance proceeds from itself, just as, on the contrary, neither in Christ does one person exist from himself. For as there the man can be from the Word because of a difference of nature or substance, one in person but not existing from itself, so here one can proceed from another, and from both of them a third can proceed, because of the diversity of persons, while they exist in one substance or nature which does not proceed from itself. But if anyone who acknowledges this procession in them should assert a personal unity, it would be necessary for him to grant a plurality of nature or substance. On the contrary, whoever would argue for a unity of nature in them, together with this procession, must acknowledge in them a plurality of persons.

Unity and what is equal to unity are not one person since, as we said, from unity there is what is equal to it. Unity is from itself, that is, not from another. Unity therefore is a person in its own right *(a se)*. What is equal to it is not from itself but from that unity, from which it is, in whatever way it is. The cause of this difference in the manner of having personhood will be the cause of them.[9] Is it the substance that is the same for both, or some property that is common, such as the fact that they produce of themselves and, so to speak, from themselves (as will be shown) the equality which they have among them? But what is identical or common to each does not establish difference among them. A singular property will be the cause that unity is of itself that person. Since, as was said, nothing in itself can come to be assigned as the cause why it is such and such apart from itself, it must be that this same being is the cause that it is itself, and, in general, that it can be said to be that very same thing. In other words, if a singular property is the cause that it is itself this [first] person, this property of singular unity will be itself personal, and in conformity with that the unity will be singularly this first person. It is the same regarding what is equal to unity: that he should be said to be necessarily another person is evident from what preceded, because he cannot not be a person. It is in line with the same reasoning that in their very equality there will be found a third person. Thus, if any one of these has a singular personality proper to himself, it will be necessary that each of the others also have its own

9. Martineau translates '*Hujusmodi igitur diffentiae in personalitatem habendo, ea[n]demque erit causa*' as '<La cause> d'une telle différence, donc, <sera> dans le fait d'avoir une personanalité <propre>, et ce sera la même cause' and explains in a note: 'même sera donc la cause 1. de la différence entre ces deux personnes et 2. de leur personnalité respective'. My translation means the same as his, but I have dropped his emendation of *ea[n]dem*.

proper and special personhood, without which on the evidence they will be unequal to him because of having less than he has.

Chapter 17. Therefore, having found in God a personal plurality which will be expressed more fully in what follows, one ought to show in what it consists, that is, what are the three persons there, whether they can be more numerous than those which have already been demonstrated, that is, three, namely, in unity, in what is equal to unity, and in the equality of both.

Chapter 18. There are two species of numbers, the even and the odd. The odd approximates the nature of unity more closely, because unity allows for no division, whereas an even number does not evade division both by even numbers and by odd numbers, that is, by any kind of number. The odd can receive only one sufficient division,[10] that is, by [un]even parts. Likewise, because the cause of that inequality is a certain special unity, unity blocks sufficient division of the odd by two equal parts; and so it alone resists division into halves. So, if where highest unity exists some number is to be established, reason suggests that it is preferable that the odd be received there, and the one which is first among those which are primary, that is, three.

Chapter 19. In accord with this kind of law of number is formed the triangle, the figure from which all arise and into which all are resolved. What number has more reason to be allowed there where the origin and end of all things is located,

10. According to Martineau, 91, n. 2, *divisio sufficiens* is division into whole numbers.

where that which is the principal and first figure[11] of the substance—namely, of the Father, the uncreated form from which and according to which are patterned and formed all things—is located?

Chapter 20. Moreover, the number in the power of which stands the force and the form of all things is the equality that comes from unity. It is taught that from equality proceed all species of inequality. This equality is constituted among three terms, and there are three rules according to which all this inequality derives. The same is also true in God: from the highest unity proceeds the equality from which all species of creatures follow, unequal to each other, and to their origin. Now, to what can this equality more aptly be assigned than to those three persons which have already been found? But reason shows that, since equality cannot exist except among several, the first equality of all is that which existed between two things, especially if it were the first of all things, so that very equality will be third from them, and will be three with them.

Chapter 21. If, however, after these three, which are perfectly equal to themselves, a fourth person is introduced in God, the equality already established in them seems to require that, since this fourth is not one of these three persons, it necessarily proceed from all of them. However, it could not remain unequal to any of the rest or to all of them together. Equality cannot exist except in many, nor can it be except from many, from those of which it is equality. It is necessary that there be found in their substance that from which the equals

11. Sermon 3.3.

can be indicated as related to each other and as responding mutually. So equality proceeds from that fourth person, if such exists there, which it was shown must proceed from equality itself. But it is impossible that something proceed from that which proceeds from it.[12]

Chapter 22. Someone may say that there is one equality from which that person proceeds, and another equality which proceeds from it. However, if two magnitudes exist there, two equalities cannot. Everywhere equality is correlative to magnitude. In God, however, there is no other magnitude than substance, and there is only one substance, and hence only one equality. It is supreme and unbounded equality. In no genus of things do reason and nature allow two things to be supreme and first. So, also, supreme wisdom and power must be one.

Thus it is impossible that there be two supreme magnitudes and equalities. If two equalities existed there, four persons would not exist there but five. One might object that what has been said[13] cannot be required, namely, that the fourth person, if it be there at all, proceed from the other three although they are equals, for only what proceeds from that unity from which the other two proceed can exist there, as we will make clear.[14] Thus, equality is equal with unity, but what is equal to unity is not from [equality] because it cannot exist except

---

12. For Richard of Saint Victor's exclusion of a fourth person in the Trinity, see *De Trinitate* 5.15, ed. Ribaillier, 213–214.

13. See Chapter 21 above.

14. In fact, Achard does not return to this topic. He seems to have included a number of promise-making cross references as reminders to himself of points needing development, but never returned to them to complete his work. See Martineau, 95, n. 3.

from unity itself. This is because equality requires necessarily that there be something equal to unity, such that situated between it and unity it requires nothing else for its proper being, if it is true that it exists fully between these two. Hence whatever else will be proposed, even if from unity—and by that fact equal to unity—will have to be from their equality also. Otherwise, their equality will not be of the same substance with those two, nor will it be fully equal to them.

Whatever is from that equality cannot be its equality in relation to something else. Nothing has or can have its being from its own equality. It is necessary that being itself be equal to something, and we must first consider a thing in itself before considering it in its equality with another, as has been shown. Later it will be shown more fully that equality necessarily proceeds from those of whom it is the equality. Hence, there cannot be a fourth which is equal to the three already discussed, and so it is necessary to confess only three persons there.

Chapter 23. In referring to these, it seems more reasonable to speak of 'Trinity' rather than of 'ternary' or 'triple'. The word 'ternary', although it indicates the plurality that is there, does not suggest the unity that exists there among the many. If God is described as 'triple' it indicates that there is something more in the persons taken together than in them singly, or that the divinity in each is imperfect, or in all superfluous. The word 'Trinity', although it is imposed to indicate plurality, still gives some suggestion of the word 'unity'. 'Trinity' seems to stand for 'tri-unity'. On the other hand, the word 'triplicity' points to the addition of quantity. We cannot, however, completely separate the number that is 'ternary' from the persons of the Trinity; otherwise we would have no grounds for calling them three, just as several of them could not be said to be two apart from duality. Just as in those three there is Trinity, duality cannot be denied in any two of them.

However, one cannot simply say that duality exists in the persons of the Divinity, especially when one asks what the persons there may be, lest we be thought to indicate that the persons there are not more than two. Concerning the number of persons reason may perhaps proceed further in what follows.

Chapter 24. Now is the time to distinguish the persons by properties, and the names in accord with properties. Regarding this distinction, whether of properties or names, if the grace of God enables us we will give a clearer reason in what follows. Also we must consider the three things in which the plurality of the Trinity has been found, that is, unity, and what is equal to unity, and equality itself. Since substance is one, we must pay close attention to how the terms can be distinguished. This cannot be nothing at all, since without it there would not be many in which there is still the highest identity.

Chapter 25. First of all, let us examine the property of unity in which there is nothing except unity itself—no distinction, no plurality of any kind. Hence nothing can be the cause and unity of that unity itself; so it cannot be from another but only from itself. It is not permitted or possible for reason to understand that there is something prior to the unity that has been indicated—that is, that is understood as exempt from all plurality—

something by which it is capable of existing. If it were from another, either it would consist solely in unity—and thus there would nothing except unity itself—or, if some plurality occurred there, unity would not be from it, but rather it would have to have its origin from unity, whence all plurality proceeds.

Chapter 26. This argument establishes that what is equal to unity is from unity. There some first distinction or primary plurality, that is duality, without which it would not be different from unity, already emerges. They would not be, nor could they be said to be, equal, if they were not somehow distinct from each other.

Chapter 27. If, like unity, what is equal to unity were from itself, there would be nothing by which it could be distinguished from it. Then no plurality would occur there, and it would not be equal to unity, but would be that very unity which has been determined.

Chapter 28. If some reason would allow what is equal to unity to have its existence from itself as unity does, although they were in all respects of the same nature and operation, by that very fact their unity would be less. This is because, even if one was or did nothing that the other was not and did not do equally, it would not follow from that that each was and did the same thing, because neither would be or would do something from the other or in the other. For example, because heat and brightness are not operative except by fire, and fire operates in both, whatever heat and brightness cause, fire causes also; thus, it never happens either that heat and brightness arise apart from fire, or even if one arises from fire, it could exist without arising from it any more.

This comparison will have no little value for understanding the procession in the Trinity and in commending the unity of the Trinity. For the highest unity of three to be there, it is required that whatever is said about any of the persons—property is an exception—can by that very fact be said equally about either and both of the others, with reference to substance, and in regard to will and operation. A fuller explanation of this unity will be given in its proper place. Here, however, it will suffice to say that between unity and what is equal to unity, this unity would be lacking, whether each proceeded from the other, or if there were one of them which at some point in time ceased to proceed from the other. Therefore, that this unity may be, and may be kept there, integrally, since perfect unity cannot be from another, it remains that what is equal to it proceeds from it, and that procession never comes to an end.

Chapter 29. Although what is equal to unity is from unity, it would not be properly said to proceed from it unless it were from it in such a way that it flowed out from its very substance. If it were not from its substance, it would be from nothing, since it would have to be first from unity, if unity is its sole principle. If, however, it were from nothing, it would no longer be God but a creature, and naturally by that very unity by which it was made from nothing it could be reduced to nothing, and so it would be corruptible. But the corruptible is no longer in any way equal to that supreme unity. Thus there comes from unity what proceeds from unity and from its very substance, but which proceeding thence cannot become of another substance, but remains utterly of the same nature with that unity from which it proceeds, and as far as possible equal to it.

Since, therefore, each is a living and feeling nature, the only kind to which the notion of generation is properly assigned, what is there to keep one from finding in them the property of generation, when, as has been said, in a nature which is living and feeling one proceeds from the substance of the other without proceeding to become another substance? These words, 'generators' and 'generated', occur in all manner of things, but the words 'father' and 'son' seem to imply something more spiritual. Insensate or inanimate things are sometimes improperly said to generate and to be generated. More precisely, since not groundlessly, or abusively, or improperly, unity is said to give birth, and what is equal to it is said to be born of it, the former is also and most rightly indicated by the word 'Father' and the latter by the word 'Son', especially since both are not only of a living and sentient nature, but also of a rational nature, of which 'father' and 'son' are spoken more frequently, and perhaps more appropriately, in accord with propriety.

Chapter 30. Now we must ask what name will be most apt for the third person, whether equality or something else, if we consider his property in relation to each of the aforementioned, since it is according to it that a name should be imposed. There is a property by which he is related to Father and Son, the equality of them both, because, since the Father, as we have shown, is from no one, and the Son from the Father alone, their equality must proceed from both. This follows from the preceding. Nevertheless, although a reason has already found for something else, here a reason more basically and specifically for this must be found.

The reasons that showed that the Son proceeds from the Father prove the same thing regarding the equality of both—that it proceeds from the Son, since the Son cannot proceed from it. Nothing, we established, proceeds from its own equality; that reasoning argued for the unity proposed above. The perfection of unity noted there would not exist among them unless one proceeded from the substance of the other. In some fashion this has been asserted generally of all the equals there. So the reason why equality is assigned to each with reference to the other must be found in the substance of the Son as of the Father.

Chapter 31. But since there is one magnitude of both, could not the same be the case if there were many? However, there would not be one, and it would not produce equality. In order for there to be equality, the first unity and the first plurality come together. Therefore, equality, in order to be from the first unity, necessarily proceeds from the first plurality. However, as there is unity in the Father, in the Son the first plurality occurs—that is, duality—not because he is two, but because his being from the Father is the reason why he and the Father can now be said to be two. For the same reason, in the equality of the Father and Son there occurs the first Trinity, which plurality proceeds from unity and from duality equally.

Chapter 32. Also for there to be many it is necessary that there be one; but the converse is not so, as we have often said. For there to be equals there must be several, but not the converse. Hence, as unity is the cause of plurality, so plurality is a cause of equality.

Chapter 33. Likewise just as it is necessary that there be a one between two so that there may be three, so duality is required that there be that equality, which cannot exist without a ternary. The equality of Father and Son is their highest and all-encompassing cohesion. Every cohesion arises from cohering things. Now one thing never coheres to another unless there is an aptness and cause of cohering in both of them. Why does the soul cohere more to the flesh than to a rock if not that it finds there a greater disposition for cohering? The body does not cohere to the soul more than to the non-soul except because of an aptitude for cohering in the soul. Similarly, the visual ray which flows out through the eye, and the solar ray which it finds in the air, would never come together there to form by their common course the sight which proceeds from them, if each did not find in the other a suitability which enabled them to mix together.

Chapter 34. Further, the Son is from the Father alone, and completely equal to him; it seems there could be a third which is from the Father and not from the Son. However, just as equality is from them alone and totally equal for them, it cannot come about, as was shown above,[15] that some fourth be from those two that does not proceed from their equality. Therefore equality is not only from the substance of the Father but also from the

15. See Chapter 21 above.

substance of the Son—which is the same—since, so that they may be equal, it remains with them of the same substance.

Chapter 35. Why is it not also designated by the name 'Son'? Because that has been given already to that other person, so that if it were given to this one equally, confusion would arise. When one was designated 'Son' there, no one would know which was meant.

Chapter 36. There is a more obvious reason: the nature of things did not allow it. The equality of Father and Son is equally related to them both, just as it proceeds equally from both. Hence if this one were their Son, he would be [the son] of the other, and thus he would have two fathers, which the nature of things does not allow. But—something else nature abhors in creatures—the same one would be both son and grandson of a single other, and again the same would be both son and brother to the same, and the same would be father and grandfather, and the same father and brother of the same. Therefore, this communion by which equality is related indifferently to the Father and to the Son denies him the name and property of Son.

It seems necessary then to attribute to him a name that calls attention to this same communion which the other name takes away, and which does not seem inferior to that other name. Thus 'communion' is the proper element of his quality in relation to Father and Son, because he is the equality of each to the other. He is equally common to both, he is indeed their very communion, by which he is common to both, something neither the Father nor the Son have. So, because he is common to them, or their very communion, he is distinct from them, and in this he has something proper to him by which he is related to both.

To indicate this a proper term must be coined, and how could this be done more fittingly than by having a name common to all especially attributed to him? Thus, by this common name specially adopted to indicate him, we will be reminded that this person has communion itself, in a specific mode, as his property, something the other persons do not have, except by this very communion. And if all have communion among themselves, it is something common, but this person alone is communion itself.

If, however, to indicate this the name of 'divinity' were accommodated to him, he might be thought of as a common nature, but not as a person singular in himself. If the word 'deity' denotes only the nature and not the personality, the name 'God,' denotes not only the nature but the personality in the nature, although it determines no person specifically. If, however, this name common to the whole Trinity here be given specially to the third person in order to denote his proper communion—since he must have a name of this sort by which he is referred in common to the Father and likewise to the Son, whose communion he is, so that in accord with what is indicated by this name he is said to be of both equally—he is not named from them in relation to this name, but they are rather named from him.

The word 'spirit' seems not unfittingly capable of receiving a proper sense to indicate that the property of this person is itself common to the others, or is the communion of the others. Nevertheless, because this name denotes only communion of nature, it also seems that another should be added to it to indicate the communion that consists of unity of will. This is not because nature is one thing there and will another, but lest it seem to be there as in others, where whatever things are one by nature are not therefore also one by will. The adding of the word 'holy' points to this unity of will, so that he is called not simply 'Spirit' but equally 'Holy Spirit', and receives as in one proper name two common elements, in order to show that while the person is one, it does not proceed singularly from one but in common from two persons. In this very fact we are to discern his distinction from them, because he is their perfect and all-embracing communion. His personal uniqueness and unique personality is this: that he is the sole common unity of the other persons.

Chapter 37. By all the reasons given thus far regarding the Trinity, a distinction seems to have been shown to exist in the Father and the Son and the Holy Spirit. The causes of their properties and names have been found in unity, and in what is equal to unity, and in equality itself—or, to say the same thing with other words, in unity, and what is like it and in their likeness; or in unity, and its equal, and in their equal; or in unity, in what coincides with or is congruent to unity in all respects, and in their coincidence or congruence, or in unity and what is one with it, and in their common unity or communion.

So that all these matters may be clearer, and the specifying of Trinity and unity may be more manifest—as well as the distinction of properties, and in accord with that the assignment of names—let us follow another way toward these same results, and take up a different mode of inquiry. This, I confess, all those to whom it was granted, indeed divinely given, to investigate and to find this by reason, have taken up. The way detailed above finds 'the invisible things of God' not through 'the things that have been made'† but from that Rm 1:20 invisible, unique nature, without reference to the things that have been made. Just as happens regarding these things that have been made, this mode pays attention to the things that have not been made, looking to their reasons and origins. Thus it considers them not in the being which they have by themselves, but there where they subsist more truly, that is, in their eternal causes.

Chapter 38. They have come here from a place whence they would not have issued unless they were also there in some other mode. However, they did not come from there so as to be absent there when they came here, or so that they were not and are not there because they came here. On the contrary, here they have come to be in a temporal way because there they were eternally, and are, not-come-to-be.[16] They are not there as things in themselves, but in their eternal reasons in which all are one, because their reasons are one reason according to substance and person, as we shall show. These are not there without differentiation, because some distinction does exist among their reasons, although they are also one substance and person.

Chapter 39. There are three reasonable causes for things—on account of which, according to which, and through which, things come to be—and these

16. Achard's word *infecta* negates the word *facta* translated 'come to be' just above.

all can be spoken of in common. The first are for the most part final, the second formal or exemplary, the third expository—these can also be called formal, for it is not only through them, but according to them, that a thing is formed in a certain way.[17] One who sees how a thing is to be made also sees of what it is to be made, but not vice versa. The first are usually called simply the 'causes' of any sort of works; the second are called the forms of things; the third, the *noûn*[18] of operations or the ways of operating.

These three appear distinctively in our works. For example, there is something [on account of] which it is written, that is, so that we or others may sometimes use and enjoy it. There is something 'according to which' it is written—that is, the form of the book which the mind intuits as conceived within by its own communication or some other revelation or as introduced from without through the body's senses. Again, through the instruments of the body this form is introduced outside into matter, so that there it may be bodily what by itself and in itself it is, and so that [the mind] may retain [the form] even as it pours [the form] out bodily. Finally, that 'through which' it is written is something else—that is, an art, this very manner of writing, which is no less in the power of the mind.

Chapter 40. To deny that these same three kinds of reasonable causes are in the wisdom of God is madness. He could [not] do at all anything he did not do for some reason, and according to some

---

17. This third kind of cause is a specific sort of efficient cause, which has to do with know-how in making or doing.

18. Martineau suggests that Archard took the Greek word *noûn* from Romans 11:34.

reason, and through some reason. This tripartite distinction seems to be set down and suggested in the very Word of God,† when it is said of him Jn 1:3–4
that 'all things came into being through him' as though through the general reason and eternal art of making all things, and that 'without him', that is, without the rational cause of all things, 'nothing came into being', and that 'what came into being, was life in him', that is, the intellectual form of what came into being. Morever, the first formal reason not only lived there, it 'was life' itself, as what follows will make more obvious.

Also perhaps on account of the three-part distinction, in the first verse a word is repeated three times: 'In the beginning was the Word, and the Word was with God, and the Word was God'.† Jn 1:1
Indeed to collect into unity whatever distinctions might be there, the theologian immediately adds not 'these' but 'this was in the beginning with God', 'this' referring to what he had just said: God the Word was in the beginning, and in the beginning was the Word with God. I think that the book of Genesis† hints at these same three, Gn 1:3, 6, 10 etc.
indicating the manner of doing by 'God said', the form of the thing to be done by 'Let there be light', or 'let there be a firmament' or this, or that, or by both, and the cause by 'God saw that it was good'.

Chapter 41. That these three aspects of the works of God not only occur to our understanding as three, but also are distinct in God, not only the authorities just quoted but also necessary and manifest reasons[19] attest. [1] The causes of the things to be done are only the causes of those things that

19. This is Achard's only use of 'necessary reasons' in this work. In 1.12 he refers to *necessariis assertionibus*.

God has decided to do. If there were in God a reason why other things should also be done, he would do the other things, and would decide to do them. Who would dare to deny that there are in his mind [2] not only the forms of the things that he does, but of those that he can do, and also [3] the modes of doing each? Otherwise, as will appear later, he would be able to do more than he could know.

Modes are distinguished from forms because there are modes only of operations, but forms of all sorts of things. The intellectual and primary modes that are there also, as will be shown, are the forms of inferior modes, so that every mode is a kind of form, but a mode of acting; modes are inferior forms. Unless there were some distinction of mode from form there, the angels could not see in the Word of God what kind of things have been made unless they could also see how they are made, nor could they see there the form of any thing without thereby seeing also the mode of its making, nor would they understand what kind of Son is born without also understanding how he is born. But we often see with much unshakable reasoning the 'what' and 'what kind' and 'why' of things to be made, while remaining ignorant of how they are to be made. Whatever things we see by reason of this kind, we see above us in the light of eternal reason, in the eternal truth which is above us, as Augustine testifies, and reason itself shows.

Chapter 42. Since it is established that the three things just discussed are distinct in God, one should consider now, regarding each of them, whether it is distinct of itself, or only according to the kinds of things, or according to individual things. Because the forms of things strike our thought before the causes and modes of acting, and the causes before the modes, not only do forms precede causes, but causes seem to precede modes. No one seeks the mode of acting without the cause. Therefore we will follow this same order in discussing them, so that we will treat first of the forms, second of the causes, and finally of the modes and the forms of things. First it must be shown that they are in the mind of God from eternity; next that they are also distinct there; then the distinctions themselves must be somewhat considered; and finally whether the same things that are here are also there, or other things than exist here, because of which things here are said to be there. But perhaps many other things will have to be investigated as well.

Chapter 43. That all the things that are here were also there from eternity, in such a way that they are understood to have been there, cannot be contradicted. Nothing is here that God did not make, nor did God do anything unknowingly; God never knew, nor can he know, anything he did not know from eternity, and will not know eternally. Otherwise some change could befall him.[20] Therefore he understood from eternity all things whatsoever that he was going to do, with time or in time, not only what, but also quantity, quality, relationship to himself and to each other, in what they would be active or passive, where and when they were going to exist, how they would come to be located in their proper places, what they would possess,[21]

20. See *De Discretione,* 13.

21. Achard here lists the categories of Aristotle. See John Scotus Eriugena, *Periphyseon: De divisione naturae* 2 (558B), ed. and tr. I. P. Sheldon-Williams (Dublin: Institute for Advanced Studies, 1972) 2: 140–141; tr. John O'Meara (Montréal: Bellarmin, 1987) 194.

and absolutely everything in things that can exist or be thought of truly. The things themselves in which these [categories] existed did not yet exist so that they could be seen in them; even if they had existed, God did not need them in order to see what was in them. God's generosity cannot arise from the existence of things, but rather the existence of things must have its cause in God's generosity.

So from eternity, before anything was, he had present to himself not only the substances of all the things he was going to make, but also the quantities and numbers, places and times, and so forth. He possessed all things in his understanding, not in act, since, as we said, they were not yet in act. Act proceeded later from intellect; intellect did not proceed from future act. Temporal things are not causative of eternal ones, nor are things made causative of what is not made, but on the contrary. Therefore it should not be said that, as here are the things made, there are the things understood, but rather that there are the things eternally understood, and here are the things temporally made; or there are the things disposed, and here the things composed. Thus, insofar as things are there as understood, and here as made, so the things understood there can fittingly be called exemplars or forms of the things made here while here are certain likenesses or copies of them.

In our usage, the term 'form' is sometimes used to name all that exists in things apart from their simple and unformed, if I may so describe them, essences. Of these there is no knowledge except through the forms of things. All knowledge of things is of their forms. God knows all things and understands them from himself; with him and in him, therefore, are intellectually all the forms of all things. One cannot deny that the essences in which the forms reside are present there in the same way. There they are understood not only in their active formation, but also in their natural simplicity, by which they are distinguished from all forms by the very privation of all forms.[22] The substances of things are, and are understood, in connection with essences and forms; their distinction from each other is observed only with respect to the forms, and it affects all understanding of them, since essences are not distinguished from one another except by the variety of forms associated with them.

Chapter 44. If these forms of things were not distinct in God, no intellect could see any distinction of things, whether essential, formal, or substantial, nor could is distinguish between a human being and an ass. But just as no distinction would exist among them there, so also none would exist among them here had they not preceded them there. There, then, they are distinct, the forms of all things, and in the forms, and in accord with the forms, both the essences on which the forms are based and the substances of things that are made up of the essences and forms.

Chapter 45. There, not only substantial but accidental forms are distinct, not only generic but specific; they are such even in accidents. In substantial forms are not only common but also singular [forms], and among all these, not only those that exist, but whatever can in any way exist—

22. On this notion of essence as the *forma simplex* or *non formata* see Augustine, *De Trinitate* 15.15.25, CCSL 50A (Turnhout: Brepols, 1968) 499–500.

that is, not only what exists or can exist in the nature of things, although they are never in them in act, but whatsoever new forms the creator can establish, either against the established nature of creatures, or beyond it. Since the power of God is measureless, and his wisdom is no less, an infinite number of things must be contained there, not only individuals, but also species, not only species, but also genera, which cannot be found in the nature of things. There is no proportion between the infinity of these genera and the totality, not only of existing genera, but also of species, which exceed the number of genera, and even of individuals, although these are far more numerous than genera and species, and even of all things simultaneously in each of the genera.

Whether here and there, or there and not here, the species there seem infinite, and exist intellectually, but they are themselves, taken individually, exceeded by the infinite number of individuals there. While here there is one sun and only one moon, there they are infinite. Single individuals are also distinct there by infinite forms, and by the infinite degrees of each form. The sky here is only round, there it is triangular, there it is square, and arranged in all sort of ways *ad infinitum*. Even in the shape in which it exists in our world, there it as beautiful as in itself, and twice as beautiful, and three times, and four times, and so on to an infinity of numbers and proportions. From this one can conclude that there any one individual has greater beauty than the whole universe of creatures has in itself, no matter at what degree occurs the limit of that beauty. There cannot be a number for all degrees; their totality exceeds infinitely the measure of every limited beauty.

Chapter 46. Since, as we have shown, the things that are here are infinite there—but nothing is here, that is, among creatures, that cannot be said to be there as well—it seems not unjustified to inquire whether things can be numerically the same in both places. If they are the same, how can those that are forms or exemplars there be the same as those that are here? Will something be the exemplar or form of itself? Will not what is made in the likeness of something necessarily be other than it, and also later? Can anything be different from itself, or precede itself? Again, if the things here and things there are completely the same, how did the latter exist when the former were not yet in existence, and how do they continue when the former perish? If they are not the same, then those that are here are not the same in the intellect of God.

This is the existence of things in the mind of God that we are considering to be there by knowledge and understanding—that is, to be known and understood there by God (he knows and understands in himself whatever he knows and understands); hence, if there is or can be nothing at all that God does not understand by number, there is nothing here which is not identical in number there. If, however, other things are there, and not the same things which are here, but forms of these things, distinct from them by number—by which forms God is said to understand them—then God no longer sees these things immediately, but as if through certain other things. Consequently he is no longer said to see them truly and properly, but only because he sees certain things different from them, but which pertain to them—or rather to which they pertain—so that it is only by desire of imitation of these for the others that in the sight of those others these too are said to be seen—or they are seen there as in mirrors rather than as things seen in themselves.

It was the opinion of some that as incorporeal things cannot be seen by the eye of the body, so also certain corporeal things cannot be seen by the eye of the understanding. They would have spoken more truly and persuasively had they said that they can be comprehended perfectly by the eye of the understanding, but that it cannot happen in a bodily way. It is unthinkable that God not see these things, or that he see them through a medium and not through himself, or that he apply to the sight of these—or seek—another eye. Since he has the eye of his nature—that is, intellect—by which he sees himself—in which and with which he sees all things, and by that very fact himself—it seems impious that it [not] be the same for him to see himself, and to see all things within or in himself.

We could also consider in regard to ourselves whether it is another verse, and not rather numerically the same one, that we have already thought out within the heart, and that, once thought out there, we bring forth orally, and that we write by hand—so that there are not three verses, in mind, voice, and book. But if the thing is not numerically the same in act and in God's intellect—in his work and in his thought—if he did not dispose from eternity the same thing numerically that he did in his work, but saw that he was going to do a thing numerically different, and did this other thing—and if he did not see that what he did was the same numerically as what he was going to do—and because what he saw that he was going to do he said he was going to do by his co-eternal Word, but did not do that same thing, or fulfill what he predicted—then in the Word, which is Truth itself, there would be falsity. Therefore, not without impossible absurdity is it said that the things in the mind or intellect of God are not exactly the same numerically as they are in the act of existing that they have in themselves.[23]

It does not follow that any thing is its own form or exemplar, although anything, insofar as it exists there, can be said to be form or exemplar for itself, just as it is in itself, or there. If an old man differs from himself as a boy, he does not differ from himself, or if anyone is better or worse in his thought or estimate than he actually is, he cannot simply be said to be better or worse in himself. Or according to the example of verse, given above, a verse is uttered or written in accord with the way it is understood by the mind—as it is inwardly, so it is formed outwardly—but it should not be said to have been formed in accord with itself on account it happens because of another mode of existing, sometimes within and sometimes without.

These, however, are much less different than the mode that anything has in itself, and that which it has above itself, in God's mind; it is as different as the divine mind is more excellent than the human mind. The verse is corporeally in the speaking or the writing, and intelligible in the mind of the one uttering or writing it, but it does exist in each mutably. The very thing that subsists in itself corporeally because variably, not only is in the mind of God intellectually, but also eternally, because immutably. But if it exists there in such

---

23. This sentence states the thesis that Achard wishes established: numerical identity here and there. The rest of the chapter will deal with erroneous interpretations. See Martineau, 121, n. 8.

a way, it cannot be said absolutely that it exists in such a way—not if it is here and there variously and contrarily—not if the same thing began here and existed there from eternity, so that the same thing both began and existed from eternity—not if the same thing ceases here and remains there, so that one thing both ceases and remains—not if it was there before it was here, or even before it was, so that it was there before it was here, or before it was at all—for if it was, or is, there, it does not follow that it was, or is, nor that being there is simply being.[24] To be there, as we said, is nothing else than to be understood there. There things that are not are understood just like things that are.

Chapter 47. Someone might be disturbed if things are truer in the divine intellect than in themselves. There they are immutable, though mutable in themselves. Why should they not be said simply to exist because of the being they have there, rather than because of the being they have in themselves? Why also since they do not have inferior or lesser being, are they said not to exist, and not rather to exist on account of that superior and greater being they have in the mind of God? Perhaps this happens because, although here they have lesser being, and that superior being as well, the inverse is not true—that if they have that being there, [they have being] here also. And so, when they have being here, they exist in every way, since they have the one and the other; and that is why they now can be said to exist more absolutely and universally. Also, the names of things have been imposed to signify this being: although that is first in nature, this precedes it in our knowledge. Hence, in accord with this,

24. See the 'Second Treatise', Chapter 10.

the first imposition of names is made by us; these we use when we apply them to that being, not in a proper sense but derivatively. 'It is' seems to have been established to signify here what is of itself; it has that meaning only with some qualification or addition, such as 'in knowledge', or 'in the Word', or 'in the intellect of God', or something of the sort.

Chapter 48. Since, then, as has been shown, the same things exist here and there, one must inquire whether those that are the same here and there are here and there the same in number, or different here and there, or the same and different in different respects, and if so, what is the same and what different.[25] Among corporeal things, a thing the same in number remains in a given time a certain thing, the same in number as it was, and [at another time] it ceases to be a certain thing that it was, and becomes a certain thing different in number than it was. Thus at different times a certain thing is now numerically one, now numerically other, remaining nevertheless afterward numerically one, and it can in different ways be called both a thing numerically the same as it was—as for example a body is numerically the same—and a thing numerically different than it was—as for example, a different statue or a different cup, or any kind of artificial product of that sort, remaining different in number, although the same as a natural work.[26]

But even in natural things it can happen, and does happen, that a body, remaining the same in

25. Martineau notes that the thesis of identity is already established, and this long chapter will consider ramifications and questions that result from it.

26. A piece of sheet metal may be fashioned first into a cookie sheet and then into a sculpture.

number, is now this tree, now that one, or now this plant, and now that one, as happens in bodies from the nature of matter.[27] Hence it is not thought that anything similar can happen in spiritual beings, which do not have matter, nor in any forms, nor even in matter alone, but only in what is composed of matter and form. In this the same matter, in accord with its type, receives and puts off various forms, so that a thing remains numerically one because of the numerical unity of its matter, but because of changes of form it ceases to be the same and becomes other. Nevertheless, in this kind of situation a thing can never be simultaneously numerically one and numerically other

Still less can this happen in a spiritual nature, that it be at this same time what it cannot be, even at different times. What occurs elsewhere in act, occurs also in the intellect. Whatever is here is also there, but not everything there is also here, and whatever things follow one another here are to be understood to be there simultaneously by reason of natural vivacity and eternality of understanding. Simultaneously—something that cannot occur in creatures—there the same thing is a certain thing numerically one and a certain thing numerically other; indeed, things can be numerically as many as God can make them—that is, numerically infinite—and nevertheless in all these there is that same certain thing that is numerically one, as was obvious in the examples above. There the body that here remains one in number, while varying the individual forms, is somehow made numerically many through succession. There, I say, the body is seen simultaneously both in its own kind

27. For example, a perennial bulb that produces a new tulip each year.

of unity of body, and in all that multiplicity—or even infinity—of forms by which, while remaining the same in number, the body changes or can be changed.[28]

Although this does not happen, nor can it happen, to anything according to nature, one must still ask whether God, to whom nothing is impossible, can make it occur in anything, so that while it remains something numerically one, at different times it is also other things numerically diverse. Now it is certain that if it pertains to possibility, God is capable of it; if however, it does not so pertain, he is not capable. For instance it does not pertain to possibility to make it happen that the same thing be simultaneously both white and black, or large and not large, or to be and not to be, and for the same to be simultaneously true and false.

If, however, God is capable of what has been said regarding all these, it could not be comprehended by reason how he is capable regarding spirits, or even regarding those things compounded of spirits and bodies, or regarding the prime matter of things, or regarding any form, or even regarding the many things composed of matter and form. Nevertheless, even in certain of these it seems to be more comprehensible because he would not be changing their nature. If he is not capable of this regarding them, it is because that same thing seems to pertain to their nature which he himself confers on them, so that he himself cannot do it regarding them while that nature remains. It is as if he has established this nature of the body so that even he cannot change it into the nature of spirit while the

28. Here the sheet metal can have only one form at a time. There, in the divine mind, all its possible forms are known simultaneously.

nature of the body remains safe and whole. Nor is his power at all diminished in this.

So if God can do regarding all things what was discussed above,[29] it is established that not only is he in those in which he does this, but all things, even if he does not do this in them, are with him; thus any of them is there, both things many in number, or even infinite, and a certain thing totally one in number. If, however, he is not capable of this in regard to all, it is clearly true that regarding many of them he is capable of what he does not do; then not all the beings there are thus, but many there are thus, because here they are things that keep themselves there as they are here; either they maintain themselves thus or, it cannot be denied, something is there that it seems ought not to be said, because the same things are one thing there and another here, but more especially because some are there which are not here. However, for things that are shown to be the same in number here and there—here by subsisting, there by understanding—it must be manifest from the above that both here and there they are numerically the same.

If, then, something was both places, and no things are here that are not there, then these things are numerically the same here and there. Things here are seen there insofar as they are the same in number as they are here, and because those are [the same] in number as these, because they are there according to the mode of existence being considered here, because there they are understood, because there they are the same in number as they are here in themselves, because they are understood to be

29. Martineau, 127, n. 10: 'that is, produce both the numerical unity and infinity of things'.

the same in number, so also it is necessary to grant that according to the same mode of existing there, and according to the same form of speaking, they are numerically the same there as they are here.

It does not follow, however, that the things said to be here and there, which are numerically the same in both places, are therefore in both places numerically the same.[30] For they are not said to be here and there in the same way or by the same property of language, but they are here, as we have often said already, because of their existence, but there only because of knowledge of them. Nevertheless they were there, although they did not subsist in themselves in the way that an animal is generally said to have been in an egg before it existed, but only according to the original cause, not according to the very substance of the animal or according to the proper subsistence which it now has in itself.

Hence, although something numerically the same is said both to exist now, and to have existed before in an egg, it was not the very same thing numerically there that it is in itself simply. Therefore because things are numerically the same in themselves actually, and in the mind of God intellectually, it cannot be inferred that they are numerically the same here and there, but only because of the other things that have been alleged—because, namely, with them to exist there is nothing else than that they are understood to be there numerically what they are in themselves. I do not say that they are understood to be there numerically the

30. Martineau sees here a distinction between the ontic and the ontological. He gives an example: It is not necessary to believe, under pretext that the donkey is numerically the same here and there, that it is the numerically the same donkey that is found here and there.

same thing that they are in themselves, but that there those things are understood to be numerically what they are numerically in themselves.

It is one thing to understand that they are there numerically the things they are in themselves, another to understand that they are in themselves numerically the things that they are in themselves, just as it is one thing to understand that they are in themselves, another, that they are in the intellect. This is so because in the intellect they are eternal, but in themselves they are not eternal. If therefore here and there things are said not only to be numerically the same, but also to be the same things numerically, because, as has been said, those that are here and are understood there are numerically the same, but also they are understood there as the same numerically as they are here, it follows that for the same reason and the same cause they are said to be of the same substance, of the same quantity, and of the same quality as these are here. There one understands the substance, quantity, and quality that they have here, and all else about them.

No one should think that this same thing is trivial and unworthy of God, namely, to see things here as they are here, although they are as nothing to him who sees all things totally in a single glance, and always in the same way, and see them without beginning or end—and not only things here, but, as has been said, simultaneously and similarly an infinite number of others, not as sense or imagination perceives things, but by intelligence or eternal reason, invariable and immense. He sees inestimable magnitude and beauty not only in all being but in each, not only in the greatest and the more beautiful, but also in the least and the less beautiful.

Although, therefore, in its way the quantity of any spirit is greater than any body by its form because it is more beautiful, there is no body is so tiny that in comparison to something else it is not as great as the whole world is in relation to it. If not, in effect, contrary to what reason shows, a body could no longer be cut up into an infinite number of bodies, of which none could be said small except in comparison with larger ones. We see, however, that some are larger than others, but we do not see those that are smaller than the same, and how these are larger than those smaller ones, and therefore we say that certain bodies are little with respect to larger ones rather than big in proportion to smaller ones. If we were able to look simultaneously upon the entire totality of the parts of any body, which reason shows to be infinite, as in the totality no scarcity occurs, so also in the whole of them in themselves no smallness would appear, but as in them is an infinity, so in the whole of them, according to the consideration of them, is a certain immensity.

Since the parts are also infinite, it is clear that by their qualities and forms—if not common then at least proper—they are distinct from each other, and each of them has its own beauty. As all the quantities of the parts flow together into the one quantity of the whole, so also the beauties of all converge in the one beauty of the whole, in which, since the distinctions of beauties are as infinite as those of the parts, what consists in a single joining together in the whole is much more beautiful yet. In the contemplation of this a certain wondrous, ineffable delight would arise, if anyone could see it as one might see equally in a single beauty, as if member by member, infinite beauties, and in each of them singly and distinct from all others, and also all connected in one—that is, both an infinity in one and one in an infinity—that is, if one could see beauties infinite in number, each in itself and discrete from the others, and all connected among themselves, so that the beauty coming from all by a unique connection, and by each distinct one in many ways—indeed, in infinite, though hidden, ways.

This is far from the body's sense, and why it attains only a small part of the beauty of things. Our reason has better access and penetrates deeper. However, it is not able to look at the whole simultaneously, or to distinguish each [beauty] part by part, which it could see together as infinite—I do not say 'see simultaneously that they are infinite', for this even our reason does grasp. At the same time to gaze on infinite things so that each is seen in itself, and each is distinguished from the others, and all are comprehended in their one interconnectedness with one simple glance of the understanding, is beyond the scope of any but the divine eye. Where perfection is greater, there every form of knowledge is more perfect. He, as has been said, can see all things, both according to their parts, and according to the whole, and how great they are, and of what sort they are, and in every other respect, with a single glance. That is why in his look or his glance things are exactly as great and such as they are.

Chapter 49. If however things are there such as they are in themselves, then it seems they are mutable there. Again, they are there as they are understood there and not solely because they are understood as such there. Consequently, to be is nothing else there than simply to be understood; for the same reason things are there as they are understood. They are understood there immutably and eternally, for they are always understood there in the same manner. God can understand nothing more, or less, or other, or otherwise, than he does understand it. All things are there immutably. Their mode of existing there is the mode of their being understood there, so that their existence there is the understanding of them there. Hence, they are immutable there because they are existing immutably there—that is, they are understood there immutably.

However, these same things are also said to be there simultaneously mutable and immutable, temporal and equally eternal. What is 'mutable' can be said to be there on account of a second quality or mode which they have, or can have, of existing elsewhere, although not of existing there, which mode is nevertheless seen there.[31] 'Immutable' also because of the mode it has of not existing elsewhere, but of existing there, which mode distinguishes things as they are in the understanding from those same things as they are in act. This mode is there not only intellectually but also essentially, just like the intellect itself, just like God himself. The mode of subsisting which creatures have in themselves, although it is said to be there because it is understood just as those creatures are, is not however there in its very act, just as neither are they. Therefore it is thought more to be believed that things are immutable or eternal there because of their prior mode, which never ceases there, than mutable or temporal because of their substance, or

31. Martineau explains: Their being there consists in their being understood there, not in being understood there such as they are, that is, mutable.

quality, or mode, or anything else, which can be said to be there only because they are understood there. If, however, they are asserted to be simply mutable there, it is not because they could change there—that is, because the mode of understanding them there could vary—but because what was understood there could vary elsewhere, and this too is understood there. This kind of speech is somewhat like what occurs from time to time when someone is said to reign in a certain region, not on account of the power of reigning there, but because he retains there the power which he has of reigning elsewhere.

Chapter 50. It is to be noted that, when created things are immutable or eternal there not because of a quality of their own, but only on account of a mode of understanding, one ought not ask which eternal beings or which immutable beings they are there. Not to them, but to their understanding, is attributed the eternity or immutability which they are said to have there. If anyone says these eternal things there are models, because they are called exemplary according to the mode of existing that they have there, in this nothing eternal is asserted, but rather eternity is applied solely to the mode of understanding. To distinguish this from that mode which things have in the act of subsisting they are called exemplaries. Hence, if some things of this kind are called exemplaries there, and other are called examples here, or there their actual eternal forms, these are to be taken in accord with modes of understanding there and of subsisting here, and not in accord with a diversity of things.

If we investigate what things are there, and their forms, in accord with the fact that they are said to be there only because there is understanding of them there, we cannot deny, as was shown earlier, that exactly what are here are there, because what are here are understood exactly there, both in substance and number. Only this regarding their mode is of relevance, namely, that here they exist variably, there they are—that is, are understood—invariably. Therefore, regarding these two modes, between the forms of things in the understanding and the forms of the same in act, this sort of distinction can be noted: those are intellectual, these actual, those immutable and eternal, these mutable and temporal; both, or rather each, is of the same substance. But to avoid immoderate prolixity regarding the forms of things, let this treatise proceed this far and no further; another disputation, another book, is to formed.

The Second Treatise

Chapter 1. The intellectual or exemplary forms of things—which have been discussed—are said to be, and are, in God by understanding alone; they are of a much different and an inferior substance than the understanding by which they are said to be. For God himself is that understanding; the forms of things, as was shown in the preceding,[32] are the same there in understanding as they are among us in act. For this reason it is not on account of, or according to, these forms of things existing solely intellectually in the Word of God that one can accept what the Evangelist says—that is, 'what came into being was life in him'.[33] Lest anyone try to turn his meaning in another direction, he specifies what he wanted understood by 'life' there by adding regarding this life: 'and the life was the light of people'. Likewise, lest anyone expound 'him' differently, calling 'light' in the Word of God

32. The 'First Treatise', chapter 48.
33. This chapter comments at length on John 1:1–14.

what came into being here, by the sole fact that we are enlightened through the understanding of things, especially when we understand them as they are there, he proceeds very carefully about this light, saying that it 'shines in the darkness', but that 'the darkness did not comprehend it', and calling it 'the true light that enlightens every human being coming into this world'. Then, indicating a relationship not to the words 'light' or 'Word' but to an understanding of the Son who is both Word and light, he adds regarding this same light—that is, regarding the Son—'he was in the world and the world came into being through him'. And finally, in designating this same light he repeats the name 'Word': 'and the Word became flesh'—that very Word about whom he had earlier written: 'In the beginning was the Word, and the Word was with God, and the Word was God'. It is not said that 'what came into being was in this Word except according to some form of it. It is necessary to seek there a form of each thing superior to the forms thus far discussed, one that is not only there immutably, but that is completely immutable with regard to its substance, and is not there because it is understood there, but rather is understood there because it is there. Because of it this is said: 'What came into being in him was life.'

Chapter 2. Those things that are here, and are said to be there because they are understood, were such there from eternity as they are now in themselves. Others were seen there from eternity, as has been shown, although not in the same state, because of the eternity of their understanding. Therefore, they were made there intellectually from eternity before they came to be in themselves, just as the prophet said of God that 'he made the things that were going to be'.† Thus, according to the statement of the prophet he made from eternity what was going to be made later in time, but then in understanding, afterward in act. Is 45:11

One should not say absolutely that God made anything from eternity. That mode of making which pertains to the act would be understood, not that which pertains to understanding. When specifying the mode, it can be said that through himself, and not in some fashion, God 'made the heavens in understanding',† and he made in himself from eternity all the things that were going to be made, or that he was going to make. Thus it is indicated that we are not to understand that he made them in the same way then as he did afterward, in the way that things are said to come to be in act. If these things had been made in that way, could they then have been said to be going to be made, or to be going to have to be made, afterward? Ps 136:5

These two modes of making can be applied, as has been said, to anything whatever that is reported to have been made there. 'God said: Let there be', and afterward is added: 'And so it happened',† or something like that. The fact that Scripture said 'God said: Let there be' signified that 'coming into being' of things which is not only from the Word but also in the Word also. He said this 'with'† him not in time but from eternity. And he does not say in advance that what he said would come into being has already come into being in the Word. If his speaking is a making, 'what came into being'† is always—that is, eternally—with him. Gn 1 passim Jn 1:1 Jn 1:3

The human artificer makes nothing by his own labor that he did not first make within himself

by a kind of interior word. It often comes to his mind to make something that not only has he not made before, but that he has not thought he would make. Although it comes to his mind, he does not immediately make it within himself, perhaps because he does not yet know how to make it. This is not the case with God, for whom there can be no new willing or any lack of knowledge. Hence, with him it is necessary that all things have come into being eternally and without beginning—all the things that at certain times have come into being in themselves, among us, in our mode—or rather all the things that have actually been presented to us and manifested to us as they could be—or better, as we could perceive them—just as they were made elsewhere intellectually. However we judge more by the mode of making that we know better, and we apply our speech patterns to it when we simply say that a thing has come into being. Hence it does not follow that if it is said that [God] made all things from eternity in the prior mode they can therefore be said to be made from eternity. In the same way, if someone has already made an ark in his heart, he has not simply made an ark. A person is said to have made a verse or letters when he has formed them only within himself in accord with that intellectual mode of making of which God speaks in Isaiah: 'The things that were first, behold they
Is 42:9 have come';† and elsewhere, 'a new heaven and
Is 65:17, 66:22, as in 2 Pt 3:13; Rv 21:1 a new earth',† new in what concerns their mode among us, not in reality but only in appearance; not altogether new in themselves, since God says
Is 66:22 they are already 'before' him.†

Someone may ask whether they are there by creation, and if it would not be more true to say that they are there through the generation of the

Son alone, through which they are also here. They are there by creation itself, but they have not yet been made there. They can also be said to be there before they are in themselves, created from nothing and intellectually fully formed. The following statement seems to be in line with this: 'He who remained forever created all things together',† and the Lord said through the prophet: 'From days of old I formed it, and now I have brought it to pass'.†

Si 18:1

Is 37:26

However, whether all the things that God can make, though they are never going to be made, or only those that he is going to make, can nevertheless be said to have been made in God in this way, is not sufficiently clear, and is not to be asserted rashly. It does not happen that Scripture assigns this mode of making to anything except what has been made or is to be made by God. That these are not only made in God, but also created and formed, is clearly attested in not a few places, as has been shown in part. It is necessary therefore that they have been made and formed there as well according to some form and exemplar that is both superior to them and prior in nature, not only as they are here, but also as they are there, as reason urges; otherwise [the exemplar] itself would have been formed there, and it would be necessary that it have another exemplar, and the exemplar could not be first. But nothing could be formed by God either here or there that was not formed according to reason, or that was formed in accord with any other reason besides the eternal and divine wisdom of God, in which he made all things before they came to be in themselves through it. Hence the Psalmist said to him: 'You have made all things in wisdom',† not according to another wisdom, but according to Wisdom itself. Wisdom

Ps 104:24

itself is neither made nor formed; it is therefore the first exemplar of all things, and the first form in which the eternal intellectual formation of all things exists; what comes from it is actually in the things made temporally, and therefore it is also made temporal here.

Chapter 3. However, if there were no distinction at all in this first and highest form of things, they would not be formally distinct either here or there. Thus according to that same form all would be different, so that two forms would be necessarily of one and the same. Who would produce the image of the horse and of the donkey from the same form? Who would fix his glances on one same exemplar, interior or exterior, when he wished to form a house and a tray, a tunic and a cape? That the first and exemplary form of things is in God Augustine asserts in many places, such as the one in his book *On the Trinity*—to take one example from among many—where he says: 'Therefore, in that eternal truth, from which all temporal things were made, we behold by the gaze of the mind the form according to which we are and according to which we do anything by true and right reason, either in ourselves or in bodies'.[34] That this can certainly not be anything other than truth itself, in which the form of each thing is distinct from the form of other things, he makes clear in his book *On Eighty-Three Questions,*[35] where he says that since God does nothing except in accord with reason, 'it is absurd' to believe that he made man and ass in accord with exactly the same reason. By this he wished to show that he intended that the

34. *De Trinitate*, 9.7.12, CCL 50 (Turnhout: Brepols, 1968) 303–304.
35. *De diversis questionibus LXXXIII,* q. 46.2, PL 40:30.

reasons of whatever things are distinct from each other are no less distinct there.

To prove their distinction we will add examples which, though many in their way, are only a few of the many available. Since things here are not said to be there except on account of their forms and reasons, which are eternally there, they can in no way be said to be distinct there if [the reasons] on whose account alone they are said to be there are utterly indistinct there. Since they are understood there in these reasons alone, they could not be seen there as distinct at all if they did not have some distinction. Moreover, since a form of this kind—that is, the formal reason of anything—is its truth, if this one form of all things were one without any distinction, the truth of all things would be in the same way one, and not distinct from any point of view. But if this were the case, and if nobody could see the truth of anything in the contemplation of God without recognizing, equally and by that very fact, the truth of any other thing whatsoever, one could not know the truth of one thing without simultaneously knowing the truth of all. There no one would understand anything about the truth of things which another did not understand, and what was entirely without distinction could not come into any participation, and it would not be clear how anyone could see it through himself and in himself except he saw it in the same way as God. He would be seeing something about the truth, or in the truth, of things which not just anybody could in some way see there.[36]

---

36. The argument of this sentence is that if there were one form for all things, there would be one truth of all things, and from this some absurd consequences would follow: (*nec si*) and if anyone in the contemplation of God could not see the truth of anything without by that very fact recognizing the truth of any other

Just as we sought above distinctions about things that are understood there, so it is necessary to distinguish the distinct reasons of those things in which they are understood there. There, moreover, not only the genera and all the species of things necessarily exist under their reasons, but also individuals, not only whole but also in parts, although these are infinite in each single thing, and all that is substantial and accidental, and in accidents both quantities and qualities, and universally all such things, and all these not only in things which exist but in the same way in all the things that could be made by God. And certainly there are distinct reasons not only of creatures and natures, but also of virtues and beatitudes, and in these things not only [the reason] of those he confers on creatures, but also all those—however many—that he can confer, whether on those he has already made, or on those

---

things, (*nec*) and one would not know the truth of one thing without at the same time knowing the truth of all, (*nec*) and one would not understand about the truth of things there anything another did not understand, (*sed nec*) but that which was completely without distinction could not come into any participation, (*nec*) and it would not be clear how anyone could see it through himself and in himself if not in the way that God alone sees, (*ipse*) he could see something about the truth or in the truth which no one at all sees there in any way.

Martineau's French translation has the following: 'and if, in the contemplation of God one could not see the truth of anything whatever without knowing equally and by that very fact the truth of every other thing, no one would know the truth of one thing without knowing at the same time also the truth of all, and one would not understand there anything about the truth of things which another did not understand, moreover, what was completely deprived of distinction could not come to any participation, and one would [not] see how someone could see through himself and in himself without seeing in the same way as God himself—who for his part (*nec* = *à son tour*) could not see something on the subject of or in the truth of things without everyone, in some regard, seeing it there too.

The point of the argument is clear, but the Latin is exasperating. Martineau has added a sixth '*nec*' to make sense of the sentence, and justifies this addition in *Éclaircissement* 9, pp. 225–228.

Assuming one does not amend the text, then (1) if God is the antecedent of *ipse*, one is tempted to make the last clause an independent declarative sentence (it is actually subjunctive), or (2) if *ipse* refers to the subject of the whole sentence, one could see the final clause as a summation of the whole sentence.

new ones which, though not yet made, he could still create.

Now the virtues of creatures which the saints receive through grace are certain forms of participation in those first and supreme virtues that are all, wholly, simultaneously, and always, in God. These are all substantially one virtue, which is not other than God himself. Likewise, the beatitudes of creatures are only certain derivatives of the highest beatitude which is in God and is God. Both [virtues and beatitudes] are nothing other than connections of the rational creature to its Creator, of the image to Unity; they also seem to be certain images of that supreme connection which exists between the persons of the Trinity. Although there seems to be a determined number of these in creatures, in the eternal reasons they exceed all number; and there, as has been said, are found not only those that have been conferred on creatures, but also those that can be granted by their omnipotent Creator to them or to others.

For this reason, if there were nothing in the virtues and beatitude of God that could not be extended downward by him for participation by the rational creature, then he would, so to speak, have proceeded wholly in infinite forms of participation of this kind, not in act, but in understanding. Thus the infinity of those virtues and of that beatitude would correspond in some way to his immensity, so that it would be there in him without end and in them without number, and nothing would be there in his unity which was not completely here in a varied and multiple—in fact, infinite—distinction.

This could make it possible to understand the peculiar nature of the Holy Spirit, if things are really thus. He is the connection of the Father and the Son, proceeding eternally from them, and it is customary in the Scriptures to refer distributions of graces and gifts, as well as the graces and gifts themselves, to him. These are nothing else than the previously mentioned forms of participation in the aforementioned things, and certain spiritual connections of Creator and his created image in the eternal reasons, proceeding in some way eternally in accord with them, and out of them and transfused into creatures in the very act from the time, or with the time, as set out from eternity by those reasons.

There they are distributed intellectually to the creatures, and conferred on the saints through providence or predestination, in accord with which 'they were also chosen in Christ before
Ep 1:4 the foundation of the world'.† There 'God knows'
2 Tm 2:19 without beginning 'who are his'† and who are
their own, or who is of God. There 'the kingdom
prepared' for them is not only 'from the origin
Mt 25:34 of the world'† but even before the origin of the
world. There also the very man taken up into unity of person by the Word of God and the supreme truth had that glory with the Father before the
Jn 17:5 world began† by which he asked to be glorified
by the Father at the time of the resurrection. There, if not into others through infinite forms of participation, then into himself according to overall fullness, the whole deity proceeded from eternity, so that from that time on there dwelt in him there, by an eternal procession, 'the whole fullness of divinity' intellectually, which afterward in the fullness of time began to dwell in him by
Col 2:9 temporal procession 'bodily'.† There too the Holy
of Holies was chosen from eternity; thus the saints were chosen there from eternity in Christ, and so

too the very Holy of Holies was chosen there from eternity, 'predestined' in God himself 'the Son of God in power'.† Rm 1:4

No one can be said to be chosen or predestined from eternity simply because of the formal reason of being chosen, so to speak, unless a causal one is there also—unless perhaps it is fitting to repeat here what was considered above,[37] that is, it is not granted that something is made there, unless it was to be made elsewhere in creatures—that is, only that which has there not only a form according to which, or a manner through which, but also a cause on account of which, it will come to pass. Hence the Prophet does not say that God made what he could make, but those things that are going to be made—namely, what he is going to make.† Is 45:11

Chapter 4. The foregoing distinctions of the reasons, although one can note them and make use of them for the distinctions of the things of which they are the reasons—just as 'the invisible things of God are seen, being understood through the things that have been made',† Rm 1:20 nevertheless they do not flow from the distinctions of things, but rather, as things flow from reasons, so too the distinctions of things flow from the distinctions of reasons. Thus it is necessary that reasons be distinct, and that they have the source of the distinctions in themselves. The origin of that distinction will be spoken of in what follows.

What is it then—that is, what are the properties according to which it exists, and not simply the correlations which the reasons of things have toward the things themselves? Are they said to be their reasons, or how does the distinction of reason

37. Chapter 2, just above.

proceed from its origin? This, as this work will show, seems not only difficult, but indeed ineffable. Moreover, according to the distinctions of reasons and things, there are also distinct understandings there: hence they also, considered in relation to the things of which they are [understandings], and the reasons from which they somehow proceed, are proven to be infinite. Nevertheless, all of them are one understanding of the understanding God, just as the reasons in accord with which they all are is the one reason of God.

The understanding of anything is a kind of connection of the one understanding and the thing understood. God understands the reasons of all things and the eternal truths, because of which and in which he is truly said to understand, and truly he does understand, all things, so that he contemplates them not 'through a mirror and in
1 Co 13:12 a riddle',† not in images and shadows, but in their very truths—or rather their very truths—which are not something other than him who understands. Therefore he sees the things not only truly, but immediately—not through another than himself, not in another besides himself; God's vision is a certain connection of God himself seeing and of the truth of the thing as seen, as has been said.

According to this, as will be shown later, as the reasons of things and the truths pertain to the Son, so too can the understandings of them can be referred to the consideration of the Holy Spirit; just as the distinction pertains to the Son, so the connection pertains to the Holy Spirit, as has been shown and still is to be shown. Since understanding in some way connects the thing understood to the one understanding, there can never be fewer connections of this sort there than distinctions of reasons or truths which are understood there, according to which and from which also, as has been said, understandings are distinguished there. Thus their distinctions regard only the reasons and truths of things that are understood there distinctly.

Chapter 5. Since these reasons are fully infinite, all numbers are necessarily found in them; numbers cannot be something different from them. They are not numbered except by themselves, because none of them is said to be one except itself. They are of a simple nature; for them to have is nothing else than to be. By this kind of numbers, which are intellectual and first, we number those who are in spirits, or in bodies, or in any sort of things, which Augustine calls numerable numbers.[38] Those numbers which, unlike inferior numbers, he calls in many places numbers by which we number, we can number only by themselves. Others are only numbered; one does not number by them. Boethius too, following Augustine, indicates this distinction of numbers in his short book *On the Trinity*.[39]

However, as all other things are from those first reasons, so the numbers of all others flow out from their numbers, which are nothing but the very reasons themselves, the first origins of things. Hence even pagan philosophers assert that God possessed the numbers and exemplars of all things, to which Boethius, the Christian philosopher, also testifies. Augustine says that six is not, or is not said to be, 'a perfect number', because 'God finished his works in six days'; rather, the works are perfect because they were done according to the reason of

---

38. *Numerables numeros*: Augustine does not seem to use this expression.

39. Boethius, *De Trinitate* 3, Loeb Classical Library (Cambridge: Harvard, 1962) 12–15.

this kind of number.[40] Nevertheless in his *Literal Commentary on Genesis* he declares that God made all things in number—that is, in himself, who is the number of all, but without number. His is the wisdom in the aforementioned reasons, which is Wisdom itself, and exceeds every number, in accord with the Scriptural statement: 'His wisdom
Ps 147:5 is without number'.[41]†

In accord with this, the same Augustine, in his treatise *On Free Will*,[42] asserts that number is the same as Wisdom, which need not be understood
Ws 7:27 to refer to the substance of wisdom. It is 'one',†
but according to the aforementioned reasons, by which one wisdom is distinguished; infinite wisdom comprehends these reasons in one.

Likewise, in Book 11, chapter 10, of *On the City of God*,[43] Augustine asserts the same thing in these words: 'The Spirit of wisdom is described in the
Ws 7:22 holy Scriptures as "manifold"† because wisdom has
many things in itself; what it has it also is, however, all is 'one'. Wisdom is not many things, but one, in which are certain infinite things—infinite treasures of things, intelligible to wisdom'. Among these are all the invisible and unchangeable reasons of things even those visible and mutable, which are made by it.' If any desire to know more fully Augustine's coherence regarding primary, true and pure numbers, let them read his *On Music*.[44]

Later numbers are like traces of the first numbers, mixed with various accidents. However, in them is no true unity, and they cannot be said to

40. *De Genesi ad litteram* 4.7.14, CSEL 28 (Vienna: Tempsky, 1894) 103, lines 16–21.
41. *De Genesi ad litteram* 4.3.7–8, 98–99.
42. *De libero arbitrio* 2.11.30 (PL 32:1257).
43. *De civitate Dei*, 11.10,3 (PL 41:327).
44. *De musica*, PL 32:1081–1194.

be true numbers, but [they are] like images of true number in minds, likenesses in spirits, shadows in bodies. Perhaps, as one can understand regarding the forms of things, one can also understand about numbers, that they are invariable in their reasons or in themselves, and uncreated, eternal, true, and first—or rather truth itself, and a kind of principle and cause of subsequent ones—but that in creatures and subject things, in relation to their quality and nature, they are variable, created, temporal, likenesses and vestiges of truth, effects of the principal cause. But where all true numbers are, the true reasons of numbers cannot be lacking, nor the proportions of numbers, which are not inferior to numbers, for without them numbers do not and cannot exist, just as they cannot exist without numbers. Numbers are causes of these [proportions] too, and from numbers these proportions of theirs proceed as certain connections of numbers. From these the proportions of things have their origin, as from higher numbers and the primary numbers of things.

If, however, all the intellectual proportions of numbers exist in the wisdom of God, all the more certain is it that all the reasons of proportions which are themselves immutable are found there. To the formal eternal reasons of things seem to pertain also all those things in which they are seen and can be seen, that is, the species of things, the quantities of things, their natures, figures, relations, movements, and whatever else is in things and can be truly comprehended. All this can only be in their reasons and truths, which must be immutable, so that from them one grasps the unshakable truth of mutable things. I do not think it unfitting to recall here by certain excerpts from *On the Trinity* what Augustine thought about their mutability, eternity, and excellence.

Chapter 6. Thus, in Book 6, chapter 9: 'But we gaze upon the inviolable truth, by means of which we define as perfectly as we can not the kind of thing the mind of any particular person is, but what kind of thing it ought to be in the eternal reasons. Likewise it is by other rules that remain immutably above our mind that we decide within ourselves to approve or disapprove the images of bodies, whenever we rightly approve anything.'[45]

Later, near the end of the same chapter, regarding the 'form of unshakable and abiding truth' which he says bathes the gaze of the mind with its inscrutable eternity, he adds this regarding bodies or their images: 'Therefore, we see concerning these things in accord with that [form of truth], and that we perceive by an insight of the rational mind, grasping by pure intelligence the reasons and the ineffably beautiful art of such figures above the sharp point of the mind.'[46]

Likewise in Book 12, chapter 2: 'But it belongs to the higher reason to judge concerning these bodily things according to incorporeal and eternal reasons, which, if they were not above the human mind, would not be immutable. . . . We judge regarding bodily things by reason of dimensions and figures which the mind knows continue unchangeably.'[47]

Likewise, in the same book, chapter 14, where he distinguishes wisdom from knowledge, he says:

45. *De Trinitate* 9.6.9–10, CCL 50, 1:301, lines 15–302, esp. line 25. Quotations are not perfectly exact. Achard added connectives, and so forth.

46. *De Trinitate* 9.6.11, CCL 50, 1:303, lines 59–60, 71–72, 77–79.

47. *De Trinitate*. 12.2.2, CCL 50, 1:357, lines 16–22, esp. line 80.

'When there is discourse about these things, I think that it is a discourse of knowledge which must be distinguished from the discourse of wisdom. To this pertains those things which neither were nor will be, but are, and because of the eternity in which they exist, they are said to have been, to be, and to be going to be, without any real change of times. They did not exist in such a way that they ceased to be, and they will not exist in such a way that they do not now exist. Rather, they always had the same being, and they will always have it. They do not remain fixed in spatial locations like bodies, but in incorporeal nature intelligible realities are present to observations of the mind, just as those localized are visible and touchable to the senses of the body. Not only the intelligible and incorporeal reasons of sensible things located in space remain without spatial locations, but also the reasons of motions passing through time stand without temporal change, and these of course are intelligible, not sensible. Few have the sharpness of mind to reach these [reasons]; and when they do reach them, as far as that is possible, they do not remain in them, but their sharpness is as it were repulsed and driven back,[48] and so there is a transitory thought about a non-transitory thing. This transitory thought is commended to memory through the disciplines by which the mind is taught, so that what is compelled to pass from there has a place it can return to. Although, if thought did not return to memory and find there what it had entrusted to it, then, it would be led back to it like a person ignorant as it had been led at first, to find it where it had first found it, in that incorporeal

48. '*Reverberata*', a classic term in mystical theology; see Châtillon's note in *Sermons inedits*, 238, n. 88; also below, 2.16.

truth, whence again it would fix a description of it in the memory. For example, if the incorporeal and immutable reason of a square body remains, but a person's reason does not remain in the same way—if one could even reach it without a spatial image—or if the rhythm of some artful and musical sound extending through time is comprehended, standing outside of time in a sort of secret and profound silence, it can be thought at least as long as that music is heard. However, what the passing glance of the mind grasps thence and puts in its memory—as though swallowing it down in its stomach—it can somehow ponder by remembering it, and turn into disciplined knowledge what it has learned in this way. But if this was destroyed by complete oblivion, by means of teaching one could come again to what was altogether lost, and find it just as it was.'[49]

Although here Augustine affirms these immutable and eternal reasons of things, in earlier chapters of the same book he spoke thus: 'And what among the eternal things is more excellent than God, whose nature alone is unchangeable?'[50] There certain eternal things are known which nevertheless do not have an immutable nature, and are therefore called 'eternal' not by their nature but only by participation in eternity. Rational created spirits and the blessed are such; above these, he states in many places, no natures exist except that by which they were made. He establishes above our mind the absolutely immutable and eternal reasons, not only in the testimony set down above where he said that they 'would not be immutable if they were not above the human mind', but also in

49. *De Trinitate* 12.14.23, CCL 50, 1:376, lines 46–377, esp. line 80.
50. *De Trinitate* 12.14.22, CCL 50, 1:375, lines 24–25.

frequent statements of the same thing in this and in other treatises. Concerning the mind and the reasons of things he adds in the following chapter:[51] 'But we should rather believe that the nature of the intellectual mind has been so constituted that, being joined in the order of nature to intellectual things by the Creator's disposition, it sees them in a kind of incorporeal light that is *sui generis*, somewhat as the eye of flesh sees what lies around it in this corporeal light, [a light] it was created capable of and compatible with.'

About the incorporeal light, what it is, and the immutability of the reasons, where they are, he makes some further statements in Book 14, chapter 15, where he speaks in this way of one who has not yet turned toward this light: 'He is reminded to turn to the Lord as to that light by which he was in some way touched even when turned away from it. Hence even the godless think about eternity, and censure with reason and rightly praise many things in the conduct of human beings. By what standards do they judge these things if not by those in which they see how a person ought to live, even if they do not live that way themselves? Where do they see these standards? Not in their own nature, since without any doubt these things are seen by the mind, and obviously their minds are mutable, while to those who have been able to see this in these standards they appear immutable. It is not in a condition of their minds, since these are standards of justice, and it is clear that their minds are unjust. Where then are those standards written? Where do even the unjust recognize what is just? Where do they see that they ought to have what they do not

51. *De Trinitate* 12.15.24, CCL 50, 1:378, lines 12–17.

have? Where are [these standards] written, then, if not in the book of that light which is called truth? From there every just law is copied and transferred into the hearts of those who do justice, not by an entrance but by a kind of imprint, as an image passes from the ring to the wax and does not leave the ring. Those who do not do [justice], but nevertheless see what they ought to do, are the ones who turn from that light by which they are touched. Those who do not see how they should live sin more excusably because they are not transgressors of an known law, but they too are sometimes touched by the splendor of the ever-present truth when, having been admonished, they confess.'[52]

These statements of Augustine have been brought forth in support of our assertion regarding the reasons of things; they are a few of many found dispersed in his various works.

Chapter 7. As to the formal reasons of things, it should be handed on that they pertain not only to those *in* which the things are known, but also to those *from* which they are known—that is, those from which it is demonstrated that concerning the demonstration of one thing, and to prove a single truth about that thing, innumerable [reasons] can converge. For example, [to show] regarding a line that it is not made up of points, or a surface, that it is not made up of lines or of a body, that it is not made up of surfaces—we understand incorporeal points and lines and surfaces that reason conceives and defines, that can never come to the senses or to imagination, but that subsist solely in the comprehensibility of reason or understanding. These,

52. *De Trinitate* 14.15.21, CCL 50, 2:450, line 35–451, esp. line 59.

perhaps, are nothing else than certain measures and intelligible forms of the length and breath that are in bodies, just as the bodies that are called mathematical, which are determined according to the power and the reasons of numbers, do not seem to be anything but certain intelligible forms of those sensible bodies which are or can be in act, or certain reasons of numbers through which a doctrine about them is constituted. Although there, in intellectual and prime numbers, we discover many things of this sort which are found in inferior numbers, the very matter of bodies, though weak, does not seem less capable of receiving them.

Chapter 8. How are universal things in the eternal reasons of things? Do they have their own reasons there, and superior forms according to which they too are formed there intellectually and here in act, just as subject things are formed according to them? Or are these first forms of things immutable in themselves and eternal, but infused by participation into things formed in accord with them in time? These are not trifling questions nor can we easily answer them. However, Augustine in Book 8, chapter 6 of *On the Trinity*,[53] where he describes the just soul, calls what is expressed by that description the 'reason' or 'truth' or 'form' after which all souls must be informed in order to be just souls; in this interior truth, which is present in all, the unjust soul sees in itself what it is not—that is, a just soul.

Also in Book 9, chapter 6,[54] he asserts that the human mind, as determined by general or special knowledge, is seen to stand in that very truth, that unchanging eternity; after that he adds:

53. *De Trinitate* 8.6.9, CCL 50, 1:283.
54. *De Trinitate* 9.6.9, CCL 50, 1:301.

'Not by seeing many minds with our bodily eyes do we collect by comparison a general or special knowledge of the human mind.' Later he says what we cited above: 'We gaze upon the inviolable truth, by means of which we define as perfectly as we can not the kind of thing the mind of any particular person is, but what kind of thing it ought to be by the eternal reasons.' He affirms that the reason of a square body is immutable, as we said above. Elsewhere he calls this its form according to which all square bodies, of whatever quantity, are judged, whether they occupy more or less space. Whence it is necessary that it adjust to every creature with regard to space, volume, and dimension, so that it can be applied in judging both greater and lesser things. It could not be related to all square things if it was not the general form of all square bodies, by participation in which they themselves become square bodies. This form which is signified by the term 'square body' is nothing else than that of the genus of all square bodies.

It seems reasonable that certain universal things exist that are immutable even in relation to subject things, however much these very things vary under the universal thing. Hence even Seneca, speaking after Plato about the exemplary and common human form, asserted that it is immutable and eternal in the mind of God: 'Therefore', he says, 'human beings perish; however humanity itself, in the likeness of which a human being is formed, remains; and, though humans labor and die, humanity suffers no change.'[55] So great is the range of each universal thing that it can, of itself, relate to an infinite number of things, and be led into an infi-

55. Seneca, *Epistola* 65.7, ed. and tr. Richard Gummere, *Epistolae ad Lucilium*, Loeb Classical Library (Cambridge: Harvard University Press, 1953) 1:448.

nite number of forms of participation, but of itself it cannot be contracted or extended, increased or diminished. It is not found larger in larger things, or smaller in smaller things; it is whole in each and one in all, not singular in each, or more universal in all. Certain of them subsist in act in nearly an infinite number of things; such is the nature of the body in all bodies, since the number of bodies is infinite; [and of] substance, genus—this is in all substances—accident in all non substances, being, or 'thing' universally in all things. The names signifying things of this kind do not denominate them as they are or are understood in themselves and separate from the subject things, but as they are attained in their participation, in accord with the way in which they are in them; in their actual existence, not in accord with the way they are in their natural and true intellectual being, where they each subsist singly in their simplicity, and then distribute themselves to others in common by participation.

Chapter 9. The question regarding true things is still more pressing. No one can deny that certain of them exist from eternity, and in eternity, and are wholly eternal, as are all the things that we understand about eternal things, apart from any consideration of temporal things. Now these seem to be numberless: for example, God is, God is God, God is triune, the Father is, the Father is God, the Father is the Father, the Father is not the Son, the Father is not the Holy Spirit; by the removal of every creature: for example, God is not the heaven, not the earth, not the sun, not the moon, not a rock, not a tree, and so forth. Now these statements must be said to exist; they are not said to be in God, but only understood there; they are not there essentially like heaven and earth and other created things; these things are uncreated, because eternal; their nature and substance are not elsewhere or in others, except in these which are eternal, although they can be understood by others. So they are there essentially, and in us only through understanding; although they are understood by us, they are not from us. Although we are changeable, and therefore temporal, these things remain absolutely immutable, hence they cannot not be eternal. There they are understood, but not from other things except from those, whatever they are, from which they exist there, and they are not of another mode than are those things from which they are understood, and which are there. As regards the truth of their immutability and eternity, they are truly there.

What are they then? For the moment I will say nothing about those formulated in accord with the way of negation, and which perhaps have another reason, because they are understood not according to the structure of any being, but only by its removal: 'God is true and good', or 'To be any being', is not less good than the thing itself, for to be is good, even in other things that are not God, although their being is a greater good than is the thing itself. We judge how good a thing is by what it is in itself; we observe how good anything is not solely according to what is in it, but rather according to what is from it, which is greater in the totality than the thing is in itself. There is nothing whose being is not good for the totality, for not only is it good that good things exist, but the bad things too are good for it; sometimes the bad things are better than the good, but among the goods sometimes those less good are preferable, and among the bad sometimes those that are worse. 'God is' not better than God himself is, but it would be better if God were not the supreme good, than which nothing better can exist, because he is himself the universal and total good of the whole universe, not only of all taken together, but also of each in particular. No good, greater or lesser, exists except by participation in the supreme good. Similarly, however, 'God is God' and 'God is just' do not seem less good than are his deity and justice, nor is the existence of the eternal reasons of things less good than is the reason itself.

Chapter 10. However, the truths pronounced regarding other things—that is, about creatures—exist eternally, like creatures, by their reasons; and, if they are said to begin and to pass away, it is not in themselves or as such, but in regard to creatures or in creatures, because of the variability of such creatures; there, however, they always remain, immobile and eternal. However it may be here, whatever is once true there is always true. Just as here [the truths] are in the connections of things, so there they are in certain connections of the reasons or the truths of the same things; and those very connections of reasons or truths are certain forms or truths of those connections which exist in things. And so the things that otherwise are only true, are not only such there, but are truths themselves. Hence, they are said to be true.

The connections in which truths exist here are by simple existence, which either connects itself to another, or another through itself, as when something is understood to be or to be something. The simple essence, as will be shown later, can be referred to the particular character of the Father according to one consideration, just as truths are connected to the particular character of the Son, and the connections themselves, or the truths, to the particular character of the Holy Spirit.

These truths, because they are, and are said to be, true both here and there because of the same truths, can therefore be said to be the same truths numerically both here and there, and in both cases essentially, even though they are not of the same substance here and there. There they are eternal; here, according to the assertion of many, they are not eternal. There alone they are intelligible, and here sensible or imaginable, that is, perceptible to the sense or to the imagination. This is not the case with all of them, however. Those concerning incorporeal creatures are open solely to the intellect.

There, also, as was said, not only true things exist, but the truths themselves. Here, however, although those same true things exist, these are not the truths themselves, but rather certain images or likenesses or even shadows of those truths. These, although different, are not truly different, because they do not come from different truths. Thus, however often one verse or proposition is uttered, even if there are many utterances or numerically different essences, there are not many or diverse verses, or many or diverse propositions. Hence, if someone says that 'heaven is', or that something else of this kind is eternal and true, it does not follow, it seems, that heaven or the other thing of this kind is eternal. But when there is mention of eternal truth, eternity can be understood to extend to the being of the truth itself, not to the being which the subject thing has in itself, and not in the truth above itself. Eternity is not said to extend to the being of the subject thing which it has in itself, or to the being of the true [statement], which it has about the subject thing—in which also there is change—as if someone, having withdrawn the term 'truth', said that this very thing, that is 'heaven is', was eternal.

This can be found in many similar instances; for example, when something is said by the addition of something else, which, however, is not said truly of this, because the meaning of the added term, whatever it is, extends in one sense when pronounced with the other term, and in another when it is set down by itself. Thus a new ring is not simply old if the gold is old, for in this statement, age is attributed only to the matter receiving the form. So too when an utterance is recent, and the verse or proposition is not recent, the stating of the latter is recent nevertheless. So too a man who plays the cithara is good at a specific time, but not absolutely good.

The same thing can be shown by an infinite number of examples. However, it is not said that something can be called eternal because of what is added to it, when in itself it is not eternal. It is not thus with other names, that something can be rightly said to be eternal in such or such a respect which it is not itself eternal. One might think this is so because others are imposed to signify the being which things have in themselves; but this is taken up by a higher being which they have in the truth itself, where things temporal in themselves are eternal, because their truths are eternal.

Chapter 11. These truths, although they are distinct among themselves in many ways, all converge in one truth, and according to their substance are one truth, and one reason, and in some way one form, and one wisdom, and one word of God.

That is why Augustine says in *On the Trinity* Book 6, chapter 10: 'This being is one-and-all, as the perfect Word, to which nothing is lacking, and a kind of art of the almighty and wise God, full of all the living and unchanging reasons. All are one in [this art], as it is one from the one, with whom it is one. There God knows all the things that he has made through it.'[56] All are the Word of God, and so is each, and each is God. None of them is not an intellectual, eternal, living, and intelligent substance, and even life itself, understanding, and the light whence we are all illumined and understand. Unlike us, God does not understand reasons by a reason which is other than they, but the eternal reasons that he understands are also the simple reason by which he understands them. When his reason is mentioned, it is his nature that is indicated; nevertheless, the reasons of things, or the eternal reasons, are distinctions in the simple reason and nature.

Chapter 12. In Augustine's opinion, these are what were called 'ideas' by secular philosophers, and first of all by Plato. The same Augustine testifies that these not only exist, but they alone truly exist, and he attributed so much force to them that without an understanding of them no one could ever be wise. Plato defined them as eternal exemplars of things that come to be by nature,[57] while Augustine wants them to be exemplars of things that come

56. *De Trinitate* 6.10.11, CCL 50, 1:241.

57. See *De diversis questionibus LXXIII,* q. 46; *De civ. Dei*, 7.28; Martineau suggests that Achard is really thinking of Seneca, *Ep*. 58.19, Leob Classical Library, 1:398.

to be through art as well. Seneca, in a letter to Lucilus, goes further: 'The third genus consists of those things which properly are countless here, but placed outside of our gaze. What are they, you ask? It is a tool proper to Plato, who calls "ideas" those from which all the things we see are made, according to which all things are formed.'[58] These are immortal, unchangeable, and inviolable, as the continuation of the letter shows. He says: 'Let us turn our mind to those things which are eternal; flying on the heights let us gaze on the forms of all things, and on God sojourning among them.'[59] And in another letter to the same recipient: 'These exemplars of all things God has within himself; he has grasped with his mind the numbers and modes of all things which are to be done, and he is full of these figures which Plato calls ideas, immortal, unchanging, untiring.'[60] In these the archetypal world is said to consist, and so Boethius, speaking of God, wrote: ' . . . being yourself most fair, a fair world in your mind you bear'.[61]

Chapter 13. These principal forms of things—that is, the ideas—Seneca distinguishes from those he calls *eidos*. He situates the latter in the act and material of the work, and the former in the mind and understanding of the artificer.[62] There too the latter, which are essentially in act, can also be said in some way to exist, because of the former, and

58. Seneca, *Epistola* 58.18, Leob Classical Library, 1:396.

59. Seneca, *Epistola* 58.27, Leob Classical Library, 1:404, where the translator (405)—unlike Martineau and the translation here—construes *volitantes* with *formas*: 'Let us look up to the ideal outlines of all things, that flit about on high. . . .'

60. Seneca, *Epistola* 65.7, LCL, 1:448.

61. Boethius, *De consolatione philosophiae* 3, met. 9, ed. H. F. Stewart, Loeb Classical Library (Cambridge: Harvard, 1962) 264, lines 7–8.

62. Seneca, *Epistola*. 58.20–21, Loeb Classical Library, 1:398; cp. *Epistola* 65.7, Loeb Classical Library, 1:448.

in the former, which are naturally there, and in which the latter are understood.

Scripture also seems to have noted these distinctions where it says: 'God said, "Let there be light",
Gn 1:3 and light was made'.† By 'said', which indicates a word, can be very precisely understood the reason and the very idea of the light that is in God's Word and that is God's Word; by the word 'light' [can be understood] the form of the light, which was there intellectually, and which came to be from all eternity when 'God said' through his Word, coeternal to himself, and therefore from eternity: 'Let there be light'; by 'and light was made' [can be understood] the form of light, created in its own act in time, or with time, and impressed on matter.

What we asserted above—that through 'said' he receives the art of making subsequently to himself—is not at all inconsistent. As we said then, in the art of making something both the form of the thing to be made and the form of each thing are seen. The first of these is in no way formed, but solely a form—in which, however, the thing itself can be said to have always been formed, but in understanding, not in act. A certain eternal intellectual formation of the thing is there, then, or a certain form of each thing, formed there intellectually and eternally. In the thing itself the form has been formed and made temporally and in the very act.

The first [form] is truly and absolutely coeternal, not mutable, and, as was said, not only in God's Word, but the very Word of God. The second, even if called eternal and immutable, as we showed above, is not so because of its substance, but only on account of the mode of existing—that is, of being understood there; it is not the Word itself,

but from out of the Word, although not yet in act. The third [form] is absolutely not in the Word, and is temporal and variable—that is, in accord with its substance, as the first is not, and in accord with its the mode of existing, as first and the second are not. The first agrees with the second in a certain manner of existing, but differs from the third both in substance and in mode of subsisting. The second agrees with the first, as has been said, in mode, but differs in substance, while it agrees with the third in substance but differs in mode. The second is nothing else but a form, in the intellect just as it is in act, but not in the same way. Only on account of the first forms of things was it said of the Word: 'What came into being'—that is, its formal
reason—'was life in him',† and 'the life' of this sort Jn 1:3–4
'was the light of people—that is, the very Word of God, immortal wisdom, reason, and eternal truth enlightening rational lives.

Chapter 14. We must consider whether perhaps that bipartite division of forms into ideas and *eidos* that was cited earlier, or this tripartite one into forms as they are in subject things and forms as they are understood—which are themselves the eternal reasons of things—should be understood according to their various states of being and modes of understanding rather than according to the number of their forms. Thus it may be wholly true if it is both expressly and properly said that 'what came into being was life' in the Word.[63] Coming into being—that is, being created—pertains to form as well as to matter. The unity of the second and

63. This punctuation of John 1:4 is characeristic of Christian exemplarists. See Stephanus Axters, *The Spirituality of the Old Low Countries* (London: Aquin, 1954) 29–30.

third form, both in substance and in number, has been sufficiently proven above, although there is a difference in number.

The numerical unity of the first with each of the others must now be briefly considered. As was said, from them—that is, from the third, but not the second—it is distinct in substance and in mode of subsisting. We must not believe that God had with himself two forms and two exemplars of whatever was to be made, in accord with which he would then form one thing in act in a unique mode. A form differing numerically from that one neither existed there, nor was understood there, in another form, but what was there truly and essentially was understood there in itself, not another in it. Again, it is those, numerically the same, that he saw, understood, and had in himself, and has poured forth into the thing to be formed, so that [a form] which had been with him until then without any matter, might be in matter here, and applied even to the matter on which it was impressed and in which it was temporally expressed. [The form] that was and is in itself eternal has become temporal here; what was and is truly immortal there has become variable and corruptible here; what [was and is] uncreated there has become created here; what [was and is] not unformed, but of supreme formal beauty though not formed, has become formed here; what was and is begotten there [has become something] made here; what was and is reason itself there has become a work of reason here; what was and is the Word expressed without sound there has become a kind of sound expressing the Word here; what was and is truth alone and uncreated mind there has becomes an image of truth in a created mind, or a likeness of truth in

a spirit, or a shade of truth in a body here; what
was and is living there is not living here, or if living
here, the life here is not like there—or if life here,
not life of the kind that is 'the light of people',† life Jn 1:5
of the kind that exists there—or even if a certain
kind of 'light of people' here, such as people's
natural reason or understanding, it is nevertheless
not 'the light' that 'shines in the darkness', which
'the darkness did not comprehend'†—or even if Jn 1:5
it be explained here in such a way that it can be
applied to created light, nevertheless 'the true light
that enlightens every human being coming into
this world'† such as it was—that is, with God, in Jn 1:9
the Word—before it came to be in the world, is
not here. That is why 'was' was said, rather than
'is'—not because it is not there now, but lest it be
thought that it did not exist before it was here.
When it began to exist here it did not cease to
exist there, but remaining where it was and what
it was there, it came to be here what it was not.
Thus in accord with what was said earlier, it is here
of another substance, truly other, yet a single form
both here and there, but not in a single substance.
This I think is that the profound mystery of the
Incarnation, in the one person of Christ and his
two natures or substances. Hence the Evangelist,
not long since had said 'what came into being, was
life in him', and he adds a little later, as if in contrast,
'The Word became flesh',† as if he was saying that Jn 1:14
what was life there, has become non-life here.

Chapter 15. Although the same form is here made, and there not made, here temporal and there eternal, it is not simply true that it is made and unmade, temporal and eternal, or that the made and temporal form is the unmade and eternal form. As the same verse, while inside—that is, according to the mode of being that it has solely in the mind through understanding and memory—is incorporeal, inaudible, and invisible, but while outside in an utterance is audible, visible in writing, and thus corporeal in both, it is not so absolutely. The same verse is thus corporeal and incorporeal, audible and inaudible, visible and invisible. Because the different modes are not determined, a contradiction is understood to be in the same things according to the same mode, which does not exist in them except according to different and contrary modes.

Similarly too, although a syllable such as the [Latin] word *do* [which means 'I give'] is significative in one place and elsewhere not significative—such as the same syllable where it is not a word, but part of a word or of some other expression, such as *donas* ['you give'] and *domus* ['a home']—nevertheless the same syllable is not both significative and not significative, nor will a significative syllable be said to be not significative. Although the verse in the mind is the exemplar according to which the same verse has been written in a book, before the copy that has been written in accord with it as it is in the mind—so that one could say that the copy is there, the exemplar here, and the reverse—nevertheless this is not a reason, as we determined above, that it could be said without qualification that the copy is the exemplar; or this, that no more can it be said fittingly that the exemplar of the verse in the book is the same copy, or the copy in the mind is the exemplar; it seems better to say that the copy here is the exemplar there, or the reverse, that the exemplar there is the copy here; and, although this could be truly said and understood, it is not said as properly and distinctly as if it were said something like this: the verse that is the model there is the copy here; or that what is the copy here is the exemplar there and the reverse.

This will be clearer if it is formulated with the words *idea* and *eidos.* One cannot say that the *eidos* is the *idea*, or the *idea* the *eidos*, nor can one correctly say that the *eidos* in the work is the *idea* in the mind, or that the *idea* in the mind is the *eidos* in the work—nor can one express it this way: the form that is the *eidos* in the work is itself the *idea* in the mind, or the form that is the *idea* in the mind is the *eidos* in the work. This seems to be expressed more clearly if, without using the word 'form', one simply phrases it something like this: what is the *eidos* here is the *idea* there, or what is the *idea* there is the *eidos* here.

That is why the Evangelist did not say that 'what was going to come into being was life', or that 'what was going to come into being was life in the world', although he could have said this truly, that 'the form that has come into being', or other expressions of this sort, but rather: 'What came into being, was life in him'. Although that was already said, not only truly, but also properly and aptly, he says more aptly and fittingly, generally and infinitely that 'what came into being was life in him'. However, if anyone insists on asking 'what', having come into being 'was life, in the Word,' requiring a certain and particular response, although a true and fitting answer would be that the form which came into being there was life. Augustine too grants that heaven and earth, or whatever has come into being here, was life there, but, 'universally', he says, 'all the things that came into being here were life there'[64]—and not by any reason propounded separately apart from this discussion—we could be constrained to a determined answer of this sort.

If, however, we say that the form that is *eidos* here is the *idea* there, we would not be forced to give some special name to form, by which it would be determined what form is called *eidos* here, and *idea* there. The name by which it is expressed must refer equally both to the *idea* and to the *eidos*. Perhaps a special name which refers to both of them equally cannot be found, as the same 'body' is now earth, now water, now a tree, now a plant. If anyone asks why the body cannot be expressed specially, since it is clear that it is something, it cannot be determined according to some one species of body because it is related equally to all, or to many, species of body.

Chapter 16. We have inquired thus far regarding the eternal reason according to which things come to be—that is, regarding their intelligible and primary forms. This has been done at some length, both because in them is established a true and solid comprehension of things and a certain knowledge of their truth, and especially because it seems on account of them that the Evangelist discerned that secret, and in some ways impenetrable, word about the Word: 'what came into being was life in him'. To perceive these reasons in whatever way they exist in relation to subject things, or in subject things where they are inserted, and to discern in them—or from them—the things themselves in some measure, at least by some weak outpouring or ray of truth proceeding from them, is quite easy, and indeed universally granted. Almost all

64. *De Genesi ad litteram* 2.6.12, ed. Zycha, 41–42.

see truths in many things and in relation to many things, although they do not understand where and whence and how they are seen, and rarely pay attention to it. To pay attention to it is much more sublime, and something only a few do. What is extremely arduous and belongs to very few is to find it by paying attention, and to contemplate as if immediately with only the eye of the understanding, the truth itself, in its true and simple purity—truth abstracted by the vivacity of the mind's insight from the things subject to it, and from every occurrence or representation of any other thing whatsoever—and to embrace it universally, naked in its beauty, with the arms, so to speak, of the inner self.

To stay there and to cling to it for very long is impossible, even to the spiritual mind while it is still in fragile flesh, burdened and pressed down of the weight of a corruptible nature and by the weakness and corruption contracted from it. [The mind] is not allowed to remain there, but immediately falls back from there into itself and under itself. For a moment it was rapt above itself, but its gaze, as if weakened and repulsed by the brightness of the unfamilier light, is returned and thrust back into its familiar and usual darkness, retaining from that light only some slight, yet not negligible, remains by which its darkness is partially illuminated. These remains quickly wither away, however, unless they are restored by a frequent return to their source.

Although in the first place we must ask and await God's grace for this return and frequent illumination of the uplifted mind, the mind's own industry cooperates with no little efficacy, as does a frequent and diligent exercise of reason in assiduous meditation on things of this kind. But also and especially necessary is purity of heart, and inner quiet away from the den of activities and the tumult of thoughts.

That is enough about these matters. Now the orderly plan proposed above[65] requires that after the reasons according to which things come to be, we diligently add something regarding the things on account of which they come to be—that is, after the forms of things, we should say something about the causes of works; what is to be said about them will be as suitably brief as our study of the former was protracted.

Chapter 17. God, who is reason itself—supreme, infinite, and boundless—can do nothing unreasonably or unreasonable. A work cannot be a work of reason itself if it is in any way unreasonable. 'Its framer gives form to what he frames', as the philosopher says.[66] That is why a work of perfect reason must be reasonable and perfect. A work is reasonable if it proceeds from some reason, that is, it must have some reasonable cause. Certainly God consults no reason but his own [to determine] why he does all that he does; he does not incline himself below himself to seek beneath himself a reasonable cause of his works; he does not locate this first and general cause anywhere but in himself, who alone is the first and supreme principle of all; no more did he consider from eternity the temporal, mutable, and transitory cause of the things he was going to do at the proper time. Instead he considered a sure, fixed cause, one co-eternal with himself; the cause of his eternal will—that is, why he willed from eternity what he did will—could not be some

65. The 'First Treatise', chapter 37.

66. Martineau identifies the source of this saying as Calcidius' translation of Plato, *Timaeus*, 28a.

other, non-eternal reason. No cause whatsoever can be later than that of which it is the cause.

Perhaps even among human beings, no reason for doing or for willing exists that has not existed for eternity, although humanity itself is as temporary as its work and will. So that humanity may will and do what is just because it is just, and because to will and to do it is itself just, a reason exists that is not temporal and does not subsist in anything temporal even though it concerns a temporal thing. Instead it remains in eternal truth itself, and is itself also eternal, and is nothing else but eternal truth itself and immutable justice itself. From eternity it was true, reasonable, and just that when humanity would exist it would will and do what, when it exists, it should will and do on account of that and on account of what it should [will and do it]—that is, because it is reasonable and just—that is, on account of reason and justice, which certainly existed in themselves before beginning to exist in [humanity]. When they begin to exist where they did not exist before, they do not for all that cease to remain where they were before—that is, when they begin to exist in a creature they do not for all that cease to exist in themselves—existing in the creature actually—in themselves substantially, in the creature by grace, in themselves by nature, in the creature by participation, in themselves by a fullness whence even if at some time the creature ceased to exist they would always persist unmovable in themselves.

Chapter 18. But if, like the forms of things, the causes of works too—the eternal reasons not only according to which, but also on account of which, God did what he does in time—were distinct in

him in unchangeable truth and his one reason, neither we nor the angels, as was said regarding the forms of things earlier, would discover in the very truth that is above us the certain and immobile cause of anything whatever that is done; instead the causes of all things to be done or already done, not only by us or by them, but even by God himself, would flow into our consciousness as if under a single ray. Indeed, not only causes, but the Cause of all things would be only one and completely indistinct, and we would no longer have to exclaim with the Apostle—for the Apostle, although
2 Co 12:2 'caught up into the third heaven'† exclaimed over
Rm 11:33 the depths of the judgments and counsels of God†
nor would the Prophet speak of the judgments of
Ps 36:6 God and the great deep;† nor would God have
greater understanding than an angel of anything that is going to be done or ought to be done.

However, one cannot deny that, as was shown in the preceding chapter, there is one general and supreme cause of all things, namely the reason of God, or God himself, who, as Scripture testifies through Solomon in Proverbs, 'has done every-
Pr 16:4 thing for himself'.† Under or in this general cause
are contained an infinite number of special causes, which all depend from this one in some way and are referred to this one. When the righteous refer everything to the divine will, as to the general and first cause of their works, nevertheless for their own sake they pay attention to the many special distinctions of reasonable causes. With reference to them they are said to make a home for one purpose—that is, that they may dwell there—and a vestment for another purpose—that is, that they may wear it—and for another purpose a book, not to inhabit or to wear, but to read. They will these things only

for God, for whom alone they seek to instruct the mind and not deny necessities to the body. But when, more specifically, a house is to be built—which is the determined reason or cause—this can also be subdistinguished through other individual reasonable causes, so that one determines why a foundation is made in the house, another why the roof is made, another the walls, another the door posts, another the doors, another the windows, and so regarding all the individual parts. It seems as if reasons can be given for each of them, yet all converge in the single superior cause of building a house. So, too, the righteous make some [causes] concur with many others in one supreme cause, which is the divine will. Similarly too the eternal reason—although in itself it is one, in accord with which all things are formed—is distinguished—as was shown above—through an infinite number of formal reasons of things which happen or can happen because of it.

What wonder, then, if this [cause], although it is the general cause of all, is nevertheless distributed through an infinity of causal reasons or reasonable causes of those things which come to be on ac-
count of it. Thus, God's wisdom, which is 'one',[†] Ws 7:27
is not vainly or falsely called 'many-shaped'[†] by the Ep 3:10
Apostle, and elsewhere a 'manifold' spirit[†] whose Ws 7:22
treasures of wisdom and knowledge are hidden in
Christ.[†] And again: 'The depths of the wisdom and Col 2:3
the knowledge of God!'[†] Divine speech would not Rm 11:33
have spoken in this way unless it wanted to suggest the existence of a kind of impenetrable and infinite multitude of all the reasons pertaining either to wisdom about eternal things or to knowledge about temporal things. From them those [reasons] on account of which it is fitting that each thing

come to be or not come to be cannot be excluded; although they concern temporal things, they themselves are not temporal but eternal, as was said earlier.

However much works must vary in conformity with things and times, the reasons of those works remain invariable, and even the reason of that variation does not vary, although the variation itself varies. Just as the same works do not always come to be, so also they do not always vary in the same way. The reasons both of works and of variations remain always the same, although the same ones are not always involved in working or in varying the works, and the reasons do not succeed one another, even if their effects cannot be unfolded simultaneously. If, along with the work, and the variation of the work, the reason of each passed, after it there would be nothing by which those things that have reasonably come about could be judged. Only in their reasons could one see here about those things in which, and when, they can be seen to be reasonable.[67]

These are the same reasons in which and from which we make a judgment regarding individual works, whether future, present, or past, and for this to happen they must be always present, never future, never past. Although there may be a reason why something happened yesterday, and no reason for it to happen the day before, or a reason for it to happen today, nevertheless there was a reason the day before and there is a reason today why it happened yesterday—indeed the reason always was

67. This sentence is difficult to translate. The Latin is: *Non enim nisi in rationibus suis hic de ipsis videri potuit in quibus et quando sint videri potest quia rationabilia sunt.* Martineau's French translates: 'It is only in the proper reasons of works that one has been able to see here those in which—and when—they could be rational' (189).

and always will be. There was not one reason that it would happen when it did happen, another when this happening was still future, and another when it was past, but the same [reason] that existed then in the doing also existed before the doing, and after what was done. If matters were not the way they are now, but different in quality and relationship, for many things there might have been a reason for them to happen then, for which there is at present no reason for them to happen, and, inversely, for many for which there is at present a reason for them to happen now, then there was no reason. However, then there was no reason for them to happen then because there is now no reason that they should have happened then, nor is there any reason for anything to happen now for which there was no reason then, nor that it happen then, but that it happen if things and circumstances be such as they now are. Thus there was no reason then which does not exist now, nor is there a reason now which did not exist then, so that reasons that exist cannot not exist, nor can there be any different from those that exist, nor in general can the number of reasons be increased or diminished, or even changed.

Thus works that are at one time reasonable, are often not reasonable at another time, because things that have a reason at one time lack a reason at another; even at the same time, however, what has a reason to be done by one has no reason to be done by another, so that the same work at the same time may be reasonable in relation to one but unreasonable in relation to another. But that what at one time is a reason may sometimes become a non-reason, or, inversely, a reason come to be from a non reason—so that what is a reason in one thing is not a reason in another—is utterly impossible, if one understands both reasonably.

If people err in the judgment of reason, they can perhaps say that what is a reason is not a reason for them, or that what is a non-reason for them is nevertheless a reason—that is, they take reason for non-reason and non-reason for reason. Nevertheless, the substance or quality of reason itself, for and in everyone—not only those who recognize and embrace it, but also those who are ignorant of it and disdain it—remains indivisible and unchangeable. It is the light that shines even in the darkness, although the darkness does not com-
Jn 1:5 prehend it.† Here it is not exactly[68] the light itself—that is, reason and truth shining in themselves, even though [they shine] by it—so that even the darkness—that is, minds darkened by ignorance or disdain—are illumined by it. When they are enlightened by it, so that they recognize and love it, they are changed and move, not in space but by a kind of alteration—because those who were only
Ep 5:8 darkness become 'light in the Lord'.† That light, by participating in which they become light, does not move, change, or alter, so that darkness would come from light itself; now it not only shines there as it did before, but it also illumines what it did not illumine before—that is, not only are reason and truth there in it, but they are also from it—that is, from its outpouring and participation of itself it makes those minds reasonable and truthful, moving and advancing them without itself being moved or advanced, diminished or increased, casting the darkness out of them, not taking it into itself, pouring itself into them, not pouring out of itself,

68. The Latin is *nimis*; Martineau translates 'truly'.

sharing without dividing—not taking what it lays aside—not losing what it bestows.

Chapter 19. Although the subject here is causal reasons, what has been said is true not only of causal, but also of other reasons as well. These statements are understood to include the other reasons. Whenever it is said about anything that there is a reason why it comes to be, the word 'reason' is to be referred to all equally. 'Reasonable cause' means not only the cause of the doing, but also the form of the thing done, and the mode of unfolding the thing done, when it is said that there is a reason why it is done. If any of these three is not reasonable there will be no reason why the work itself should come to be. A form is said to be, and is, reasonable, from the genus of reasons with which we dealt sufficiently above, and the mode from the genus about which we will deal subsequently. The form is observed to be reasonable in accord with the formal reasons, the cause in accord with the causal reasons, the mode in accord with the explanatory or, so to speak, modal reasons. Of nothing is it said that there is a reason that it happens, because that very same thing—that is, the coming to be of the thing—is the reason (it is temporal, and reason is eternal), but because there is a reason in accord with which and on account of which the thing can or must happen.

Chapter 20. Although they are eternal, we consider some reasons of this kind according to what is not eternal as well. Thus, for example, because of what we want others to do for us, we notice what we must do for others, and when we see or hear what others do, and why and how, from this we sometimes gather also the rational form, cause, and mode of the thing to be done. Again, in particular regarding those things that are our concern here—that is, the causal reasons that are our only subject—they are, like the others, always present without any succession because of their simplicity and eternity; they have in themselves no anterior or posterior reason. Certain ones of them from among the works of God are designated only according to what is done, but others according to what in some way precedes what is to be done; and among these latter, some according to what is in God alone, others according to what is in another thing; and of these, again, some according to what is of nature, and others according to what is from the free will—that is, from good or bad will—that is, some according to the natural qualities of things, others according to the merits of will or even of works. Those considered in accord with what is in God alone can not inappropriately be referred to as 'original' reasons or causes; those, on the other hand, considered in accord with natural things, can be referred to as 'natural' reasons or causes; those considered in accord with the merits, can be referred as to 'judicial' reasons and causes; finally, those considered in accord with the merits of what is done—that is, in accord with their consequences—can be referred to as final reasons or causes.

Chapter 21. The original causes of the things done by God arise solely from his gracious goodness. The nature or justice of no other thing requires him to act. He does things solely at the invitation of his natural and innate kindness, not because of need or coercion, not because impelled or drawn by some usefulness or increment accruing to himself, but solely, as someone said, 'by the innate form of the supreme good',[69] that is, solely because he is good, or rather because he is supreme goodness itself. A deed or act of will proceeding from this goodness of his cannot lack a reason; this is itself a reason; it is absolutely becoming to his supreme goodness that the good God should will to do good, and do good, simply because he is good. Although his goodness is one in itself, from it alone—by various distributions, so to speak, and multi-channeled derivations—all his gracious goods and gifts flow to and arrive at creatures like innumerable streams from a single spring.

In great part these are collected and flow together in two principal and general rivers, of which one flowed in the creation of the world and the other in the redemption of humanity. No nature or justice of a creature could have existed which could have required that what was not yet should come to be, or that it come to be good, since, although it was made good, it had by its own vice and contrary to [God's] will, made itself evil instead of good, and in what concerns his justice made itself unjust instead of just. Hence, not only did it not deserve to be redeemed and freed by [divine goodness], it even deserved to be damned. Although it did not deserve to be created when it did not yet exist, neither did it deserve not to be created when it had not yet done or willed anything evil.

The grace in redemption was greater than that in creation. In Sacred Scripture grace is usually indicated by the name of the Holy Spirit. Hence

69. Boethius, *De consolatione philosophiae*, III, metr. 9, Loeb Classical Library, 272, lines 5–6.

in order to indicate that grace alone is prior cause of both creation and redemption, it is said [in the Old Testament] that 'the Spirit of the Lord traversed the
Gn 1:2 waters'† and we read [in the New Testament] that the very author of redemption, that is, Christ, 'was
Lk 1:35 conceived by the Holy Spirit'.†

Besides these two rivers of graces, so to call them, there seem to be two others, which are perhaps lesser: a superior one in the justification of the angels, and an inferior one in the granting of the temporal benefits of God. These latter he extends even to the wicked, seeing that 'he makes his sun rise' not only 'on the good' but also 'on the evil', and 'he sends rain' not only 'on the
Mt 5:45 just' but also 'on the unjust'.† He freely grants numberless other things in the same way, not only on the worthy, but also on the unworthy, often conferring even more and greater temporal goods on the unworthy than on the worthy, and among the unworthy sometimes more on those who are more unworthy. Of this grace we cannot doubt that it is less than any of the other three.

Regarding the third, clearly it is less than the second—that is, it is less than the grace of redemption. This one—that is, the grace of angelic justification—precedes all merit, both good and bad, and so, although it is prior to merit, it is not contrary to merit.

The [second]—that is, the grace of human redemption and justification—not only existed prior to good merit but also existed after bad merit; not only for conferring good merit but for taking away and destroying bad merit; not only for forming unformed nature, but for reforming deformed nature; it was strong enough not only for leading human beings to heaven from earth but also for leading

God to earth from heaven; not only that a servant might receive the form of God but also that God might receive the form of a servant;† not only that Ph 2:6–7 humanity might be made righteous by God, but also that a human being might himself become that justifying God; not only that the justifying God, and justice itself, might become a just human being, but also one justified—that is, made just—not by someone unjust—not just by himself, but just by the assuming God—that is, just not by human nature but solely by the grace of God—not only a humanity not made just by herself but even a humanity weak in itself—that is, a humanity prone to suffering and death, but even dying, not only by the most bitter death, but by the most disgraceful death.

Regarding the first grace and the third grace—that is the grace of the creation of the world and the grace of angelic justification—there seems to be some question which of the two of them is greater and which less. The form of justice is more excellent than the form of nature, the form given here freely is more excellent than the form made there freely. The mode there, however, seems to be more excellent there than here, and more wondrous. Creation does not occur in anything, nor from anything, nor out of anything, preexisting, but simply from nothing, or out of nothing. The justification of the angels, although it cannot be said to have occurred from anything, did not occur from nothing; it occurred out of something, though not from something, and it occurred in something. Although it did not occur from anything, such as matter, yet it occurred out of something, that is, justice, as though out of a formal cause, and it occurred in something, that

is, in the angelic nature, which although not yet just was capable of being justified, and by a certain natural form in which it was made 'in the image
Gn 1:26 and likeness of God'†—that is, by the property of being justifiable—which was in a certain way calling forth, or, as it were, inviting—although not meriting, or exacting as something due it—the form of justice for justifying itself more excellently by justifying grace than it had been earlier formed by creating grace.

Here ends 'On the Unity [of God] and the Plurality of Creatures', in the year of the incarnation of the same Lord, 1352. Amen.

Index

Editorial Offices & Customer Service

- Cistercian Publications
  WMU Station, 1903 West Michigan Avenue
  Kalamazoo, Michigan 49008-5415 USA

  Telephone 616 387 8920
  Fax 616 387 8390
  e-mail cistpub@wmich.edu

Canada

- Novalis
  49 Front Street East, Second Floor
  Toronto, Ontario M5E 1B3 CANADA

  Telephone 1 800 204 4140
  Fax 416 363 9409

U.K.

- Cistercian Publications UK
  Mount Saint Bernard Abbey
  Coalville, Leicestershire LE67 5UL UK

- UK Customer Service & Book Orders
  Cistercian Publications
  97 Loughborough Road
  Thringstone, Coalville
  Leicestershire LE67 8LQ UK

  Telephone 01530 45 27 24
  Fax 01530 45 02 10
  e-mail MsbcistP@aol.com

Website & Warehouse

- www.spencerabbey.org/cistpub

- Book Returns (prior permission)
  Cistercian Publications
  Saint Joseph's Abbey
  167 North Spencer Road
  Spencer, Massachusetts 01562-1233 USA

  Telephone 508 885 8730
  Fax 508 885 4687
  e-mail cistpub@spencerabbey.org

Trade Accounts & Credit Applications

- Cistercian Publications / Accounting
  6219 West Kistler Road
  Ludington, Michigan 49431 USA

  Fax 231 843 8919

Cistercian Publications is a non-profit corporation. Its publishing program is restricted to monastic texts in translation and books on the monastic tradition.

A complete catalogue of texts in translation and studies on early, medieval, and modern monasticism is available, free of charge, from any of the addresses above.